MONTEREY AND CARMEL

Eden by the Sea

Help Us Keep This Guide Up to Date

Every effort has been made by the authors and editors to make this guide as accurate and useful as possible. However, many things can change after a guide is published—establishments close, phone numbers change, facilities come under new management, etc.

We would love to hear from you concerning your experiences with this guide and how you feel it could be improved and kept up to date. While we may not be able to respond to all comments and suggestions, we'll take them to heart and we'll also make certain to share them with the authors. Please send your comments and suggestions to the following address:

The Globe Pequot Press
Reader Response/Editorial Department
P.O. Box 480
Guilford, CT 06437

Or you may e-mail us at:

editorial@globe-pequot.com

Thanks for your input, and happy travels!

HILL GUIDES™ SERIES

MONTEREY AND CARMEL

Eden by the Sea

Second Edition

by Kathleen Thompson Hill
&
Gerald Hill

The Globe Pequot Press

Guilford, Connecticut

Hill Guides is a trademark of Kathleen Thompson Hill and Gerald N. Hill.

Cover painting entitled *Mission at Carmel* by Judy Theo Lehner, M.F.A. Studio address: 134 Church Street, Sonoma, CA 95476; (707) 996–5111. Medium: monotype.
Cover and text design by Lana Mullen
Maps by Lisa Reneson
Photos by Kathleen and Gerald Hill except Big Sur Coastline and Colton Hall courtesy Monterey Peninsula Visitor's and Convention Bureau
Historic photos: John Steinbeck courtesy Pat Hathaway Collection and National Steinbeck Center; Alvarado Street in 1888 courtesy Pat Hathaway; Steinbeck's 1960 pickup Rocinante courtesy National Steinbeck Center; archival pictures of Vizcaino, Larkin, Alvarado, Colton, Jacks, Devendorf, and Carmel in 1909 by Louis S. Slevin

Library of Congress Cataloging-in-Publication Data is available.

ISBN 0-7627-0914-6

Manufactured in the United States of America
Second Edition/First Printing

CONTENTS

PREFACE

*A*gain and again we have been drawn to Monterey and Carmel. For several summers in her preteens, Kathleen vacationed with her parents in Carmel Valley, where she rode horseback, fished, caught crawdads, swam in the Carmel River, and accompanied her mother on endless tours of Carmel's shops and galleries.

Jerry first rode through on a motorcycle trip along the coast in his twenties, and a few years later attended a wedding at the Carmel Mission. A friend introduced him to the joys of salmon fishing (and the horrors of seasickness) on a charter boat berthed in Monterey. Later he spent time here as a consultant to the city of Seaside. Another friend invited him into the inner sanctum of Ed Ricketts's renovated laboratory on Cannery Row, and twice he participated in conferences at Asilomar in Pacific Grove.

Carmel, Monterey, and Big Sur were stops on our honeymoon—we always stayed within sight or sound of the ocean. As part of our political lives, we came to work for Sam Farr (now a U.S. representative) in his first campaign for the state assembly. We brought our teenage children here to experience the aquarium, Cannery Row, the Santa Cruz boardwalk, and the Carmel beach and restaurants. Little did we know that less than ten years later, in 1997, our son Mack Hill would be honored as one of an Emmy-winning team on the television special *Monterey: Wonders of the Outer Bay.*

We returned when Kathleen wrote an article on food festivals for *Cook's* magazine that included the Castroville Artichoke Festival, and again when we both interviewed World War II air hero General Jimmy Doolittle, who was living at Pebble Beach. By that time we were completely in love with this remarkable stretch of California coast.

So when the senior editors of Globe Pequot asked us what place we would like to write about next, without a moment's hesitation we answered in one voice: Monterey and Carmel. We have been delighted to reexplore Eden by the Sea for this second edition. Any excuse will do!

—Kathleen Hill
—Gerald Hill

Our Father who art in nature.

—John Steinbeck, *Cannery Row*

ACKNOWLEDGMENTS

*O*ne early morning during our exploration of old Monterey we stood blinking in the bright sunlight on the corner of Alvarado and Pearl Streets. Up walked a well-dressed gentleman who asked, "Can I help you?" We told him what we were doing and, as if he had nothing but time, he pointed out various older buildings and recited brief histories of each. It turned out he was Carmel Martin, one of the deans of the Monterey County Bar, a resident of Carmel, and a member of the Martin family, whose Martin Ranch dated back almost 150 years.

Mr. Martin's courtesy and helpfulness were symbolic of the generous and cooperative attitude we found in Monterey, Carmel, Pacific Grove, and Salinas during our work on this book.

Amy Herzog of the Monterey Peninsula Visitors Bureau was helpful beyond the call of duty, as was Amanda Holder of the National Steinbeck Center. Volunteers and staff members of the Carmel Business Association, the Pacific Grove Chamber of Commerce, the Monterey County Vintners and Growers Association, the Salinas Chamber of Commerce, and other groups were always generous in their assistance.

Our special thanks go to Ken Peterson and his staff at the Monterey Bay Aquarium, Bert Cutino of the Sardine Factory Restaurant in Monterey, and Pat Hathaway of California Views, a remarkable historic photograph collection. Our old friends Garth Eliassen (who grew up in Monterey) and Jane Lowrey Weisser (chronicler for Carmel High alumni), Carmel artist Rochana Cash, and Michelle Pollack, manager and wife of famed woodworker Andrew Pollack, all gave us insight and materials invaluable to our efforts.

Kathleen and Tom Anderson, proprietors of Sparrow's Nest, the popular Sonoma bed-and-breakfast, kindly scouted restaurants and accommodations on the Monterey Peninsula. Again our friends Susan Weeks and Sue Holman sacrificed their bodies and tasted their way around on our behalf.

And most of all we thank the proprietors and employees of the shops, galleries, and restaurants who patiently answered our questions, the chefs who were generous with their recipes, the vintners and tasting room managers who were so hospitable, and all those people who, like Mr. Martin, volunteered local information and advice.

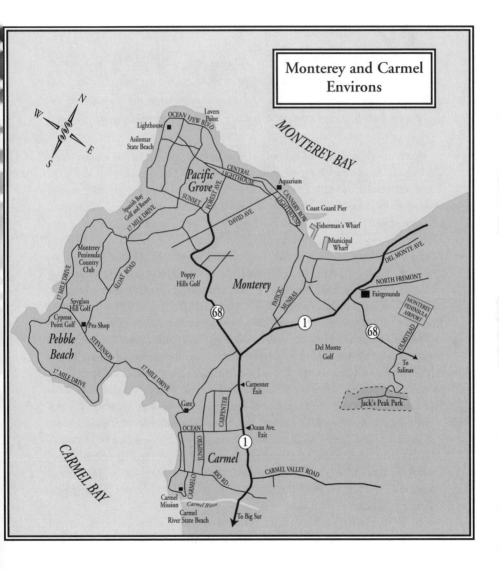

Monterey and Carmel Environs

N
W · E
S

Lovers Point

OCEAN VIEW BLVD

Lighthouse

Asilomar State Beach

MONTEREY BAY

Pacific Grove

CENTRAL

LIGHTHOUSE

SUNSET

FOREST AVE.

Aquarium

CANNERY ROW

LIGHTHOUSE

Coast Guard Pier

DAVID AVE.

Spanish Bay Golf and Resort

17 MILE DRIVE

Fisherman's Wharf

Municipal Wharf

Monterey Peninsula Country Club

SLOAT ROAD

Poppy Hills Golf

Monterey

PACIFIC

MUNRAS

DEL MONTE AVE.

NORTH FREMONT

Fairgrounds

17 MILE DRIVE

Spyglass Hill Golf

Cypress Point Golf ■ Pro Shop

STEVENSON

68

1

68

MONTEREY PENINSULA AIRPORT

OLMSTEAD

Pebble Beach

17 MILE DRIVE

17 MILE DRIVE

Del Monte Golf

To Salinas

Carpenter Exit

Gate

CARPENTER

Ocean Ave. Exit

Jack's Peak Park

OCEAN

JUNIPERO

1

Carmel

CARMEL VALLEY ROAD

CARMEL BAY

CARMELO

RIO RD.

Carmel Mission

Carmel River

Carmel River State Beach

To Big Sur

INTRODUCTION

In Carmel Valley a few decades ago, rustic cabins hid under tall trees, and fish darted around in crystal-clear streams. The air was hot, the leaves on the ground were hot, the pavement on the way to the store was hot, but evenings in the little log cabin were delightfully cool.

Every day Kathleen and her pal Gary went fishing. One day Kathleen made the mistake of catching the most fish, all of which she saved in her bucket. That night, exhausted and full of fresh air, she climbed into her sleeping bag, moved around to find her usual comfort zone, felt something cold, tried to move it, and yelled loud enough to wake the neighbors when it moved. Gary had put a live crawfish in Kathleen's sleeping bag.

As we grew up, we became acquainted with the more sophisticated Carmel, often staying with parents at the Normandy Inn, and enjoying a Thanksgiving or Easter feast at the Pine Inn. Carmel still nurtured an artists' colony then, but as more and more people came to love Carmel and its historical charm, some of that flavor disappeared in favor of more upscale galleries and boutiques.

Monterey, once an intense sardine-fishing village loaded with California history, has become an extremely popular destination for exploring nature at the Monterey Bay Aquarium and at the Butterfly Gardens in nearby Pacific Grove, as well as a spot for sampling fine foods and wines. Skin divers and those who just want to try the experience for the first time can be seen backing into the water (quite a sight!) with instructors nearby, at the south end of Cannery Row.

In 1542 Don Juan Cabrillo, a Portuguese explorer in search of California's fabled riches (weren't the rumors true, though?), sailed into La Bahia de los Pinos (the Bay of Pines), but the adventurers never stepped on the land. Sixty years later, however, in 1602, Sebastian Vizcaino did land briefly, making him the first European to set foot on the peninsula.

In 1770 Father Junipero Serra, founder of the California missions, and Commander Don Gaspar de Portola arrived in Monterey, where they set up a mission and a presidio guarded by Spanish troops. In 1777 Monterey became the official capital of both Alta (Upper) and Baja (Lower) California, remaining head of Alta California under both Spanish and Mexican rule in 1822 when Mexico gained its independence from Spain. Pablo Vincent de Sola became the first Mexican governor of California. Years of dispute between Mexico and the United States ended when Commodore John Drake Sloat arrived in Monterey and raised the American flag over the Custom House, ending Mexican rule on July 7, 1846.

John Steinbeck gave most of us our first glimpse of the sardine business in his renowned *Cannery Row*, which we highly recommend to anyone who wants to get a fun, if only slightly romanticized, perspective on Monterey.

The Monterey Peninsula has often been called "the most beautiful place on earth." The Pacific Ocean meets the land with mutual respect, and human beings have done well to develop their needs with sensitivity. Man, and an occasional woman, has made the most of nature on Monterey and Carmel Bays with the exquisite 17-Mile Drive and Pebble Beach Resort and Golf Course.

A wide, blunt appendage to mainland California, the Monterey Peninsula sticks out into the Pacific Ocean between Monterey Bay to the north and Carmel Bay to the south, just 120 miles south of San Francisco, 60 miles south of San Jose, and 280 miles north of Los Angeles.

On the Monterey Peninsula itself, you must investigate the cities of Monterey (including colorful Cannery Row), Pacific Grove, Carmel-by-the-Sea, Carmel Valley, Seaside, Marina, Sand City, and lush Pebble Beach. North of the Monterey Peninsula you can enjoy Santa Cruz, Capitola, and Moss Landing, while to the south Big Sur is well worth the 28-mile trip for its breathtakingly and unequaled dramatic natural beauty.

Native Americans had thrived in the area for thousands of years. Following the Spanish pioneers, settlers on the Monterey Peninsula included Americans, Chinese, Portuguese, Italians (Sicilians and Genovese), and Japanese. The heritage and customs these groups brought with them form the basis for much of the area's culture. The permanent population of the Monterey Peninsula hovers around 128,000, and most of those people live in the peninsula's cities. But eight million visitors flock to the area's natural wonders, historical sites, and shops every year. And we are among them.

Despite the number of outsiders visiting Monterey and Carmel, we never feel particularly crowded, partly because the region's small cities are separated by people-created and natural splendors, and partly because we avoid the huge event weekends, such as the Monterey Grand Prix at Laguna Seca Raceway and the Monterey Jazz Festival. If you do want to attend these events, be sure to book reservations several months (even a year) ahead.

Among the peninsula's hundreds of public events you might enjoy, especially spectacular are the Monterey Jazz Festival, the AT&T Pebble Beach National Pro-Am Golf Tournament, Cannery Row's annual John Steinbeck Birthday Festival, the Monterey Wine Festival, and the Old Monterey

Seafood &Music Festival. (See "Annual Events" in our "Lists of Lists" for detailed information on local events worth planning your trip around.)

One of Monterey and Carmel's greatest attractions is its climate. Its cooling fog is famous, refreshing, and reliable, keeping average summer temperatures ranging from 51° to 68°F, with occasional warm days up to 85°F. Winter temperatures keep a moderate 44° to 61°F. The year-round average temperature is 57°F. Most of the area's 18 inches of rainfall drop from November through April, although the "dripple" from fog can't be measured. Spring and fall months usually have the most pleasant weather. In the summer warm temperatures inland often draw the fog in over this part of California's Pacific coast.

This is definitely a sweater climate. We recommend that you "don't leave home without one"—or a jacket or coat. The weather may appear to be clear as you approach the coast, but plan for that comforting blanket of fog covering the Monterey Peninsula.

Carmel still retains a slightly genteel and formal atmosphere, with an abundance of fine clothing stores. Ties and coats are still worn occasionally in better restaurants, although casual and comfortable clothes are perfectly acceptable. Monterey and Pacific Grove are more informal, but it would still be wise to bring along your best travel clothes.

We prefer to travel in the area during the off-season, i.e., not summer, because fewer visitors means less crowding everywhere, and more chances to actually converse with local shopkeepers, chefs, and winemakers.

Painters, sculptors, photographers, actors, writers, and musicians have moved or visited here for decades to capture and express the extreme sensations they experience in the unusually gorgeous landscape and climate of the Monterey Peninsula. Perhaps the best-known contemporary artist to live here is actor Clint Eastwood, who served as mayor of Carmel from 1986 to 1988. Once a well-known artists' colony, Carmel now boasts more than a hundred art galleries, some of which offer the work of noted local artists, while others concentrate on regional landscapes and art from around the world.

Most communities along the peninsula offer golf courses, beaches, scuba diving, whale watching, fishing, horseback riding, hiking, and biking—to say nothing of exquisite dining, wine tasting, strolling, and beachcombing. Can you handle it all? Come on.

HOW TO GET HERE

Monterey and Carmel are not places you just happen to stop at unless you are wandering up or down Highway 1. So pay attention to our easy directions.

We give you instructions by car from San Francisco, San Jose, Oakland and the East Bay, and Los Angeles. Then we tell you how to get here by commercial airline, bus, and Amtrak.

Approaches by car provide the most beautiful and cultural experiences and allow you to traipse through artichoke fields (and buy minuscule to giant ones from local farmers), talk to fishermen in Moss Landing, stop for lunch overlooking the ocean at famed Nepenthe in Big Sur, or commune with John Steinbeck in Salinas. But if you want to get here quickly and easily, three commercial airlines land at Monterey Peninsula Airport.

ON THE ROAD FROM SAN FRANCISCO AND OAKLAND/BERKELEY

For your own sanity and blood pressure control, we highly recommend that you take Highway 280 south from San Francisco to San Jose to get to the Monterey Peninsula from northern California. You can also take Highway 1 down the western edge of the United States from San Francisco, either by going west on Geary Boulevard to the Great Highway and heading south, or by taking Highway 280 south and taking the Pacifica and Highway 1 exit. Highway 1 affords one of the most spectacular drives in the world, but we avoid traveling south on this section of it because we are occasionally queasy driving along cliff edges. If you don't have this problem, go for it. Otherwise, save Highway 1 for the return trip, when you will be on the inside hugging the mountains.

The easiest way to get to Highway 280 in San Francisco is by taking Nineteenth Avenue heading south, past Stonestown Mall and San Francisco State University, and turn south (right) onto Highway 280 through Daly City and the cemetery center of Colma, and keep going south.

You have several choices once on Highway 280. One is to go straight to San Jose and take the turnoff to Highway 17, which takes you over 23 miles of lush winding road across the Santa Cruz Mountains. While this is a beautiful route, every Bay Area radio commute report warns drivers of accidents on Highway 17. Less than newish cars often overheat (there are lots of pullouts to let your engines and tempers cool), and road signs caution drivers to turn off their air-conditioning to give their cars a chance. Highway 1 and Highway 17 will take you into Santa Cruz, from which you can rejoin and follow Highway 1 south to Monterey.

A real benefit of taking Highway 17, which we love, is that you can visit many wineries along the way, including Bonny Doon, in the Santa Cruz and Soquel areas.

Highway 280 passes through quasi-rural parts of San Mateo County, now covered principally with Silicon Valley suburban housing offering glorious views of rolling hills around San Francisco's Crystal Springs Reservoir. Thirty-eight miles south of San Francisco State University (Nineteenth Avenue and Holloway) in San Francisco, you can take Highway 85 (often crowded during Silicon Valley commute hours) to Gilroy. We suggest you continue on Highway 280 to San Jose and take Highway 101 south.

Continue on Highway 101 south of San Jose for 27 miles into Gilroy, the "Garlic Capital of the World," where the aroma of "the stinking rose" from nearby processing plants permeates the air for miles around. Stop at Garlic World or the Garlic Shoppe on the east side of the road; both specialize in fresh and preserved garlic in every form imaginable. We usually stock up here. Be very careful turning in and out of these shops. This long stretch of 101 between San Jose and Gilroy used to be called "Blood Alley" until recent improvements were made.

About 7 miles south of Gilroy is the turnoff to Mission San Juan Bautista, where the climactic scenes of Alfred Hitchcock's 1958 classic *Vertigo* were made with Kim Novak (a Carmel resident) and Jimmy Stewart.

Continuing south on Highway 101 about 10 miles, you might want to check out the red barn Flea Market and Antiques on the left side of the road. At 5.7 miles south of the red barn, take Highway 156 west toward Castroville, the "Artichoke Center of the World."

Six miles beyond Castroville you begin to see sea mist and sand dunes along Marina State Beach. In the next 8 miles to Monterey, you will pass through Sand City and Seaside.

Another Highway 101 alternative is to continue on it south to Salinas to visit the National Steinbeck Center and Steinbeck House, and then turn west on Highway 68 and pass scenic Laguna Seca Raceway, home of the Monterey Grand Prix, and proceed right into Monterey.

If you come down Highway 1 from San Francisco, you get to visit Pacifica (now a San Francisco suburb), Montara and Montara State Beach, El Granada Beach (especially easy beach access and camper parking), Miramar Beach and Resort, Moss Beach and the Moss Beach Distillery, Half Moon Bay (try the down-home local Flying Fish Grill just east of Highway 1), San Gregorio State Beach, Pescadero State Beach and Pescadero, Dunes and Venice Beaches, and Pidgin Point Lighthouse, now a rarefied hostel with daily tours just south of Bean Hollow State Beach. About 67 miles south of San Francisco you might want to stop to view the Henry Cowell Redwoods or visit Davenport's Whale City Bakery Bar & Grill overlooking the Pacific.

Three and a half miles south of Wilder Ranch State Park you find the University of California, Santa Cruz, to the west, and Santa Cruz city limits about 5 miles farther. All of the small coastal towns between Santa Cruz and Monterey are interesting and worth a stop. You might want to visit wineries (see Chapter 6, The Grape Escape). We like Soquel, Capitola (with its quaint artistic village on the ocean), Aptos, Zmudski State Beach, and Moss Landing State Beach.

It's definitely worth a slight detour into Moss Landing to visit a solid fishing village. Do not miss Phil's Fish Market and Eatery, loaded with shrimp and fish and chips, burgers, and almost local brews, or the Lighthouse Grille. Antique and collectible shops carry curious curios. Be sure to visit the natural wonders of Elkhorn Slough National Estuarine Reserve. We like to stop at Pezzini Farms 5 miles south of Moss Landing for artichokes and strawberries on our way back to San Francisco.

South of Moss Landing follow Highway 1 past the former Fort Ord, which is now the newly founded California State University at Monterey, and right into Monterey.

FROM OAKLAND/BERKELEY AND THE EAST BAY

As Dionne Warwick sings, "Do you know the way to San Jose?" Getting there is easy, but heavily trafficked. Just follow Highway 680 or Highway 880 south to San Jose, take Highway 101, and proceed south 60 miles through Gilroy.

Either take Highway 156 west through artichoke capital Castroville and then head south on Highway 1, or stay on Highway 101 to Salinas and take Highway 68 west past Laguna Seca Raceway to Monterey.

FROM LOS ANGELES

Three routes can take you from Los Angeles to the Monterey Peninsula. You can make your choice based on your taste in driving speed and sightseeing.

The speediest, most gas-guzzling of all routes is to take Highway 5 north nearly 300 miles, then turn west near Los Banos on Highway 152 over Pacheco Pass toward Gilroy. You can either go to Gilroy and garlic and then head south on Highway 101, or take Highway 101 to Salinas and Highway 68 past Laguna Seca Raceway to Monterey.

The slightly slower and much more pleasant route is Highway 101, which takes you through Thousand Oaks, Ventura, Carpinteria, Santa Barbara, Goleta, along the coast below the Santa Ynez Mountains, then inland and northward through Santa Maria, Pismo Beach, and to San Luis Obispo with its mission and California Polytechnic State University.

From here, if you have any height queasiness, you can continue north on Highway 101 for 90 miles, but if you want a slower and definitely the most beautiful scenic route, you can pick up Highway 1 at San Luis Obispo and follow it up the coast to Morro Bay and adjoining Atascadero State Beach, Cambria, San Simeon and the Hearst Castle, a northern section of Los Padres National Forest, Big Sur, and then Carmel and Monterey 23 miles north of Big Sur.

From San Luis Obispo on Highway 101, you pass through Santa Margarita, Atascadero (best known for a California state prison), Paso Robles, the Camp Roberts Military Reservation, and King City. About 5 miles north of King City you can visit your first area winery, Scheid Vineyards, and then visit Jekel Vineyards just north of Greenfield.

Here you have another choice, particularly if you want to taste local wines. From Greenfield you can turn west on Elm Avenue, then west on Arroyo Seco Road, and north on Carmel Valley Road to Joullian Vineyards, Galante Vineyards, River Ranch Vineyards, Bernardus, Durney Vineyards, and Chateau Julien Wine Estate, all in the Carmel Valley. Be warned that this is a narrow, winding road through Los Padres National Forest that takes a good hour and a half. Or you can continue north from Greenfield to Soledad and visit Chalone Vineyard, Paraiso Springs Vineyards & Cobblestone, Smith & Hook, and Cloninger Cellars near Gonzales. From Gonzales you can drive farther north on 101 to Salinas, and take Highway 68 west to Ventana Vineyards and Monterey.

FLYING TO THE MONTEREY PENINSULA

Three commercial airlines fly nearly a hundred arrivals and departures daily between San Francisco or Los Angeles, and Monterey Peninsula Airport. Contact American Eagle, America West, and United/United Express.

Monterey Peninsula Airport (831–648–7000, www.montereyairport.com) is located on Olmsted Road off Highway 68, 4 miles east of Monterey and 19 miles west of Salinas. Avis (800–831–2847), Budget (800–527–7000), Hertz (800–654–3131), and National (800–227–7368) car rental agencies all have cars available at the airport. Monterey Salinas Transit (831–899–2555) runs buses every hour to and from Monterey and Carmel and the Monterey Peninsula Airport, with the last bus leaving the airport at 6:50 P.M. From the airport take the No. 21 Monterey, which becomes the No. 4 Carmel. On your return to the airport, take the No. 4, which becomes the No. 21 Salinas. Fare is $1.50 one-way. Taxis are also available at the curb.

The Monterey Salinas Airbus (831–883–2871) makes twelve trips daily between Monterey, Marina Municipal Airport, Salinas, San Francisco

International Airport, and San Jose International Airport. The fare is $35 one-way, $55 round-trip, and less for two or more passengers. When the Monterey Peninsula Airport is fogged in, the airlines hire the Airbus to take passengers to the San Jose and San Francisco airports, so you are rarely truly stuck. Shucks!

GETTING HERE BY TRAIN

Amtrak's star train, the Coast Starlight, travels between Los Angeles and Seattle, with a convenient stop in Salinas and free bus service from the Salinas train station to downtown Monterey and Carmel. The Coast Starlight travels along more than 200 miles of Pacific Coast, sometimes practically hanging over crashing waves, gliding past volcanic mountains and homes of movie stars, and cruising through nuclear bases. Amtrak has restored crystal and linen table-cloths to Coast Starlight dining cars, and we find the food to be startlingly good. For more information, call Amtrak at (800) USA–RAIL.

GETTING HERE BY BUS

Greyhound Bus Lines, 1042 Del Monte Avenue, Monterey (831–373–4735), runs three buses daily between San Francisco and Los Angeles and the Monterey Peninsula.

From San Francisco, the bus goes through Santa Cruz and Watsonville and costs $19. From Los Angeles, bus riders get off in Salinas and transfer to Monterey or Carmel, with a one-way fare totaling $35.

GETTING AROUND ONCE YOU'RE HERE

Car Rentals

The Monterey Peninsula is definitely a place where having a car is the most convenient way to get around. If you don't have your own and prefer this mode of transportation, contact one of the following:

Alamo, 2030 North Fremont Street, Suite D, Monterey; (800) 327–9633

Auto Rental Gallery, Dolores and Fifth Avenue, Carmel; (831) 624–3438 in Carmel or (831) 648–1261 in Monterey (for collector automobiles, including convertibles, coupes, and sedans from the forties, fifties, and sixties)

Avis Rent A Car at the Monterey Peninsula Airport; (831) 647–7140 or (800) 831–2847

Budget at the airport; (831) 373–1890 or (800) 527–7000

Enterprise at the airport; (831) 649–6300 or (800) 736–8222; 1191 Echo Street, Seaside, (831) 372–4200.

Hertz at the airport; (831) 373–3318 or (800) 654–4173

National Car Rental at the airport; (800) 227–7368 or (831) 373–4181

Rent-A-Wreck of Monterey, 95 Central Avenue, Pacific Grove; (831) 373–3356

Sears at the airport; (831) 373–1890 or (800) 527–7000

Buses

Monterey Salinas Transit (831–899–2555) offers excellent bus service throughout the Monterey Peninsula that is cleaner and safer than any other we have experienced in the United States. Between Memorial Day weekend and Labor Day, Monterey Salinas Transit operates one of the best deals in public transportation for visitors anywhere. The WAVE (Waterfront Area Visitors Express) blue-and-white buses run from 9:00 A.M. to 6:30 P.M. on a circular route from downtown Monterey through Pacific Grove. Tickets are good for same-day unlimited rides, and rides include a taped presentation of the area's history and highlights. WAVE buses stop at most major hotels and motels, the Monterey Conference Center, the Monterey Bay Aquarium, Fisherman's Wharf, and the American Tin Cannery. Fares are $1.00 for adults; 50 cents for children six to eighteen, seniors sixty-five and older, and disabled persons; and free for children five and younger.

Taxis

You'll have better success calling a cab than you will trying to hail one on the street. Yellow Cab (831–646–1234) is everywhere. Carmel also has Joe's Taxi (831–624–3885) and Carmel Yellow Cab (831–626–3333). Specializing in airport rides are Monterey Airport Taxi (831–626–3385) and Marina Taxi Co. in Marina (831–384–3894).

Limousines

Definitely the luxurious way to go. Try American International Transportation Service, 1999 Aguajito Road, Monterey 93940 (831–649–0240, fax 831–649–3534); Main Event Limousines, PO Box 2751, Monterey 93942 (831–646–LIMO); or Your Maitre d', PO Box 221696, Carmel 93922 (831–624–1717, fax 831–625–1699).

HOW TO BE A VISITOR AND NOT A TOURIST IN MONTEREY AND CARMEL

Monterey Peninsula residents are extremely tolerant of visitors and tourists—right up there with residents of Victoria, British Columbia.

Visitors are so welcomed in Carmel and Monterey, where they are in the majority on the streets, that you will forget you are one. Tourists contribute significantly to the livelihoods of the locals, and many of the salespeople you encounter are "outsiders" themselves—they live where housing is more affordable. Some old-timers regret the commercialization of Carmel and of Monterey's Cannery Row, while others celebrate sharing their treasures and enjoying the profits of your visit in their community.

But what does strain the patience of Carmel and Monterey residents is poky pedestrians who saunter out into the street, wait for their companions who haven't yet left the curb, and then slowly stroll across the street as if it's their own driveway.

To appear local and get along comfortably and well, be considerate of others—while driving your car, reading your map, or walking the streets. Stop at stop signs and wait your turn, based on who got there first. If you've arrived more or less simultaneously, California state law allows the car on the right to go first. Out-of-towners are easily pegged if they act belligerently toward other motorists.

Parking limits are enforced vigorously and occasionally profitably for the cities' coffers. Tickets and fines are great sources of revenue, and are usually paid by folks from elsewhere.

It is probably wise to avoid wearing a Carmel or Monterey T-shirt, although Monterey Bay Aquarium shirts are worn by all because even locals support its noble educational endeavors.

Try to experience the Monterey and Carmel vicinity from a local's perspective. While it is fun to visit the great tourist restaurants, hangouts, and shops, to follow Steinbeck's tales and trails, and to look for movie stars and pick local produce, it is also fun to explore those places frequented by locals—a real chance to discover their favorites, the best the local community produces, or the best of local products. Those tidbits are what we offer you as guidance.

While shorts are fine during summer days, many Carmel establishments expect everyone to look ever so slightly more presentable at dinner. Outwardly touristy restaurants will take you any way you come.

Residents of Carmel and Monterey would prefer to have you visit and leave, rather than to support their communities with more housing. Local politicians have risen and fallen with current development attitudes and moods, including former Carmel Mayor Clint Eastwood.

When walking slowly and browsing the shops, go ahead and enjoy yourself, but don't take up the whole sidewalk. Some locals actually do shop here, as well as in popular local shopping centers, which are of better quality than those in many towns and well worth your time to investigate.

Avoid these pitfalls, remember you are ladies and gentlemen, follow your Hill Guide, and you'll be sure to enjoy Monterey, Carmel, the rest of the Monterey Peninsula, and the entire central coast of California.

The prices and rates listed in this book were confirmed at press time. We recommend, however, that you call establishments before traveling to obtain current information.

CHAPTER 1

MONTEREY

et yourself right into the heart of things: Go directly to the city of Monterey. The natural focal point of historic as well as much current life is the smiling crescent of Monterey Bay itself. While a smaller percentage of locals now work in seafood industries, more work in conservation and preservation endeavors.

Beginning with Old Monterey, we'll then take you through Fisherman's Wharf and Wharf No. 2 (also known as Municipal Wharf), Cannery Row, and New Monterey. But to start, from Highway 1, take the Monterey/Fisherman's Wharf exit if you are driving south, and the Munras Avenue/Monterey exit if you're driving north from Carmel. Follow the excellent signage to Old Monterey.

OLD MONTEREY

We love the beautifully and carefully restored Spanish adobes and historic buildings of Old Monterey and the Monterey Bay National Marine Sanctuary. Visits to the restored Custom House and nearby Stanton Center/Maritime Museum afford entirely different and worthwhile experiences.

Self-propelled and -guided tours of Old Monterey are the best way to discover Monterey's and California's history, with the grand pleasures of lovely local shops and restaurants thrown in.

Our tour begins below, at the Stokes Adobe Restaurant, but you may want to precede it or complement it with others, perhaps the Path of History Walking Tour, a 2-mile stroll thoughtfully created by the city of Monterey. You can self-start the tour at any historic building by locating the yellow tiles in several languages set into the sidewalk. Large tiles and signs mark points of special interest. You may want to take the annual Adobe Tour in April (see "Events and Festivals" in "List of Lists") or the Historic Garden Tour of Old Monterey, which leaves from the courtyard of the Cooper-Molera Adobe at 1:00 P.M. the second and fourth Tuesday and Saturday, May through September ($2.00 per adult).

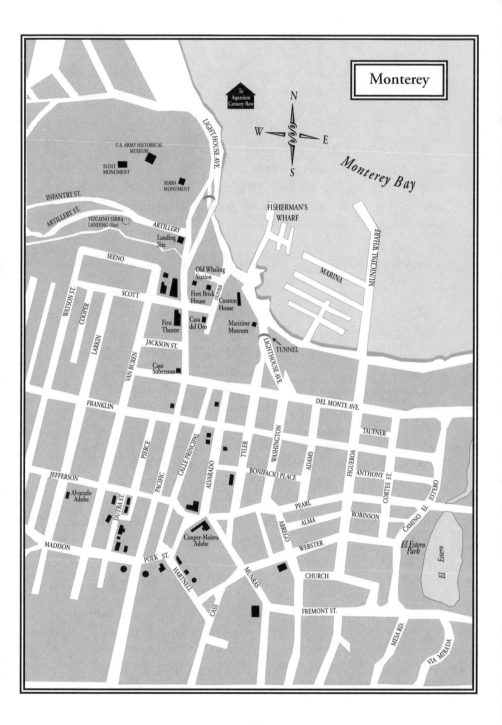

You may want to begin the Path of History Walking Tour at the Stanton Center/Maritime Museum at Custom House Plaza, where a free fourteen-minute film is shown three times every hour. From here you can also take a Monterey State Historic Park Association guided tour departing hourly from 10:00 A.M. to 4:00 P.M. daily. Tour choices include the Robert Louis Stevenson House, the Cooper-Molera Adobe, and California's First Theatre. Volunteers at individual historic sites also conduct guided tours, with the hours varying widely by building. For general information on Monterey's historic buildings, call (831) 649–7118.

A $5.00 all-day pass gains you admission to all of the state historic park buildings the same day. Historic buildings for which there is no admission charge include Pacific House (10:00 A.M.–5:00 P.M. daily); Custom House (10:00 A.M.–5:00 P.M. daily); First Brick House (10:00 A.M.–5:00 P.M. daily); Old Whaling Station Garden (10:00 A.M.–5:00 P.M. daily); Boston Store (Casa del Oro) (11:00 A.M.–3:00 P.M. Thursday–Sunday); First Theatre (1:00–5:00 P.M. Wednesday); Colton Hall (10:00 A.M.–5:00 P.M. daily); and Royal Presidio Chapel (8:30 A.M.–6:00 P.M. daily).

Monterey has accomplished the finest restoration and integration of historic buildings in a functioning business district that we have seen. The newer hotels and businesses have been designed to fit in with the historic buildings tastefully and subtly.

Interesting restaurants abound in Old Monterey, particularly along Alvarado and Calle Principal. There are two good ways to attack this intensely interesting district, and both include lunch at STOKES ADOBE RESTAURANT. Either begin with that treat, and then explore the surrounding historic buildings, walking down Alvarado's east side and then back up the west side (maybe with a sidetrack to Calle Principal and cross streets); or begin with the walk, from near the Monterey Conference Center, proceed up Pacific to Jefferson and explore the historic buildings in the vicinity, and conclude with lunch at Stokes Adobe.

We'll start with the restaurant, and then tell you about the historic buildings, including the one that houses it. Stokes Adobe offers the best in California-Mediterranean cuisine, delivering flavors from southern France, northern Italy, and Spain. You may enter the historic adobe through Hattie's Bar and stop to commune with Hattie's photo and ghost. Locals (including singles) hang out here comfortably and enjoy their lunch alone or in groups.

The dining room is cheerful and light, with bright, colorful paintings on the walls, and its windows afford views of greenery and other historic Monterey facades.

Co-owners Chef Brandon Miller and Kirk and Dorothea Probasco bring back the buzzing success enjoyed for thirty years in this building by Gallatin and

STOKES ADOBE RESTAURANT, MONTEREY

Lou Powers. The new team brings an unusual collection of California culinary credentials to this winning effort.

Miller is a San Francisco native who worked cracking crabs at Fisherman's Wharf during high school. At age twenty he took over the Pacific Heights Oyster Bar & Grill, and a year later began working in Fog City Diner, quickly becoming sous-chef to Cindy Pawlcyn. In 1987 he moved on to executive sous-chef under Michael Chiarello at Tra Vigne in the Napa Valley (from whom he learned food history and traditional dishes), after which he left for Europe, where he worked for three months with Georges Blanc, France's chief proponent of nouvelle cuisine. Returning after a month of eating his way around Italy, Miller worked as sous-chef under Jan Birnbaum (now owner/chef at Catahoula in Calistoga) at Campton Place. Later he became chef at LuLu Bis and executive chef at Paragon in San Francisco.

Kirk Probasco started as a high school busboy at Al and Jack's Rocky Point Restaurant and worked his way through restaurants and the University of California, Berkeley, to enter an investment career. His entry into restaurant management began at the Real Restaurant group's Rio Grill in Carmel. He then assisted with Tra Vigne's opening in Napa Valley and Bistro Roti and Bix in San Francisco, before coming back to Rio Grill in 1990.

Stokes Adobe's signature dishes include a fabulously tender seared hanger steak served with a perfect spinach cheese tart ($18.25); succulent garlic-marinated (yes!) grilled chicken under a brick with garlic mashed potatoes ($14.00); grilled lavender-infused pork chop with savory bread pudding and pear chutney ($17.50); and rustic pasta tubes with house-made fennel sausage and fresh Manila clams ($13.00).

Splendid lunch entrees range from ravioli of the day ($11.00), a perfect smoked pork tenderloin sandwich with black mission fig chutney and scrumptuous house-made chips ($7.50), and (Jerry's favorite) grilled steak sandwich on house potato roll with pommes frites ($7.75), to vegetable Napoleon made of crepes layered with homemade ricotta and smoked tomato sauce ($9.00). A dish of at least four flavors of imported olives arrives the minute you sit down, followed by house-made bread and informed, charming servers.

Stokes Adobe's wine list is relatively brief and direct, with excellent selections from Napa Valley (including Silver Oak, Hess Collection, and Pine Ridge Cabernets), Monterey and Central Coast, and Oregon, as well as Italian, French, and Australian wines. Prices range from less than $20 to the $191 Chateau Pichon Lalande 1988 Pauillac.

How many times did we say perfect? Never enough.

❧ *Stokes Adobe Restaurant, 500 Hartnell Street, Monterey 93940; (831) 373–1110, fax (831) 373–1202; e-mail stokes@mbay.net. Open 11:30 A.M.–10:00 P.M. Monday–Saturday, 4:00–10:00 P.M. Sunday. Full bar. Visa, MasterCard, American Express, Discover, Diners Club. Wheelchair accessible.*

HATTIE GRAGG BOUGHT STOKES ADOBE IN THE 1890S. HER GRANDCHILDREN OWN IT TODAY.

WHOLE ROASTED BABY PUMPKIN
WITH WINTER MUSHROOM RISOTTO
from Executive Chef Brandon Miller, Stokes Adobe, Monterey

½ cup (1 stick) sweet butter

½ cup brown sugar

4 Baby Bear pumpkins, topped and seeded

salt and pepper to taste

3 oz. sweet butter

2 sweet yellow onions, diced

1 bay leaf

1 tsp. each of fresh thyme, sage, and marjoram, chopped

2 oz. dried porcini mushrooms, rehydrated

1 lb. chanterelle mushrooms or other wild mushrooms (careful—K.T. Hill)

2 cups arborio rice

1 cup white wine

8 cups vegetable or chicken stock, hot

1 cup peeled fava beans or English peas

1 cup boned duck confit (optional)

salt and pepper to taste

1 cup grated Parmesan cheese

Preheat oven to 375 degrees.

Melt ½ cup of butter and add sugar, brush mixture inside pumpkins and season with salt and pepper. Roast pumpkins for 45 minutes on a greased cookie sheet until tender. Keep pumpkins warm.

In a large saucepan melt 3 oz. butter and add onions, bay leaf, and herbs. Sauté onions with herbs until sweet and translucent. Add mushrooms and sauté for 10 minutes at medium heat. Add rice and sauté for 2 more minutes.

Add white wine and cook out alcohol. Cooking at medium heat, add hot stock 4 oz. at a time, stirring constantly for 15 minutes.

Add beans and duck, season to taste with salt and pepper. Cook for 5 more minutes, finish with Parmesan cheese. Fill warm pumpkins to the rim with risotto and serve. Serves four.

We will begin our walking tour at Stokes Adobe at the intersection of Calle Principal and Hartnell, just an angled block from the beginning of Alvarado Street, Old Monterey's main street. It's also across from Casa Gutierrez and the wonderful Monterey Museum of Art.

From Stokes Adobe you can walk straight down Calle Principal (which is not Monterey's main street, despite what the name implies) to view Casa Gutierrez, the Monterey Peninsula Museum of Art, the House of Four Winds, William Tecumseh Sherman's headquarters, and the Larkin House, all in the same block between Madison and Jefferson.

Then turn left on Jefferson, and left again on Pacific, where broad lawns create dramatic foregrounds for Colton Hall and the Old Monterey Jail. We love to pause in the brick-pathed gardens of Friendly Plaza adjoining Colton Hall and climb the few stairs to Dutra Street behind Colton Hall to remind ourselves of what life must have been like in the late nineteenth century.

Theater enthusiasts may want to take a short walk to California's First Theatre at the corner of Pacific and Scott Streets, (831) 375–4916.

The **STOKES ADOBE**, which houses the restaurant, was built by English sailor James Stokes, who arrived in California in about 1833 and bought the one-room house that was located on this site. By 1842 Stokes had enlarged it to two stories, entertained here, and acted as town physician and pharmacist to many people, including Governor Jose Figueroa. He acquired two land grants and married Maria Josefa Soto in 1844.

ROASTED BUTTERNUT SQUASH SOUP

from Executive Chef Brandon Miller, Stokes Adobe, Monterey

---

2 butternut squash
olive oil
salt and pepper to taste
4 Tbs. sweet butter
1 yellow onion, sliced thin
1 Tbs. thyme
1 Tbs. sage
½ tsp. nutmeg, grated
1 qt. chicken or vegetable stock
4 Tbs. maple syrup
1 cup heavy cream
4 Tbs. apple cider vinegar

Cut squash lengthwise and seed. Rub with olive oil and season with salt and pepper. Roast face down on sheet pans at 375 degrees until tender, approximately 45 minutes.

Meanwhile, combine butter and onion in a large saucepan, cover and cook until onion is translucent. Add thyme, sage, and nutmeg.

Peel squash and combine with onions in saucepan. Add chicken stock and simmer for 1 to 1½ hours. Season with salt and pepper. Add maple syrup, cream, and cider vinegar. Puree in food processor and serve. Serves four.

CALIFORNIA'S FIRST THEATER,
PACIFIC AND SCOTT STREETS, MONTEREY

Stokes was active in the 1846 American takeover and eventually moved to San Jose.

CASA GUTIERREZ was built in 1843 and was a Mexican restaurant in its latest incarnation. You can best view its courtyard from Pacific Street and imagine what it must have been and could be.

The MONTEREY PENINSULA MUSEUM OF ART runs through the block from Calle Principal to Pacific. Here you will see work of some of the region's best artists, from Armin Hansen to Hank Ketcham, creator of Dennis the Menace.

❧ *Monterey Peninsula Museum of Art, 550 Calle Principal or 559 Pacific Avenue, Monterey; (831) 372–7591. Open 11:00 A.M.–5:00 P.M. Wednesday–Saturday, third Thursday until 8:00 P.M., 1:00–4:00 P.M. Sunday. Admission: $3.00 adults, $1.50 students and active military, children under twelve free. Visa and MasterCard in the gift shop. Wheelchair accessible.*

The HOUSE OF FOUR WINDS (Casa de los Cuatro Vientos) was built in 1835 by Thomas O. Larkin and was named for Monterey's first weathervane, made of wrought iron and mounted on its hipped roof. During the 1850s Monterey County used the building as its Hall of Records. In 1914 the Monterey Women's Civic Club bought and restored it. The Monterey Civic Club still maintains it. Thank you!

SHERMAN QUARTERS is a one-room adobe erected by people hired by Thomas O. Larkin in the late 1830s. After the American takeover in 1847, William Tecumseh Sherman, then a lieutenant with Company F of the Third U.S. Artillery, lived here. He and two pals, Henry W. Halleck and Edward O. C. Ord, for whom Fort Ord was named, all became generals in the Union Army during the Civil War.

LARKIN HOUSE was the home of Massachusetts native Thomas Oliver Larkin, who arrived in Monterey in 1832, soon married Rachel Hobson Holmes, prospered in business, and built the Custom House, endearing himself to most locals. He served as U.S. consul to California from 1843 to 1846, as a secret agent of the U.S. government for the peaceful acquisition of California. His later holdings in San Francisco (Larkin Street), Monterey, Benicia, and the Sacramento Valley made him extremely wealthy, so he moved to New York, but eventually returned to San Francisco, where he died.

Larkin House shows prevalent New England architectural influences, such as the hip roof, central hall, and interior stairway, with Mexican architectural features blended in, such as adobe walls, second-floor balcony with overhanging roof, and walled garden, all resulting in what is known as Monterey Colonial style.

A short block west is Pacific Avenue with another entrance to the Monterey Peninsula Museum of Art and, across the street, Friendly Plaza and the expansive

WILLIAM TECUMSEH SHERMAN QUARTERS AND LARKIN HOUSE

lawns in front of Colton Hall, the Old Monterey Jail, and current City Hall.

COLTON HALL was built in the late 1840s by Walter Colton, a Vermont-born writer and editor who came to Monterey with Commodore Stockton in 1845. After the American conquest of the area in 1846, Colton was appointed *alcalde* (mayor), a post he occupied for four years. Together with Robert Semple, Walter Colton founded California's first newspaper, a four-page weekly called *The Californian.*

As alcalde, the most important position in town, Colton personally designed his building as a meeting place for the California Constitutional Convention in 1849. A two-story structure built of stone with a plaster outer coat by local jail inmates, it was funded by the sale of town lots, taxes on liquor shops, and fines on gamblers (so what else is new?). After statehood it became a schoolhouse. The downstairs is used by the city of Monterey for overflow offices from nearby City Hall.

Forty-eight delegates from throughout California, which was not yet a territory and no longer a Mexican province, met at Colton Hall in 1849 to draft a constitution. The document was sent to Washington in September 1849 with a plea to make California a state. A year later, on September 9, 1850, the petitioners' request was granted. Hence Colton Hall's sobriquet: "the Cradle of Statehood."

On Dutra Street behind and just north of Colton Hall are the Vasquez Adobe and Casa de Alvarado (Alvarado Adobe).

Famed bandit and Monterey native (1835) Tiburcio Vasquez lived in the VASQUEZ ADOBE most of his childhood and then became an outlaw after California became part of the United States. He was known as a Mexicano free spirit and sort of Robin Hood type famous throughout California, before he was captured, tried, and hanged.

Businessman and early Monterey postmaster Felipe Gomez owned the house from about 1849, and later owner Louis Hill added the second story. The city of Monterey now owns the building and uses it for office space.

Right next door to the Vasquez Adobe, at the corner of Dutra and Jefferson, is the ALVARADO ADOBE (Casa de Alvarado), built by Juan Bautista Alvarado in the early 1830s for his mistress, Raimunda Castillo, with whom he had three children. She refused to marry him because she said he drank too much! He later married Martina Castro—by proxy, because he was too busy with "diplomatic affairs" (read drunk). In 1843 Raimunda married Mariano Soberanes, a prominent Monterey citizen, and they moved to his land grant, Rancho Los Ojitos, near San Luis Obispo, where she lived until her death in 1880.

After Raimunda moved out of Alvarado's house, he sold it to Portuguese trader Manuel Dutra; a later owner, Mrs. Wesley R. Heard, donated it to the

ALVARADO ADOBE, DUTRA STREET

state of California in 1978 as a residence for park personnel. It now houses an insurance agency.

CASA AMESTI, in the first block down Polk Street from Stokes Adobe, is a two-story adobe built by Jose Amesti, a Spanish Basque who came to Monterey in 1822, married Prudenciana Vallejo, the daughter of Don Ignacio Vallejo, in 1824 and became one of Monterey's leading citizens as a merchant and alcalde in 1844. Casa Amesti, an exceptional example of Monterey Colonial architecture, now houses the Old Capital Club (private).

The **COOPER-MOLERA ADOBE AND GARDEN** complex is at the head of Alvarado Street, and its colorfully painted side faces Polk Street. You can enter the blissful adobe and courtyard through the shop, with docents available to provide tours. The Cooper Store in the old Spear Warehouse is operated with love, care, and charm by the Old Monterey Preservation Society.

John Rogers Cooper was born in 1792 in Alderney (one of the British Channel Islands) and emigrated to Massachusetts with his mother, who gave birth to Cooper's half brother, Thomas Oliver Larkin, in 1802. Cooper arrived in California in 1823 as master and part owner of the merchant ship *Rover,* settled in Monterey in 1827, changed his name to Juan Bautista Cooper, and married Encarnacio Vallejo, another Vallejo daughter. In the late 1820s Cooper bought this land, built a house, and invited Larkin to join him, which he did in 1832.

EXTERIOR OF THE COOPER-MOLERA STORE

Cooper's granddaughter, Francis Molera, left the property to the National Trust for Historic Preservation, and it now belongs to the California Department of Parks and Recreation.

⊁ℑ *Cooper Store and Cooper-Molera Adobe and Garden, 525 Polk Street, Monterey 93940; (831) 649–7118. Open 10:00 A.M.–5:00 P.M. daily June–August, 10:00 A.M.–4:00 P.M. daily September–May. Guided tours 10:00 and 11:00 A.M. and noon Tuesday–Sunday June–August. No admission fee. Visa, MasterCard. Wheelchair accessible.*

CASA DE ALVARADO, at the head of Alvarado Street across from the Cooper-Molera Adobe, was a large house built in 1834 by Juan Bautista Alvarado, the first Monterey-born governor of California. This adobe, where Alvarado lived with his wife, Martina, is not to be confused with the other Alvarado Adobe on Dutra Street, in which Alvarado kept his mistress. When the house was completed, it and Thomas O. Larkin's were the only two-story houses in Monterey.

Alvarado was a real wheeler-dealer before the American takeover of California from Mexico, having led the revolt against Governor Gutierrez in 1836 and then serving as provisional governor until 1839, when the provisional government named him governor. He was replaced as governor by Brigadier General Manual Micheltorena in 1842, who also became military commander. Alvarado promptly organized the effort to get rid of Micheltorena, who ruled with his *cholos*, a local army of ex-convicts.

After the American takeover in 1846, Alvarado and his wife, Martina, moved to Rancho San Pablo (northeast of Berkeley and Oakland) to property his wife's family had received as a land grant. Alvarado died there in 1882.

Although it is slightly off the beaten track, you might want to visit the ROYAL PRESIDIO CHAPEL (founded by Father Junipero Serra in 1770 and the original church of Mission San Carlos Borromeo) that runs between Church and Freemont Streets; **ROBERT LOUIS STEVENSON'S HOUSE** at 536 Houston Street; and **CASA SOBERANES**, often called the "House with the Blue Gate." Casa Soberanes, at the corner of Pacific and Del Monte, was built by Rafael Estrada, half brother of Governor Juan Alvarado and nephew of General Mariano Vallejo. It has particularly charming gardens and a collection of early New England, Chinese, and Mexican furnishings.

CALLE PRINCIPAL AND ALVARADO STREET

As early as the 1830s Calle Principal (Main Street) and Alvarado were the center of activity for all of Monterey, northern Mexico, and the new state of California. Today they are the commercial center of Old Monterey and the site of its vibrant year-round Farmers Market from 4:00 to 8:00 P.M. Tuesdays. Here you can sample Brazilian delicacies or ostrich and eggs, along with ripe vegetables and fruit, aromatic cinnamon buns, breads, barbecued chicken, and beef kabobs.

A few of the original adobe buildings and lovely walled gardens that used to line the streets remain, with businesses or service industries employing locals, and computers to connect them to visitors from around the world.

We will now walk you from Stokes Adobe down Calle Principal and up Alvarado Street, as well as point out "don't misses" on Old Monterey's cross streets.

As we said earlier, despite its translation to principal or main street, Calle Principal is not that. Its primary attractions are four: an excellent city parking garage between Franklin and Jefferson Streets; Montrio bistro; the First Noel; and Chambers Sports Bar in the Marriott Hotel.

Along with Tarpy's and Rio Grill, the sensuous **MONTRIO** is part of the Downtown Dining group of restaurants owned by Tony Tollner. Montrio's interior design within a historic firehouse accomplishes with flair what many other restaurant designers only attempt. The restaurant's undulations and curves set up a pleasant experience for many senses, although the noise level at times may dull one or two. You can't miss the puffy white clouds hanging from the ceiling, the copper and iron sculpture, and the hand-carved curved bar and bar stools.

Designated "Restaurant of the Year" by *Esquire* magazine in 1995, Montrio combines urbanity with country-fresh ingredients without overdoing nouvelle cuisine. At lunch Chef Tony Baker (yes!) produces a rotisserie chicken niçoise salad, basmati rice cakes, delightfully light mahi mahi ($9.90), a portobello and Tillamook with grilled onions sandwich ($7.95), and grilled salmon with

MONTRIO GRILL'S
INTERIOR DESIGN

cucumber and watercress mayo ($8.25). Dinner offers range from grilled pork chops at $16.85 to Chilean sea bass ($17.75).

❧ *Montrio, 414 Calle Principal, Monterey 93942; (831) 648–8880; www.montrio.com. Open 11:30 A.M.–10:00 P.M. weekdays, until 11:00 P.M. Saturday with lunch until 5:00 P.M., and Sunday from 5:00 P.M. Full bar. Visa, MasterCard, American Express. Wheelchair accessible.*

At the corner of Calle Principal and Franklin is FIRST NOEL, a Christmas store. For lovers of ornaments and Christmas scenes, this store is year-round heaven, featuring Christopher Radko, Possible Dreams santas, Seraphim Classics angels, Department 56 villages, Pooh Classics, and Fontanini Heirloom nativities. (It has a sister store in Pacific Grove.)

❧ *First Noel, 201 West Franklin, Monterey 93942; (831) 648–1250. Open 9:30 A.M.–6:00 P.M. Monday–Saturday, 11:00 A.M.–4:00 P.M. Sunday. Visa, MasterCard, American Express. Wheelchair accessible.*

BYTES INTERNET CAFE, across Calle Principal from Montrio and First Noel, is a great place to pick up your e-mail, play computer games, communicate, and enjoy some casual food and coffee. A very mellow place. You can also enter Bytes through the Osio Cinema.

❧ *Bytes Internet Cafe, 403 Calle Principal, Monterey 93942; phone/fax (831) 644–0743. Open 9:00 A.M.–9:00 P.M. daily. Visa, MasterCard. Wheelchair accessible.*

Chambers Sports Bar & Grill in the Marriott is exactly what it says it is. Now turn the corner down the little hill onto West Franklin Street heading toward Alvarado Street. In this short block you will find that the most interesting businesses have to do with food. Surprise!

A couple doors down Franklin at the corner of Alvarado is our favorite local coffee place, **PLUME COFFEE**, whose address is actually on Alvarado. Here every cup of coffee is ground and brewed when you select from thirty-two varieties of beans and such blends as Heart of Darkness, Smooth French, Sweet Italian Organic, and Bean of the Earth. Tea lovers can choose from huge Republic of Tea jars. All this and an abundance of delectable pastries from local bakers.
➳ *Plume Coffee, 400 Alvarado, Monterey 93940; (831) 373–4526. Open 6:30 A.M.–11:00 P.M. Sunday–Wednesday and till midnight Thursday–Saturday. Visa, MasterCard. Wheelchair accessible.*

Just to complete this block of Franklin, we point out **JAMBA JUICE** at the corner on the north side of Franklin. When you walk in the door of this bright, slightly industrial juice grindery, the air smells heavenly with fruit aromas. While the service is fast food and not very friendly, the smoothies ($3.50) are hugely popular and excellent. The noise makes the crowd move in and out fast. (No Rollerblades allowed!)
➳ *Jamba Juice, 380 Alvarado Street, Monterey 93940; (831) 655–9696. Open 7:00 A.M.–10:00 P.M. Monday–Thursday, 8:00 A.M.–11:00 P.M. Saturday, 8:00 A.M.–10:00 P.M. Sunday. No credit cards. Wheelchair accessible.*

Back up Franklin a couple doors is our favorite local pub, **CROWN & ANCHOR ENGLISH PUB,** downstairs underground. Englishish stuff beckons you down the stairway, and the collection of miniature ships, maps, and drawings is worth the visit. An early photo of Queen Elizabeth II and her Duke of Edinburgh greets you at the bottom of the stairs. Locals hang out at the substantial old English bar, and the atmosphere is both dignified and fun. British-owned and -operated, the Crown & Anchor believes in the important role of the pub in welcoming home sailors and travelers from everywhere, with the credo "You'll be a stranger here but once."
All entrees come with a historic description of their traditional origins, plus fries, mushy peas, mashed potatoes, or salad. You can choose from a wide range of salads (all under $9.00), fish and chips (up to $7.95), calamari and chips ($7.95), burgers or veggie burgers, sirloin of beef with Yorkshire pudding or corned beef and cabbage ($8.95), or lamb shanks, steak and mushroom or chicken pie, bangers and mash ($7.95), curries, and even New York steak ($13.95). Sandwiches range from a Philly steak to curry chicken, banger on a roll, or shrimp salad, all under $7.00 and served with chips. Twenty beers on tap.

❧❧ *Crown & Anchor English Pub*, *150 West Franklin Street, Monterey 93940; (831) 649–6496. Full bar. Visa, MasterCard, American Express. Not wheelchair accessible.*

Now on to Alvarado Street. We must warn you that Monterey in general, and specifically Alvarado Street, seems to have an interesting food establishment of some kind in nearly every other storefront. Brace yourselves.

We suggest that you head down Alvarado for 1 block to **BAY BOOKS & CAFE**. Bay Books is the ultimate independent bookstore in Monterey, with a full-service espresso bar, great salads, sandwiches, bagels, pastries by T. Fred Baker, Carmel Valley Coffee Roasting Company's excellent coffees and teas thrown in, and an open mike forum at 7:00 P.M. on the third Wednesday of every month.

This is where you get your newspapers from all over the world and country, local and foreign-language magazines, and an excellent collection of foreign-language books, such as *Arabian Nights* in Arabic and John Steinbeck's works in Japanese. Individual special orders placed during the week are available in one day, a highly unusual turnaround time.

Manager Anne Congleton, who keeps the service and aura going, also has strong roles in organizing the Monterey Bay Book Festival to benefit Reading Is Fundamental, now held in early November. The festival attracts such participating authors as Jane Smiley and Andrew Cleary. Publishers host booths, characters from kids' books give readings, and workshops enlighten authors on how to get published.

❧❧ *Bay Books & Cafe, 316 Alvarado Street, Monterey 93940; (831) 375–1855. Open 7:30 A.M.–10:00 P.M. Sunday–Thursday, till 11:00 P.M. Friday–Saturday. Visa, MasterCard, American Express. Wheelchair accessible.*

HEDI'S is a lovely new addition, with Mephisto, Clarks, H.S. Trask, and Cole Haan shoes. Hedi's also has a magnificent store in The Barnyard shopping center south of Carmel.

❧❧ *Hedi's, 350 Alvarado Street, Monterey 93940; (831) 655–3080. Open 10:00 A.M.–6:00 P.M. daily. Visa, MasterCard, American Express, Discover. Wheelchair accessible.*

Just up Alvarado from Hedi's is the open space entrance to Osio Cinema & Cafe, a multiscreen theater with an entrance to Bytes Internet Cafe.

The **MONTEREY PENINSULA VISITORS & CONVENTION BUREAU** and Congressman Sam Farr have the good fortune to occupy the Rodriguez–Osio Adobe, built in 1849 by Jacinto Rodriguez as a large house and store where one

copy of California's first constitution was signed. Eventually Rodriguez's sister-in-law lived in the house and inherited it. Both offices welcome your visit.
❧ *Monterey Peninsula Visitors & Convention Bureau, 380 Alvarado Street, Monterey 93940; (831) 649–1770. Open 8:30 A.M.–5:00 P.M. Monday–Friday, 10:00 A.M.–4:00 P.M. Saturday July–August. Wheelchair accessible.*

After you pass Jamba Juice, cross Franklin Street again and continue up the west side of Alvarado. Just beyond Plume Coffee you come to **HATS & CAPS**, one of a very local "chain's" four stores. Hat lovers will enjoy the best of Stetson, Scala, derbies and bowlers, Greek fisherman's hats, books, postcards, magnets, sweatclothes, and gloves.
❧ *Hats & Caps, 402 Alvarado Street, Monterey 93940; (831) 645–9556. Open 9:00 A.M.–6:00 P.M. daily. Visa, MasterCard, American Express, Discover. Wheelchair accessible.*

Hats & Caps is technically in the **MONTEREY HOTEL** building, a restored historic downtown hotel with leaded-glass windows and English decor. Next door and within the hotel is **AIELLO JEWELERS & IMPORTS**. The Aiello family has been in business here since 1961. They feature diamonds, pearls, Italian designer jewelry, religious articles, and Bulova clocks.
❧ *Aiello Jewelers & Imports, 408 Alvarado Street, Monterey 93940; (831) 375–4260. Open 10:00 A.M.–5:30 P.M. Monday–Saturday. Visa, MasterCard, American Express. Wheelchair accessible.*

VIVA MONTEREY, an openly wild cabaret cafe in the historic and slightly altered Casa Sanchez, has aqua stools and walls and boasts live music seven days a week. It also claims to be "locals' favorite pool house," and they don't mean swimming.
❧ *Viva Monterey, 414 Alvarado Street, Monterey 93940; (831) 646–1415. Open 4:00 P.M.–2:00 A.M. Visa, MasterCard, American Express, Discover. Wheelchair accessible.*

Hot popcorn smells waft out the door onto the sidewalk from the United Artists' Theatre, one of the old single-screen movie houses, surviving under the same ownership as the State Theatre across the street. In fact, to watch movies playing here, you get your tickets across the street.
SWENSON & SILACCI FLOWERS & GIFTS is an elegant, feminine florist with lots of stuff for sale that people who like to arrange flowers need and also lots of interesting gifts for people you left at home. Designers in this fifty-year-old establishment are AIFD certified, and you will enjoy their work even if you only want to walk in for the experience.

❧ *Swenson & Silacci Flowers & Gifts, 432 Alvarado Street, Monterey 93940; (831) 375–2725. Open 8:00 A.M.–5:30 P.M. Monday–Friday, 9:00 A.M.–4:00 P.M. Saturday. Visa, MasterCard, American Express. Wheelchair accessible.*

ROSINE'S RESTAURANT is a classic small-townish family restaurant that is packed all the time because it offers slightly better than down-home cooking, from meat loaf and sandwiches to calamari and broiled salmon. What catches your eye as you walk in are the tallest-you-have-ever-seen cakes, the most popular of which are their candy bar cakes (which may include whole Oreo cookies in the icing). You'll also find Snickers pie; Kit Kat, Rocky Road, and Almond Joy cakes; carrot cake; German chocolate, or, yes, chocolate chocolate. Enormous slices range from $4.83 to $5.09. Hearty breakfast, lunch, and dinner. Tall plants and flowered paintings and upholstery set the tone.

❧ *Rosine's Restaurant, 434 Alvarado Street, Monterey 93940; (831) 375–1400, fax (831) 375–2636. Open 9:00 A.M.–9:00 P.M. Monday–Thursday, 7:30 or 8:00 A.M.–10:00 P.M. Friday–Saturday, 8:00 A.M.–9:00 P.M. Sunday. Visa, MasterCard, American Express, Discover, Carte Blanche, Diners Club. Wheelchair accessible.*

BRITANNIA ARMS offers twenty-four draft beers, darts, European soccer matches and many other sports on big screens, and substantial pub grub: meat pies, corned beef and cabbage, beef braised in Guinness, salads, soups, and the Moby Brit, eighteen ounces of cod fried in beer batter. Live Music Friday–Saturday.

❧ *Britannia Arms, 444 Alvarado Street, Monterey 93940; (831) 656–9543; www.britanniaarms.com. Full bar. Open 11:00 A.M.–2:00 A.M. daily. Visa, MasterCard. Wheelchair accessible.*

Bonifacio Plaza wanders west between Alvarado and Calle Principal with primarily offices lining it. Just south of it is the BAGEL BAKERY, one of a small local chain of shops with tender fresh bagels and great quick bagel sandwiches. You're safe at any one of their sites on the peninsula.

❧ *Bagel Bakery, 452 Alvarado Street, Monterey 93940; (831) 372–5242, fax (831) 372–5249. Open 6:00 A.M.–6:00 P.M. Monday–Saturday, till 7:00 P.M. Tuesday, 7:00 A.M.–5:00 P.M. Sunday. Wheelchair accessible.*

DICK BRUHN A MAN'S STORE moved into the old Woolworth's store from Carmel in 1998 to bring formal wear and elegant sportswear for men and women to Alvarado Street. It features Monterey Peninsula's own Robert Talbott, Pendleton, Alan Edwards, Street Croix, and Hickey-Freeman, as well as uniforms to meet your needs. Henry the mannequin greets you dressed as a security guard and occasionally Nigel the butler, dressed in tails, makes a formal appearance. Ladies will enjoy the new M'Lady Bruhn adjoining the men's store. There is also a store in Salinas.

❧ *Dick Bruhn A Man's Store, 458 Alvarado Street, Monterey 93940; (831) 647–1100. Open 9:00 A.M.–6:00 P.M. Monday–Saturday, 11:00 A.M.–4:00 P.M. Sunday. Visa, MasterCard, American Express. Wheelchair accessible.*

Just south of Dick Bruhn's, try **PAPA CHANO'S TAQUERIA** for an informal family-style sample of "autentica comida Mexicana." And they mean authentic Mexican cuisine, featuring wildly fresh ingredients and your choice of meats with every order, including shredded pork, carne asada (marinated flank steak), green chili pork, chicken, tongue, pollo asado (marinated barbecued chicken), or chorizo (Mexican sausage). Burritos begin at $4.25, and the most expensive combination plates top out at $6.99, with an excellent selection of Mexican beers. Hand-chopped salsa and bowls of succulent radishes await you at every table.

❧ *Papa Chano's Taqueria, 462 Alvarado Street, Monterey 93940; (831) 646–9587. Open 10:00 A.M.–midnight daily. Beer. No credit cards. Wheelchair accessible.*

R. G. BURGERS is the closest thing to a gourmet burger shop we have seen. Self-dubbed "A 'real good' Place to Eat," r. g. serves "real good burgers," natch. But we can get over the language. Best thing: The burgers are all available in six-ounce beef or turkey patties, boneless, skinless chicken breast, or vegetarian falafel patties. Seasoned fries or salads are extra. Winter makes the fresh home-made soup and salad platter tempting ($6.25).

The basic burger is a whopping $3.95, with prices escalating slightly through mushroom-cheddar and guacamole-Swiss at $5.25, to a double burger ($6.60), or a burger with blue cheese, chili, red pepper, or lemon pepper (all $5.50 and under). Thick milk shakes with four basic flavors are yummy and $3.00, while more exotic flavors are a quarter more and malts another fifty cents.

❧ *r. g. burgers, 470 Alvarado Street, Monterey 93940; (831) 647–3100. Open 10:30 A.M.-10:00 P.M. weekdays, till 11:00 P.M. weekends. No credit cards. Wheelchair accessible.*

Our favorite camera store in Monterey is **GREEN'S CAMERA WORLD**, where they will sell you a wide range of cameras, bags, equipment, albums, frames, and film, and fix the simplest camera problem for dummies like us. They will even change your battery or film for you, with a pleasant, not teeth-gritting, smile.

❧ *Green's Camera World, 472 Alvarado Street, Monterey 93940; (831) 655–1840. Open 9:30 A.M.–6:00 P.M. Monday–Saturday, 11:00 A.M.– 4:00 P.M. Sunday. Visa, MasterCard, American Express, Discover. Wheelchair accessible.*

LALLA PALOOZA is a confessed "Big American Menu and Martini Bar" that features all sorts of colors and flavors of martinis that would make older generations gasp. But if you ask, you can even get a real martini (you know, the gin with olives kind?). This is definitely a place aiming at twenty- to thirty-somethings.

We like the salmon niçoise salad ($14.95) or the Dagwood Sandwich (like Dagwood and Blondie never knew)—apple-smoked bacon, ham, turkey, and chicken ($9.95). You might prefer a wide range of pastas or Black Angus prime steaks ($16–$24).

✿ *Lalla Palooza, 474 Alvarado Street, Monterey 93940; (831) 645–9036. Open 11:00 A.M.– 11:00 P.M. Monday–Saturday, 4:00–11:00 P.M. Sunday. Full bar. Visa, MasterCard, American Express. Wheelchair accessible.*

One of the best Oriental (read Persian) rug and furnishing stores we have seen in tourist places is NO MADS FINE RUGS & ART, wedged between Lalla Palooza and Avalon Beads. No Mads has elegant rugs and extremely interesting imported furniture and accessories.

✿ *No Mads Fine Rugs & Art, 486 Alvarado Street, Monterey 93940; (831) 373–1009. Open 10:30 A.M.–5:30 P.M. daily. Visa, MasterCard, American Express. Wheelchair accessible.*

Tiny AVALON BEADS has a fun collection of bead necklaces (and all the equipment to make your own), candleholders, hand-carved mirrors, Celtic symbols and jewelry, and Indian sarongs! The decor is constantly changing. You might want to check it out.

✿ *Avalon Beads, 490 Alvarado Street, Monterey 93940; (831) 372–3550. Open 10:00 A.M.–7:00 P.M. Monday–Saturday, 11:00 A.M.–5:00 P.M. Sunday. Visa, MasterCard. Wheelchair accessible.*

At the top of Alvarado Street is DO RE MI, a music store that also sells videos but does not rent them. This is an extremely cool place for music lovers and hipsters.

✿ *Do Re Mi, 498 Alvarado Street, Monterey 93940; (831) 372–8460. Open 10:00 A.M.–9:00 P.M. daily. Visa, MasterCard, American Express, Discover. Wheelchair accessible.*

Now we will bring you down Alvarado Street's east side, with an almost hidden Ordway Drug Store in an old bank building.

MONTEREY ICE CREAM is an extremely popular in-and-out purveyor of Dreyer's ice cream, specializing in those fabulous old Dreyer's standards like mud pie and Butterfinger ice creams, with the updated additions of smoothies, frozen yogurt, espresso drinks, and Italian sodas.

❧ Monterey Ice Cream, 491 Alvarado Street, Monterey 93940; (831) 375–1531. Open 11:00 A.M.–10:00 P.M. Monday–Thursday, till 10:30 P.M. Friday–Saturday. Visa and MasterCard for purchases over $5.00. Wheelchair accessible.

One door down Alvarado is many locals' favorite informal dining spot: OLD MONTEREY CAFE, voted "Best Breakfast" in Monterey for several years running. Must-tries are the chocolate chip pancakes, sumptuous waffles, lush fresh blueberry or lemon-coffee muffins, banana bread, and 6-inch high slices of coffee cake. Kathleen likes the spinach and mushroom omelette topped with avocado and artichokes. Lunchtime specials include crab sandwiches, salads, and Mexican specialties (try the chilis rellenos). Well-polished wood and dangling plants enhance the crowded, cluttered funk that hundreds of visitors and locals come back daily to enjoy. Definitely kid friendly.

❧ Old Monterey Cafe, 489 Alvarado Street, Monterey 93940; (831) 646–1021. Open 7:00 A.M.–2:30 P.M. daily. Visa, MasterCard, American Express, Diners Club, Carte Blanche, JCB. Wheelchair accessible.

Just north of Old Monterey Cafe, the MONTEREY BIBLE BOOK STORE does more than sell bibles. It also offers a large collection of Celtic music, religious and spiritual books, jewelry, gifts, videos, and bible dictionaries.

❧ Monterey Bible Book Store, 487 Alvarado Street, Monterey 93940; (831) 375–6487. Open 10:00 A.M.–5:30 P.M. Monday–Saturday. Visa, MasterCard, American Express, Discover. Wheelchair accessible.

The wonderful MONTEREY BAY PIE COMPANY, the adored baby of Richard Lampner, is rapidly becoming a locals' favorite. Be sure to sample the piecrust cookies, pies, and espresso, inside or out, and take home a plastic pie cutter. Slices are $1.95, pies $9.95. Pies include Otter Bay Olallie berry, mixed berry, apple, no-sugar-added apple, peach-apple crumb, strawberry-rhubarb, pecan, cherry, and pumpkin. All the berries and rhubarb are grown nearby.

❧ Monterey Bay Pie Company, 481 Alvarado Street, Monterey 93940; (831) 656–9PIE. Open 10:00 A.M.–6:00 P.M. Monday, till 9:00 P.M. Tuesday–Thursday, till 10:00 P.M. Friday–Saturday.

We quickly change gears with the MUCKY DUCK BRITISH PUB next door. Voted by locals the "Best Pub of 1998," the Mucky Duck has a great enclosed patio in back with live music on farmers' market and other nights. Dark wood booths fill the room, with the bar on your right as you enter, and a dart alcove just beyond the bar. Singles gather at the fireplace in the round in the back room.

Thursday night is Trivia Night when you pay $1.00 to play trivia for a whole evening, with the bartender asking the questions. Regulars come by for the contest and feast on roast beef and Yorkshire pudding, English mixed grill, bangers and mash, fish and chips, steak and mushroom pie, and Scotch eggs, all under $12. A good place to sample British ales.

❧ *Mucky Duck British Pub, 479 Alvarado Street, Monterey 93940; (831) 655–3031. Open 11:30 A.M.–11:30 P.M. Sunday–Thursday till 1:00 A.M. Friday–Saturday. Full bar. Visa, MasterCard, American Express, Discover, Carte Blanche, Diners Club. Mostly wheelchair accessible.*

FUTONS & SUCH sells futons—surprise. The "such" includes wall beds and some hilarious needlepoint pillows that are small enough to take home if you don't want to pack a whole futon.

❧ *Futons & Such, 475 Alvarado, Monterey 93940; (831) 373-2443. Open 10:00 A.M.–6:00 P.M. daily. Visa, MasterCard, American Express, Discover.*

North and down from Futons & Such is the COIN SHOPPE, a musty emporium of bought-and-sold collectibles, swords, clocks, golf memorabilia, gold and silver bullion, sports cards, Nikon and Hasselblad cameras, and prints. A forty-eight-star American flag covers the glass in the door.

❧ *Coin Shoppe, 471 Alvarado, Monterey 93940; (831) 646–9030. Open 10:00 A.M.–5:00 P.M. Monday–Friday. Visa, MasterCard, American Express, Discover, Diners Club. Wheelchair accessible but a tight squeeze.*

TUTTO BUONO offers a bright contrast to the Coin Shoppe, bringing locals and visitors into the colorful present and future with wholesome, creative California Italian food. John Spadaro, who also owns the terrific Spado's in Salinas, presides over this adventurous yet reliable eatery. White-and-black tile floors set off light wood fixtures, murals of the Italian Riviera, and photos of good customer John Tesh. The GT Grand Prix (at Laguna Seca) recommends Tutto Buono, which also sponsors the Bookmobile at the farmers' market.

Particularly if you are from out of California, you might want to try the very local Castroville artichoke served with an unusually good balsamic Dijon vinaigrette ($6.95), the vast and tempting antipasti bar, the polenta torine with layers of polenta and eggplant, light, thin brick-oven pizzas (try the Gorgonzola with chicken, Roma tomatoes, and caramelized onions at $11.50), and Italian salads. We particularly like the Insalata di Noci e Gorgonzola of local (Salinas) romaine lettuces, toasted walnuts, mushrooms, and pancetta with blue cheese dressing ($6.95).

The Monterey Bay calamari and tomatoes over linguini is excellent ($12.95), as are the half roasted range chicken (actually, it's a completely roasted half chicken) ($13.95) and La Nostra Bistecca, a melt-in-your-mouth sixteen-ounce New York Black Angus porterhouse steak marinated in olive oil and fresh rosemary and topped with a cabernet-mushroom beurre-blanc sauce ($16.95). You might want to share this.

➤ *Tutto Buono, 469 Alvarado Street, Monterey 93940; (831) 372–1880. Open from 11:00 A.M. with dinner from 5:00 P.M. Full bar. Visa, MasterCard, American Express, Carte Blanche, Diners Club, JCB. Wheelchair accessible.*

The espresso is good at Tutto Buono, although **STARBUCKS** addicts can get their coffee fixes right next door and sit at sidewalk tables watching the tourists go by.

➤ *Starbucks, 461 Alvarado Street, Monterey 93940; (831) 373–8575. Open 6:00 A.M.–11:00 P.M. Monday–Thursday, till midnight Friday–Saturday, 7:00 A.M.–11:00 P.M. Sunday. Visa, MasterCard, American Express. Wheelchair accessible.*

CARMEL CREAMERY, just down from Tutto Buono, makes ice cream right here and has a great bench to rest on in its entranceway. Feast your eyes on the yellow and black Model A, stuffed animals, Jelly Bellies, chocolates, and yes, that yummy ice cream. (You can also find one in Carmel at Carmel Plaza on Ocean Avenue.)

➤ *Carmel Creamery, 459 Alvarado Street, Monterey 93940; (831) 372–4720. Open 11:00 A.M.–9:00 P.M. Monday–Thursday, till 10:00 P.M. Friday–Saturday, noon–7:00 P.M. Sunday. Visa, MasterCard. Wheelchair accessible.*

You might venture into the Consignment Gallery set back between the Creamery and Gasper's.

GASPER'S JEWELERS is a delightfully old-fashioned jewelry store specializing in custom designs, diamonds, colored stones, watches, and Lladro figurines. And they are nice to visitors "just looking."

➤ *Gasper's Jewelers, 447 Alvarado Street, Monterey 93940; (831) 375–5332. Open 10:00 A.M.–6:00 P.M. Monday–Saturday. Visa, MasterCard, American Express, Discover. Wheelchair accessible.*

Detour to your right down Bonifacio Place for two very special off-the-beaten-path-of-life shops. **MONTEREY BOOK COMPANY** is a book lover's bookstore. We never want to leave. Oriental rugs, elegant library tables, and fine books set the ambience. Here you can find old, rare, and out-of-print books, either through their search service or in the store. Appraising and bookbinding are also available. *❧ Monterey Book Company,* 136 Bonifacio Place, Monterey 93940; (831) 372–3111, fax (831) 372–5537. Open "about 10:00 A.M.–5:00 P.M." Wednesday–Saturday. Visa, MasterCard. Wheelchair accessible.

For a push-the-edge experience, venture next door into the **OUTER EDGE HAIR STUDIO**, where hairdresser and collector supreme Michael Keenan does his thing the last ten days of every month. He spends the rest of his time in New York and Kansas City and comes back to Monterey to cut pals' hair by appointment only. But that's not the point.

Just walk into this place. Men and women, both. Hair studio? Where? You have never seen or lived with such funk and junk: old radios, pink kitchen stools and phones, clocks from the thirties to the fifties, bikes hanging from the ceiling, old televisions everywhere, a clothes wringer on the sidewalk. To top it all off, the haircutting subject looks into an open 1947 Norge refrigerator with the salon mirror in the back of the fridge. Michael and his creation are enough to make us all question society's design restraints!

❧ Outer Edge Hair Studio, 146 Bonifacio Place, Monterey 93940; (831) 649–4151. Open 7:00 A.M.–9:00 P.M. the last ten days of each month. Visa, MasterCard. Wheelchair accessible if some stuff is moved out of the way.

Right next to Outer Edge, The Blue Moon Trading Company sells vintage and contemporary clothing.

Across Tyler at Bonifacio is the terrific, colorful, and inexpensive **TURTLE BAY TAQUERIA**, an offshot of the earthy and excellent Fishwife (see p. 67). Turtle Bay makes different salsas daily (help yourself), from roasted tomato to avocado tomatillo. Order at the counter and servers bring steaming salmon tacos, wraps, burritos, calamari, quesadillas, and unbelievable chicken-, fish-, steak-, or shrimp-topped salads.

❧ Turtle Bay Taqueria, 431 Tyler at Bonifacio, Monterey 93940; (831) 333–1500. Beer and wine. Open 11:00 A.M.–9:00 P.M. Monday–Thursday, till 9:30 P.M. Friday–Saturday, noon–8:30 P.M. Sunday. Visa, MasterCard, American Express, Discover. Wheelchair accessible.

For interesting pastries and sandwiches, try tiny **JOSEPH'S PASTISSERIE AND DELI**, which reflects Joe's Malta background, as well as his experience at the Lodge at Pebble Beach, Palm Beach Polo Club, and Carmel Valley Ranch.

❧ Joseph's Patisserie and Deli, 435 Alvarado Street, Monterey 93940; (831) 373–1108. Open 9:00 A.M.–4:00 P.M. Monday–Saturday. No credit cards. Wheelchair accessible but tight.

Check out **RED'S DONUTS SINCE 1950,** an early-part-of-the-day place with David Goins posters, stools at the counter, and hot chicken breast sandwiches. This may look like just an urban deli and donut place, but Red has cooked at the Sheraton Hotel in Boston and served as pastry chef at several Hawaiian resorts as well as at Pebble Beach Lodge, Carmel Valley Ranch, and the Palm Beach Polo Club. So you're in for a surprise.

❧ *Red's Donuts Since 1950, 433 Alvarado Street, Monterey 93940; (831) 372–9761. Open 6:30 A.M.–1:30 P.M. daily. Visa, MasterCard. Wheelchair accessible.*

TSING TAO CHINESE RESTAURANT serves Mandarin and Szechuan cuisine and food to take back to your hotel room. Specialties include mushu shrimp ($8.50), hot braised fish, eggplant with hot sauce, fried bean curd with Tsing Tao brown sauce ($6.25), and fried chicken with garlic sauce ($6.50). Combination dinners range from $7.75 to $9.75 per person. Lunch specials and rice plates range from $4.25 to $5.25 (including soup, tea, and fortune cookies).

❧ *Tsing Tao Chinese Restaurant, 429 Alvarado Street, Monterey 93940; (831) 375–3000. Open 11:00 A.M.–10:00 P.M. Monday–Friday, 11:30 A.M.–10:00 P.M. Saturday–Sunday. Beer and wine. Visa, MasterCard. Wheelchair accessible.*

Kids of all ages enjoy the masked D.J. in the front window of **MUSIC UNLIMITED,** which supplies much of the Monterey peninsula with hot instruments, from every-color-of-the-rainbow Fender and Taylor guitars to drums and organs. Nostalgia?

❧ *Music Unlimited, 425 Alvarado Street, Monterey 93940; (831) 372–5893. Open 10:00 A.M.–7:00 P.M. Monday–Friday, till 6:00 P.M. Saturday, 11:00 A.M.–5:00 P.M. Sunday. Visa, MasterCard, American Express. Wheelchair accessible.*

While we don't urge anyone to smoke, a trip into **HELLAM'S TOBACCO SHOP** is a trip into the past. Our grandfathers were everywhere.

Lee Hellam's father, Frank, opened the shop, originally across the street, in 1893. Lee carries on the tradition while he watches the store and the customers perusing his imported cigarettes, an enormous pipe collection, canisters of loose tobacco priced by the ounce, a multipiece lighter collection displaying symbols of most men's interests, all sorts of pocketknives, chess sets, magnifying glasses, and quickie candy bars right by the door.

❧ *Hellam's Tobacco Shop, 423 Alvarado Street, Monterey 93940; (831) 373–2816. Open 9:00 A.M.–9:00 P.M. Monday–Thursday, till 10:00 P.M. Friday–Saturday, 10:00 A.M.–6:00 P.M. Sunday. Visa, MasterCard, American Express, Discover. Wheelchair accessible.*

Now we come to the United Artists GOLDEN STATE THEATRE, whose sister is across the street. This is where you buy your tickets for both venues. A historic landmark designed by Reid Brothers and built in 1926, this was the first theater on the Monterey Peninsula to show talking pictures (1929).
❦ *Golden State Theatre, 417 Alvarado Street, Monterey 93940; (831) 372–4555. Open 11:00 A.M.–midnight daily. No credit cards. Mostly wheelchair accessible.*

The largest sushi bar in Monterey is at elegant JUGEM JAPANESE RESTAURANT next door to the movie theater. While the restaurant has a full Japanese menu, the sushi bar is the attraction for most locals. Jugem also features fresh local seafood as well as a whole low-calorie menu. Great for drop-ins.
❦ *Jugem Japanese Restaurant, 409 Alvarado Street, Monterey 93940; (831) 373–6463. Open for lunch 11:00 A.M.–2:30 P.M. Monday–Friday, dinner 5:00 P.M.–10:00 P.M. Monday–Saturday, 5:00 P.M.–9:30 P.M. Sunday. Beer and wine. Visa, MasterCard, American Express, Discover. Wheelchair accessible.*

FISHERMAN'S WHARF AND
MUNICIPAL WHARF (WHARF II)

Monterey Fisherman's Wharf consists of two piers (one called Fisherman's Wharf and the other called Wharf II or Municipal Wharf No. 2) that stretch out into the harbor. This is where Commodore John Drake Sloat landed in 1846 to raise the U.S. flag and where Monterey's once thriving cargo and whaling industry boomed from the mid-1800s into the early 1900s.

To get to Fisherman's Wharf, take Del Monte Avenue along the waterfront and turn north into one of the municipal parking lots. The eastern parking lot (nearest Wharf II) has some free parking close to the working pier. The western parking lot ($1.00 an hour) provides the easiest access to the Custom House, Fisherman's Wharf, and the recreation path that leads all the way through New Monterey to Pacific Grove. There is also metered parking on Wharf No. 2.

Fisherman's Wharf is the amusement park part of the whole wharf, with oodles of souvenir shops, restaurants, hawkers, and occasional food samples. Little remains of the old-style sale of fresh fish right off the boat at stands in front of restaurants. Wharf II is still a working fishing pier, with a large processing plant at the end of the pier and two restaurants you might want to try on the way.

We especially like ELVES' GRILL BOAT HOIST & RESTAURANT, the first restaurant you come to on your left going out Municipal Wharf II. It's a tiny triangular diner with a takeout window on its left end, three or four booths, and a

ELVES' GRILL BOAT HOIST & RESTAURANT, MONTEREY

counter with stools full of local former and current fishers and blarney throwers. Booth tables allow you to look eastward and watch diving sea otters and crazy people who like cold water. Counter tables let you watch Lloyd and friends whip up those famous omelettes and waffles. Often one conversation dominates the whole place.

Owner-chef Lloyd Elves was born into this place where his mother used to reign as president of the local fishermen's association. Try his fruit-filled Belgian waffles, squid and eggs, local artichoke omelettes, fresh fish, oysters and squid with chips, Philly cheesesteaks, burgers, hot crab melts, crab or shrimp Louie salads, and hot dogs for the kids. All range from $2.50 to $8.95.

Elves' Grill Boat Hoist & Restaurant, Wharf No. 2, Monterey 93940; (831) 375–6201. Call ahead for hours as establishment is seasonal. Beer and wine. No credit cards. Wheelchair accessible.

Practically next door to Elves' is the **SANDBAR & GRILL**, a slightly-under-the-pier local hangout with an old-fashioned piano bar complete with live singer, fabulous views (try sunset, kids) looking west at the yacht club's finest, some good seafood, and a happy hour from 4:00 to 6:00 P.M. Monday to Friday. Sea otters romp before your eyes, even without the cocktails. Because of the air spaces between boards on the pier and stairs to the Sandbar, we suggest you keep your car keys in your pocket, or you may never see them again.

Owner and South Philly native John Anderson worked as carnie and Broadway stage manager for twenty-three years, which accounts for his fascinating display of Broadway show posters.

Local and not-so-local fish fill the menu, with an occasional concession to the carnivore such as baby back ribs, burgers, chicken breasts, and a half-pound filet mignon ($18.95) that comes with salad, sourdough bread, rice pilaf or potato, and seasonal veggies. Everything's a good deal here, including the locals' atmospheric conversation and the music.

Lunch ranges from seafood or chicken salads (to $11), grilled sand dabs ($8.95), deep-fried oysters ($9.95), and ribs ($9.95–$12.95), to a crab club sandwich ($7.95), a crab, shrimp, and avocado melt sandwich ($7.95), a crab burger, and oyster or calamari sandwiches ($7.95). Dinner features a popular deep-fried shrimp lover's sampler of prawns, scampi, and crab ($16.95), sautéed prawns ($14.95), or a Dungeness cracked crab ($18.95). There's a children's menu available too. Try it (the restaurant, not the children's menu).

✢ *Sandbar & Grill, Wharf No. 2, Monterey 93940; (831) 373–2818. Open continuously 11:30 A.M.–11:00 P.M. daily, weekend and holiday brunch 10:30 A.M.–4:00 P.M. Full bar. Visa, MasterCard, American Express. Not wheelchair accessible.*

As you leave Wharf No. 2, turn right (west), wander through the parking lots, take a ticket, and park as close as you can to the Stanton Center and Maritime Museum of Monterey (same building), which connects by a large cement plaza to the Custom House and Fisherman's Wharf.

The **STANTON CENTER AND MARITIME MUSEUM OF MONTEREY** is a newish building housing a fascinating nautical museum with loads of historical photographs, ship prints and paintings, ship wheels, all sorts of ship equipment, and models of Commodore Sloat's flagship, *Savannah*. The Stanton Center focuses on the now disappeared sardine and whaling industries, Ohlone Indians, and the lore of local shipwrecks. It is also the gathering place for some Path of History Walking Tours.

✢ *Stanton Center and Maritime Museum of Monterey, 5 Custom House Plaza, Monterey 93940; (831) 375–2553. Open 10:00 A.M.–5:00 P.M. daily. Admission: $5.00 adults; $4.00 seniors and disabled; $3.00 ages thirteen to eighteen; $2.00 ages two to twelve. Visa, MasterCard, American Express. Wheelchair accessible.*

Just west of the Stanton Center and museum is **PACIFIC HOUSE,** a classic Mexican California adobe with a beautiful courtyard in back that once served as a seaman's boarding house. Its historic museum, which is open daily from

TWO DUDES PAINTED ON THE BALCONY OF PACIFIC HOUSE

10:00 A.M. to 4:00 P.M., focuses on Monterey's four historical phases: Indian, Spanish, Mexican, and early American. Check out the dudes painted on the outside walls.

Just north of Pacific House, the CUSTOM HOUSE is a great example of a classic California adobe building that you should see if you don't have time to go downtown to Old Monterey. Built in 1814 to collect admission tolls, it may be the oldest government building on the West Coast. This is where Commodore Sloat actually raised the American flag to take over California for the United States. Its museum features period nineteeth-century artifacts.

🍂 *Custom House, Custom House Plaza, Monterey 93940; (831) 649–2909. Open 10:00 A.M.–4:00 P.M. daily. Free admission. Partly wheelchair accessible.*

Now walk slightly northward to Fisherman's Wharf itself, for a contrast of style and taste. Here you can get everything from cotton candy to T-shirts, shrimp cocktails, and espresso, as well as some very good seafood at a wide range of quality and prices.

Abalonetti and Domenico's are the two best restaurants on Fisherman's Wharf. They both belong to John Pisto, who also owns the Whaling Station and Paradiso on Cannery Row.

ABALONETTI SEAFOOD TRATTORIA is the more casual of the two, with a substantial bar, an antipasto bar at which everything is sold separately (from roasted

VIEW FROM NO. 1 FISHERMAN'S WHARF, JOHN STEINBECK'S
FAVORITE WHARF HANGOUT

garlic, $2.25, to six oysters on the half shell, $6.95), and a great view facing west, looking at part of Monterey Harbor, otters and sea lions, and tour boats of tourists looking at the otters and sea lions. The animals are not feaful of the boats—they often follow them into the wharf for the scraps thrown over by the fishers. So enjoy.

Abalonetti uses Carmel Valley baby greens in its salads, which range from a Sicilian bread salad ($4.95) to shrimp Louie ($12.95) and blackened salmon salad ($14.95). We enjoy the calamari sandwich or the abalonetti, defined as calamari fillets french-fried with a light lemon butter sauce. Servers here will tell you honestly if the calamari is truly local that day. The cioppino and bouill-abaisse are worth a try (seasonal prices). Reliable pizzas (under $10) from the wood-burning oven are also good, as are the crab and clam pastas. The children's menu offers a burger or calamari and fries, spaghetti, or pepperoni pizza, all under $6.00.

Abalonetti Seafood Trattoria, 57 Fisherman's Wharf, Monterey 93940; (831) 373–1851. Open for lunch and dinner daily. Full bar. Visa, MasterCard, American Express. Wheelchair accessible.

DOMENICO'S ON THE WHARF, across the pier, looks east at Monterey's spectacular yacht collection. Notice that the restaurant's blue upholstered chairs match the blue of the yacht's mast covers. Tiled walls and an inviting oyster bar just inside the door create a casually elegant atmosphere.

The oyster bar serves oysters, clams on the half shell ($7.95), cracked Dungeness crab ($9.95, half; $19.95, whole), marinated calamari, octopus and scallops, ceviche, seafood cocktails, escargots ($7.95), and steamed artichokes ($4.95). New England clam chowder and seafood Louie salads are popular, as are the calamari steak sandwich ($9.95), bay shrimp salad sandwich ($11.95), and Domenico's cioppino. You will also enjoy a wide range of local seafood pastas, Domenico's bouillabaisse, seafood paella Barcelona, calamari every which way, and sea scallops, all in the $20 range. You might also want to check out John Pisto's own cookbook, which is available here.

✢ Domenico's on the Wharf, *50 Fisherman's Wharf, Monterey 93940; (831) 372–3655. Open for lunch and dinner daily. Full bar. Visa, MasterCard, American Express. Wheelchair accessible.*

TRADITIONAL POLENTA
from John Pisto, Abalonetti Seafood Trattoria and Domenico's, Monterey

---

1 Tbs. salt

8 cups water

2 cups ground cornmeal

1 tsp. salt

¼ tsp. each crushed red and black pepper

½ cup butter

1½ cups Reggiano cheese, grated

Add 1 Tbs. salt to the water; bring to a rapid boil. Slowly add corn-meal to boiling water and stir with a whisk over high heat. Add remaining 1 tsp. salt, red and black pepper, butter, and cheese and mix thoroughly. After cornmeal is thoroughly mixed in, reduce to medium flame. Stir almost continuously for 45 minutes.

Remove from heat and serve warm, or pour into a large sheet pan, spreading evenly to cool. The mixture will harden in approximately 20 minutes. Cut into serving-size squares. Preheat large grill or skillet until smoking. Brush polenta with olive oil. Brown on both sides and serve with sauce of your choice or none at all. Serves 4–6.

As you leave Fisherman's Wharf, either get back in your car and drive to Cannery Row, or follow the paved **RECREATION TRAIL** by foot or wheelchair from Fisherman's Wharf around to Breakwater Cove and its marina. The path runs from Pacific Grove to Seaside, sometimes following the former railroad bed.

The city of Monterey publishes a *Recreation Trail Etiquette and User Rules* brochure. Basically the rules say that you can't ride a skateboard on the Recreation Trail "between the head of Fisherman's Wharf and the city limit of Pacific Grove." You may ride skates or bikes or use a wheelchair in a "safe manner." Stay "on the right-hand side in the direction you are going." The brochure implores you to be courteous and cautious, and patient in congested areas, to look both ways, and "walk or jog or skate only two abreast." In addition, don't "block the Trail" or "step into the flow of traffic on the other side of the Trail," and do ride bikes single file, signaling "with bell or horn, loudly announcing 'passing on left'" when passing. Skateboarders must skate individually in a forward movement "and not swagger," perform "no acrobatic tricks," and "not damage public or private property with your skateboard." Now, got that?

We love the fact that Monterey gives this path a neutral name, so that bike path enthusiasts don't get bent out of shape when walkers, joggers, and wheelchair users invade their pleasure territory.

On your way to Cannery Row, stop for a few refreshing minutes at the Breakwater Cove Marina, where you can watch divers taking lessons and backing into and out of the water at San Carlos Beach to commune with the otters. (You can also watch the otters watching the divers performing this odd maneuver.) Here you can also launch your boat, have lunch at the Bijan Restaurant, pick up snacks and drinks at the market and deli, or rent kayaks for bay tours.

Just above the San Carlos Beach is a beautifully landscaped terrace with picnic tables and benches where you can join other visitors and lots of local regulars who come here to inhale the air and enjoy Monterey Bay's natural wonders.

To get to Breakwater Cove Marina and San Carlos Beach by car, take Del Monte Avenue from the east or Lighthouse Avenue from the west and follow the signs to Cannery Row, turning east on Foam Street, then right (south) on Reeside Avenue. Turn right to the beach parking lot or left at the bottom of the hill to Cannery Row and the Monterey Bay Inn, Monterey Plaza Hotel, and the Sardine Products Company Inc.

For a charming detour to entertain the kids, old and young, we recommend DENNIS THE MENACE PARK right downtown near Fisherman's Wharf and along Lake El Estero. Dennis the Menace creator and local resident Hank Ketcham created the park's stuff with local sculptor Arch Gardner. It's some of the wildest and best fantasy playground equipment anywhere. Dennis the Menace fans of all generations will enjoy this place with nostalgic warmth, regardless of the weather conditions.

Enjoy climbing on a real train's steam engine, a hedge maze, a swinging rope bridge, lots of Dennis's friends, loads of benches for parents and grandparents, and a snack bar facing the parking lot on Pearl Street.

Either the ambience of the Monterey Peninsula attracts artists with a sense of humor or there is something in the air that brings out the funny side of those with a strong artistic gene. The trend apparently started in 1929 with Jimmy Hatlo, who created the daily feature They'll Do It Every Time, *a wonderfully funny commentary on human foibles, and then in 1941 launched* Little Iodine, *the ultimate in brat humor. Hatlo lived in Carmel at what is now the Tally Ho Inn for six years before the Hatlos moved to a house at Pebble Beach named "Wits End."*

The world's most famous lovable brat, Dennis the Menace, *debuted in 1951 from the ink bottle of Hank Ketcham, a former Disney animator, who was living in Carmel Woods. He moved to Switzerland for a time before settling in Pebble Beach in 1977. Dennis the Menace Park, a children's special playground in downtown Monterey, was inspired and promoted by Ketcham. Dennis also hit the television and movie screens, and is an image ingrained in the American consciousness.*

Another one-time Hollywood animator, Gus Arriola, moved to the area following World War II, after having begun Gordo *in 1941, the hilarious and human story of Gordo, his relatives, friends, and beautiful young women in a Mexican village. Praised for its excellent graphics and strong characterizations,* Gordo *was a favorite of Jerry's and comics experts. Arriola finally married off perpetual bachelor* Gordo *in the 1980s and retired from the daily drawing board, but is still a popular personage around the peninsula.*

A local product is Eldon Dedini, whose distinctive cartoon style and humor (sometimes scatalogical) is regularly seen in Esquire, The New Yorker, Playboy *and other magazines as well as book illustrations. After an apprenticeship as a Walt Disney animator he returned to his roots and became one of America's most successful single-panel cartoon artists. One of the panels in the wall mural on Cannery Row is a Dedini.*

Pebble Beach's Alex Anderson was the creator of the pioneering TV cartoon Crusader Rabbit *("the plot sickens") and the long-running* Bullwinkle. *Another animator, Preston Blair of Carmel, has won awards for his work, as did Anderson.*

Monterey Peninsula Herald *editorial cartoonist Vaughn Shoemaker of Carmel was awarded a Pulitzer Prize in this very competitive field.*

And last, but far from least, is Carmel's Bill Bates. His cartoons on the pages of the Carmel Pine Cone *for more than two decades incisively catch the spirit and mood of Carmelites. Many hang in the Carmel Post Office. Bates's drawings reveal that cartooning is just one aspect of his artistic talent. He joined with local artist Carol Minou in creating the humorous mural at the corner of San Carlos Street and Seventh Avenue in Carmel.*

DENNIS THE MENACE PARK, MONTEREY

❧ *Dennis the Menace Park,* Pearl Street at Lake El Estero, between Camino Aguajito and Camino El Estero, Monterey 93940; (831) 646–3860. Open 10:00 A.M.–dusk daily. Partly wheelchair accessible.

SIGNIFICANT OTHERS

One restaurant in Monterey that is not on your natural walking path but which we don't want you to miss is the highly reputed **FRESH CREAM**, a classic French restaurant whose walls are lined with romantic Impressionist prints. There are three private dining rooms for intimate dining reminiscent of Jack's or Ernie's in San Francisco, perfect service, a fabulous view, and creative French-California food.

You walk up a spiral staircase to the bar/lounge and dining rooms to take full advantage of all that Monterey Bay offers in the view department. Chef Tim Nugent's menu changes daily but always offers several appetizers and sumptuous veal, local and imported seafood (love that ahi tuna, which they will cook more than rare if you wish), and perfect salads of local greens. There are always plenty of vegetarian selections too. Don't miss the Grand Marnier soufflé, one of those marvelous traditional desserts we rarely see anymore. The wine list offers excellent local and French wines.

San Francisco Focus Magazine Readers' Poll has voted Fresh Cream "Best in Monterey County" for seven consecutive years.

✤ **Fresh Cream,** *100-C Heritage Harbor, 99 Pacific Street, Monterey 93940; (831) 375–9798; www.freshcream.com. Full bar. Open for dinner 6:00–10:00 P.M. nightly; cocktails from 5:00 P.M. Visa, MasterCard, American Express, Carte Blanche, Diners Club, Discover. Wheelchair accessible.*

CANNERY ROW AND NEW MONTEREY

A plethora of new shops and restaurants now prevails in Cannery Row, where Monterey's sardine canneries used to be. New Monterey, up the hill a couple of blocks from Cannery Row, is where many locals do their business and where adventurous visitors find some intriguing shops and restaurants.

You can approach Cannery Row from two perspectives: what it is now and what it was then, during the era of the sardine culture and John Steinbeck. In this chapter we take the former approach and guide you through today's Cannery Row and New Monterey. In the chapter "Travels with Steinbeck," we will take you door-to-door through Steinbeck's haunts in that earlier time.

In 1998 the National Trust for Historic Preservation named Cannery Row one of America's most endangered historic places, apparently threatened by overdevelopment in entrepreneurs' eagerness to restore and

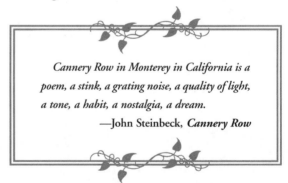

Cannery Row in Monterey in California is a poem, a stink, a grating noise, a quality of light, a tone, a habit, a nostalgia, a dream.

—John Steinbeck, *Cannery Row*

capitalize on history and lore. So please enjoy this onetime "Sardine Capital of the World" with care and respect, regardless of how you feel about sardines.

We take you from the southern end of Cannery Row (San Carlos Beach end) northward to the Monterey Bay Aquarium. The street now called Cannery Row was originally called Ocean View Avenue.

The best parking garage available for visitors to Cannery Row, the aquarium, and Recreation Trail offers 1,000 spaces (a whole city block) on Foam and Wave Streets and between Hoffman and Prescott Streets. It includes spaces with handicapped access. There is also a smaller parking facility closer to the aquarium between David and Irving Avenues and Foam and Wave Streets.

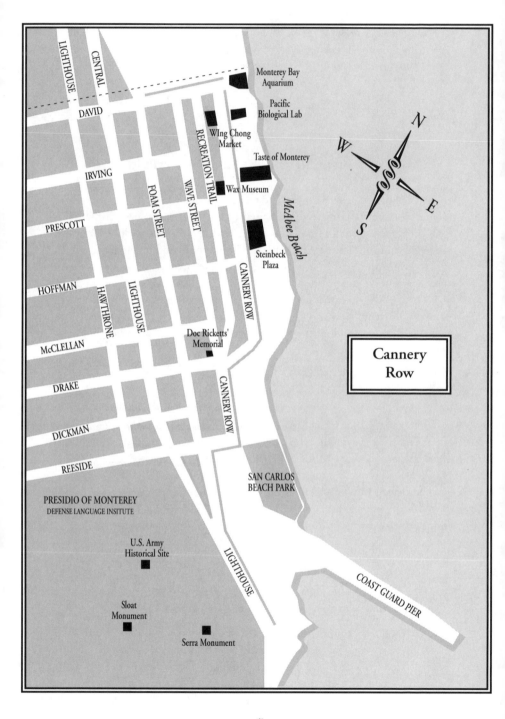

LIGHTHOUSE
CENTRAL
DAVID
IRVING
PRESCOTT
HOFFMAN
HAWTHRONE
LIGHTHOUSE
McCLELLAN
DRAKE
DICKMAN
REESIDE

FOAM STREET
WAVE STREET
RECREATION TRAIL
CANNERY ROW

Monterey Bay
Aquarium

Pacific
Biological Lab

WIng Chong
Market

Taste of Monterey

Wax Museum

McAbee Beach

Steinbeck
Plaza

Doc Ricketts'
Memorial

CANNERY ROW

SAN CARLOS
BEACH PARK

PRESIDIO OF MONTEREY
DEFENSE LANGUAGE INSITUTE

U.S. Army
Historical Site

Sloat
Monument

Serra Monument

LIGHTHOUSE

COAST GUARD PIER

N
W
E
S

Cannery
Row

CANNERY ROW WITH MONTEREY PLAZA HOTEL, MONTEREY

To see the whole spectrum of Cannery Row, take Reeside Avenue down the hill (east) from Lighthouse Avenue or Foam Street. After you turn left onto Cannery Row, you will first see the Monterey Bay Inn, the old Sardine Products Company, Monterey Rent-a-Roadster, and the elegant Monterey Plaza Hotel.

Within the Monterey Plaza Hotel is one of the peninsula's most elegant restaurants, the DUCK CLUB. On entering you immediately see the bright, polished copper counter around the right-out-there kitchen with its wood-burning ovens. Jackets are required for men, and if you forget yours the staff will graciously loan you one (but take no responsibility for how it looks!).

The view of Monterey Bay is sparkling and romantically breathtaking, as are the room and service. Every night there is a menu du jour three-course prix fixe if you want to try specialties ($32). Otherwise, starter standouts include the Dungeness crab cakes on dill-marinated fennel salad ($11.50), the Chef's Raw Bar of tuna tartare, smoked Atlantic salmon, oysters, caviars, and crudités ($11.50), Caesar salads with pickled white anchovy and garlic crackers served at your table ($15 for two), and artichoke and shiitake soup ($6.50).

Excellent dinner entrees include pumpkin seed crusted halibut ($23), tagliolini pasta with wood-roasted baby vegetables with truffle oil and Reggiano cheese ($19), Steinbeck's Duck air-dried and wood-roasted with caramelized orange sauce ($22), pancetta and herb wrapped filet mignon with a cabernet glaze ($24), and of course excellent steaks and veal and lamb chops.

Irresistible to us for desserts are the cappuccino crème brûlée ($6.25) and the Chocolate Chocolate Pyramid with a ball of malted milk ice cream ($6.50). Kathleen especially loves the Parisian touch of the French press coffee featuring Italian Viaggio coffee, priced by the number of diners to indulge.

If you enjoy elegant brunch buffets, do not miss this one!

➳ *Duck Club, Monterey Plaza Hotel, 400 Cannery Row, Monterey 93940; (831) 646–1706. Open for breakfast 6:30–10:30 A.M. Monday–Friday, till 2:00 P.M. Saturday–Sunday; dinner 5:30–10:00 P.M. daily. Full bar. Visa, MasterCard, American Express, Diners Club, Carte Blanche. Wheelchair accessible.*

As you wind your way to the more commercial part of Cannery Row, you pass the **CHART HOUSE** restaurant, which is open only for dinner and focuses on fresh seafood, steaks, prime rib, and its fabulous view of the harbor. Once the site of the Western Sardine Company and for many years the home of Willy Lum's China Row restaurant, the Chart House is now a great place for those good old old-fashioneds, martinis, and a taste of cholesterol heaven.

➳ *Chart House, 444 Cannery Row, Monterey 93940; (831) 372–3362. Open from 5:00 P.M. daily. Full bar. Visa, MasterCard, American Express. Mostly wheelchair accessible.*

As Cannery Row straightens out, huge **EL TORITO MEXICAN RESTAURANT & CANTINA** hangs right over the water on the east side of the street across from where Hoffman Avenue ends. You will know it by its colorful sign and huge parking lot between the street and the restaurant. El Torito occupies what was once the site of the Custom House Packing Corporation, which opened just before the Wall Street crash of 1929 and burned in 1953, and of Carmel Canning Company, which opened to process sardines during World War I, closed when the sardines disappeared in the early 1950s, and burned in 1967.

While this is not exactly known as a gourmet Mexican restaurant, it is fun, colorful, and reasonable, and the drinks are good. After all, everyone needs a little Mexican food once in a while to purify their systems.

➳ *El Torito Mexican Restaurant & Cantina, 600 Cannery Row, Monterey 93940; (831) 373–0611. Open to 9:00 P.M. Monday–Thursday and Sunday; Friday–Saturday till 10:00 P.M. Full bar. Visa, MasterCard, American Express. Wheelchair accessible.*

Across the street at the corner of Hoffman and Cannery Row is a new comedy and dance club called Club Gemini. In the seafaring atmosphere you'll also find Captain's Cove restaurant, featuring fish and chips and burgers, and the terrific Rocky Mountain Chocolate Factory and its soda shop.

SPADARO'S, which overlooks Monterey Bay and the diving sea otters and wet-suited human types, is frequented by lots of locals and visitors alike both because the family is so well known in the community and because their restaurant has such tasty Italian food, ranging from $10 to $20. (We love John Spadaro's Spado's in Salinas and highly recommend it when you go to Salinas to visit the National Steinbeck Center.) Do try his restaurant right here. The family also owns Tutto Buono on Alvarado Street in downtown Monterey. You never leave their restaurants hungry. ❧ *Spadaro's, 650 Cannery Row, Monterey 93940; (831) 372–8881. Open 11:00 A.M.–10:00 P.M. daily. Full bar. Visa, MasterCard, American Express. Wheelchair accessible.*

One of our favorite places to sit by the water and savor lunch is **PARADISO TRATTORIA**, one of John Pisto's four Monterey restaurants. Paradiso is in the Spindrift Inn building (which also has an outpost of San Francisco's renowned Ghirardelli Chocolate Factory). The Spindrift was built in 1927 by the Wu family as the Ocean View Hotel.

Paradiso's excellent Caesar salad

BABY ARTICHOKE RISOTTO
from John Pisto, Paradiso Trattoria

24 baby artichokes
2 Tbs. olive oil
3 Tbs. butter
1 large yellow onion, coarsely chopped
4 cloves garlic, coarsely chopped
1 lb. Italian short grain (arborio) rice
½ cup white wine
salt and black pepper
6–8 cups beef broth
pinch of saffron
¼ cup heavy cream
¼ lb. prosciutto, cut into small cubes
½ cup Reggiano cheese, grated

Clean artichokes; remove outer leaves. Cook in rapidly boiling water for 5–10 minutes. Pour olive oil into preheated large skillet and add butter. When butter has melted, add onion and garlic. Sauté until soft. Add rice to skillet and stir until brown. Add white wine and stir until wine reduces; add salt and pepper to taste. Begin to add broth, one cup at a time, reducing it before you add the next ingredients. Add saffron and heavy cream and stir continuously. Fold in artichokes, prosciutto, and cheese. Top with more cheese and black pepper and serve. Serves 4.

---

is only $4.95, but try the Sicilian calamari salad ($6.95) or the eggplant cannelloni ($4.50). The Dungeness crab and shrimp salad is a bargain at $11.95, and we especially enjoy the fire-roasted ahi tuna sandwich ($8.95) with

Caesar salad. The softshell crab sandwich melts in your mouth, and the One-Pound Bag of steamed clams or mussels is just that ($7.50).

You might also want to try the artichoke frittata, smoked salmon scramble, or the vegetarian polenta tower. Wood-burning-oven-baked pizzas and a special kids' menu (for special kids, of course) round out Paradiso's appeal. The Franciscan bread is an excellent, light but textured sourdough.

As important as the food is the valuable romantic experience of watching the seals and otters on the rocks and practically inhaling the blues and greens of the waves and the gold of the sand below.

*⋌ *Paradiso Trattoria, 654 Cannery Row, Monterey 93940; (831) 375–4155. Open for lunch and dinner daily. Full bar. Visa, MasterCard, American Express. Wheelchair accessible.*

Steinbeck Plaza No. 2 is a newish building owned by The Cannery Row Company and designed to reflect Monterey's Spanish Colonial heritage. It's full of elegant shops and is also the gateway to Steinbeck Plaza and McAbee Beach. Wander down and get your feet wet. It feels good after all that walking. You can also walk across the street to Steinbeck Plaza No. 1 via a replicated crossover to the warehouse side of Cannery Row to explore a wide range of specialty shops, galleries, gift shops, cafes, and a billiard parlor.

MONTEREY CANNING COMPANY, CANNERY ROW, MONTEREY

Between 1860 and 1900, McAbee Beach was where Portuguese shore whalers from the Azores launched their longboats to chase blue and humpback whales migrating close to shore. The whales' blubber was rendered into whale oil right on this beach until kerosene replaced whale oil around 1900.

Canadian John B. McAbee eventually rented tent cabins and boats on the beach, but when Monterey's Chinatown at China Point burned down in 1906, the Chinese established a small Chinatown here that remained until the mid-1920s.

Just north of the little plaza is a reproduction of the Monterey Canning Company cannery, now referred to as 700 Cannery Row. The original was built during World War I to meet military demands for sardines as a cheap and healthy ration. The original building burned down in the 1970s and the replica was reconstructed carefully by the Cannery Row Company with the original crossover. Now forty businesses bustle with visitors' curiosity.

Some of our favorite stops inside 700 Cannery Row include the Garlic Shoppe, with everything garlic from braids to pickles, as well as aprons, jams, crunchies, and some cool drinks too. The Spirit of Monterey Wax Museum features more than one hundred life-size figures, many modeled after Steinbeck's *Cannery Row* characters (including "Doc" Ricketts, Lee Chong, Sam Mally, and Dora Flood).

At **A TASTE OF MONTEREY** you can sip Monterey County's finest wines while looking out over the bay. The wine and produce tasting room is on the top floor, and there is a good elevator as well as rest rooms in the center of the complex. A Taste of Monterey also has an excellent collection of local cookbooks and guidebooks, aprons, pot holders, and posters. You can order a cheese and cracker platter ($5.50), or enjoy gourmet snacks such as relatively local almonds, pistachios, and Gil's garlic sauces and salsas. The wine processing and history photo exhibit is fascinating. (See page 157 for list of local wineries whose wines you can only taste here.)

✾↩ *A Taste of Monterey, 700 Cannery Row, Monterey 93940; (831) 646–5446; www.tastemonterey.com. Open 11:00 A.M.–6:00 P.M. daily. Tasting fee: $5.00 for six tastes. Visa, MasterCard, American Express, Discover, Diners Club, Carte Blanche. Wheelchair accessible via elevator.*

Sly McFly's Refueling Station Bar & Grill on the ground floor facing the plaza and Cannery Row is exactly what it says: a great place to have a good American lunch and drink at a reasonable price.

On the north side of 700 Cannery Row at the back of the attractive garden and little courtyard is the popular **BUBBA GUMP SHRIMP COMPANY**, an obvious crustacean outgrowth of Tom Hanks's and Forrest Gump's tremendous cinematic success. First built in 1916, the building originally housed the company's reduction plant, where sardines were ground and baked into fishmeal and fertilizer.

This is a fun restaurant for the whole family, with lots of Bubba stuff around and for sale, down-home casual warmth, and nothing much to break. Shrimp come billions of ways, such as "peel 'n' eat," scampi, kabobs, and cocktails, and there's even local salmon, crab legs, rib-eye steaks, and pork chops. And there's an occasional chocolate. Lots of choices in the $10–$15 range.

❧ Bubba Gump Shrimp Company, 720 Cannery Row, Monterey 93940; (831) 373–1884. Open Sunday–Thursday until 10:00 P.M.; Friday–Saturday until 11:00 P.M. Full bar. Visa, MasterCard, American Express. Wheelchair accessible.

Take the time to study the murals painted on wooden fences along both sides of Cannery Row in this block. All painted by local artists, the murals depict the history of Cannery Row and Monterey, often through the eyes of John Steinbeck's characters.

The primary remaining landmark on the water side of the street between here and the Monterey Bay Aquarium is a private club once used as "Doc" Ricketts's Lab (800 Cannery Row) as memorialized by Steinbeck in *Cannery Row*.

Cross the street to browse. You'll find Mackeral Jack's Trading Company, Flora Woods' Lone Star Cafe, Bear Flag Restaurant, Amarin Thai Cuisine, Flavors Cafe & Grill, Resort Works, Kristonio's T-shirts and souvenirs, and Alicia's Antiques.

KALISA'S serves economical, easy meals, including herring and potatoes, German head cheese sandwiches, stuffed salmon with potatoes, meat loaf sandwiches, a pot of beans and bread for only $3.95, and Lappert's Hawaiian ice cream. In the Steinbeck tradition.

❧ Kalisa's, 851 Cannery Row, Monterey 93940; (831) 372–3621. Open for lunch and dinner. Visa, MasterCard. Wheelchair accessible.

For many locals and visitors alike, the **MONTEREY BAY AQUARIUM** is the highlight of a visit to Cannery Row and the Monterey Peninsula. The aquarium is located at the juncture of David Street and Cannery Row and occupies the site of the original Hovden Food Products cannery (of which Portola Sardines was one label) and its neighbor, Sea Pride Canning Company. Here Norwegian Knute Hovden, a protégé of Frank Booth ("Father of the Monterey Sardine Industry"), developed innovations and inventions that improved the speed and efficiency of the industry's off-loading and canning processes. Hovden was such a leader that he became known as "King of Cannery Row."

The aquarium, the world's largest devoted to a single region, exists because

MURALS ALONG
CANNERY ROW,
MONTEREY

EDWARD F.
"DOC"
RICKETTS'S
LAB

of the efforts of Julie Packard, the David and Lucile Packard Foundation, loads of contributors, large and small, and 800 volunteers. Their mission "to inspire conservation of the oceans" is accomplished with dignity, humor, sensitivity, and devotion to our natural world.

Monterey Bay's 10,000-feet-deep drop affords the bay the rare, diverse collection of marine species that we love to watch, study, and learn from at the aquarium. The Monterey Bay National Marine Sanctuary is the largest protected marine area in the northern hemisphere, and the largest in the world by water volume. The aquarium's interpretive exhibits and galleries highlight the colorful and complex array of marine life found here.

David and Lucile Packard donated the entire $55 million to build the original aquarium. Half the funds ($27 million) needed to construct the fabulous Outer Bay Wing came from other private and business donors. A rare community effort for northern California and visitors from around the globe!

San Francisco architects Esherick Homsey Dodge and Davis designed both wings in keeping with the old Hovden buildings. Note the rough cement and corrugated metal roofing. Both you and the animals will feel comfortable here.

You can see and, in some cases, touch more than 300,000 animals and plants representing 571 species of fishes, invertebrates, mammals, reptiles, birds, and plants found in Monterey Bay. Yes! Many people head right for the three-story kelp forest where sardines, leopard sharks, and other fish weave among fronds of kelp, which grows up to 8 inches a day in the bay. You can even watch divers hand-feed the fish, with narration by a volunteer guide and two-way communication between the diver and the audience. View some orphaned and rescued sea otters, part of the total population of 2,300 individual California sea otters that live right here in Monterey Bay.

Don't miss the Marine Mammals Gallery, the Great Tide Pool, Deep Reefs, the Wharf, bat rays, moon jellies, octopus and friends, the new Outer Bay Galleries (where you feel like you are underwater at times but in no danger), and a look through the largest window on the planet, which allows you to view the tallest aquarium exhibit in the world. Flippers, Flukes & Fun offers interactive exhibits for children four to seven years old and their families. Kids can wear flippers and flukes to feel how whales swim, and crawl though a blubbery elephant seal. Whales sing and dolphins squeak to the delight of kids of all ages.

We also suggest you investigate the aquarium's gift shop and the Portola Cafe, all of whose tables have ocean views. The restaurant has a very reasonably priced cafeteria/cafe with lots of good food, from clam chowder in a sourdough-bread bowl and garlicky pizza to hamburgers and healthy salads. The more formal part of the restaurant includes white linen tablecloths and flowers, and well-prepared seafood, pastas, and an oyster bar, mostly under $15. The newer Outer Bay Wing offers a snack window and the Bay View Coffee Bar. Self-guided audio tours and maps are available in English, Chinese, French, German, Italian, Japanese, and Spanish.

Ꮳ Monterey Bay Aquarium, 886 Cannery Row, Monterey 93940; (831) 648–4800, fax (831) 648–4810; www.mbayaq.org. Open 10:00 A.M.–6:00 P.M. daily in winter except Christmas, 9:30 A.M.–6:00 P.M. daily May 23–September 7. Admission: adults (eighteen and over) $15.95; seniors and students (thirteen to seventeen or with college ID) $12.95; children (three to twelve) and disabled $7.95. Group rates available for twenty or more. Visa, MasterCard, American Express, Discover. Wheelchair accessible except for the Sea Otter mezzanine. Assisted listening devices are available for the hearing impaired and most exhibit videos are close-captioned. Advance tickets highly recommended through the Aquarium's Web site. Audio tours $3.00. Call advance ticket numbers: toll free within California, (800) 756–3737; toll-free from outside California, (831) 648–4937.

If you walk up David Street from the aquarium to the corner and turn right, within a block you come to **AMERICAN TIN CANNERY PREMIUM OUTLETS**, Monterey's outlet center. The outlets, actually in Pacific Grove, occupy most of a block between Eardley, Ocean View, Sloat, and Dewey Streets.

Originally this facility opened as the American Can Company, which supposedly produced twenty-six million cans for sardines in its first season of operation. Today it's the site of California's first factory outlet complex.

Here we have found quality garments and shoes at Anne Klein's Factory Store, Danskin, G.H. Bass, Izod, Jones New York, London Fog, Van Heusen, Joan & David, Rockport, Vans, the Book Warehouse, Royal Doulton, Osh Kosh B'Gosh, and loads of leathers, luggage, sporting goods, and clothing, as well as a good collection of fast foods, ranging from all-American diner to Japanese sushi.

American Tin Cannery Premium Outlets, 125 Ocean View Boulevard, Pacific Grove 93950; (831) 372–1442. Open 10:00 A.M.–6:00 P.M. Sunday–Thursday, till 8:00 P.M. Friday–Saturday. Credit cards vary by store. Wheelchair accessible.

Two of our favorite restaurants in this part of Monterey are nearby on Wave Street. You can't miss the Sardine Factory's red awning.

The **SARDINE FACTORY**'s co-owner Bert Cutino is probably the most active restaurateur in America, and he turns out fabulous food too. A native of Carmel whose father was in commercial fishing, Cutino attended high school and college in Monterey while working from age thirteen in every job in the restaurant business.

He and his partner Ted Balestreri opened their restaurant here in 1968 in what had been an old cannery workers' canteen. Both Cutino and the restaurant have received a long list of awards from American, French, and Italian culinary associations, including a recent Grand Award from *Wine Spectator*. The Sardine Factory was one of fifty restaurants selected to serve at President Ronald Reagan's inaugurations. It has one of the finest wine lists in the world.

Cutino and his partners own several restaurants, shopping centers, office buildings, and 70 percent of Cannery Row. Their newest company, Pacific Hospitality, owns franchise rights of Wendy's International in a tricounty area. Do they cover the waterfront, Monterey and otherwise!

Cutino's penchant for perfection and excellence shows in the Sardine Factory. The atmosphere in every room is different, ranging from deep reds and brass to the elegant round conservatory atrium surrounded by plants. The round glass dome is reminiscent of the garden court at San Francisco's Palace Hotel.

Don't miss the photos in the Captain's Room up a few stairs to your left as you walk in the front door. Here you will see Bert with the pope, Bert with

PRAWNS SAMBUCA
from Bert Cutino, the Sardine Factory, Monterey

4 oz. olive oil

1 Tbs. fresh garlic, chopped

1 Tbs. fresh shallots, chopped

16 fresh Monterey Bay prawns

3 oz. chardonnay or dry white wine

2 oz. Sambuca liqueur

¼ cup diced tomatoes

1 Tbs. fresh tarragon, finely chopped

2 tsp. salt and pepper

4 oz. sweet butter

12 oz. angel hair pasta, cooked

2 chives

In a sauté pan, heat oil, add garlic, shallots, and prawns. Cook for 1 to 2 minutes. Add wine and Sambuca. Flambé.

Add tomatoes, tarragon, salt, and pepper, and cook for 2 more minutes. Add butter and reduce.

Put each serving over 3 ounces of pasta. Garnish with tarragon leaf and chives. Serves four as an appetizer.

California Governor Edmund G. "Pat" Brown, Bert with President Gerald Ford. In the bar check out the Clint Eastwood photo with brass plaque commemorating the filming of Eastwood's directorial debut, *Play Misty for Me,* here at the Sardine Factory. Catch the great photo of John Steinbeck under the large television set. Those martinis can't be beat. The Steinbeck Room houses a collection of canning era photographs.

Practically when you arrive at your table, small squares of focaccia bread crisped with pesto pinato appear, followed by long, thin, crisp breadsticks. Perfect.

The only sardine on the menu is in the house salad of purple endive and bib lettuces with caper dressing (be sure to ask for the crumbled Stilton cheese for $2.00 extra).

On your must-try list should be the Sardine Factory's signature abalone bisque—a rich, delightfully smooth taste experience—as well as anything with prawns. Portions here are sumptuous, and many special entrees are rich and large enough to feed the whole family tomorrow. The fresh catch of the day can be twelve ounces of halibut, or the steak can be an eighteen-ounce crisp filet ($27.50). Perfect Monterey sand dabs ($18.95), the Factory's famous lobster and prawns on crescent pasta in brandy-lobster sauce ($27.95), and the certified Angus New York steak with Brie, prosciutto potato cake, and green peppercorn and pear sauce ($25.95) are all extravagantly wonderful, as is the vegetarian Napoleon with layers of potato with portobello mushrooms, artichokes, and other local vegetables ($15.95).

The Sardine Factory's renowned wine list is good enough to sit and read at the table, pardon me please. The wines range from a 1996 Sutter Home White

Zinfandel ($13) to an 1826 Chateau Mouton–Rothschild Bordeaux ($10,000). Among the selections in between you will find a Leonetti Cabernet ($80), a Dom Perignon 1955 Brut ($550), a 1959 Chateau d'Yquem Sauterne ($1,500), and a bargain 1870 Chateau Lafitte Rothschild Bordeaux ($6,000), as well as many local and more affordable wines to please your palate.

Eat sparingly during the day to maximize your full enjoyment potential here. Oh, how we wish they were open for lunch!

☙ *Sardine Factory, 701 Wave Street, Monterey 93940; (831) 373-3775; www.sardinefactory.com. Open 5:00–10:30 P.M. Monday –Thursday, till 11:00 P.M. Saturday, and till 10:00 P.M. Sunday. Full bar. Visa, MasterCard, American Express. Wheelchair accessible from parking lot.*

Another of John Pisto's restaurants, the **WHALING STATION**, emphasizes prime steaks and seafood with an elegant old-world flair. Pisto's trademark antipasto bar and house-made pastas share top billing for locals. The building was originally Mow Wo's Store, a Chinese grocery and dry-goods store in the 1920s, and later a general store and boardinghouse.

Here's one place where you can get a wedge of iceberg lettuce with creamy Roquefort dressing ($6.50) like my mother used to make it. Or you can try a more adventurous crab, tomato, avocado, and mango for some local flavor ($9.50) or fire-grilled vegetable salad ($5.95). Traditional (read fifties) appetizers include oysters Rockefeller or on the half shell, crab cakes, and oak-grilled scallops.

The Dungeness crab fettuccine with roasted garlic, red peppers, and spinach ($19.95) is rich and very good. The garlicky fresh clams and linguine ($15.95)

CALAMARI PUFFS
from Bert Cutino, the Sardine Factory, Monterey

2½ lbs. cleaned squid, fillet only
½ medium onion, chopped
1 bunch green onions, finely chopped
1 egg
1 Tbs. parsley, chopped
salt and pepper
½ Tbs. granulated garlic
¼ cup cracker meal
¼ cup bread crumbs
parchment paper
oil for frying

Chop squid into pieces and place in a bowl. Add chopped onion, green onions, egg, parsley, salt and pepper, and granulated garlic. Mix thoroughly. Add half of the cracker meal and bread crumbs into the mixture. Form into little 2 oz. oval balls and roll balls in remaining cracker meal and bread crumb mixture. Lay on sheet pan with parchment paper. Let set.

Cook balls in a deep fat fryer (350 degrees) until golden brown. Serve hot with your favorite cocktail sauce. Serves four.

is one of Kathleen's favorites, along with the Sicilian-style wood-fired swordfish. And those famous local sand dab fillets are irresistible ($16.95). But many people come here for their meat fix—Nebraska corn-fed beef grilled with John Pistos's seasoning, roasted garlic mashed potatoes, and sautéed spinach. What happened to the creamed spinach?

The steaks range from an eight-ounce petite filet mignon ($25.95) to a twenty-two-ounce porterhouse ($32.95), with a few other choices of steaks, rack of lamb ($28.95), a brace of quail ($18.95), or semiboneless fire-roasted half chicken with forest mushrooms ($15.95). Good, clean, yummy cholesterol heaven.

✿ *Whaling Station, 763 Wave Street, Monterey 93940; (831) 373–3778. Open from 5:00 P.M. daily. Full bar. Visa, MasterCard, American Express. Wheelchair accessible.*

NEW MONTEREY

To locals, New Monterey consists of several blocks of restaurants, shops, and galleries that are slightly off the beaten path of Cannery Row and Old Monterey. The area technically runs up David Street from the Monterey Bay Aquarium 3 short blocks to Lighthouse Avenue, which also runs from Old Monterey to the ocean in Pacific Grove. This is where lots of Monterey residents do their business, and we encourage you to explore it for some outstanding aesthetic experiences.

Along Lighthouse you might enjoy the Monterey Boot Company (800), Monterey Baking Company (598), and four bookstores, including Books & Things (224), Lighthouse Books (801), and Old Capitol Books (639A). This is where you find fast-food chains (from Baskin Robbins to Carrows), tacos, used clothing and collectibles, a few nightclubs, and several restaurants, of course.

Try the Bulldog British Pub (611) for fun, food, and music, or Consuelo's Mexicano Restaurante (361) for fun drinks, atmosphere, and food. For Japanese, there's Ichiban Japanese (514) or Sakura Japanese (574); for Korean, Won Ju (570). There's also Gallery Bistro (615), Lighthouse Bistro (529), and the popular noodle house, The Loose Noodle (538).

Golf, biking, diving, and surfing enthusiasts will find great stores to buy or rent everything they need while vacationing here.

CHAPTER 2

PACIFIC GROVE

ortunately underdiscovered is one of our favorite communities on the Monterey Peninsula, Pacific Grove, whose city mothers and fathers call it both "Butterfly Town U.S.A." and the "Last Hometown." Here you will feel and live local history, enjoying people who have lived here for generations, buildings and institutions that have been here for generations, and young families who are creating new generations.

Pacific Grove basically begins at the Monterey Bay Aquarium and ends at the 17-Mile Drive gate, connected by streets as well as by the Recreation Trail. You have several options for getting to Pacific Grove. From Monterey, take Lighthouse Avenue—off Davis Street—from Cannery Row. From Highway 1, take either the Del Monte Avenue Exit into downtown Monterey and Lighthouse Avenue, or take the exit for Ocean View Drive, which wanders along the coast to Pacific Grove. From Carmel, you can take the Highway 1 exits or follow the elegant 17-Mile Drive ($7.00 per car). Lighthouse Avenue is Pacific Grove's main street.

You can park on the street for two hours (there's an active meter watcher patrol), or in a public parking facility on Fountain Avenue behind Lighthouse Cinema.

Perhaps locals should also call Pacific Grove "Migration City," since thousands of monarch butterflies appear every October at their designated sanctuary in the eucalyptus trees. At the same time, gray whales swim by a couple of blocks away on their migration from Alaska to Mexico. All of this adds up to a natural extravaganza, even for the casual observer.

The weather in Pacific Grove is often the best of the year when these small and large smart beasts pass through (October–March), a lesson we should learn. Surfers and cyclists know this, and locals know to grow plants that will attract and entertain the swarms of monarchs, so that the butterflies can, in turn, entertain the locals. Coastal California often has its worst weather in the spring and summer, when hot temperatures in the state's interior valleys pull that natural air-conditioner, fog, across the beaches and coastal towns. Get the message?

Butterfly worship is rampant here, complete with "Butterfly Crossing" signs and a city ordinance proclaiming it "unlawful for any person to molest or inter-

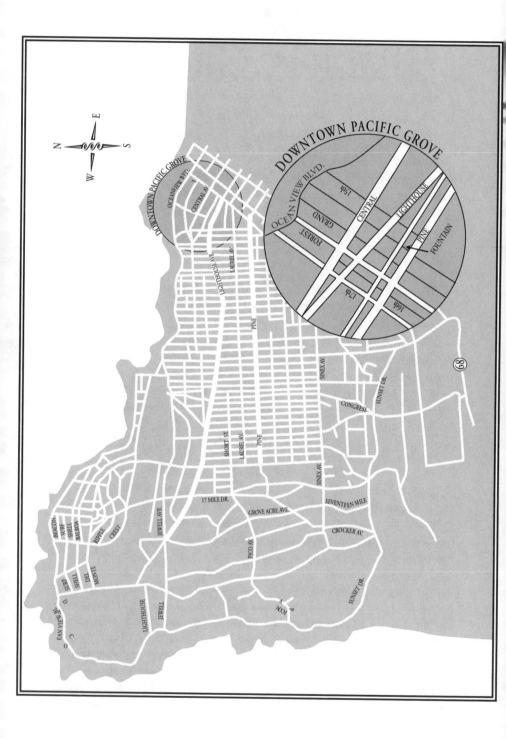

> *Pacific Grove has a law that requires you to pull your shades down after sun-*
> *down, and forbids you to pull them down before. Scorching on bicycles is forbid-*
> *den, as is sea bathing and boating on Sundays. Hijinks are or is forbidden.*
>
> —John Steinbeck in *Sweet Thursday* (sequel to *Cannery Row)*

fere with in any way the peaceful occupancy of the monarch butterflies on their annual visit to the city of Pacific Grove."

Pacific Grove was founded originally as a Methodist summer vacation center, and Grove locals and visitors now relish the glorious Victorians built subsequent to the tent city's great success and popularity. People swim in bikinis, surfers surf, cyclists wear Spandex, and restaurants serve alcohol, thank god and goddess. As the last city in California to remain dry after Prohibition, holding out until 1969, the Last Hometown used to sit in stark contrast to the wild and woolly nearby Cannery Row. Now its attraction is good taste, great artistic projects, beautiful buildings, lovely parks, a few excellent restaurants, and a plethora of natural wonders.

Pacific Grove has a couple of don't-misses we want to alert you to before we take you on a walking tour of downtown.

The **MONARCH BUTTERFLY SANCTUARY** is a grove of eucalyptus and cypress trees where you can go to look at the butterflies from October to March, give or take a few days or weeks. Drive west on Lighthouse Avenue from downtown Pacific Grove, turn south on Ridge Road, and park your car on the street. Then walk down a paved path beside the Butterfly Grove Inn to the grove in back. Descriptive signage helps you learn almost everything you could want to know. The Butterfly Souvenir Shop to benefit Friends of the Monarchs is in Wilkie's Inn at 1038 Lighthouse Avenue (831–375–0982). You might enjoy the Butterfly Parade on the first Saturday in October (831–646–6540) and the Victorian Home Tour on Sunday of the same weekend (831–373–3304).

The **PACIFIC GROVE MUSEUM OF NATURAL HISTORY** is truly worth a visit to see an outstanding collection of local wildlife, minerals, and artifacts from now extinct local Indian tribes, all housed in a delightful California–Spanish-style building. You'll know you're there when you see *Sandy the Gray Whale*, Larry Foster's life-size sculpture, in front of the museum. An excellent museum gift shop is full of great local-interest books, posters, minerals, and Pacific Grove memorabilia relating to local birds, mammals, reptiles, amphibians, insects, and geology. Occasionally, selected traveling exhibitions from the Smithsonian Institution visit too.

The museum's native plant garden contains rare and endangered species whose total life range is confined to the Monterey Peninsula. Many people plan their trips around the annual wildflower show, held the third weekend in April.

Kids love the hands-on and cold saltwater aquarium.

Pacific Grove Museum of Natural History, corner Forest and Central Avenues, Pacific Grove 93950; (831) 648–3116. Open 10:00 A.M.–5:00 P.M. Tuesday–Sunday. Free admission. Visa and MasterCard. Wheelchair accessible.

We also highly recommend getting yourself down to the **POINT PINOS LIGHTHOUSE** and walking or rolling along the path by the waterfront and Sunset Drive. Go west on Lighthouse Avenue and turn right (north) on Asilomar Avenue. Or approach from Ocean View Boulevard (Cannery Row's continuation from the American Tin Cannery Premium Outlets), from which you turn left (south) onto Asilomar Avenue.

The stone lighthouse, one of six lighthouses originally funded by the U.S. Congress, is on the northernmost tip of the Monterey Peninsula and was meant to signal the entrance to Monterey Bay. Its beacon has beamed since February

POINT PINOS LIGHTHOUSE, PACIFIC GROVE

1, 1855. Listed on the National Register of Historic Places, it is the oldest continuously operating lighthouse on the West Coast. You can see old ship and shipwreck records of events that occurred nearby. Just come out here to breathe the air and watch the deer romping in the ice plant.

❧ *Point Pinos Lighthouse, Asilomar Avenue north of Lighthouse Avenue, Pacific Grove 93950; (831) 648–5716; www.pgmuseum.org. Open 1:00–4:00 P.M. Thursday–Sunday. Admission free. Partly wheelchair accessible.*

Please take the time to walk or roll along the well-compacted pebble or wooden walkway along the National Marine Sanctuary of Monterey Bay. To get here, either follow Ocean View Boulevard around to where it becomes Sunset, or take Lighthouse Avenue straight out to Asilomar Avenue, and make a little jog to the left on Asilomar and then right again down to Sunset. Asilomar State Beach and Conference Center are reachable by Sunset Avenue. Do not disturb or feed the deer, please.

Oh yes, Pacific Grove has a respected eco-etiquette advisory, and we encourage you to pay attention and follow it. Please stay on pathways, walkways, and boardwalks to minimize impact to dunes, plants, trees, and wildlife. Enjoy looking at everything, but please do not remove anything from its natural habitat. Do not feed wild animals or birds, as feeding degrades both the health and habitat of these creatures. Ride your bikes, but stay on paths without riding on walking paths, path shoulders, or vegetation. Enjoy boating and other water sports, and please do not approach marine animals. Picnic along the shoreline or in parks; please stay in designated areas and dispose of litter properly. Explore the tide pools, being very gentle with the sea creatures you touch; put them back exactly where you find them. Please stay on designated roads, park in designated parking areas and turnouts, and turn off engines while enjoying scenic views or loading and unloading passengers. Excellent ecoetiquette for everyday living!

Now we will take you on our street walking tour of downtown Pacific Grove. Are you ready? We'll first take you along the northern side of Lighthouse Avenue, cross the street, and then come back up the southern side, followed by a few explorations of the cross streets.

We begin at **FAVALORO'S** restaurant at the corner of Lighthouse and Fountain in the Holman Building. Lots of locals stop in here for at-home-feeling Italian and American cooking and dining, including gourmet specialty pizzas, imported veal and chicken, house-made pasta, and rich-looking desserts. Try the Sicilian sandwich of eggplant, portobello mushroom, and mozzarella ($7.50), the sand dabs or calamari sandwich ($6.50), or a huge sandwich of mini meatballs ($6.95). The house specialty is gnocchi with tomato cream or any other sauce ($11.95). There are also loads of veal or chicken selections with soup or salad under $15.

❧ *Favaloro's, corner of Lighthouse and Fountain Avenues (in the Holman Building), Pacific Grove 93950; (831) 373–8523. Open for lunch 11:00 A.M.–2:00 P.M. Tuesday–Saturday, dinner 5:00–9:30 P.M. Tuesday–Sunday. Beer and wine. Visa, MasterCard. Wheelchair accessible.*

Next door, **HOLMAN ANTIQUE PLAZA & CONSIGNMENT CENTER** occupies what used to be a mainstay of Pacific Grove. In 1924 Rensselaer Luther Holman built a three-story department store, and during the Depression added two more stories to give work to men in town and demonstrate his confidence in Pacific Grove as a good location for business. The original "putting your money where your mouth is" guy!

After its second completion, Holman's became the largest department store between Los Angeles and San Francisco, with mail-order clients all over the world. Local clients included John Steinbeck, who particularly liked to hang out in the hardware department.

After Holman died, his heirs sold the building to Ford's Department Store, which later went bankrupt, putting the building into demolition jeopardy. To the rescue came developer Nader Aga, who purchased it in 1996, gave it back its old name, and created its current incarnation as an antiques collective and consignment center. Now collectibles from Holman's original period are sold at the fifty stalls, as well as furniture, jewelry, coins and stamps, swords, glassware, gold, watches, dolls, china, quilts, Tiffany and Meissen, prints, and books.

A sign in the window warns you to "BEWARE OF THE CAT—HE IS A DOG CATCHER."

If you need to call home, or anywhere else for that matter, there's a pay phone at the corner.

❧ *Holman Antique Plaza & Consignment Center, 542 Lighthouse Avenue, Pacific Grove 93950; (831) 646–0674 or (831) 646–1677. Open 10:00 A.M.–5:30 P.M. Monday–Thursday, till 6:00 P.M. Friday–Saturday, till 5:00 P.M. Sunday. Visa, MasterCard. Mostly wheelchair accessible.*

Just west of Holman's is the **FIRST NOEL**, a sister store to the one in Monterey. For fans of Christmas decorations, this is the place for limited-edition ornaments and Christmas scenes. Check out their specially decorated seashore tree, vintage tree, and gardening tree. They also sell Heavens' Treasures, Snow Village by Department 56, Crabtree & Evelyn stuff, stained glass and houses, the Disney series, Maruri world travelers, and Piphan original figurines.

❧ *First Noel, 562 Lighthouse Avenue, Pacific Grove 93950; (831) 643–1250. Open 10:00 A.M.–6:00 P.M. Monday–Saturday, 11:00 A.M.–4:00 P.M. Sunday, with special holiday hours. Visa, MasterCard, American Express. Wheelchair accessible.*

Ladies will enjoy **ANELLE WOMEN'S APPAREL** for Action Gear, Only, Cotton Cotton, Cramicci, Royal Robbin, Mishi, Ecosport, Potato, socks, handbags, and all the backups of women's casual wear.

❧ *Anelle Women's Apparel, 566 Lighthouse Avenue, Pacific Grove 93950; (831) 333–9277. Open 10:00 A.M.–6:00 P.M. Monday–Friday, till 5:00 P.M. Saturday, 11:00 A.M.–4:00 P.M. Sunday. Visa, MasterCard. Wheelchair accessible.*

If you can, we insist that you walk upstairs to the **PACIFIC GROVE ART CENTER**, the epitome of what a community art center should be, and the largest gallery on the central coast. Here you will find the studios of eight working artists, many open to the public so you can watch the artist at work. There are also four elegant galleries and three exhibit halls displaying a wide variety of art. The center, housed in a former Masonic building, offers classes, lectures, forums, and activities for kids.

For the annual Pacific Grove Artists Studio Tour (usually the last weekend in September), eighty local artists open their studios to the public. The event begins with a gala kickoff party at the Pacific Grove Art Center the Friday evening before the tour. Maps of the studio tour are available in the Monterey *Herald's* Art and Leisure section, as well as at the kickoff and the art center.

❧ *Pacific Grove Art Center, 568 Lighthouse Avenue, Pacific Grove 93950; (831) 375–2208. Open noon–5:00 P.M. Wednesday–Saturday, 1:00–4:00 P.M. Sunday. Not wheelchair accessible.*

For a unique Hallmark experience, try the huge **HALLMARK CARDS** at the corner of Lighthouse and Forest Avenues. It feels like a former hardware store, but now it's strictly soft ware, as in cuddlies.

❧ *Hallmark Cards, 570 Lighthouse Avenue, Pacific Grove 93950; (831) 373–2024. Open 10:00 A.M.–6:00 P.M. daily. Visa, MasterCard, American Express.*

As you cross Forest Avenue, consider whether you are ready for some delightful Mexicali food for lunch and a hot time generally. Even if you're not, walk down just to take a look at **PEPPERS MEXICALI CAFE**. Locals stream in here every day for lunch and dinner, and we suggest you try it.

We love the decor—chili peppers everywhere (including on the walls)—and the huge La Espanola Grocery neon sign over the counter. Wood tables, woven straw seat chairs, and crunchy chips invite you inside.

Starters include three huge nachos choices, red pepper gazpacho ($2.50/3.50), quesadillas ($4.95–$8.95), and Mexican sausage pizza ($6.95). Combination plates range from one main item ($6.50) to three items ($10.95)

with your choices of mixes and matches and refried beans and rice. Seafood ranges from snapper three ways (all $9.50) to prawns three ways (all $12.50) and grilled seafood tacos.

And of course there are the required but fresh fajitas and specialties. Try the Chicken Caribe with citrus habañero marinade ($9.95), grilled and smothered southwestern sausage, or the Mission District burrito platter ($8.95). Lots of vegetarian choices, as well as heat choices and filtered water on request.

Special sides can include avocado salsa fresca, Melinda's habañero sauce, and black beans. Gotta sample the flan, Mexican chocolate cake, and sopapillas. Mexican coffee and local microbrews too.

᛭ *Peppers MexiCali Cafe, 170 Forest Avenue, Pacific Grove 93950; (831) 373–6892. Open 11:30 A.M.–10:00 P.M. Monday, Wednesday–Thursday, 11:30 A.M.–11:00 P.M. Friday–Saturday, till 4:00 P.M. Sunday. Beer and wine. Visa, MasterCard, American Express, Diners Club, Discover. Partly wheelchair accessible, although the sidewalk in front is a little steep.*

Back to Lighthouse Avenue. The first store you come to, **CUBBY HOLE**, is in an old Spanish-style bank building. Cubby Hole's interior murals and shingles were put up there by friends on scaffolding loaned by the Chamber of Commerce. Here you will find interesting mosaic tables, painted furniture, watering cans, garden seeds, linens, and other home and garden accessories, all jumbled together to make you want to browse. (You can also visit their Carmel store at Dolores and Ocean Avenue.)

᛭ *Cubby Hole, 580 Lighthouse Avenue, Pacific Grove 93950; (831) 648–5344. Open 10:00 A.M.–5:00 P.M. daily. Visa, MasterCard, American Express. Wheelchair accessible.*

The next stop you should make is at the extremely local **LIGHTHOUSE CAFE** for truly hometown atmosphere, flavor, and prices at breakfast or lunch. There are fluffy omelettes, great burgers (with add-ons such as cheeses or mushrooms), a marvelous cucumber sandwich ($5.25 or $3.95), with separate prices for sandwiches alone and slightly higher if accompanied by fries, potato salad, or cole slaw. Since they assume you don't want a lonely sandwich, they list the "with" prices first. Try the calamari steak sandwich ($6.50 or $5.25) or a yummy charbroiled marinated chicken breast sandwich ($6.25 or $5.25). Cappuccino and espresso are handy also. More importantly, here's where you hear local chitchat.

᛭ *Lighthouse Cafe, 602 Lighthouse Avenue, Pacific Grove 93950; (831) 372–7006. Open 7:00 A.M.–2:00 P.M. daily. Visa, MasterCard, American Express. Wheelchair accessible.*

Just south of the Lighthouse Cafe is a fun photo-processing place called QUICK SILVER FAST PHOTO, worth walking into even if you don't need any film developed. Pick up beautiful note cards and postcards with partner Daniel Danbom's remarkable photos—great souvenirs and greeting cards to take home, as are his framed photographs and those ever-present photo refrigerator magnets.
❧ *Quick Silver Fast Photo, 606 Lighthouse Avenue, Pacific Grove 93950; (831) 375–1997. Open 9:30 A.M.–5:30 P.M. Monday–Friday, till 4:00 P.M. Saturday. Visa, MasterCard. Wheelchair accessible.*

SAND PEBBLE GIFTS majors in cards, Hello Kitty stickers, and Classic Pooh everything. At the risk of sounding sexist, this is a little girl's heaven.
❧ *Sand Pebble Gifts, 608 Lighthouse Avenue, Pacific Grove 93950; (831) 372–7024. Open 11:00 A.M.–5:00 P.M. Monday–Saturday. Visa, MasterCard. Wheelchair accessible.*

Local character Gene Allen presides at his GENE'S BARBER SHOP, at which he sells bags of golf balls for $4.00 a dozen. A self-annointed (confirmed by print media) movie critic and Academy Award predictor, Gene particularly considers himself to be an expert on Clint Eastwood movies. Go in just to listen!
❧ *Gene's Barber Shop, 610 Lighthouse Avenue, Pacific Grove 93950; (831) 375–2335. Open 9:00 A.M.–4:00 P.M. Tuesday–Saturday. No credit cards. Wheelchair accessible.*

At the P. G. BUSINESS CENTER you can do all the faxing, photocopying, and Airborne Expressing you could possibly want. The staff here really knows what they're doing.
❧ *P. G. Business Center, 612 Lighthouse Avenue, Pacific Grove 93950; (831) 375–2073, fax (831) 375–2075. Open 8:30 A.M.–6:00 P.M. Monday–Friday, 9:00 A.M.–1:00 P.M. Saturday. Visa and MasterCard. Wheelchair accessible.*

The COUNTRY STORE next to the copy place has exquisite taste and country furniture and accessories, from armoires to children's chairs, hutches, bookcases, and round dining tables. (There's also one in the Barnyard Shopping Center in Carmel.)
❧ *Country Store, 618 Lighthouse Avenue, Pacific Grove 93950; (831) 375–8049, fax (831) 375–2330. Open 10:00 A.M.–5:00 P.M. Monday–Saturday, noon–4:00 P.M. Sunday. Visa, MasterCard, American Express. Wheelchair accessible, but tight.*

At the corner of Lighthouse and Seventeenth you will find Pacific Grove Plaza, a complex of professional offices, and **NEW YORK PIZZA**, an informal counter service restaurant featuring salads, pizzas, sandwiches, Italian pastas, and Greek salads and gyros.

❧ *New York Pizza, 620 Lighthouse Avenue, Pacific Grove 93950; (831) 646–0447. Open 11:00 A.M.–9:00 P.M. daily. Visa, MasterCard, American Express, Discover. Not wheelchair accessible. Or try the new Shnarley's Bronx Pizzeria at 650 Lighthouse.*

Be sure to cross Nineteenth Street to the **RED HOUSE CAFE**, an adorable redone house that feels like a tearoom and also sells gorgeous pastries (don't miss the fudge brownies) and food to go. Yes, it *is* red (and so is the Radio Flyer wagon in front of the fireplace), the walls are avocado green, and the floors are beautiful old pine. At the back of the second room is a sign that blares "HERE IT IS!" to mark the rest room. Must-tries are the tomato basil soup and the Caesar salad with Dungeness crab ($9.95).

❧ *Red House Cafe, 662 Lighthouse Avenue, Pacific Grove 93950; (831) 643–1066. Open 8:00 A.M.–3:00 P.M. Tuesday–Sunday. Beer and wine. No credit cards. Not wheelchair accessible.*

We insist you wander downstairs below the Red House Cafe to **MISS TRAWICK'S GARDEN SHOP**, in what used to be the basement and backyard of the red house. Here you will find the most tastefully elegant and rustic garden and home accessories shop we have seen. Old clock reproductions, iron fixtures, garden benches, birdhouses and birdbaths abound. It's just fun.

❧ *Miss Trawick's Garden Shop, 664 Lighthouse Avenue, Pacific Grove 93950; (831) 375–4605. Open 10:00 A.M.–5:00 P.M. Monday–Saturday, noon–4:00 P.M. Sunday. Visa and MasterCard. Not wheelchair accessible.*

Now we suggest you cross Lighthouse to its south side, one half at a time. Under the big oak tree be sure to find your way into **BOOKWORKS BOOKSHOP, COFFEE & TEA HOUSE**, an excellent bookstore owned by Wouter and Walter Van Rossum, both of whom are still on university faculties in the Netherlands. Bookworks specializes in first editions, children's books (from Mulberry Children's Bookshop), classics, and popular novels, and also has a large collection of foreign and domestic magazines, newspapers, and cards.

Be sure to wander past the magazines to the back of the store where you will find the Coffee & Tea House, with its excellent desserts and pastries, espressos, and teas the Van Rossums fly in from the Netherlands. Check out the accoustic guitar music Tuesday and Friday evenings from 7:00 to 9:00 P.M.

❧ *Bookworks Bookshop,
Coffee & Tea House, 667
Lighthouse Avenue, Pacific
Grove 93950; (831) 372–
2242, fax (831) 372–9184.
Open 9:30 A.M.–9:30 P.M.
daily. Visa and MasterCard.
Wheelchair accessible.*

Antiques fans will
find their mecca just up
from Bookworks at the
four-dealer **ANTIQUES** collective. Anjane's Antiques
and Front Row Center
combine with others to
offer great conversation,
estate jewelry, furniture,
books, quilts, silver, glass,
china, stamps, linens, and
jewelry appraisals. We
love this place.

❧ *Antiques (Anjane's
and Front Row Center),
663 Lighthouse Avenue,
Pacific Grove 93950;
(831) 375–5625. Open
10:30 A.M.–5:30 P.M.
Monday–Saturday,*

BOOKWORKS BOOK STORE,
COFFEE & TEA HOUSE, PACIFIC GROVE

noon–5:00 P.M. Sunday. Visa and MasterCard. Wheelchair accessible.

One of Pacific Grove's best and hottest restaurants is **CYPRESS GROVE**, where
area chefs like to dine. So do critics from the *San Francisco Chronicle.* Everything
at this restaurant, owned by Rosemarie and Kurt Steeber, is out of this world,
so we will point out more unusual selections you might want to try. The menu
changes to take advantage of each season's bounty.

Appetizers might include sautéed foie gras with port poached pear and
Maytag blue cheese ($14.95), ahi tuna tartare with marinated cucumber and
frizzled leeks and wasabi cream ($13.95), or an onion and fennel tart with pea

shoots and lemon beurre blanc ($6.95). Adventurous diners might even try the abalone with sea urchins! Tasting menus are also available.

Entrees to sample have been grilled Alaskan ivory salmon wrapped in bacon with beluga lentils and corn pudding ($18.95), grilled Sonoma duck breast with black Mission fig and porcini mushroom compote ($22.95), Ming-Kee Sierra foothills quail with foie gras, chanterelle mushrooms, and ginger aioli ($26.95), vegetarian risotto ($14.95), and Fresno venison tenderloin with spaetzle and fava bean puree ($10.95).

All desserts are $6.00 and range from honey grits flan with whiskey sauce to orange-scented mascarpone cheesecake, chocolate mousse, or seasonal fruit tartlets. The imported French cheese plate is $8.95, or $12.95 with a glass of Graham's Six Grapes Port. Oh my!

❧ *Cypress Grove, 663 Lighthouse Avenue, Pacific Grove 93950; (831) 375–1743, fax (831) 375–0370. Open for lunch 11:30 A.M.–2:30 P.M. Tuesday–Friday, brunch 11:30 A.M.–2:30 P.M. Saturday–Sunday, dinner 5:30–9:30 P.M. Tuesday–Saturday. Wine and beer. Visa, MasterCard, American Express. Wheelchair accessible.*

GERNOT'S VICTORIA HOUSE RESTAURANT occupies what was once Dr. Andrew Hart's office, as the lead stained-glass window pane over the door notes (1894). Gernot's has often been voted "Best European Restaurant" in the area.

Here you can feast on escargots ($6.95) or a Castroville artichoke with curry mayonnaise ($5.45), among other appetizers. Entrees include breast of duck ($20.95), rack of lamb ($24.95), wild boar bourgignon ($19.95), Austrian Wiener schnitzel ($18.95), and veal piccata ($18.95). As you can see, this is home of hearty European food, and lots of it, prepared with traditional care. Nothing nouvelle here. Arrive hungry.

❧ *Gernot's Victoria House Restaurant, 649 Lighthouse Avenue, Pacific Grove 93950; (831) 646–1477. Open from 5:30 P.M. Tuesday–Sunday. Wine and beer. Visa, MasterCard. Not wheelchair accessible.*

Just north of Gernot's is the antique-filled GOSBY HOUSE INN, with twenty rooms and two carriage houses. Delighting overnight guests for more than one hundred years, the inn is a splendiferous Queen Anne Victorian mansion where you can enjoy sumptuous breakfasts and afternoon teas. On request (and on your charge), decadent truffles and champagne can "magically" appear in your room, to gild the lily of fireplaces and views.

❧ *Gosby House Inn, 643 Lighthouse Avenue, Pacific Grove 93950; (831) 375–1287 or (800) 527–8828. Wine available. Visa, MasterCard, American Express. Two rooms wheelchair accessible.*

GOSBY HOUSE INN, PACIFIC GROVE

Between Eighteenth and Seventeenth Streets, you might want to walk up to CAROLE'S CUTS & COLLECTIBLES BARBER SHOP, where she cuts a little hair, sells a few collectibles, and chats it up for fun.

✦ *Carole's Cuts & Collectibles Barber Shop, 624 Lighthouse Avenue, Pacific Grove 93950; (831) 375–4444. Open when she's open. Visa and MasterCard. Not wheelchair accessible.*

Seventeenth Street is worth exploring on your own, particularly if your goal is to reach FANDANGO BISTRO, RESTAURANT & BAR—which it should be. Pierre Bain and Rene Cruz have created this fun and elegant Mediterranean ambience. You enter through what was originally the living room of a house and wander back to the small, engaging bar (with huge arrangements of sumptuous roses) and narrow dining room that seems to go on forever. We love the Hotel de Bain (bath house), the Cochon & Babe French posters, and the charming Basque atmosphere and servers. These people are seduction conspirators!

You might also enjoy the *Fandango Cookbook*, available at the restaurant for $18.75.

Fandango's Cuisines of the Sun reflect the shining Basque, Algerian, and Spanish influences of the owners' backgrounds and are supplemented by mesquite-grilled fresh seafood, steaks, and rack of lamb, along with house-prepared pastries, cakes, soufflés, and creams. Be sure to try the hearts of palm salad ($3.75) or poached artichoke ($3.95), both served with an outstanding vinaigrette dressing. We love the couscous Algerois and the paella Fandango ($16.95). The who's who of the area flock here for the perfect petrale sole served with creamed spinach and new potatoes ($14.95), bouillabaisse Marseillaise ($21.50), and the always outstanding and large fresh salmon fillet grilled over mesquite and served with Cafe de Paris butter ($14.75). The Fandango house wine is from Napa's Round Hill Vineyards.

❧ *Fandango Bistro, Restaurant & Bar, 223 Seventeenth Street, Pacific Grove 93950; (831) 372–3456. Open for lunch, brunch, and dinner daily. Full bar. Visa, MasterCard, American Express. Wheelchair accessible.*

At the southeast corner of Lighthouse and Seventeenth, in what was once a deli and looks as if it might also have been a service station, Frank G. Morris III (see Juice n' Java, below) has opened his **FRANK'S 17TH STREET GRILLE**. The Ohio native serves lunches and dinners from an open grill kitchen; indoor and outdoor seating in good weather. With-it meals include wraps, burritos, burgers, and salads, mostly under $7.00.

❧ *Frank's 17th Street Grille, 617 Lighthouse Avenue, Pacific Grove 93950; (831) 373–5474. Open 11:00 A.M.–8:00 P.M. daily, brunch Saturday–Sunday. Visa, MasterCard, American Express. Wheelchair accessible.*

As you continue north on Lighthouse Avenue to the northeast corner of Sixteenth Street, relax at the **PACIFIC GROVE JUICE N' JAVA**, the pride of Frank G. Morris III and Marlana Nico. This is the place in Pacific Grove for that urban San Francisco coffeehouse feeling with the aroma of oatmeal raisin cookies wafting through the air, stuffed sofas and big chairs, lots books on shelves, a table with guys playing cards in the back, hardwood floors, and excellent bread pudding and eclairs.

Juice n' Java hosts open mike evenings Fridays from 7:00 to 10:00 P.M., and jazz and folk rock Saturday evenings, same time and place (undoubtedly the doing of Frank, a triple-threat musician—guitar, flute, and piano).

❧ *Pacific Grove Juice n' Java, 599 Lighthouse Avenue, Pacific Grove 93950; (831) 373–8652. Open 7:00 A.M.–8:00 P.M., till 10:00 P.M. Friday–Saturday. No credit cards. Wheelchair accessible.*

Adventurous soles (!) among you may want to hike the stairs to **STOWITT'S MUSEUM AND LIBRARY**, where you might see performance painting on the second floor of the 591 Building.

PAELLA FANDANGO
from Pierre Bain of Fandango Bistro, Restaurant & Bar,
Pacific Grove

La mejor salsa del mundo es el hanbre. (The best sauce in the world is hunger.)

—Miguel de Cervantes

If you asked people outside Spain what's the most typical Spanish dish, the majority would probably say 'paella.' This delicious dish gets its name from the special metal pan that the cooks of Valencia use to prepare rice dishes. If you don't have a paella pan, you can use a large skillet or a wok—and you can still call the finished product paella. Why not? You're the cook.

—Pierre Bain

½ cup olive oil

1 large onion, chopped

2 cloves garlic, chopped

2 large tomatoes, diced

2 bell peppers, 1 red, 1 yellow (you can substitute green for either), cut in strips

2 cups white rice

8 cups chicken broth

3 Tbs. chopped parsley

2 large pinches saffron threads

2 chicken breasts (each cut in 4–5 pieces)

1 chorizo sausage (about ½ lb.), cut in ½-inch slices

½ lb. scallops

½ lb. calamari

½ lb. shrimp, peeled, tails intact

8–10 littleneck clams

8–10 mussels

1 cup peas, fresh or frozen

salt, pepper, cayenne

In a skillet heat olive oil and add onion, garlic, tomatoes, and bell pepper strips. Sauté until limp. Add white rice and chicken broth and bring to a boil. Add the chopped parsley and the saffron threads and cook for 20 minutes at a simmer. Add chicken, sausage, seafood, and peas, and cook to doneness, probably about 20–40 minutes. You're the cook (see above), so you decide. Season to taste with salt, pepper, and cayenne, and serve. Serves eight.

Otherwise, another of Pacific Grove's traditional coffee shop/restaurants is right next door at the BAY CAFE. Extremely popular with locals for nearly twenty years, Mimi and Chris Defeo's restaurant serves big, unpretentious food

at breakfast and lunch, including steak and eggs ($7.95); one egg, fries, and toast ($4.95); and three-egg, three-filling omelettes ($6.95). Lunch includes lots of sandwiches from chicken-fried steak to squid, and burgers. Donut freaks, get your fix here. A star indicates which menu selections are kosher.
✴❧ *Bay Cafe, 589 Lighthouse Avenue, Pacific Grove 93950; (831) 375–4237. Open 7:00 A.M.–2:00 P.M. daily. Visa, MasterCard. Wheelchair accessible.*

Near the corner of Lighthouse and Forest is an interesting gift shop called **LASTING MEMORIES**, owned by Olivia Moti, who paints and sells hand-decorated plates and entire table settings with colorful flower motifs. Olivia's husband, Michael, fires the plates in the kiln in the barn of their home in near-by Prunedale, which is a long way from home for one of her best clients, Barbra Streisand. Her plates are also used at the famous Casanova Restaurant in Carmel, Monterey Joe's, and many others.

Eclectic as it is, Lasting Memories features other local artists' creations and serves as the local J. C. Penney catalog store. Keep your purses and children close here so nothing gets broken. Plate prices range from a bargain $9.00 to $51.00.
✴❧ *Lasting Memories, 581 Lighthouse Avenue, Pacific Grove 93950; (831) 655–9736. Open 9:30 A.M.–5:30 P.M. Monday–Saturday, 11:00 A.M.–2:00 P.M. Sunday. Visa, MasterCard, American Express, Discover. Wheelchair accessible.*

At the corner of Grand Avenue, **PRIM AND PROPER** is an appropriately named ladies' clothing shop featuring petite sizes and fine sweaters.
✴❧ *Prim and Proper, 553 Lighthouse Avenue, Pacific Grove 93950; (831) 372–5563, fax (831) 372–6563. Open 10:00 A.M.–5:30 P.M. daily. Visa, MasterCard, American Express. Wheelchair accessible.*

ORLANDO'S SHOE STORE is an old and special place, founded in 1941 by Peter Orlando and currently run by Peter's daughter Marlene Orlando Kellog, with a new generation about to take over the shoestrings. Peter began with an old-world-style shoe repair shop (an entity extremely important to us but a disappearing craft in our throwaway world), and eventually began selling excellent quality shoes, such as Cobbies, Easy Spirit, Selby, Naturalizer, Soft Spots, Clarks, and Keds. Clogs too. The family has also recently introduced women's clothing.
✴❧ *Orlando's Shoe Store, 547 Lighthouse Avenue, Pacific Grove 93950; (831) 373–4650. Open 10:00 A.M.–5:00 P.M. Tuesday–Saturday. Visa, MasterCard. Wheelchair accessible.*

SCOTCH BAKERY,
ONE OF STEINBECK'S FAVORITES, PACIFIC GROVE

Just east of Orlando's is one of John Steinbeck's and our favorite places, the
SCOTCH BAKERY, the "Sweetest Place in Town." This 1930s historic bakery has
only had two owners in its sweet life—who could leave it? Just catch a whiff of
the sweet buns Steinbeck mentions in *Cannery Row*, donuts, cookies, pastries,
fresh breads, and coffee, with a four-tiered wedding cake in the window. This is
a truly old-fashioned bakery that proudly touts its use of fresh eggs, pure cream,
creamery butter, and 100% vegetable shortening. We dare you not to buy something.
✢ *Scotch Bakery, 545 Lighthouse Avenue, Pacific Grove 93950; (831)
375-3569. Open 6:00 A.M.–8:45 P.M. Tuesday–Friday, 6:00 A.M.–6:00 P.M.
Saturday, 6:00 A.M.–4:45 P.M. Sunday. No credit cards. Wheelchair accessible.*

At **GROVE NUTRITION**, certified massage therapist Ann Coleman has turned
an old, empty health food store into a truly complete establishment selling alter-
native health products and nutrition supplements and foods. Her slogan,
"Health Food and More," is definitely on target since she took the place over in
1995.
✢ *Grove Nutrition, 543 Lighthouse Avenue, Pacific Grove 93950; (831)
372-6625. Open 9:00 A.M.–6:00 P.M. Monday–Friday, 10:00 A.M.–5:00 P.M.
Saturday. No credit cards. Wheelchair accessible.*

In a brightly painted Victorian building dating from 1893 is the crown princess of this end of Lighthouse Avenue, **VICTORIAN CORNER**. Its comfortable ambience suggests an old family restaurant, which it has been since 1977, with its wooden flooring and chairs, bright colors, friendly staff, and good solid food at reasonable prices. It's also worth the meal just to see the historic photos on the walls.

Victorian Corner is a good place to stop for breakfast or lunch, which includes a daily special for $6.95 with soup or salad, bread, and soft drink or coffee and tea. Soups are hearty and excellent, salads are reasonable, and specialties include creative takeoffs on standard sandwiches, ranging from grilled cheese with Monterey Jack, cheddar, and Swiss cheese ($4.75), to the Asilomar: healthy sprouts, fresh mushrooms, tomato, and sesame seeds topped with Swiss cheese on wheat bread ($5.75). You can also get a New York steak sandwich with sautéed mushrooms and garlic bread ($7.95). All sandwiches come with homemade french fries and salad. Burgers, quiches, and omelettes are all under $7.00. Check out the cheescake, cannoli, or mud pie, and the espresso drinks. Run right over. Try the homemade pastas and seafood specials at dinner.

❧ Victorian Corner, 541 Lighthouse Avenue, Pacific Grove 93950; (831) 372–4641. Open 7:45 A.M.–3:00 P.M. and from 5:30 P.M. daily except Sunday evening. Beer and wine. Visa, MasterCard. Wheelchair accessible; might need some help if you need to use the restroom.

Slightly east of this main shopping area of Pacific Grove is one of its most popular restaurants, **PASTA MIA TRATTORIA**, voted "Best Italian Restaurant" for nine years in a row. In this older home above Lighthouse Avenue, the atmosphere is still casual and happy, with light wood decor. The trattoria features Northern and Southern Italian specialties: grilled local seafood and scampi al modo mio ($15.50); pollo marsala (15.50); osso buco ($13.50); and yummy lasagna, gnocchi, pizzas, and Linguini Marini with seafood and sun-dried tomatoes ($11.75). All served with soup or salad. Don't miss the tiramisu, tora di noci, profiteroles, and tora di formaggio. A great chance to try some unusual Italian and local wines.

❧ Pasta Mia Trattoria, 481 Lighthouse Avenue, Pacific Grove 93950; (831) 375–7709. Beer and wine. Open 4:00–10:00 P.M. daily. Visa, MasterCard, American Express. Not wheelchair accessible.

SIGNIFICANT OTHERS

There are some restaurants off the beaten path that are well worth the trouble of finding. We want to make sure you know about them.

The **BRAZILIAN CAFE & RESTAURANT** may well be what it claims to be: the "best authentic Brazilian restaurant in California." We really don't have many comparisons, unfortunately, so Argentine cuisine would be welcomed too. You will enjoy the lively colors, music, and fun atmosphere as well as pastas, fresh seafood, and marinated steaks.

Brazilian Cafe & Restaurant, 1180 Forest Avenue, Pacific Grove 93950; (831) 373–2272. Full bar. Open from 5:00 P.M. daily. Visa, MasterCard, American Express. Wheelchair accessible.

One of the new stars on the Monterey Peninsula restaurant scene is definitely **PASSIONFISH**, by the same owners and in the same location as the old Crocodile, just at the end of the Lighthouse Avenue's business section. Winery staffs throughout the county recommend Passionfish, partly because it offers Napa and Monterey wines at close to retail price, without the sometimes outrageous markup that many restaurants charge. *Wine Spectator* magazine has blessed Passionfish with its "Award of Excellence."

Unfortunately, Passionfish is only open for dinner, but suffer your way through succulent crab cakes with lime salsa ($8.00), coconut-crusted prawns with pepper rum sauce ($7.00), or portobello mushroom fritters with aioli ($6.00) for starters. Main courses are equally reasonable for the quality. Try duck confit with Tasmanian honey sauce ($15), maple-cured prime rib ($14), Monterey Bay rock cod or sand dabs ($14), local swordfish ($16), sweet corn ravioli ($12), or carnivore's delight of short ribs over horseradish smashed potatoes ($15).

Passionfish, 701 Lighthouse Avenue, Pacific Grove 93950; (831) 655–3311. Open 5:00–9:00 P.M. Sunday–Monday and Wednesday–Thursday, 5:00–10:00 P.M. Friday–Saturday. Wine and beer. Visa, Thursday, 5:00–10:00 P.M. Friday–Saturday. Wine and beer. Visa, MasterCard, American Express. Wheelchair accessible through back door.

The **FISHWIFE AT ASILOMAR BEACH** is just as much fun as its name suggests. You can enjoy award-winning California cuisine with a Caribbean accent in this gorgeous restaurant designed to highlight the natural wonders of the trees, beach, and ocean right outdoors. Fabulous pastas, local fresh-catch seafoods, sautéed prawns Belize, grilled snapper Cancun, calamari steak, and fettuccine Alfredo with prawns, scallops, or crab, all at surprisingly reasonable prices (under $15). Don't miss the Key lime pie or chocolate truffle torte.

Be sure also to check out the Fishwife's terrific and informal Turtle Bay Taqueria in Monterey, as well as its new Taqueria and Fishwife side-by-side in Seaside.

Fishwife at Asilomar Beach, 1996 Sunset Drive, Pacific Grove 93950; (831) 375–7107; www.fishwife.com. Open 11:00 A.M.–10:00 P.M. Wednesday–Monday. Full bar. Visa, MasterCard, American Express. Wheelchair accessible.

Since it opened in 1969, **TILLIE GORT'S CAFE**, just 2 blocks from the aquarium, has often been voted to have the "Best Vegetarian Food in Monterey County," and for good reason. Carnivores can also get excellent burgers and pastas, and the homemade desserts delight everyone. Espresso drinks are great.

Tillie Gort's Cafe, 111 Central Avenue, Pacific Grove 93950; (831) 373–0335. Open 11:00 A.M.–10:30 P.M. daily. Beer and wine. Visa, MasterCard. Wheelchair accessible.

The **TINNERY** is a true family restaurant overlooking Monterey Bay—kids can have pizza or an excellent hamburger and parents can have a real drink. With an outdoor patio, cocktails, and live entertainment nightly, the Tinnery tries to cover all bases for all people.

Different rooms set different tones, from a pub with a bar menu and atmosphere to more formal dining with white linens and warm stone fireplaces. Breakfast may include eggs in all styles served with croissant and potatoes beginning at $5.99 and up to $10.99 for eggs with filet mignon. Cheese blintzes are good ($6.99), as are Belgian waffles with walnuts or strawberries and whipped cream ($6.50).

Shrimp and crab Louie salads are available at lunch and dinner, and you might also enjoy the Monterey Bay snapper, sand dabs, fish and chips, calamari, roasted tom turkey, or fabulous steaks and roasted prime rib available in three cuts, from $7.95 at lunch to $18.99 at dinner.

Tinnery, 631 Ocean View Boulevard, Pacific Grove 93950; (831) 646–1040; www.thetinnery.com. Open 8:00 A.M.–11:00 P.M. daily. Full bar. Visa, MasterCard, American Express. Wheelchair accessible.

TOASTIE'S CAFE right on Lighthouse serves excellent breakfasts if you want an alternative to the one at your hotel. Also good, reliable all-American lunches and dinners, including great pancakes, omelettes, and even California creations like huevos rancheros. All-day breakfast.

*⅍ *Toastie's Cafe,* 702 Lighthouse Avenue, Pacific Grove 93950; (831) 373–7543. Open 7:00 A.M.–3:00 P.M daily, and for dinner Tuesday–Saturday. Beer and wine. Visa, MasterCard. Wheelchair accessible.

If you're looking for the best pizza in town, locals have voted **AMELIA'S GOURMET PIZZA** (formerly known as Allegro) "Monterey's Best Pizzeria" since 1988. You can dine inside, on the patio, or in your hotel room via their delivery service. Calzones, wonderful seafood pastas and risottos, everyone's favorite garlicky Caesar salad (Kathleen loves it), and, oh yes, those gourmet pizzas. Some pizzas are even passable by the American Heart Association standards, meaning little or no cheese and whole wheat pizza dough on request. Kids can play with real dough and feast on peanut butter and jelly, although even they usually go for the pizza.

*⅍ *Amelia's Gourmet Pizza,* 1184 Forest Avenue, Pacific Grove 93950; (831) 373–5656. Open 11:00 A.M.–9:00 P.M. Sunday–Thursday, till 10:00 P.M. Friday–Saturday. Beer and wine. Visa, MasterCard, American Express, checks. Wheelchair accessible.

Often voted Monterey's "Most Romantic," "Best View," "Best Service," "Best Place to Kiss," and "Best Fine Dining Menu," the **OLD BATH HOUSE RESTAURANT** at Lovers Point Park may be a must-stop for you if you're in the mood or want to be. This is a gorgeous Victorian with elegant drippy interior decor with lots of candles and slightly nouvelle American cuisine. At the healthier end of the menu spectrum, try the mesquite-grilled local fish. If you want to go for rich and wonderful, it's the veal or duck Merlot, ranging from $18 to $35. Reservations almost a must.

*⅍ *Old Bath House Restaurant,* 620 Ocean View Boulevard, Pacific Grove 93950; (831) 375–5195. Open for cocktails at 4:00 P.M., dinner from 5:00 P.M. Monday–Friday, from 4:00 p.m. Saturday–Sunday. Full bar. Visa, MasterCard, American Express. This historic building is not wheelchair accessible, although staff happily and frequently carry wheelchair guests upstairs.

CHAPTER 3

17-MILE DRIVE AND PEBBLE BEACH

*P*ebble Beach and the 17-Mile Drive are two of the most beautiful creations anywhere on this big earth.

We suggest you drive it slowly, in any kind of weather, just to take in the fresh air, water, coastal cliffs, sand dunes, golf courses, cypress trees, and engaging wild animals, from deer to cormorants. It is recommended but unlikely that you keep your eyes on the road.

Get on the 17-Mile Drive in Pacific Grove where it intersects with Lighthouse Avenue about 10 blocks west of Pacific Grove's commercial area. Turn left (south) on 17-Mile Drive and you are on your way, at first cruising (slowly, please) through residential neighborhoods. Or you can begin the 17-Mile Drive at its southern end in Carmel, at the west (ocean) end of Ocean Avenue. Please respect locals' needs to get where they need to go. They are not necessarily on vacation. There are no food or gasoline concessions or commerce of any kind, so go prepared. The whole drive with stops everywhere can take from forty-five minutes to as many hours as you wish to ecstasize.

Be warned that the water and beaches along here are extremely dangerous. Monterey Bay's 10,000-foot drop, called its Grand Canyon, is at its deepest off the shore along 17-Mile Drive. It is not even safe to frolic on the rocks, because, as the signs warn, sudden unexpectedly high waves can sweep you right off your feet and off the rocks and you're on your way to China and beyond.

Soon you arrive at a tollhouse (no cookies, sorry) where you pay $7.00 per car to enter the Pebble Beach Company's property and the Del Monte Forest. Incidentally, the company owns the 17-Mile Drive, Pebble Beach itself, the shopping center in Pebble Beach, Spyglass Hill, the Inn at Spanish Bay, the Links at Spanish Bay, and Pebble Beach Golf Links, as well as private Cypress Point golf courses, the site of the AT&T Pebble Beach National Pro-Am Golf Tournament. An excellent and well-maintained (everything here is) bicycle route begins off the road next to the tollhouse.

A mile into the drive you come to the Inn at Spanish Bay and in another mile Spanish Bay beach and picnic area, with a parking lot and portable toilet. A gorgeous golf course is everywhere, with deer romping occasionally on the course while you watch; gardeners mow, and golfers swing and putter along on golf carts.

In another three-tenths of a mile you can join the nature trail where signs warn RESTLESS SEA, HIGH SURF, SUBMERGED ROCKS. Within the next mile you come to Point Joe and China Rock, both great points from which to take photos. Point Joe became an accidental burial ground as explorers crashed into the rocks, thinking it was the entrance to Monterey Bay.

Our favorite place to stop is at Bird Rock, where there are great photo opportunities, inexpensive (25 cents) long-range telescopes so you can watch the sea lions and cormorants on Bird Rock, and deer romping in grass across the road. We also love the pelicans and gulls, who seem quite comfortable with all these funny-looking people around. The pecking order on Bird Rock places birds toward the top, with seals, sea lions, and otters lower down. The deepwater canyon promotes a welling-up of sea life to feed local marine life. Great free public rest rooms are at the southern end of the parking lot, with true wheelchair access.

BIRD ROCK

Next you come to Spyglass Hill Golf Course and Grill, and then we encourage you to stop at Fanshell Beach to look at the seals.

Just 6 miles along the drive, you pass through Cypress Point Golf Club, and then after you wander through an area of enormous and occasionally ostentatious homes, you come to a pullout on the water side of the road to view the Lone Cypress, a breathtaking sight. If you can, take the wooden stairs down the cliff for closer viewing.

Soon you come to Pescadero Point, where the flattop cypress trees are particularly unusual. In another few tenths of a mile you come to Pebble Beach, with its fabulous golf course, shopping center, restaurants, and lodge.

Among the Pebble Beach resort shops, we suggest you check in at the Pebble Beach Market to experience how the locals shop and cook and to pick up a few picnic supplies or Pebble Beach clothing yourselves. The Pebble Beach Golf Shop is the ultimate for golf fans and the ideal place to find a gift for your favorite golfer, even if it's yourself. Westwinds features the latest in women's golf apparel and accessories and casual resort wear for on and off the golf course. Reflections offers elegantly casual gifts and clothing, jewelry, goodies for children, and Pebble Beach souvenirs. The Dutches features the elegant, funny paintings by Diana Willson, along with elegant clothing for women.

Catering to the plethora of golfers passing through, the Spanish Bay Golf Shop sells a wide variety of men's and ladies' golf apparel and equipment. Morse & Co., named for Del Monte Company founder (and previous owner of Pebble Beach) Samuel F. B. Morse, offers exclusive fine clothing and furnishings for men, including upscale classic fashions.

Breezes sells gifts and resort clothing and jewelry, children's clothing and necessities, Spanish Bay mementos, that necessary aspirin and Pepto-Bismol, film, and snacks. And the Spyglass Hill Golf Shop features the latest in men's and women's attire, mostly with Spyglass Hill's logo, as well as golf clubs and bags and more gifts. All are elegant and contribute to the pleasant Pebble Beach experience.

The two primary restaurants to try at Pebble Beach are Bay Club at the Inn at Spanish Bay and Club XIX at the Lodge at Pebble Beach.

Perfect describes everything about the semiformal **BAY CLUB AT THE INN AT SPANISH BAY**. The service is as elegant as the setting (love those orchids) in this restaurant nestled within the dignified resort. Bay Club's wine list is worth the trip in itself, having received *Wine Spectator*'s coveted Grand Award several times recently.

Chef Drew Previti presents contemporary Northern Italian cuisine against spectacular views and warm soft candlelight. Artichokes from nearby Castroville and local Dungeness crab show richly over pastas, as does lobster. You can also enjoy perfect meats and fowl, with a prix fixe option.

❧ Bay Club at the Inn at Spanish Bay, *2700 17-Mile Drive, Pebble Beach 93953; (831) 647–7433. Open 6:00–10:00 P.M. daily. Full bar. Visa, MasterCard, American Express, Carte Blanche, Discover, Diners Club. Wheelchair accessible.*

CLUB XIX AT THE LODGE AT PEBBLE BEACH (Club 19) is the most posh restaurant in the area. Named for the hangout after every golf course's eighteenth hole, Club XIX overlooks the spectacular and famous eighteenth hole of the Pebble Beach Golf Links. Try the patio in good weather, or try to sit near the window inside to watch unmatchable sunsets.

Chef Hubert Keller, formerly of San Francisco's Fleur de Lys, and chef Lisa Magadini present new lighter features on Club XIX's traditional American menu, and with great success. Vegetarian selections are always available, as are a la carte selections and two prix fixe menus. Dungeness crab is always available, as are duck, elegant meats, and seafoods. Jackets are required for men downstairs at dinner.

❧ Club XIX at the Lodge at Pebble Beach, *17-Mile Drive, Pebble Beach 93953; (831) 625–8519. Open for lunch 11:30 A.M.–4:00 P.M., dinner 6:00–10:00 P.M. daily. Full bar. Visa, MasterCard, American Express, Diners Club. Wheelchair accessible.*

More affordable dining experiences exist, thank heavens, at the Inn at Spanish Bay's Clubhouse Bar & Grill (great informal chocolate desserts), where you can get a refund for your $7.00 17-Mile Drive entrance fee, or at the Dunes, a romantic garden-room setting, where entrees hover around $20.00 and Fridays feature a clambake. The Lodge at Pebble Beach also offers the Cypress Room or Tap Room, an English pub with lots of golf stuff and a tame sports bar feeling. The Tap Room has been voted "Best Late Night Restaurant" in the area, of which there are darned few.

From 17-Mile Drive you can enter Carmel down near the beach and follow North San Antonio to Ocean Avenue, Carmel's central focus.

CHAPTER 4

CARMEL AND BIG SUR

hat is a Carmel? It is sometimes a Carmel-by-the-Sea. It is not a caramel. Think Carmelite friars. In 1602, three Carmelites accompanying Spanish explorer Sebastian Vizcaino found their way to the top of a forested hill and saw the white sand beach below; a clear-water river sparkled nearby. In the Carmelites' honor, Vizcaino named their discovery Rio Carmelo, known today as the Carmel River. It enters the Pacific Ocean just south of the village of Carmel, a 1-square-mile area still nestled in a pine forest above the still spectacular, still white sand beach. South of Highway 1 from Carmel is Big Sur, a dramatically wild and lovely seacoast.

Carmel is both quirky and elegant, nouvelle and staid, avant-garde and traditional, large and small.

Its quirkiness includes no street addresses and a law requiring a permit to wear high heels (due to its urban forest nature). Many houses have names, or are known or described by their location, usually as being north or south of Ocean Avenue. The city regulates facades and colors of houses, and there is no home mail delivery. Everyone goes to the post office on Fifth Avenue between Dolores and San Carlos, prolonging the "tradition of regularly meeting one's neighbors in town," according to city hall's *Carmel-by-the-Sea A to Z*. Be sure to check out the work of local cartoonist Bill Bates on the post office walls. Recent controversial proposals to number houses and offer home mail delivery met with resounding defeat.

City hall's little book also says that "the natural sounds of surf, birds, and breeze are preferred to man-made noises." Most streets in the residential area and, occasionally, downtown, meander around trees, rock walls, and landscaping. A whole section of Carmel's municipal code deals with protection of its urban forest; it is the first community in California to employ a full-time professional forester. Dogs must be on leashes except in city parks and at Carmel Beach, where plastic disposal bags for poop are supplied, as they are in the Mission Trail Nature Preserve along the eastern border of town.

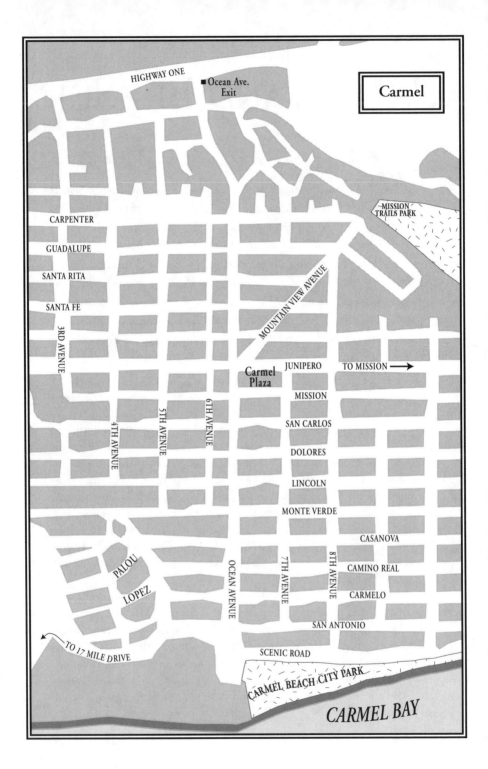

You must have on your exploring shoes because many of Carmel's most intriguing shops are in its tiny courtyards between and behind buildings, and in most cases the courtyards are, themselves, intriguing. Hundreds of boutiques, about seventy art studios and galleries, and oodles of antiques shops, small cafes, bistros, and restaurants are there for you to find.

Carmel's elegance is pretty obvious in its meticulous and often expensive shops, galleries, and restaurants where the finest clothing, china, silver, jewelry, art, and gourmet foods are offered. Both nouvelle and staid styles of dressing and cooking exist side by side in Carmel, with the hottest new chef and restaurant practically next door to the most ladylike English tearoom.

Although Frank "Devvy" Devendorf filed the first subdivision map to create Carmel in 1902, it was the 1906 San Francisco earthquake that put it on the map when well-known artists, writers, and musicians flocked here on the urging of George Sterling, a resident and California's poet, to seek quiet and camaraderie. Others eventually gravitated here, including John Steinbeck, Robinson Jeffers, Lincoln Steffens, Jack London, Sinclair Lewis, Ansel Adams, William Saroyan, Frank Norris, Dashiell Hammett, Katherine Anne Porter, and Wallace Stegner.

Carmel lives by its own, as well as residents' perceptions of, European traditions. Traditionally, people obey the laws here, and they go to the post office, and they dress well at all times. They also take tea or an afternoon glass of sherry or wine. Carmelites also participate in the tradition of activity in civic affairs; in reverence for and preservation of the environment, the urban forest, and their cherished village; and in supporting the arts in many ways, including staging the Carmel Art Festival, the Carmel Art Walk, Carmel Bach Festival, Performance Carmel, and Carmel Shakespeare Festival.

Carmel has all the amenities and elegant urban stores of a large city without being a large city, as well as nearby shopping centers with the usual chains represented. Both the Barnyard and the Crossroads have different designs, auras, and tastes, and offer different styles of restaurants and shops. So no one, of any taste, is ever deprived here.

While Carmel has a semiarid climate (even though it's right on the Pacific Ocean), it is often foggy and cool, so bring sweaters and jackets to dress in layers. Eating on the street, especially ice cream, is strongly discouraged. Ties are rarely required. Parking is available in a free lot at Vista Lobos Park, Third Avenue and Torres Street, as well as on the street, and parking laws are strictly enforced, particularly in the summer.

Carmel's beaches are down by the water (see Bill Bates's great cartoon on this topic at the post office). At the foot of Ocean Avenue is Del Mar Beach, also known as Carmel Beach. Carmel River Beach is at Carmelo and Scenic Drive. Monastery Beach is 2.5 miles south of Carmel on Highway 1, and Point Lobos

State Reserve is 3 miles south of Carmel, also on Highway 1, which basically goes down the coast.

So get your sweater, don't forget your camera, and let's go.

We will now take you on our walking tour of Carmel-by-the-Sea. First we will take you down the north side of Ocean Avenue, then up the south side. Then we give you descriptions of interesting points on the cross streets. You will find that you tend to explore on one side of Ocean, then cross it and continue to prowl around on the other. A restful and restorative meal or two in between is strongly advised! Rest assured that you will have plenty of opportunities.

Remember, there are no street addresses in Carmel. So we will tell you which side of the street a business is on: *ns* for north side, *ss* for south side, *es* for east side, and *ws* for west side. West is toward the ocean, east is up the hill.

OCEAN AVENUE

Let's begin at the top of Ocean Avenue on the north side of the street. Several shops have come and gone at Ocean and Mission, including the venerable Mediterranean Market, which we miss.

WISHART'S BAKERY EST. 1945 is a don't-miss for the feeling and tastes of an old-fashioned, small-town bakery. Locals duck in here for yummy homemade soups ($2.50–$3.50), Bud's Ice Cream, hot grilled sandwiches ($5.25), gooey blueberry and raisin scones, pecan super swivels, soft drinks and pretzels (with sesame seeds, salt, or plain), espresso drinks, and help-yourself coffee. We have never seen such huge handmade biscotti—a must-try!

These people also own Caffe Napoli on the south side of Ocean and Lincoln (great pizza and pasta) and Little Napoli on Dolores between Ocean and Seventh. Do they know what they're doing!

Wishart's Bakery Est. 1945, Ocean Avenue ns between Mission and San Carlos, Carmel 93921; (831) 624–3870. Open 6:30 A.M.–6:00 or 7:00 P.M. daily. No credit cards. Wheelchair accessible.

West of Wishart's is **SPEEDO AUTHENTIC FITNESS**, a whole store of clothing and equipment, with salespeople dressed in the clothing, not all of which is skin-hugging. Everything you need to wear for certain sports, including the one that consists of sitting in front of the television, is here.

Speedo Authentic Fitness, Ocean Avenue ns between Mission and San Carlos, Carmel 93921; (831) 626–0295. Open 9:30 A.M.–6:00 P.M. daily. Visa, MasterCard, American Express, Diners Club. Wheelchair accessible.

CONCEPTS GALLERY features wonderfully colorful visual art, from abstracts with bold colors to bold photographs of San Miguel de Allende, Patscuaro, and Carmel, along with exquisite local jewelry and sculpted glass art.

ᵏᵕ Concepts Gallery, Ocean Avenue ns between Mission and San Carlos, Carmel 93921; (831) 624–0661. Open 10:00 A.M.–6:00 P.M. daily. Visa, MasterCard, American Express. Partly wheelchair accessible.

Kids and hip-hop fans will love BIG DOG SPORTSWEAR, a shop dedicated to Big Dog label clothes and personal accoutrements. Here both kids and adults will find their sizes, as will big and tall folks or kids who buy those very big pants that hang around their ahems. Great music in here.

ᵏᵕ Big Dog Sportswear, Ocean Avenue ns between San Carlos and Mission, Carmel 93921; (831) 624–5477. Open 10:00 A.M.–6:00 P.M. daily. Visa, MasterCard, American Express. Wheelchair accessible.

Kathleen particularly loves COACH AT CARMEL at the corner of Ocean and San Carlos. Men—this is not a sports store. It's a low-key factory outlet of one of the finest leather goods producers in the United States. Beyond its outlet discount feature, the store also has monthly rotating sales, meaning some group of bags or accessories is on sale all the time. We didn't really need a yellow or purple leather bag when we dropped in, but maybe you do.

Special note: Coach at Carmel has Japanese-speaking staff members working at all times.

ᵏᵕ Coach at Carmel, Ocean Avenue ns at corner of San Carlos, Carmel 93921; (831) 626–1777. Open 10:00 A.M.–7:00 P.M. daily. Visa, MasterCard, American Express, JCB. Partly wheelchair accessible.

To continue down Ocean Avenue, cross San Carlos and walk right into DANSK II, a factory outlet of the fine Dansk kitchen and dining equipment manufacturers. This place always has great deals on cotton napkins, kitchen utensils, dishes, cookware, cobalt blue glassware, picture frames, and abstract design flatware. Dansk now makes much of its products in lower-cost countries around the world such as Portugal and the Philippines instead of Scandinavia. The store also always has a "warehouse tabletop sale" going on.

ᵏᵕ Dansk II, Ocean Avenue ns at the corner of San Carlos, Carmel 93921; (831) 625–1600. Open 10:00 A.M.–6:00 P.M. Sunday–Thursday, till 7:00 P.M. Friday–Saturday. Visa, MasterCard, American Express, Discover. Wheelchair accessible.

HANSON ART GALLERIES are well known for offering high quality contemporary artwork, particularly that of Scott Hanson, David Richey Johnson, Frederick Hart, Thomas Pradzynski, and Manuel Anoro, as well as limited edition prints. We especially like gallery owner Scott Hanson's U.S. map made of the states' license plates. You can also visit Hanson galleries in San Francisco, Sausalito, and New Orleans.

❧ *Hanson Art Galleries, Ocean Avenue ns near San Carlos, Carmel 93921; (831) 625–6142. Open 10:00 A.M.–6:00 P.M. Sunday–Wednesday, 10:00 A.M.– 7:00 P.M. Thursday–Friday, 10:00 A.M.–9:00 P.M. Saturday. Visa, MasterCard, American Express, Discover.*

CARMEL DRUG STORE is the good, old-fashioned drugstore we all need and many of us lack in this age of chains and boxes. Here you can get prescriptions filled, as well as newspapers, candy, emergency umbrellas, playing cards, Ray-Ban sunglasses, shampoo, Band-Aids, and loads of magazines. Oh yes, film.

❧ *Carmel Drug Store, Ocean Avenue ns between San Carlos and Dolores, Carmel 93921; (831) 624–3819. Open 8:00 A.M.–10:00 P.M. daily. Visa, MasterCard. Wheelchair accessible.*

JEWELRY ATELIER is a very low-key, no-hype twenty-seven-year-old jewelry store featuring estate to contemporary jewelry. The staff makes more than half the jewelry sold in the shop. Worth a look.

❧ *Jewelry Atelier, Ocean Avenue ns between San Carlos and Dolores, Carmel 93921; (831) 624–7591. Open 10:30 A.M.–5:30 P.M. daily. Visa, MasterCard, American Express. Wheelchair accessible.*

GALLERY NASH features serious art and serious staff, with elegant burgundy carpet. The lighting is dark enough in here that you may not see the invisible incline ramp between the front and rear gallery rooms. Enjoy the contemporary art, including bronze sculpture, art glass, amber jewelry, paintings, and limited-edition graphics. Artists featured include Pino, Greg Singley, Hessam, Oleg Zhivetin, and Sabzi; art glass by John Lotton.

❧ *Gallery Nash, Ocean Avenue ns between San Carlos and Dolores, Carmel 93921; (831) 662–9009. Open 10:00 A.M.–6:00 P.M. daily. Visa, MasterCard, American Express, Discover. Wheelchair accessible.*

Grandparents will find heaven at **BIB 'N TUCKER FINE CLOTHES FOR CHILDREN**. We love the Carmel bibs and Florence Eisman, Petit Bateau, Sylvia Whyte, Catamini, and Miniman clothes for kids in sizes from newborn to 6X for girls and 7 for boys. Catch the cute cards, toys, Eden and Gund stuffed animals, baby books and shoes, baby furniture, little rugs, and adorable sun hats.

➳ *Bib 'n Tucker Fine Clothes for Children, Ocean Avenue ns between San Carlos and Dolores, Carmel 93921; (831) 624–2185. Open 10:00 A.M.–5:00 P.M. daily. Visa, MasterCard, American Express. Wheelchair accessible.*

GARCIA GALLERY features Danny Garcia's (surprise) jewelry and bronze wall hangings of cypress trees, as well as designs by Garcia's daughter Linda and son Gary.

➳ *Garcia Gallery, Ocean Avenue ns between San Carlos and Dolores or Sixth between San Carlos and Dolores, Carmel 93921; (831) 624–8338 or (831) 624–1662. Open 10:00 A.M.–5:00 P.M. daily. Visa and MasterCard. Wheelchair accessible.*

PALOOSH GOURMET WOMEN'S CLOTHING is the new sister store to Girl Boy Girl, featuring Diesel, Diane Von Furstenberg, Betsy Johnson, Nicole Miller, and Earl Jeans.

➳ *Paloosh Gourmet Women's Clothing, Ocean Avenue ns near Dolores, Carmel 93921; (831) 626–2773. Open 10:00 A.M.– 6:00 P.M. daily. Visa, MasterCard, American Express. Wheelchair accessible.*

Carmel Forecast is the newest incarnation of the revolving T-shirt and sno-globe shop next door.

As you pass BURCHELL HOUSE PROPERTIES, you might look in its windows or go in for a chat. We rarely mention real estate offices in our walkabouts, but this one is unusual. Known locally as "the real estate office with the clock," Burchell House uses feng shui to assess properties' appropriateness for potential buyers.

➳ *Burchell House Properties, Ocean Avenue ns at corner of Dolores, Carmel 93921; (831) 624–6461. Open 9:30 A.M.–5:00 P.M. daily.*

PROMISES BOUTIQUE specializes in hats, knits, velvets, costume jewelry and watches, and an "I'm not going out of business" sale.

➳ *Promises Boutique, Ocean Avenue ns near Dolores, Carmel 93921; (831) 626–3904. Open 10:00 A.M.–5:00 P.M. Visa, MasterCard. Wheelchair accessible.*

If you love light, colorful, pastel floral paintings and posters, wander upstairs to the LILLIANA BRAICO GALLERY. Her paintings will cheer up the most dreary day anywhere in the world. The studio where she paints is on Sixth Avenue at the corner of Delores and can be visited by appointment.

❧ *Lilliana Braico Gallery, Ocean Avenue ns between Dolores and Lincoln, Carmel 93921; (831) 624–2512. Open 10:00 A.M.–6:00 P.M. daily. Visa, MasterCard, American Express. Not wheelchair accessible.*

One of our favorites is **GREAT THINGS ANTIQUES**, majoring in English and French antiques and furnishings, which they import directly, and have been for more than twenty-five years. It is rare to find so many fine antiques of such beautiful quality outside big cities. You will find tempting armoires, glassed bookcases, marble-top chests, and other dreamy delights that take you back to France and England or help you create your own version at home. (You can also consult and visit Great Things Interiors on Lincoln between Fifth and Sixth.)
❧ *Great Things Antiques, Ocean Avenue ns between Dolores and Lincoln, Carmel; (831) 624–7178. Open 10:00 A.M.–5:30 P.M. Monday–Saturday, 10:30 A.M.–5:00 P.M. Sunday. Visa, MasterCard, American Express, Discover. Wheelchair accessible.*

GRILL ON OCEAN AVENUE is a refreshing addition to Anton Salameh and Csaba Ajan's restaurant ventures in Carmel. A delightfully cheerful restaurant with a large stone fireplace and crisp white linens, the staff's creative twists on simple food make this restaurant a must-try.

For starters, try the salmon quesadillas ($8.75) or wood-grilled portobello mushroom and polenta with goat cheese ($8.75). We are Caesar salad freaks, but you might want to try the heart of romaine and tomato with Gorgonzola vinaigrette for something different. Taste-treat entrees include duck ravioli ($13.75 lunch, $16.75 dinner), sautéed tuna ($15.50), free-range chicken with mustard and rosemary cream sauce ($17.50), great steaks, rack of lamb, salmon, and several vegetarian selections, from sandwiches to pastas. Interesting wine list including many locals.
❧ *Grill on Ocean Avenue, Ocean Avenue ns between Dolores and Lincoln, Carmel 93921; (831) 624–2569. Open for lunch 11:30 A.M.–3:00 P.M., dinner 5:00–10:00 P.M. Full bar. Visa, MasterCard, American Express. Wheelchair accessible.*

Tucked in the quaint corner shop facing the library's garden is elegant Rittmaster for men's clothing. Their women's shop is down in the next block at the Pine Inn.

Just west of the restaurant is a charming corner of natural vegetation and Carmel's charming public **HARRISON MEMORIAL LIBRARY**. While there are rest room signs pointing in the library's direction, you are *not* welcome to use the library's. Their rest rooms are *not* open to the public, repeat *NOT*.

M. J. Murphy designed the library with a little help from architect Bernard Maybeck, whose influence definitely shows in the lovely building. The Park Branch of the library at Mission Street and Sixth Avenue has tomes of local history and lore that entertain as well as educate.

❧ *Harrison Memorial Library, Ocean Avenue ns corner of Lincoln, Carmel 93921; (831) 624–4629; Park Branch, Mission and Sixth, Carmel 93921; (831) 624–1366. Open 10:00 A.M.–8:00 P.M. Monday–Wednesday, 10:00 A.M.–6:00 P.M. Thursday–Friday, 1:00–5:00 P.M. Saturday–Sunday. Wheelchair accessible from Lincoln Avenue.*

Across Lincoln and down the hill is the whole Pine Inn complex of shops, the hotel, and a fine California chain restaurant.

The first shop is SUNDANCE OF CALIFORNIA, an upscale downstairs boutique featuring fine leather jackets, St. Croix, Axis, Rift Balley, N.E. Wear, Coogi sweaters, Enro L'Uomo, and Cutter & Buck clothing.

❧ *Sundance of California, Ocean Avenue ns at Lincoln, Carmel 93921; (831) 624–4424. Open 9:30 A.M.–9:00 P.M. Visa, MasterCard, American Express. Not wheelchair accessible.*

Also visit Fourtané Estate Jewelers for interesting antique jewelry.

Down the bright orange geranium-, alyssum-, and pink and purple petunia-lined alley between Sundance and the Pine Inn is the well-known IL FORNAIO CUCINA ITALIANA, usually referred to as Il Fornaio, which means baker, which suggests bread. Il Fornaio is often voted "Best Bread Bakery in Monterey County."

At the back of the short path, you can enter the round cafe and bakery display room where you can sit with locals, sip espresso, and nibble on your favorite bread or pastry selected at the counter. Il Fornaio's cafe is where many Europeans living in Carmel get their daily bread and stop for a ritual espresso. Lots of singles feel totally comfortable sitting at the round table in the center of the cafe, sipping, noshing on crepes, salads, sandwiches, and pizzas while watching the fire and reading newspapers. Visitors who know the Il Fornaio chain feel comfortable here.

The restaurant itself is to the left, and you see the vast open kitchen and wood-burning ovens on the right side of the room as you enter. Our favorites here are the roast chicken and creative pizzas (from $8.95). Pastas begin at $9.95, with fresh fish from $16.95.

❧ *Il Fornaio Cucina Italiana, Pine Inn, Ocean Avenue ns at Lincoln, Carmel 93921; (831) 622–5100. Cafe open 7:00 A.M.–5:00 P.M., restaurant open 11:30 A.M.–10:00 P.M. Full bar. Visa, MasterCard, American Express. Wheelchair accessible via the alleyway.*

The **PINE INN**, the first hotel in town, is one of Carmel's great elegant and traditional landmarks and the site of many a romance. This is where John Steinbeck met his last wife, Elaine, and began their love and long marriage.

Moved down the hill to this site by developer "Devvy" Devendorf when it was the Hotel Carmelo, the Pine Inn has the most splendiferously elegant (and recently redecorated) lobby in town. Rooms and public rooms are decorated with turn-of-the-century charm. Unusual for a hotel, the Pine Inn has a library from which guests are welcome to select and enjoy a book.

꙰ *Pine Inn, Ocean Avenue ns near Lincoln, Carmel 93921; (831) 624–3851 or (800) 228–3851. Open always. Visa, MasterCard, American Express. Wheelchair access from Ocean Avenue. One fully accessible room with king-size bed ($175) and accessibility to Il Fornaio Restaurant.*

While you are in the Pine Inn Courtyard, be sure to wander through Magpie Antiques and Toppers for Women.

Do not stop here. Go one more shop down Ocean toward the water to see **PIERRE DEUX**, a delightful emporium of French country furnishings and home accessories. You will find Le Cordon Bleu cooking school videos, mustards, fish, and Provençal sauces; French country china, lamps, unusual wrapping papers, fabrics in the back, scarves, picture frames, loads of quilt bags, and hard-to-get books on Provence. One of Kathleen's favorites.

꙰ *Pierre Deux, Ocean Avenue ns between Lincoln and Monte Verde, Carmel 93921; (831) 624–8185. Open 9:30 A.M.–5:30 P.M. Monday–Saturday, noon–5:00 P.M. Sunday. Visa, MasterCard, American Express. Partly wheelchair accessible.*

Now we suggest you cross Ocean to reach its south side. To see everything, start with Candlesticks of Carmel and Fideaux.

FIDEAUX has quickly become a destination "outfitter for cats and dogs" like no other, except for its barely older sister store in Napa. A former teacher, proprietor Jennifer Blevens certainly knows how to catch your eye and your passion for pets. Another Jennifer cheers and manages the Carmel shop. This may well be the happiest place to visit in Carmel. People here passionately love their jobs and their dogs. Manager Jennifer brings hers to work.

You can spoil yours with bracelets, collars, Fideaux Futons, washable beds, locally made pottery bowls, dog clocks with tongues wagging, and guidebooks for traveling pets and their owners. Visiting dogs are welcome, but must be on a leash and "friendly at all times. Dogs who are not will be asked to leave."

꙰ *Fideaux, Ocean Avenue ss at Monte Verde, Carmel 93922; (831) 626–7777, fax (831) 626–5484; www.fideaux-bestselections.com. Open*

PINE INN

10:00 A.M.–6:00 P.M. daily. Visa, MasterCard, American Express. Entrance floor wheelchair accessible. Dog friendly.

CARMEL GALLERIES is one of this elegant town's more quirky establishments, offering imports from many countries, finger and tea towels, old costume jewelry, and thousands and thousands of figurines everywhere—everywhere. This place looks as if it belongs in the New York garment district. It's fun, and a wee bit spooky.

❧ *Carmel Galleries, Ocean Avenue ss between Monte Verde and Lincoln, Carmel 93921; (831) 624–5588. Open 10:00 A.M.–5:00 P.M. daily. Visa, MasterCard. Wheelchair accessible but difficult to get around.*

In the Court of the Golden Bough complex, originally designed in 1925 by Edward G. Kuster for bohemian author Harry Leon Wilson, be sure to check out Dovecote II for ladies' wear with a British feeling (Dovecote I is up the street at Ocean ss and Dolores); Cottage of Sweets for custom chocolates and fudge; the Impulse Shoppes for miniatures; the French Collection apparel and accessories upstairs; and Chez Christian Bistro, Arawan Thai Cafe, Carmel Golf, and Porta Bella Restaurant.

CHEZ CHRISTIAN is a casual restaurant with an obvious "Frenchy" emphasis. Try the breast of duck salad ($8.75)—although the duck fat rather offsets the salad's health effects; the spinach and tuna salad with caper dressing ($8.00) is interesting, and we like the crotins de chèvre en salade ($7.75). There are lots of omelette and sandwich choices, and dinner offerings include pastas, sand dabs meunière ($15.50), frog legs Provençale ($18.75), calf's liver and onions ($13.50), sweetbreads simmered in Madeira wine, cream, and mushrooms ($17.50), and loads of meats, from breast of duck ($15.75) to the chef's filet and rack of lamb (both $19.95). The wine list features French and California wines.

✦✧ *Chez Christian, Court of the Golden Bough, Ocean Avenue ss between Monte Verde and Lincoln, Carmel 93921; (831) 625–4331. Open for lunch 11:30 A.M.–2:30 P.M. Friday–Saturday only, dinner 5:00–9:30 P.M. Tuesday–Sunday. Beer and wine. Visa, MasterCard. Wheelchair accessible.*

Also in the British-fantasy-designed Court of the Golden Bough and facing Ocean Avenue is the fun PORTA BELLA, part of Csaba Ajan and Anton Salameh's excellent four-restaurant mini empire. Porta Bella is a dog-friendly restaurant, unusual in these parts. Enjoy the tables and people-watching on the flagstone heated patio in front, or in the brick rooms with fireplaces and flagstone floors. Cigars are sold and tolerated on the front patio. Be sure to check out the historic photos on the walls.

Voted "Best New Restaurant" and mentioned in the *New York Times* as the "newcomer garnering praise" (July 1997), Porta Bella (Beautiful Door–not large mushroom) features Mediterranean country cuisine, meaning regional dishes from Italy, southern France, and Spain. Hold on!

As an appetizer, believe it or not, try the panfried goat cheese and sun-dried tomato ravioli ($7.75) or the terrine campagnarde of duck and veal pâté ($7.50). We also like the salad niçoise with seared rare tuna, although we prefer the tuna cooked through for health reasons, which the chef is happy to do on request. Lunch main plates include lots of pastas with seafood, duck, and feta ravioli ($12.25), free-range chicken paillard ($11.95), Monterey Bay sand dabs ($11.75), and various chickens. Irresistible sandwiches include one of grilled portobello mushrooms and Cachagoa goat cheese on made-here pizza bread ($10.75), a focaccia steak sandwich ($14.75), or provolone burger with country fries ($8.95). Dinner main courses include many of the above plus scampi Basquaise ($21.75), roasted free-range chicken ($16.75), veal, filet mignon, pork tenderloin, grilled salmon, and three cheese polenta with Asiago, mozzarella, and Gorgonzola, all in the $15–$25 range. Oh yes, there's a special kids' menu for your very special kids.

Crème brûlée, chocolate mousse cake, tiramisu, floating island, brioche bread pudding, and fruit sorbets (all $6.75) round out the menu and you.

❧ *Porta Bella, Ocean Avenue ss between Monte Verde and Lincoln, Carmel 93921; (831) 624–4395. Open for lunch 11:30 A.M.–3:00 P.M., dinner 5:00–10:00 P.M., cocktails 11:00 A.M.–midnight daily. Visa, MasterCard, American Express. Wheelchair accessible.*

Venture upstairs to the Enchanted Attic for cutesy home accessories. MERLOT WINE COUNTRY BISTRO is the newest endeavor of the Salameh-Ajan partnership, as in Anton & Michel, The Polo Club, and several more. Recently transformed from their Cafe Americana in the same location, a change of name and slight changes in the menu by the same chef have turned this spot into a great success.

Lunch includes the requisite but delicious Castroville artichoke ($5.95), portabella mushroom risotto ($5.75), salads, including a Caesar with grilled free-range chicken ($9.95), pizza and calzones, pasta such as gnocchi with Gorgonzola cream sauce and seedless grapes ($10.50), spicy fried chicken ($10.95), Monterey calamari steak with lemon caper sauce, sun-dried toma-toes, and risotto ($9.95), filet mignon, and burgers at lunch. Dinner may include escargot ravioli with mushrooms and tomato coulis ($8.50), home-smoked sturgeon tartare ($8.25), pasta and pizza, vegetarian plates, seared fresh tuna ($18.25), roasted rack of lamb ($21.95), and braised young rabbit and tamale dumplings with cabernet red cabbage ($16.95). A kids' menu is avail-able at all times, and breakfast begins at 8:00 A.M.

❧ *Merlot Wine Country Bistro, Ocean Avenue ss between Lincoln and Monte Verde, Carmel 93921; (831) 624–5659; www.carmelsbest.com. Open 8:00 A.M.–midnight. Full bar. Visa, MasterCard, American Express. Wheelchair accessible.*

A great place just to stop for some good coffee, a pastry snack, and some colorful artwork is the CARMEL VALLEY COFFEE ROASTING COMPANY. Brick floors covered with Oriental rugs set the tone to enjoy gourmet coffees, bagels, breakfast pastries; there's a microwave and toaster to heat up your purchases. Notice the Shanghai Trading Company replica clock on the wall. Repeat cus-tomers get little wooden tokens for an occasional free coffee.

❧ *Carmel Valley Coffee Roasting Company, Ocean Avenue ss between Lincoln and Monte Verde, Carmel 93921; (831) 626–2913. Open 7:30 or 8:00 A.M.–8:00 P.M. Visa, MasterCard. Not wheelchair accessible (one step up).*

The CARMEL BAY COMPANY is a cook's paradise with loads of mustards, Burton stoves, Emile Henry pitchers and kitchenware, scone mixes, garden tools, flatware, tea towels, cookbooks, place mats, furniture, another Shanghai clock, and wonderful French food posters.

❧ *Carmel Bay Company, Ocean Avenue ss at corner of Lincoln, Carmel 93921; (831) 624–3868. Open 10:00 A.M.–6:00 P.M. Monday–Saturday, till 5:00 P.M. Sunday. Visa, MasterCard. First floor is wheelchair accessible.*

Cross Lincoln and continue up Ocean's little hill and come back to Lincoln's shops later.

The primary business of JEWELS ON OCEAN is fourteen-karat gold, semi-precious and precious stones, and Lunch at the Ritz earrings, but our favorite feature is the photography on the walls—dramatic Carmel area beach scenes and trees.

❧ *Jewels on Ocean, Ocean Avenue ss at Lincoln, Carmel 93921; (831) 625–6747. Open 10:00 A.M.–6:00 P.M. daily. Visa, MasterCard, American Express, Discover, Diners Club, Carte Blanche. Wheelchair accessible.*

Next up the street is a fun little Italian restaurant called CAFFE NAPOLI, loaded with Italian provincial flags and banners (an Italian flag suspended below the skylight gives an interesting lighting effect), Chianti bottles, and terrific pizzas and pastas. This place is so popular with locals and visitors alike that a larger sister restaurant, called Little Napoli, has been opened on Dolores between Ocean and Seventh, serving the same menu.

The bruschetta (decorated bread wafers) are large and fabulous, as are the carpaccio, salads (all under $8.00), Tuscan soups, and risottos. If you're not having pizza, try the special cannelloni tricolore, which come in half ($12.00) or dinner ($16.95) portions; the pescatore—fresh clams, mussels, tiger prawns, sea scallops, bar shrimp, calamari, and Dungeness crab on fresh egg tagliatelle ($15.95); or the salmon and vegetable risotto ($14.95). You can also select from six other seafood pastas, and a lucky thirteen meat and vegetarian pastas. Napoli's breads come from its brother business, Wishart's Bakery, where you can get a certificate for a free glass of wine with lunch or dinner at either Napoli. Check out the extensive Italian wine list.

Of course they tempt you with tiramisu, crème brûlée, cannoli, lemon cheesecake, spumoni, and chocolate mousse. Oh well.

❧ *Caffe Napoli, Ocean Avenue ss between Dolores and Lincoln, Carmel 93921; (831) 625–4033; www.littlenapoli.com. Open 11:30 A.M.–10:00 P.M. daily. Beer and wine. Visa, MasterCard. Wheelchair accessible.*

BOATWORKS features everything for boating folks and the people who give them gifts. An overhead sign laments: "A wife and a steady job have ruined many a good fisherman." Here you will find boat sweaters, books, equipment, hats, and old ship posters. Somehow the Jimmy Buffett tapes playing seem totally appropriate! Even if you don't go on boats, it's fun to look around and laugh with the amusing staff.

❧ *Boatworks, Ocean Avenue ss between Dolores and Lincoln, Carmel 93921; (831) 626–1870. Open 9:30 A.M.–6:00 P.M. Sunday–Thursday, till 7:00 P.M. Friday–Saturday. Visa, MasterCard, American Express. Wheelchair accessible.*

VILLEROY & BOCH is the home store of a large 250-year-old chain, which allows it to sell at 20 percent to 30 percent off retail. The German company produces decorated china, and elegant crystal and flatware. It's fun to browse, but watch swinging arms and purses.

❧ *Villeroy & Boch, Ocean Avenue ss between Dolores and Lincoln, Carmel 93921; (831) 624–8210. Open 10:00 A.M.–6:00 P.M. Monday–Saturday, 11:00 A.M.–5:00 P.M. Sunday. Visa, MasterCard, American Express. Wheelchair accessible.*

Everyone's favorite is CARMEL BAKERY just up from Villeroy & Boch. Carmel Bakery is yet another of Wishart Bakery's outposts, and the quality shows. We love Dorothy Spangler's bright, colorful floral paintings on the walls, to say nothing of the cannoli with chocolate chips, great bagel sandwiches made to order, gingerbread cookies with white chocolate topping, custard napoleons, three-seed pretzels, and chocolate-dipped macaroons. Water thy mouth! Travelers can get nice, cool water and good espresso drinks too.

❧ *Carmel Bakery, Ocean Avenue ss between Dolores and Lincoln, Carmel 93921; (831) 626–8885. Open 8:00 A.M.–6:00 P.M. daily. No credit cards. Mostly wheelchair accessible.*

Next up the street is B & G JEWELERS where much of the jewelry is made by resident genius Alex, whose work mingles with that of Limoges boxes and collectors' objects, including Limoges Volkswagens, ice-cream cones, and telephones. B & G also buys and sells fine diamonds.

❧ *B & G Jewelers, Ocean Avenue ss between Dolores and Lincoln, Carmel 93921; (831) 625–2235. Open 10:00 A.M.–5:00 P.M. daily. Visa, MasterCard, American Express. Wheelchair accessible.*

At HART GALLERY, Eva Hart represents contemporary European artists such as Vosvard, Haegele, Fenkle, Hueckstaedt, and Paul Wunderlich. Eva and her sister have a sister gallery in Chicago called Hart Hohmann.

❧ *Hart Gallery, Ocean Avenue ss between Dolores and Lincoln, Carmel 93921; (831) 622–7110, fax (831) 622–7113, e-mail hartgall@pacbell.net. Open 10:00 A.M.–6:00 P.M. Monday–Saturday, 11:00 A.M.–5:00 P.M. Sunday. Visa, MasterCard, American Express, Discover. First floor is wheelchair accessible.*

Next up the street you will find Dovecote I and the ubiquitous Thomas Kinkaide Gallery.

Do stop in at **ST. MORITZ SWEATERS FOR LADIES & GENTLEMEN**, a mecca for people who like patterned sweaters, elegant cashmere, angora and cotton sweaters, and special designs by Claudia Richards and Oona.

❧ *St. Moritz Sweaters for Ladies & Gentlemen, Ocean Avenue ss between Dolores and Lincoln, Carmel 93921; (831) 624–4788. Open 10:30 A.M.–6:00 P.M. daily. Visa, MasterCard, American Express, Discover. Wheelchair accessible.*

One of our lifelong favorite Carmel stores and products is **ROBERT TALBOTT**, where Kathleen used to buy her father a tie every year. The classic original store, which opened in the 1950s and was run by Robert Talbott himself, was down the street, and this newer, bigger, gorgeous incarnation brings the whole operation into the twenty-first century with white walls, blond furniture and floors, white-skirted chairs, and white-and-beige checked carpet. Feast your eyes on hundreds of elegant real bow ties and standard ties ($50 on up), silk bathrobes, and other men's accessories. The staff is nice to look at too.

❧ *Robert Talbott, Ocean Avenue ss near Dolores, Carmel 93921; (831) 624–6604. Open 10:00 A.M.–6:00 P.M. Monday–Saturday, till 5:30 P.M. Sunday. Visa, MasterCard, American Express. Wheelchair accessible.*

On the southwest corner of Ocean and Dolores, the Corner Cupboard Gift Shop carries a variety of doodads you can see from the window.

Congratulations. You have arrived at Dolores Street.

COOGI AUSTRALIA sells that famous down-under special sportswear, including patterned sweaters, casual wear coats, pants, and skirts.

❧ *Coogi Australia, Ocean Avenue ss and Dolores, Carmel 93921; (831) 625–5507. Open 10:00 A.M.–6:00 P.M. daily. Visa, MasterCard. Wheelchair accessible.*

LLOYD'S SHOES is definitely one of Kathleen's favorites, featuring styles from Via Spiga, Peter Kaiser, Kenneth Cole, Steve Madden, Rieker, and Sacha of London. You will also drool over elegant belts and Park Avenue leather handbags. Gorgeous leather for all tastes from twentysomethings to their mothers.

❧ *Lloyd's Shoes, Ocean Avenue ss near Dolores, Carmel 93921; (831) 625–1382. Open 10:00 A.M.–5:30 P.M. Monday–Thursday, 10:00 A.M.–6:00 P.M. Friday–Saturday, 11:00 A.M.–5:00 P.M. Sunday. Visa, MasterCard, American Express. Wheelchair accessible.*

Many regular visitors to Carmel make an annual stop at **SCOTCH HOUSE** (the "oldest Scottish store in the country") to pick up Ballantyne sweaters, tartan ties and scarves, family crest blazer badges, and kilts. Scotch House even rents kilts in case you need one only temporarily. Visiting Scotch House is like taking a trip within a trip.

❧ *Scotch House, Ocean Avenue ss between Dolores and San Carlos, Carmel 93921; (831) 624–0595. Open 10:30 A.M.–6:00 P.M. Monday–Saturday, noon–5:00 P.M. Sunday. Visa, MasterCard, American Express. Wheelchair accessible.*

CAFFE CARDINALE is down a little pathway in the Doud Arcade just west of Fresh Produce clothing store and worth the walk. A small, slightly funky cafe, Caffe Cardinale has brick patio seating at round wrought-iron and marble tables at its entrance. The coffee beans are roasted here, so you get very fresh coffee, whether you order espresso drinks or one of five brewed coffees. The baked goods are divine, especially the vanilla and Dutch chocolate cheesecakes. We enjoy the Parisian prints throughout the cafe and the side room through the arched doorways where trompe l'oeil murals decorate the walls. Apparently Cardinale refers to the cardinal red trim on the doors and windows.

❧ *Caffe Cardinale, Ocean Avenue ss between San Carlos and Dolores, Carmel 93921; (831) 626–2095 or (800) 595–2090. Open 7:30 A.M.–6:00 P.M. (and they mean it) daily. No credit cards. Not wheelchair accessible (one small step up at entrance).*

Also in the Doud Arcade you will find Peppercorn gifts and needlepoint pillows, A.W. Shucks Oyster Bar, Wicks & Wax candles, Kris Kringle of Carmel, Village Sport Shop, the Rockport Shoe Shop, Winters Gallerie, Doud Craft Studio, and Port of Carmel—all fine small shops and galleries worth browsing on your personal investigative tour. The Doud Arcade is loaded with inexpensive cafes and arts and crafts.

FRESH PRODUCE is right on the street and features bright, hot-colored dresses, T-shirts, and hats for kids and adults—most with animals or plants printed on them. No fresh produce, meaning vegetables, is sold here. Too bad.

❧ *Fresh Produce, Ocean Avenue ss between San Carlos and Dolores, Carmel 93921; (831) 626–6043. Open 10:00 A.M.–6:00 P.M. daily. Visa, MasterCard, American Express, Discover. Wheelchair accessible.*

AW SHUCKS OYSTER BAR has lots of bar and not so many oysters. You might try the crab cakes ($10.95) or the local steamed artichoke ($5.95), especially if you have never had one.

Crossing San Carlos on Ocean, you come to African Odyssey, in a storefront we remember as a great creamery and ice-cream store, gone from this site since Carmel effectively outlawed eating ice-cream cones on the street. Tucked into the building's crevices you will now also find Trojan Art Gallery, Bittner Fine Pens, and Bornstein & Sigg Fine Art Gallery.

Just up from the corner of Ocean and San Carlos you will find a fascinating store, **MUSIC BOXES OF CARMEL**. On the surface it looks like a rather intimidating place, but go right in. Carl and Evelyn Sigg welcome browsers just because they love what they do so much that they want to share their excitement with you.

Poke around the Reuge wooden music boxes, other new and antique music boxes of all sizes, and new and old Swiss clocks.

❧ *Music Boxes of Carmel, Ocean Avenue ss at San Carlos, Carmel 93921; (831) 622–9120. Open 9:30 A.M.–6:00 P.M. Sunday–Thursday, till 9:00 P.M. Friday–Saturday. Visa, MasterCard, American Express, Discover. Wheelchair accessible but a little crowded.*

NORTH COUNTRY CARMEL LEATHERS has good-looking leather jackets, wallets, bags, and good prices.

❧ *North Country Carmel Leathers, Ocean Avenue ss at San Carlos, Carmel 93921; (831) 625–1282. Open 10:00 A.M.–5:30 P.M. daily. Visa and MasterCard. Wheelchair accessible.*

Another Green's Camera World is handy for film.

Just up from the leather shop is **CARMEL BEACH CAFE**, a slightly underattended casual Mediterranean cafe and restaurant with interesting European posters, a great bar, and tables along the walls like a true bistro. An extremely independent restaurant, Carmel Beach Cafe offers an incredible deal: dinner for two with a bottle of wine for a total of $28.95.

Breakfast begins with two eggs any style with potatoes and toast ($4.95), with Belgian waffles, fresh fruit and yogurt, and sides of meats all available. Clam chowder, organic greens salads, and good Caesar salads highlight the starters at lunch, which features calamari piccata ($7.95), 17-Mile Drive chili ($5.45), burgers and other sandwiches under $7.00, and pastas. Dinner main dishes include salmon a la Italiano ($12.95), pork loin ($11.95), filet mignon ($15.95), and eggplant Parmesan ($10.95). The Young Beach Comber menu includes peanut butter and jelly sandwiches, burgers, hot dogs, and chicken nuggets with soup or salad, all under $5.00.

❧ *Carmel Beach Cafe, Ocean Avenue ss between Mission and San Carlos, Carmel 93921; (831) 625–3122. Full bar. Visa, MasterCard. Wheelchair accessible.*

As you work your way toward the fabulous Carmel Plaza, you pass a T-shirt shop, Carmel Sport (sporting goods and equipment), and Primrose of Carmel (home and personal accessories).

When you come to Mission Street, cross it and enter **CARMEL PLAZA** from Ocean Avenue. We will take you up and down Mission Street in a few minutes.

Carmel Plaza is an elegant shopping mall whose fifty shops include Saks Fifth Avenue at both ends of the complex, Ann Taylor, Banana Republic, Benetton, Georgiou, Laura Ashley, Mark Fenwick, Mondi International, and Talbots. Sockshop Carmel is lots of fun, as are several jewelry stores, Do Re Mi Music and Video, Crabtree & Evelyn, and Books Inc. Loads of specialty shops like Come Fly a Kite and the Game Gallery make our day.

All of Carmel Plaza is wheelchair accessible by elevator. Enter the complex from Ocean Avenue and shop till you drop.

CROSS STREETS SOUTH OF OCEAN AVENUE

Mission Street

Carmel Plaza marks the intersection of Ocean Avenue and Mission Street. The exploration labors of food fans will be richly rewarded by a brief walk down Mission Street.

Near the Mission Street entrance to Carmel Plaza is the **FLYING FISH GRILL**, which presents a true medley of Pacific Rim and California taste experiences. We love the steamed Castroville artichoke with wasabi mayonnaise ($4.75), as well as the made-here sushi. We don't quite have the nerve to try spicy tuna tartare (with raw fish causing problems in tender tummies), but some people have become addicted. The black bean catfish ($13.75) and salmon ($16.75) are divine, as is the rare peppered ahi tuna, which you can have cooked more well done ($19.75). For a fun and fiery experience, try the "clay pots" full of vegetables and the meat or tofu of your choice ($19.95). They sizzle and steam at your table, with lovely garlic smells wafting all around.

❧ *Flying Fish Grill, Carmel Plaza, Mission and Ocean, Carmel 93921; (831) 625–1962. Open for dinner from 5:00 P.M. daily in summer, closed Tuesdays in winter. Visa, MasterCard, American Express, Discover, Diners Club. Not wheelchair accessible.*

Just south of the Mission Street entrance to Carmel Plaza is every sweet tooth's dream destination: **PATISSERIE BOISSIERE**, where sumptuous European pastries and espresso are served all day or as takeout. The chocolate eclairs are unlike any you have ever seen, let alone tasted, but don't miss the Paris Brest pâté doux either, along with tea breads by the slice, tarts, cakes, and real fruit bars. Patisserie Boissiere also has a whole picnic menu featuring many of its regular selections and others handy to eat in your fingers and available Monday–Friday.

You can also indulge in lunch and dinner here, as do many local regulars. Both proper meals may include quiche de maison with fresh fruit ($8.95), double-cream Brie, pâté, and fresh fruit ($7.95), a prawn and Castroville artichoke salad ($8.95), snow crab and avocado salad ($9.95), and a reliable Cobb salad ($8.95). Patisserie Boissiere specialties include shepherd's pie with ground beef and veggies with bacon and wine, topped with fluffy mashed potatoes, served with salad ($8.95), chicken pot pie, vegetable fillo triangle, and the classic coquilles Saint Jacques of fresh scallops and rock shrimp in a light cream sauce, julienned vegetables, and rice ($10.95). Of course there are sandwiches, and some even come on the bakery's brioches.

Patisserie Boissiere, Mission es near Ocean Avenue, Carmel 93921; (831) 624–5008. Open for lunch 11:30 A.M.–4:30 P.M. Monday–Friday, dinner from 5:00 P.M. Wednesday–Sunday, brunch 10:00 A.M.–4:30 P.M. Saturday–Sunday. Beer and wine. Visa, MasterCard. Not wheelchair accessible.

One of Carmel's premier restaurants, **ANTON & MICHEL**, is across the street and down a couple of doors facing Mission Street and bordering the interesting Court of the Fountains. There is lots of parking in the garage on the east side of Mission under the mall. Recipient of a *Wine Spectator* award, as well as many others, Anton & Michel is the flagship of Anton Salameh and Csaba Ajan's small group of excellent Carmel restaurants. Chef Kisayuki (Max) Muramatsu, who trained at Maxim's in Paris and was named Best Chef in Tokyo five times, creates a Euro-Asian cuisine mixed with mesquite charbroiling like nothing you have ever tasted anywhere.

The primary entrance faces Mission Street, and as Kathleen entered the elegant vestibule, she felt as if she were in the old L'Etoile in San Francisco's Huntington Hotel (the first restaurant of Claude Rouas, owner of Auberge du Soleil and Piatti). Soft pinks with large gold-framed classic paintings, mirrors, and general elegance dominate here. The back room and patio look out on the fountains in the courtyard and its bright orange pompon zinnias.

Here you will enjoy impeccable service, fresh Monterey Bay seafood, melt-in-your-mouth filet mignon, farmed abalone (they're honest), and rack of lamb carved at your table. Heaven! The Dungeness crab cakes with celery root and pesto aioli are different and excellent ($11.50), and the Dungeness crab cakes with saffron ratatouille slaw and rouille aioli ($11.50) are outstanding. Kathleen particularly likes the endive and Gorgonzola salad ($8.75), since it includes two of her favorite food groups, but we also enjoy the classic Caesar salad prepared at the table for two ($17.50).

Anton & Michel offers two dinners for two, both of which are carved at tableside: rack of lamb with Dijon mustard ($65.50) and chateaubriand with your choice of sauce béarnaise or bordelaise—tough decision—($59.50). Those prices are for two people.

Otherwise, the salmon and ahi tuna are exquisite, as are the lamb medallions, ostrich scallopini, venison steak flambé (in Armagnac), pheasant breast chasseur, or filet mignon with sautéed shiitake and oyster mushrooms. All entrees are in the $20–$28 range.

If you're going to try dessert, the Charlotte mango cake is different and interesting. Traditionalists may want to sample the cherries jubilee ($17.50 for two) or the crepes Suzette ($19.50 for two).

Be sure to check out the award-winning wine list, for imported as well as local wines. Anton & Michel also has a daily happy hour with complimentary hors d'oeuvres. No wonder so many locals come here.

✢✤ *Anton & Michel, Court of the Fountains, Mission Street ws between Ocean and Seventh, Carmel 93921; (831) 624–2406; www.carmelsbest.com. Open for lunch 11:30 A.M.–3:00 P.M., dinner 5:30–9:30 P.M., happy hour 4:00–7:00 P.M. daily. Full bar. Visa, MasterCard, American Express. Not wheelchair accessible.*

Browse around the Court of the Fountains and wander through the Mole Hole; Girl Boy Girl, for men's and women's new and vintage clothing; Maxine Klaput antiques, featuring Mary Engelbreit and glass paperweights; Bittner Fine Pens and Papers; Lisa's Studio, to see her sketches; the happy and lively It's Cactus of Carmel, for Mexican imports; and the Rosamond Art Gallery.

Working your way back toward Ocean Avenue along the west side of Mission Street, stroll around jewelry and knit shops and wander down the bright bougainvillea-lined little brick path to teensy and cute CAFFE DEL MARE, an extremely informal local cafe serving whole rotisserie chickens to go or halves with fries and salad ($6.25), focaccia pizzas or caramelized onion tart with goat cheese (both $5.50), steamed veggies with brown rice in a sesame or peanut glaze, and a roasted tomato tart in a pesto glaze served with local greens (both under $6.00).

Owners Celia and Scott Trambley also produce excellent sandwiches, burgers, rotisserie chicken on a French baguette, crème brûlée ($4.25), and brownies a la mode topped with ground espresso ($4.75).

ANTON & MICHEL RESTAURANT AND
COURT OF THE FOUNTAINS

❧ *Caffe del Mare, Mission Street ws between Ocean and Seventh, Carmel 93921; (831) 625–4043, fax (831) 625–4037. Open 11:00 A.M.–3:30 P.M. Wednesday–Monday. Beer and wine. Visa, MasterCard. Wheelchair accessible.*

Nearly at the corner of Ocean Avenue, be sure to indulge in two contrasting experiences: a visit to On the Beach Surf Shop and Classic Surfboard Museum and to the Edward Montgomery Fine Art gallery.

San Carlos Avenue

One of our favorite new additions to Carmel is **TRIBES**, the elegantly beautiful and inexpensive gallery of Huichol Indian arts, including beaded masks, jewelry, rugs, and those of indigenous peoples of other countries and continents. Mary and Alan Wreyford also have the Historic Line Camp Gallery and Huichol Indian Museum outside Santa Fe, New Mexico, in an old nightclub and dance hall in Pojoaque. Enjoy the Wreyfords as hosts, as well as their treasures from Peru, Brazil, Colombia, and Asia at this must-stop.

ROAST RACK OF LAMB
*from Chef Hisayuki (Max) Muramatsu,
Anton & Michel, Carmel*

2 lamb racks with 6 ribs each	6 garlic cloves, chopped finely
salt and ground pepper	3 Tbs. butter, softened
2 Tbs. olive oil	2 Tbs. Dijon mustard
1½ cups fresh bread crumbs	2 cups of brown veal stock
1 cup finely chopped parsley	

Trim all but half an inch of the fat from the lamb. Cut the strip of fat from under the chine bone. Remove the chine bone. Trim and scrape off all meat between the ribs. Season with salt and pepper.

Heat olive oil in roasting pan, add lamb racks and cook until lightly browned on all sides. Remove lamb and let cool slightly.

Mix bread crumbs, parsley, garlic, butter, and salt and pepper to taste.

Spread the upper side of the lamb evenly with Dijon mustard. Cover the mustard with the bread crumb mixture. Place lamb in the pan and roast in a 425 degree oven for approximately 15 minutes. Remove lamb from pan and keep warm.

Remove all excess fat from the pan and deglaze with veal stock over stove top. Reduce until concentrated; strain into saucepan and keep warm.

Carve lamb between the ribs and place on warm dinner plates. Serve sauce over the lamb. Garnish with fresh seasonal vegetables. Serves six.

Tribes, San Carlos Avenue es at Ocean Avenue ss, Carmel 93921; (831) 625–5100, e-mail art1@tribalgallery.net. Open 10:30 A.M.–6:00 P.M. daily. Visa, MasterCard, American Express. Wheelchair accessible.

On San Carlos you might want to visit **NICO RISTORANTE MEDITERRANEO,** a cozy contemporary restaurant with orange walls and a delightful brick fireplace, where you can sample hot turkey layered with Bermuda onions and smoked Gouda cheese ($6.95), pizza, whole wheat linguine with clams and garlic ($12.95), crab ravioli with scallops ($14.95), loads of salmon, sea bass, and swordfish, and New York steak with portobellos ($19.95).

❧ *Nico Ristorante Mediterraneo, San Carlos ws between Ocean and Seventh Avenues, Carmel 93921; (831) 624–6545. Open 11:00 A.M.–9:00 P.M. daily. Full bar. Visa, MasterCard. Wheelchair accessible.*

At Winters Gallery Jerry Winters features his own work and that of a few other artists.

Dolores Street

Dolores Street offers opportunities for intense browsing if you are so inclined, particularly in this first block south of Ocean Avenue.

Here you will find several shops, including Angel Things, Lady Fingers Jewelry, and the interesting **HOWARD LAMAR STUDIO**. Lamar is a graduate of the Art Institute of Chicago and features work of Jurgen and Petra Birkenstock, Mary Steenbergen, and his own whimsical "jumble of color."

❧ *Howard Lamar Studio, Dolores ws between Ocean and Seventh, Carmel 93921; (831) 626–6725. Open when Howard is in, but definitely closed Tuesday. Visa, MasterCard, American Express, Discover. Wheelchair accessible.*

GALLERY 1000 features (relatively) affordable impressionistic and impressionistic-realism work of Edward Fawcett, Mo Van, Nadine Sacha, Nina Mikhailenko, Marina Zavalova, Gloria Rite, Judy Greenberg, Natalie Levine, and the whimsical figures of Malcolm Moran. Have a look for your viewing pleasure.

❧ *Gallery 1000, Dolores ws between Ocean and Seventh, Carmel 93921; (831) 624–9094, fax (831) 624–2950. Open 10:00 A.M.–6:00 P.M. daily. Visa, MasterCard, American Express. Wheelchair accessible.*

SPORTSWISE carries ladylike resort wear of the crinkly, bright color, matching sets variety. It looks like athletic clothes for people who are not athletes. The Sonoma store has closed, and this one (the original) is all the better for it.

❧ *Sportswise, Dolores ws between Ocean and Seventh, Carmel 93921; (831) 624–6813. Open 10:00 A.M.–6:00 P.M. daily. Visa, MasterCard, American Express, Diners Club. Wheelchair accessible.*

One of the zaniest stores in town, and we love it, is Daniel and Jennifer Herron's the **WHITE RABBIT**, a store and two lives dedicated to Alice in Wonderland. Here is surely the largest selection of Alice and Wonderland everything in the country, from chess sets to sweaters. Daniel even makes backward clocks, which sell like hotcakes. Don't miss the White Rabbit, and check their Web site for their on-line catalog.

⋇ *White Rabbit, Dolores ws between Ocean and Seventh, Carmel 93921; (831) 624–2556; www.thewhiterabbit.com. Open "whenever I get here," from around 10:30 A.M.–5:30 or 6:00 P.M. daily. Visa, MasterCard, American Express. Partly wheelchair accessible.*

Just south of Aliceland is **TOOTS LAGOON**, a popular local restaurant with walls painted brown to look like wood. These people are really good at alive, with-it, noisy restaurants—they also have Club Jalapeño.

The salads are good, the coconut prawns and Toots artichoke are great, but Toots is best known for steak and smoked ribs, the latter of which are the best in town. Several choices of steaks and ribs top the menu, and specialties include potato crusted trout ($12.95), calamari piccata ($12.95), hot and sassy shrimp ($12.95), Toots special meat loaf ($11.95), jerk chicken ($12.95), and good grilled yellowfin tuna ($14.95). All come with steamed veggies and potatoes or rice. Kids will enjoy the brick-oven pizzas ($5.95 plus 75 cents per topping), burgers, a special kids' menu, and loads of logo shirt mementos.

⋇ *Toots Lagoon, Dolores ws between Ocean and Seventh, Carmel 93921; (831) 625–1915. Open 11:30 A.M.–midnight daily. Full bar. Visa, MasterCard, American Express. Wheelchair accessible.*

Herb and Leslee Beckett's **CUBBY HOLE** is sister to its store in Pacific Grove, but carries a wild collection of curly-rimmed dishes and mosaic and painted furniture. A different experience, right next to New Masters Gallery.

⋇ *Cubby Hole, Dolores ws between Ocean and Seventh, Carmel 93921; (831) 624–9595, fax (831) 624–6899. Open 10:00 A.M.–5:30 P.M. daily. Visa, MasterCard, American Express. Wheelchair accessible but crowded.*

As fans of Asian art, we enjoy **CONWAY OF ASIA**'s large emporium (next door to the Cubby Hole) with its elegant Asian furniture, rugs, jewelry, painted wood, brass figurines, covered pillows, necklaces, and old long guns. Great browsing with affordable prices.

⋇ *Conway of Asia, Dolores ws between Ocean and Seventh, Carmel 93921; (831) 624–3643. Open 9:30 A.M.–5:30 P.M. daily. Visa, MasterCard, American Express. Wheelchair accessible.*

We especially like to spend some time in the **CHINA ART CENTER** in a Comstock-designed former bank building. The high ceilings and vast open space make an interesting setting for a rare collection. This was Comstock's second building in Carmel (the Tuck Box was his first). Run by a sister of Mother Teresa's order, China Art affords a chance to see and purchase truly rare pieces, including rugs, large pieces of furniture, mah-jongg sets, silks, and jade jewelry. Be sure to have a conversation with the proprietress, and your entire trip to Carmel will be worth it.

❧ *China Art Center, Dolores ws near Seventh, Carmel 93921; (831) 624–5868. Open "irregular hours." Visa, MasterCard, American Express. Wheelchair accessible.*

RESTAURANT LA BOHÈME next door to China Art is a little Parisian oasis in Carmel where owners Kati and Alan Lewis, who spend as much time as they can in Paris, have created an outdoor-cafe-like experience within a small Carmel bistro. On the left side of the room is a romantic miniature dining room that pretends it's a private little house. If you come alone, or even if you don't, there are plenty of *Paris Match* magazines to entertain you.

La Bohème serves a prix fixe dinner with soup and salad and one entree selection nightly, although there is always a vegetarian dinner available. Entrees might include tournedos forestière, magret de canard Masala, scampi aux échalotes, or carre d'agneau. Seafood, lamb, veal, pork roast, duck breast, and wonderful seafoods. Dinner usually costs $25–28.

Call ahead for the menu, although reservations are not taken. Get on their mailing list to receive the monthly menu calendar or get it off La Bohème's Web site.

❧ *Restaurant La Bohème, Dolores ws and Seventh, Carmel 93921; (831) 624–7500, fax (831) 624–6539; e-mail alan@laboheme.com; www.laboheme.com. Open for dinner from 5:30 P.M. nightly. Beer and wine. Visa, MasterCard.*

The last business at the corner of Dolores and Seventh is WINGS AMERICA, which does as tastefully and funly for airplanes what Boatworks does for boating. Even if you don't like airplane stuff, you will enjoy this place, which is upbeat. The music is good, the people are knowledgeable and look as if they're hanging out instead of selling things, and the quality of merchandise is high.

❧ *Wings America, Dolores ws at Seventh, Carmel 93921; (831) 626–9464, fax (831) 626–0902, e-mail: wings@wingsamerica.com, Web site: www.wingsamerica.com. Open 10:00 A.M.–6:00 P.M. daily. Visa, MasterCard, American Express. Wheelchair accessible.*

Now cross Dolores and start up the other (east) side.

Wander back in the courtyard of the El Paseo Building to little shops and Showplace North, a small chain of upscale interior design and large furniture stores.

LITTLE NAPOLI serves the same food as its sister restaurant, CAFFE NAPOLI, meaning excellent pastas featuring a variety of meat and seafood sauces, thick pizzas, and fabulous risottos. Little Napoli enjoys a *Wine Spectator* Award of Excellence, so be sure to try something from the excellent Italian wine list. We enjoyed the signed photo of Luciano Pavarotti but won't mention that they sell good cigars.

✦✬ *Little Napoli, Dolores es between Ocean and Seventh, Carmel 93921; (831) 626–6335. Open 11:30 A.M.–10:00 P.M. daily. Visa, MasterCard, American Express. Wheelchair accessible.*

You might want to look into another ever-present-in-California Thomas Kincaide Gallery, featuring his own art, or check out his gallery at the Rabbit Corner within the Tuck Box building.

Oh yes, the **TUCK BOX**. Kathleen used to come here several times a year when she was visiting Carmel with her parents, and we had breakfast here on our honeymoon. Something seemed to be different when we walked in about nine o'clock on a dreary weekday morning. No longer was there a line out in front, but maybe everyone else was at work. The food wasn't quite what we remembered, but that's OK. We loved it again anyway.

Designed by Hugh Comstock (his first in this dollhouse English style) and built in 1927, the Tuck Box passed from family to employee ownership until it was purchased in 1996 by Dianne and Zigmont J. Le Towt, who used to own Le Bistro here in Carmel. The Tuck Box has been best known for its scones, preserves, and marmalades. But when we tried to buy scone mix and preserves as displayed on shelves and mentioned in table tents, we were told there was none in stock. Oh, oh.

So try it all while you're here. They truly are unsurpassed. Try the Olallieberry, raspberry, strawberry, or orange marmalade. We also like the two- egg omelettes because they aren't too large, all $6.50–$7.90 with fillings. The waffle was thin ($4.00) and tasty, but Jerry prefers the waffles at Katy's Place (on Mission Street, east side; see page 111). You can still get omelettes at lunchtime, plus good, old fashioned nondeli sandwiches, hot chicken salad, fruit salad with cottage cheese ($6.50), and their famous Welsh rarebit ($6.50). And don't miss the daily specials, such as shepherd's pie, fish chowder, meat pies, scalloped potatoes with ham (all $6.95), and Sunday's roast beef and Yorkshire pudding ($9.50).

Afternoon tea consists of one dessert, piece of pie, or scone at about $6.00.

Dinner branches out to filet mignon ($14.95), herbed pot roast ($11.90), fettuccine and calamari ($10.90), and fresh fish and chicken breasts.

✦✬ *Tuck Box, Dolores es between Ocean and Seventh, Carmel 93921; (831) 624–6365, fax (831) 626–3939. Open for breakfast, lunch, afternoon tea, and dinner until 9:00 P.M. daily. Visa, MasterCard, American Express. Outside patio (weather permitting) is wheelchair accessible.*

THE TUCK BOX, DOLORES STREET, CARMEL

Just up from the Tuck Box is **FOCUS PHOTOGRAPHIC GALLERY**, dedicated to the memory of Hella Langer, with the fascinating work of Roger Moore, Mark Kayne, Steve Shapiro, and Al Weber.

❧ *Focus Photographic Gallery, Dolores es between Ocean and Seventh, Carmel 93921; (831) 624–2102. Open 11:00 A.M.–5:30 P.M. Wednesday–Monday. Visa, MasterCard, American Express. Wheelchair accessible.*

DAVID LEE GALLERIES is an art gallery devoted solely to the work of—ready?—David Lee. Enjoy the precise lineal delineations and exquisite colors in his florals and meditative traditional landscapes.

❧ *David Lee Galleries, Dolores es between Ocean and Seventh, Carmel 93921; (831) 622–9992 or (800) 879–0711, fax (831) 622–9991. Open 10:00 A.M.– 6:00 P.M. daily. MasterCard and Visa. Wheelchair accessible.*

One of the most exciting new shops in Carmel is a whimsical yet practical one started recently by two French Basque women with incredible flair and charisma. **JAN DE LUZ'S** household linens are based on traditional Basque cattle blankets, which were used by shepherds and farmers to protect their cattle against sun and insects. Seven stripes cross the original blankets (and many of the linens sold here), signifying the seven Basque provinces, with colors identifying native villages. The wider the stripes, the richer the owner.

The women design their fabrics and have them made in France, bringing back all-natural fibers in tablecloths, plaid towels, luxurious bath towels and robes (all embroidered in the shop to order), aprons, and curtain fabrics, many of which can be ordered with matching Limoges china. Now you will also find copper pots, furniture, and whole doors and walls for sale.

We strongly encourage you to wander into Jan de Luz, just for the cultural experience and to enjoy the fun of the people who design, run, and own it.

☆ち *Jan de Luz, Dolores es between Ocean and Seventh, Carmel 93921; (831) 622–7621, fax (831) 622–7250; e-mail JANdeLUZ@aol.com. Open 10:00 A.M.–5:00 P.M. daily. Visa and MasterCard. Wheelchair accessible.*

As you walk toward Ocean Avenue, you might want to check out the T-shirts at Sascha's or the bunny and cypress tree jewelry at Giles of Carmel, if those suit your tastes. In between them, **OLD WORLD ANTIQUES** offers a large selection of seventeenth-, eighteenth-, and nineteenth-century European furniture and antiques, Asian art, Oriental rugs, antique paintings and prints, and early twentieth-century California art. A lovely experience.

☆ち *Old World Antiques, Dolores es between Ocean and Seventh, Carmel 93921; (831) 626–1820. Open 10:00 A.M.–5:00 P.M. daily. Visa, MasterCard, JCB. Wheelchair accessible.*

GALLERY 21 is the hometown gallery of Carmel resident and internationally acclaimed Disney artist Eyvind Earle (1916–2000). The gallery features his unusual and fantasy-oriented paintings, serigraphs, and sculptures. Earle was the exclusive background artist on Walt Disney's *Sleeping Beauty* and also worked on nine other Disney films in the 1950s. This is a must-see!

☆ち *Gallery 21, Dolores es between Ocean and Seventh, Carmel 93921; (831) 626–2700, fax (831) 626–2788. Open 10:00 A.M.–5:00 P.M. daily. Visa, MasterCard, American Express. Wheelchair accessible.*

One of Carmel's happening restaurants is **MONDO'S TRATTORIA**, serving northern and southern Italian cuisine—great pastas and salads, great celebrity watching, and great local conversation. A hangout for Clint Eastwood, Bryant Gumbel, Jay Leno, Michael Douglas, and even former President Gerald Ford, this is still an unpretentious, informal, fun place.

And with all that, the pasta is excellent and the prices are even better. Beyond the expected, try the Monterey Bay calamari salad ($6.75), the bruschetta (toasted bread rounds with toppings) with pesto, prosciutto, roasted garlic, or goat cheese (under $6.00), wonderful antipasti such as carpaccio (thin slices of raw beef with capers and shallots) at $7.25, or polenta with Italian sausage ($6.95). The combination antipasto mondo ($7.95) lets you try them all. Twenty-five pasta sauces complement your choice of fettucine, linguini, penne, farfalle (bow ties), or fusilli, all under $14.00. You can also get a sixteen-ounce T-bone steak ($18.95), roasted chicken ($14.95), and a dozen kinds of pizza, healthy and not so.

We even like the omelettes at lunch, especially the fresh sautéed vegetables of the day and the Italian sausage and mushroom, both under $8.00 and served with sautéed potatoes. Lunch also includes sandwiches from tuna to meatballs, salami, and vegetarian. There's also hot or not prosciutto di Parma with tomatoes and melted mozzarella for $7.25, including salad. Deal!

Mondo's Trattoria, Dolores es between Ocean and Seventh, Carmel 93921; (831) 624–8977, fax (831) 624–4102; www.mondos.com. Open for lunch 11:30 A.M.–4:00 P.M., dinner 5:00 P.M.–10:00 P.M. daily. Beer and wine. Visa, MasterCard, American Express. Wheelchair accessible.

One of the fun things about the **BLEICH GALLERY OF IMPRESSIONISM** is that George J. Bleich travels around the world, often taking his young son, who he says may be "the youngest artist to paint at Monet's Giverny in France" and his older surfer/painter son to paint along with him. Ever questing after his "mastery of light and color," Bleich apparently gained his travel lust from his late seafaring father, Captain Harry Bleich, and from his mother, Helen, who sailed professionally as a stewardess until the age of seventy. She's now in her nineties and works in the gallery. You can order a custom Bleich painting, with a videotape of your family participating in its creation and listen to the artist playing his guitar and singing.

Bleich Gallery of Impressionism, Dolores es near Ocean, Carmel 93921; (831) 624–9447; www.bleich4art.com. Open 11:00 A.M.–5:00 P.M. daily. Visa, MasterCard, American Express, Discover. Wheelchair accessible.

One of our favorite galleries anywhere, simply because we passionately love the photographers involved, is **PHOTO WEST GALLERY**, which features the work of Ansel Adams, Brett Weston, Ruth Gernhard, Imogen Cunningham, Carol Henry, and Christopher Burkett. You can also purchase photography books, posters, and cards. Heaven. This is a major photographic gallery.

Photo West Gallery, Dolores es near Ocean, Carmel 93921; (831) 625–1587, fax (831) 625–1288. Open 10:00 A.M.–5:00 P.M. daily. Visa, MasterCard, American Express. Wheelchair accessible.

Lincoln Street

Lincoln Street, like many others in Carmel, is full of little paths and courtyards, and we encourage you to explore them all. Remember, this is shoppers' paradise.

The south side of Lincoln offers a wide variety of shops, including Rainbow Scent, the Mischievous Rabbit, which thoughtfully has benches for husbands while wives look at kids' and infants' clothes, and (one of two in Carmel) Augustina, for gorgeous leather coats and bags.

While we don't encourage smoking in any form, the **CARMEL PIPE SHOP** is one teensy little box of fascination and atmosphere in a total of 170 square feet. And men are clamoring to get in. This is where Bing Crosby was, and Jack Lemmon is, a loyal customer. You can buy imported cigarettes, tobaccos, pipes of several kinds, and pipe equipment, all while listening to interesting conversation (free). *Carmel Pipe Shop, Lincoln ws between Ocean and Seventh, Carmel 93921; (831) 624–9737. Open when owner "feels like it," somewhere between 9:00 A.M. and 5:30 P.M. daily. Visa, MasterCard, American Express. Barely wheelchair accessible.*

Explore La Rambla Courtyard, stopping at the Garden Shop for wonderful, whimsical garden accessories.

Be sure to visit the Church of the Wayfarer and its adjoining garden at the corner of Lincoln and Seventh. It is a charming and world famous site for weddings.

In the next courtyard Anderle Gallery displays beautiful antique furniture; the Cranden Shop has chimes; and two galleries of exquisite Asian furnishings focus on the central fountain and interesting quiet browsing.

Doris Day's **CYPRESS INN** is a quiet landmark of old Carmel with its Moorish Mediterranean exterior. Staying at the Cypress Inn is like spending time in Doris Day's casually elegant home, with its "living room lobby," private cozy courtyard, and intimate and fun cocktail lounge lined with Doris Day movie posters. Enjoy afternoon tea, even if you aren't staying here, from 2:00 to 3:45 P.M. with reservations ($12). Each individualistic room comes with newspapers and a decanter of sherry, and continental breakfast in the inn's breakfast room or garden courtyard. Rooms range from $125 to $275, depending on season.

The Cypress Inn welcomes pets and offers a "pet friendly dining list" and "pet sitter list." First pets stay for $20 per night, additional pet for $12 (maximum of two pets). *Cypress Inn, Lincoln and Seventh, Carmel 93921; (800) 443–7443 or (831) 624–3871. Visa, MasterCard, American Express. Wheelchair accessible.*

On the east side of Lincoln, wander into Morgan Court to the G.H. Rothe Gallery, which displays Rothe's mezzotints; Loes Hinse Timeless Clothing; and the Avalon Gallery, devoted to fine printmaking, etchings, aqua-tints, and stone lithographs. Buff La Grange is a somewhat dark, subdued, and casually elegant boutique featuring Peserico, Lamberto Losani cashmeres, and simple, straight-lined women's clothing.

Now, next door to all this is one special spot, folks. **SADE'S COCKTAILS** is the locals' bar, where loud voices solve the world's problems and those proverbial cracks occasionally hang over bar stools facing the front window. Great drinks, great prices, great conversation.

❧ *Sade's Cocktails, Lincoln es near Ocean, Carmel 93921; (831) 624–0787. Open morning till closing. No credit cards. Wheelchair accessible.*

PAT AREIAS STERLING SILVER makes and displays a wide array of dramatic and elegant silver belt buckles (arranged by color), as well as silver trays. Pat is often here in the gallery and it's fascinating just to listen when she answers other people's questions about her background.

❧ *Pat Areias Sterling Silver, Lincoln es near Ocean, Carmel 93921; (831) 626–8668. Open 10:00 A.M.–5:30 P.M. daily. Visa, MasterCard, American Express, Discover. Wheelchair accessible.*

CROSS STREETS NORTH OF OCEAN AVENUE

Junipero Street

Junipero Street is a little up Carmel's slight hill for some people, but worth the trip food wise. Here we found three great spots: Bruno's Market, the French Poodle, and the General Store and Forge in the Forest.

DORIS DAY'S CYPRESS INN, CARMEL

One evening when Jerry was being consumed by something he consumed, Kathleen went out in the dripple and dark, looking for the trusty pink stuff and some soup and found, thank god and goddess, **BRUNO'S MARKET & DELI**, Carmel's gourmet grocery store habituated primarily by locals and occasionally by visitors who find it and its fabulous foods to go. If you don't want to walk up there, there's a small parking lot and parking on the street.

Yes, they had all the necessary cures, for both of us. Jerry got his Pepto-Bismol and Kathleen got some memorable deli-made chicken soup that was actually a divine chicken stew with wide noodles, beans, zucchini, carrots, and chunks of chicken roasted here. Spoons, crackers, napkins—the works. The roasted chickens were sold out already, but the sandwiches are so big and fully packed that you might have trouble getting your mouth around them—the fresh roasted turkey ones ooze cranberry sauce. And worst (best) of all, Bruno's has personal-size pies, cakes, and other irresistible pastries in a little rack right by the checkout stands, of course. Criminey sakes!

✣ *Bruno's Market & Deli, Junipero and Sixth, Carmel 93921; (831) 624–3821. Open 7:00 A.M.–9:00 P.M. daily. Visa, MasterCard. Wheelchair accessible from the parking lot.*

Down at the corner of Junipero and Fifth Avenue are the French Poodle and the General Store and Forge in the Forest, and they couldn't be more contrasting.

The **FRENCH POODLE** is the pride and joy of Anamaria and Richarch Zoellin, who belongs to the Chaine des Rotisseurs, and for good reason. In this superbly elegant little restaurant, extremely popular with locals who come back time and time again, Chef Zoellin specializes in his sauces, as the best French chefs do. If you eat meat, try the lamb with Dijon mustard and thyme sauce ($22), the côte de veau with morel mushrooms ($26), tournedos Rossini ($27), or the abalone meunière, whose price varies with availability.

Appetizers include perfectly steamed Castroville artichoke ($5.50), real escargots de Bourgogne ($8.00 per half dozen), or the excellent foie gras de Strasbourg ($16).

✣ *French Poodle, Junipero Street ws at Fifth, Carmel 93921; (831) 624–8643. Open for dinner from 5:30 P.M. Beer and wine. Visa, MasterCard, American Express. Wheelchair accessible.*

Just across Fifth on Junipero is the more lively and fun **GENERAL STORE AND FORGE IN THE FOREST**, where you hear laughing voices on the patio at all hours. A great fireplace warms outdoor diners enjoying the pub-style atmosphere and informal, good food. The onetime general store's original board and batten walls warm up the dining room, which feels like a wine cellar. This place has terrific salads, burgers, grilled prawns, varied quesadillas, and daily specials that include rotisserie chicken ($14, half; $11, quarter), meat loaf ($14), lamb shanks on Thursdays ($13), and Yankee pot roast with garlic mashed potatoes on Fridays. It is now employee-owned and managed.

❧ *General Store and Forge in the Forest, Junipero and Fifth, Carmel 93921; (831) 624–2233. Open from 11:30 A.M. Full bar. Visa, MasterCard, American Express. Wheelchair accessible.*

Mission Street

Your most interesting stops on the north side of Ocean Avenue will be on the cross streets between Sixth and Fifth Avenues.

At the northwest corner of Sixth and Mission is ZANTMAN ART GALLERIES, an almost overwhelmingly large collection of Renaissance-style to contemporary paintings and sculpture primarily by living American, European, and Asian artists. Note the work of Jie Mei Wang and impressionist Duane Alt. You can also visit Zantman Art Galleries in Palm Desert, California.

❧ *Zantman Art Galleries, Sixth Avenue ns and Mission, Carmel 93921; (831) 624–8314; www.zantmangalleries.com. Open 10:00 A.M.–5:00 P.M. daily. Visa, MasterCard. Wheelchair accessible.*

We now take you to Mission Street between Sixth and Fifth Avenues, where we begin at APPAREL & COMPANY, a branch of an East Bay minichain; it opened here in 1996. Local manager Nancy McNett sells Peruvian jackets and original rare American designs of women's clothing, including skirts, dresses, and jackets, ranging from $55 to $200.

❧ *Apparel & Company, Mission ws near Sixth, Carmel 93921; (831) 625–8626. Open 10:00 A.M.–5:30 P.M. Monday–Saturday, till 4:00 P.M. Sunday. Visa, MasterCard, American Express. Wheelchair accessible.*

Stop in at Pamela Levin for exquisitly artistic silver jewelry.

Don't miss Bates Cafe, lined with local cartoonist Bill Bates's drawings, where you can enjoy inexpensive breakfasts and lunches from 8:30 A.M. to 2:00 P.M.

Up the street ARCADIA ANTIQUES offers teacup aficionados a great chance to add to their collections. Osaka native Sinobu (Amy) Tabata, who came to California as a graduate student in education, also offers beautiful antique silver, furniture, and household accessories. As an antique hunter herself, Amy says she even makes house calls if you have something wonderful to sell or buy.

❧ *Arcadia Antiques, Mission ws near Sixth, Carmel 93921; (831) 624–5938. Open 10:00 A.M.–5:00 P.M. daily. Visa, MasterCard, Discover. Wheelchair accessible.*

ALEXANDER OF FLORENCE owner Alexander Magazzini (should he be selling magazines?) displays his own work as well as contemporary Italian fine art, such as that of Beniamino Coccotelli, whose work is similar to some old masters'; Salvatore Magazzini, who paints North African and Italian landscapes; and Rolando Vivarelli and Bruno Smocovich, both sculptors.

⚘ Alexander of Florence, Mission ws between Sixth and Fifth, Carmel 93921; (831) 620–0732. Open 10:00 A.M.–6:00 P.M. Sunday–Thursday, till 10:00 P.M. Friday–Saturday. Visa, MasterCard. Wheelchair accessible.

Jerry is an admirer of the artist whose work is found at the next gallery, **AMBROSE POLLACK, WOODWORKER**. Pollack is occasional woodworker to the pope and a featured artist on the Discovery Channel's Lynette Jennings Design Show. With his special joining technique, Pollack created an altar and podium at the request of Pope John Paul II for his visit to the Carmel Mission in 1987.

Once a master guitarist, Pollack decided to give up late hours in smoky saloons for his peaceful woodshop, and we all benefit. A purist with a grand respect for nature, Pollack takes his designs from the trees whose wood he crafts, producing always interesting wooden candelabra, dining-room sets, and chairs. Both Pollack and his wife/gallery manager, Michele Pollack, are involved in local politics, so you can learn lots on several fronts here.

⚘ Ambrose Pollack, Woodworker, Mission ws between Sixth and Fifth, Carmel 93921; (831) 625–6554. Open 11:00 A.M.–5:00 P.M. Monday–Saturday "or anytime by appointment." Visa, MasterCard, American Express, Discover. Wheelchair accessible.

Be sure to browse through one of Carmel's most charming courtyards, Mission Patio, which is lined with little art studios/galleries and shops. **CARMEL NEEDLE ARTS**, which faces Mission Street, specializes in needlepoint and some one-of-a-kind hand-painted canvases by outstanding local artists. England native Amanda Lawford brings this nearly 600-year-old art to the Monterey peninsula, and Michele Czaja offers bags, tapestries, seat coverings, and fiber and thread—and just about anything else needlepointers might need(le). Check out the canvases on the ceiling.

⚘ Carmel Needle Arts, Mission Patio, Mission between Sixth and Fifth, Carmel 93921; (831) 626–1545. Open 10:00 A.M.–4:30 P.M. Monday–Saturday, and later "if business is lively." Visa, MasterCard. Wheelchair accessible.

Shirttail Custom Clothing produces handmade men's quality clothing, but is open sporadically.

To watch a lively artist at work, visit **ROCHANA'S STUDIO GALLERY**, where Rochana Cash paints and draws in the center of her studio surrounded by walls covered with her work. Rochana delights in explaining what she's doing. The Texas native studied painting in Europe, New York, and San Francisco, and returned to full-time artistry after raising her daughter. Her paintings of beach scenes showing a Turner influence have become an instant success. Her series *Aspects of a Woman* is especially interesting. Rochana is one of the few truly local artists still exibiting in downtown Carmel.

❦ *Rochana's Studio Gallery, Mission Patio, Mission between Sixth and Fifth, Carmel 93921; (831) 625–0449; brelsford.net/rochana; e-mail rochana@c.s.com; Open 10:00 A.M.–5:00 P.M. daily. Visa, MasterCard. Wheelchair accessible.*

Le Verissage features contemporary French artists Claude Idlas, Eduard Karaz, Lana Askanazi, and Vartan Asadur.

As you return to Mission Street from the Mission Patio courtyard, turn left (north) to continue our stroll. Next to Carmel Needle Arts is **MUSEUM JEWELRY & FINE ART**. Michael S. Agassi makes platinum and gold jewelry for clients and interviews his customers to understand their taste and personality to make sure his creations will suit them. Also exhibiting in this gallery are sculptor Karl Saunders, who made models for *Jurassic Park* and several other movies, and landscape painter Ardett J. Smith. Gallery manager Tamara Oganesyan's personality and Ph.D. in linguistics guarantee an interesting visit.

❦ *Museum Jewelry & Fine Art, Mission between Fifth and Sixth, Carmel 93921; phone and fax (831) 625–1001. Open 10:00 A.M.–6:00 P.M. daily. Visa, MasterCard, American Express. Wheelchair accessible.*

At the southwest corner of Mission and Fifth, Christmas enthusiasts will enjoy **HOLIDAY HUTCH**, a year-round Christmas store with ornaments and Christmas scenes from Germany, Italy, Russia, Asia, and thirty local craftspeople; also, Department 56 houses, wood-carved crèches ($24–$1,600), and decorations made of corks from Monterey County wineries.

After serving in Vietnam, Colonel Charles Hutchins and his floral designer wife, Janet, "retired" to Carmel in 1974 and opened Holiday Hutch, now a locally popular institution. Four of the Hutchinses five children and their offspring work in the business, which now includes a branch at the Crossroads shopping center and St. Nick's Loft in the Barnyard center.

❦ *Holiday Hutch, Mission ws at Fifth, Carmel 93921; (831) 624–5105. Open 10:00 A.M.–6:00 P.M. daily, till 5:00 P.M. Sunday. Visa, MasterCard, American Express, Discover. Wheelchair accessible.*

Before we take you around the corner to Casanova's for one of the most romantic dining experiences anywhere, we want you to know about the best breakfast place in Carmel, in our humble opinion, right across Mission Street. KATY'S PLACE, which you enter by the side door (around the wooden deck), has a wild array of furniture, people, and collectibles, from old Schilling spice cans and samplers to old-world paintings and a brass rail under the wall benches to rest your feet in case you can't reach the floor.

For breakfast lovers, and lovers of all sorts, Katy's Place is divine and a local hangout. Katy's specialties include blintzes with fresh berries ($8.95); Swedish pancakes with mixed berries, raspberry sauce, and whipped cream; corned beef hash and eggs; huevos rancheros; a breakfast burrito; a Carmel Joe's Special with extra lean ground beef; and The Mission Cookout, a casserole of poached eggs, melted cheese, sautéed onions, and refried beans (all about $8.95). A daily special might be the smoked turkey, chicken, and artichoke with smoked garlic, lean sausage, eggs, potatoes, and toast ($8.95). Yes, that's all one breakfast.

Kathleen particularly likes the Basque omelette, but you can order any egg combo with everything from choice New York steak to lox and chives, as well as trout or calamari steak and eggs. Steaming oatmeal is exceptional for mush, as are the ten varieties of eggs Benedict made with three eggs (about $10). Try the many variations on waffles or French toast, or the buttermilk pancakes galore. Whew! Perfect place to stoke yourself up before those long walks around Carmel.

Lunch ranges from a calamari Jack burger to quesadillas, and interesting twists on standard sandwiches served on marble rye, branola, or sourdough French bread. Great salads too. Try the classic Caesar with grilled chicken.

❧ *Katy's Place, Mission Street es between Sixth and Fifth, Carmel 93921; (831) 624–0199. Open 7:00 A.M.–3:00 P.M. daily. No credit cards. Wheelchair accessible.*

Now, if you want to go to CASANOVA RESTAURANT go north on Mission and turn left (west) on Fifth Avenue, and it's the second place on the left (south).

This Italian/French/Spanish restaurant feels like a Spanish cave. Its maze of rooms wanders downstairs and back around to Mission Street. We find the downstairs rooms the most romantic of all, or the heated patio even on a dripple day for lunch. Oprah Winfrey, Kelsey Grammer, and Jack Nicholson drop in when they're in town, and Andre Agassi and Brooke Shields enjoyed their prewedding (predivorce) dinner at Casanova. Plenty of unknown happy locals enjoy it too, although some visitors consider it to be overpriced and overrated. If money is a consideration, we suggest you try Casanova at lunch or Sunday brunch instead of dinner. The Georis family owns Casanova as well as Georis winery in Carmel Valley.

Lunchtime appetizers might include bruschetta di prosciutto ($5.75), sautéed fresh mussels ($6.25), or homemade duck pâté with foie gras and marinated celery root ($5.25). Salads include a warm duck salad with lentils and beets ($9.75), a salade de poulet à l'avocat (do they mean avocado or attorney?) ($10.75), and a smoked salmon salad ($11.75). Traditional entrees include wonderfully light spinach gnocchi with Parmesan cream sauce ($8.75), lamb tenderloin on a skewer with herbs de Provence and garlic ($12.75), grilled salmon ($12.75), or marvelous cannelloni ($9.75). You can add a small green salad or cup of soup for only $1.25.

Chef Didier Dutertre's evening menu offers pastas, filet mignon au poivre ($38.75), linguine with lobster, prawns, and shellfish ($35.75), charbroiled fillet of grouper marinated in garlic Meyer lemon olive oil ($29.95), roasted leg of duck with braised sweet and sour red cabbage ($27.75), rack of lamb ($37.75), veal medallions with chanterelle mushrooms ragout ($37.75), and a classic irresistible paella Valenciana with saffron rice, chicken, lamb, chorizo sausage, and assorted seafood ($28.75 per person, two or more). All dinner prices are for a three-course dinner.

Casanova's imported and local wine cellar is famous, and with a polite request you may be able to see it. Say pretty please. Casanova also offers Nights of the Long Tables dinners on Tuesday evenings, so call ahead to inquire.

⁂ *Casanova Restaurant, Fifth Avenue ss between Mission and San Carlos, Carmel 93921; (831) 625–0501; www.casanovarestaurant.com. Open for lunch 11:30 A.M.–3:00 P.M. Monday–Saturday, dinner 5:00–10:00 P.M. daily, brunch 9:00 A.M.–3:00 P.M. Sunday. Visa, MasterCard. Front is wheelchair accessible, downstairs rooms are not. Pets welcome outdoors, has heaters.*

San Carlos Avenue

Now we will take you back to Sixth Avenue so that you can explore San Carlos between Sixth and Fifth. We recommend that you walk up the east side of San Carlos to visit its three galleries in and around the San Carlos Mall, and then back down the west side, so that you can explore Sixth Avenue itself on the way to Dolores Street.

EUROPEAN GALLERIES is just what it says, with contemporary European artists' work (Jerry's favorite is Matthew Morillo) and originals by some of the masters, such as Pierre-Auguste Renoir and Edouard Cortes. Two other local galleries also have Cortes originals.

⁂ *European Galleries, San Carlos es between Sixth and Fifth, Carmel 93921; (831) 624–2010. Open 10:00 A.M.–6:00 P.M. daily, till 10:00 P.M. Friday–Saturday. Visa, MasterCard, American Express. Wheelchair accessible.*

At **MUDZIMU GALLERY** you can touch and feel the smooth contours of native sculpture from Zimbabwe (formerly Rhodesia), with its traditional and unique sensuous curves and local materials. Zimbabwean artists are paid according to standards set by their government, which may or may not be anywhere close to what you pay for their gorgeous work in the States.

❧ *Mudzimu Gallery, San Carlos es between Sixth and Fifth, Carmel 93921; (831) 626–2946. Open 10:00 A.M.–6:00 P.M. Wednesday–Monday. Visa, MasterCard, American Express. Wheelchair accessible.*

Now we suggest you walk up to the corner at Fifth Avenue, cross the street, and begin your browsing at **CARMEL CAMERA**, one of the most congenial and informative camera stores we have encountered.

At Carmel Camera you can get everything you might need in cameras, from film to battery replacement, digital or throwaway cameras, and one-hour prints. Now owned by the national Wolf Camera chain of Atlanta, Georgia, the store has retained its friendly local staff and interesting displays.

❧ *Carmel Camera, San Carlos at Fifth, Carmel 93921; (831) 624–8880. Open 9:30 A.M.–6:00 P.M. Monday–Saturday, 10:00 A.M.–4:00 P.M. Sunday. Visa, MasterCard, American Express. Wheelchair accessible.*

Heading south on San Carlos, next we come to **MARK AREIAS JEWELERS**. Mark is an authorized Cartier dealer and designs and makes most of the other jewelry himself right here. He'll even replace your watch battery if you're desperate. A lovely place to drool.

❧ *Mark Areias Jewelers, San Carlos ss near Fifth, Carmel 93921; (831) 624–5621 or (800) 624–2214. Open 10:00 A.M.–5:30 P.M. Tuesday–Saturday. Visa, MasterCard, American Express. Wheelchair accessible.*

In the Eastwood (read Clint) Building you can't miss **G.J.'s WEST** and **G.J.'s WILD WEST**, specializing in glamorous Western and dude and dudette wear. The staff is gorgeous, the clothes, hats, and boots are gorgeous, and the prices are appropriately gorgeous. Look for Double D Ranch and Hairston-Roberson clothes, Charlie Tweedle hats, and Lucchesi boots.

❧ *G.J.'s West and G.J.'s Wild West, San Carlos ws between Fifth and Sixth, Carmel 93921; (831) 625–9453. Open 10:00 A.M.–6:00 P.M. Monday–Saturday, 11:00 A.M.–5:00 P.M. Sunday. Visa, MasterCard, American Express. Wheelchair accessible.*

After Clint Eastwood closed his **HOG'S BREATH INN** in 1999 down a little path just south of G.J.'s West and G.J's Wild West, it reopened as its old self

in 2000 with a slightly more exciting
menu and higher prices, natch.
Burgers, sandwiches, salads, and crab
cakes ($9.95) surface at lunch, with the
Humongous Fungus portobello mushroom ($7.95), Castroville artichoke
soup ($4.00), Hog's salad, prime rib,
Hog's baby back ribs ($19.95), chicken
piccata ($15.95), Dirty Harry Dinner
of chopped sirloin, wild mushrooms,
horseradish, and whole-grain mustard
sauce with garlic smashed potatoes
($14.95), peppered seared ahi tuna
($19.95), and vegetable lasagna
($15.50) at dinner. There's also a kids'
menu. Enjoy the lively courtyard and
warmer indoor fun room. Hog's
Breath Inn souvenir shirts and hats are
available, of course.

MASTER JEWELER
ORLANDO FERIOZZI

🌸 *Hog's Breath Inn, San Carlos ws between Fifth and Sixth, Carmel 93921;
(831) 625–1044, fax (831) 625–2188. Open 11:00 A.M.–11:00 P.M. daily. Full
bar. Visa, MasterCard, American Express. Wheelchair accessible via elevator in
Eastwood Building (at back between the two Western stores).*

Adjoining the path just south of the Eastwood Building are the stairs to the
offices of the Carmel Business Association, which serves as the local visitors
bureau as well. While they have loads of brochures available on their walls, we
have most of the information here, of course!

One of our favorite cultural experiences in Carmel is a visit to the next shop,
FERIOZZI OF ROME, where silver-headed maestro Orlando Feriozzi presides as
one of the world's last renaissance artists working with metal and jewels—his art
resembles that of Cellini. He first apprenticed to a master jeweler in Rome in
1931, when he was eleven years old. That gives you an idea.

Orlando made Margaret Truman's wedding ensemble jewelry while still
working and living in Rome, having been trained by world-renowned artists
such as Fabergé and Castellani. If you are lucky, Marcella Feriozzi will let you
watch her husband's surgeon's hands at work in the back room, which is an
experience in itself. We lucked out and were invited to sit in on his bimonthly
gathering of California's finest jewelers. They gather in this shop to enjoy a little of Orlando's cooking and discuss artistic problems, examining pieces they

have brought from their studios. If you happen to be in Rome, visit the Feriozzis' sons at Feriozzi di Roma, Via delle Vergini 17, Rome.

❧ Feriozzi of Rome, San Carlos ws between Fifth and Sixth, Carmel 93921; (831) 624–6515. Open 10:00 A.M.–5:00 P.M. Monday–Saturday. Visa, MasterCard, American Express. Wheelchair accessible.

Next on San Carlos is Carlson Gallery, which features twentieth-century paintings, glass, and sculpture, and is an excellent place to browse if it is open.

The impressive Fingerhut Gallery of Carmel offers prints of works by Chagall, Matisse, Miró, Picasso, and Rembrandt.

In the charming McFarland Court, you can wander through several shops, with **SIMIC GALLERIES** facing San Carlos. Mario Simic travels the world looking for fine nineteenth-century artworks, and his findings include a Van Gogh graphite drawing, Pissarros, and Cantonese artist An He. Simic also sells some local and other contemporary paintings in this extremely elegant gallery with lush deep carpeting and grandly European ambience, with prices ranging from $2,000 to $250,000. Simic also has the New Renaissance Gallery around the corner on Sixth Avenue.

❧ Simic Galleries, McFarland Court, San Carlos between Fifth and Sixth, Carmel 93921; (831) 624–7522. Open 10:00 A.M.–6:00 P.M. Sunday–Thursday, till 10:00 P.M. Friday–Saturday. Visa, MasterCard, American Express. Wheelchair accessible.

Down the path behind the Simic Galleries is the **SECRET GARDEN**, a charming little nursery that is itself a garden dominated by a Plexiglas geodesic dome made from a kit in the seventies. You can take home custom-made paving stones, pottery, wind chimes, and other garden accessories you might only see here. Lee Goodenough and Mark Burger are the resident green thumbs.

❧ Secret Garden, McFarland Court, San Carlos ws between Fifth and Sixth, Carmel 93921; (831) 625–1131. Open 10:00 A.M.–5:00 P.M. daily. Visa, MasterCard. Not wheelchair accessible.

Walk back to San Carlos and turn right (south) to **RICHARD MACDONALD GALLERIES**, definitely one of Jerry's favorites. MacDonald's most widely viewed work is the giant *Flair Across America* bronze he created for the 1996 Olympics entrance in Atlanta, Georgia. Here you can view and purchase MacDonald's original sketches, paintings, lithographs, and hand-drawn serigraphs of ballet, mime, and architectonic sculpture. This gallery feels like a museum of sensuous curves on a large scale. Small editions of "The Flair" are available for a mere $2,500 from this cum laude graduate of the Los Angeles Art Center.

❧ *Richard MacDonald Galleries, San Carlos ws between Fifth and Sixth, Carmel 93921; (831) 624–8200. Open 10:00 A.M.–6:00 P.M. Sunday–Thursday, till 9:00 P.M. Friday–Saturday. Visa, MasterCard, American Express. Wheelchair accessible.*

JONES & TERWILLIGER GALLERIES offers romantic paintings of European city scenes and vineyards, many by Missy Jenkins Lord and Kent Wallis.

❧ *Jones & Terwilliger Galleries, San Carlos ws between Fifth and Sixth, Carmel 93921; (831) 626–7300. Open 9:00 A.M.–6:00 P.M. Sunday–Thursday, till 10:00 P.M. Friday–Saturday. Visa, MasterCard, American Express. Wheelchair accessible.*

Definitely one of Kathleen's favorites is **AUGUSTINA LEATHERS**, with its rich leather aroma practically wafting out the door. Here you can inhale leather jackets from white fringe to green bomber, leather evening wear, belts, hats, and novel creations by Augustina's in-house leather artist and seamstress, all ranging from $25 to $7,000. Paula Lishman turns fur into yarn and creates unusual outfits from the resulting fabric. Yes, this is the sister store to Augustina's at Ocean and Lincoln.

❧ *Augustina Leathers, San Carlos ws between Sixth and Fifth, Carmel 93921; (831) 626–6353. Open 9:30 A.M.–5:30 P.M. daily. Visa, MasterCard, American Express. Partly wheelchair accessible.*

KERRY LEE INC. occupies the northwest corner of San Carlos and Sixth and you can hope to find Lee himself creating his custom jewelry pieces, usually with diamonds and pearls.

❧ *Kerry Lee Inc., corner Sixth Avenue and San Carlos, Carmel 93921; (831) 624–9222. Open daily but hours vary. Visa, MasterCard, American Express. Wheelchair accessible.*

Pernille is a fairly good family restaurant for breakfast, sandwiches, pasta, and seafood.

Now we will walk you down (west) Sixth Avenue's north side, up and down the hot block of Dolores, down the next block of Sixth Avenue's north side, and then back up 2 blocks of Sixth Avenue's south side, ending with the Birkenstock store, which you may well need by then!

Heading west on the north side of Sixth Avenue from San Carlos, you will find Classic Art Gallery (another locale of the Simic Gallery) and **HOWARD**

PORTNOY GALLERIE. (Where do these people get their French spelling of gallery?) The Portnoy gallery features local artists such as Larry Miller, Miguel Dominguez, and C. A. Minou, as well as guest artists like Jack Lestrade and his watercolors. Portnoy also highlights classics by Edouard Cortes, master of rainy Paris street scenes, Thomas William Jones, Colorado acrylic artist William Hook, and sensuous figures by sculptress Shray. Howard Portnoy is an interesting character himself, having worked as a movie writer and for the William Morris Agency before opening this gallery in 1991. With artwork priced from $950 to $125,000, this Portnoy has no complaints! Sorry—couldn't help it.
➥ *Howard Portnoy Gallerie, Sixth Avenue between San Carlos and Dolores, Carmel 93921; (831) 624–1155. Open 10:00 A.M.–5:00 P.M. daily. Visa, MasterCard, American Express. Wheelchair accessible.*

At the northeast corner of Sixth and Dolores Avenues, wander into the **VILLAGE CORNER** Mediterranean bistro, which advertises "Dine with the stars on our heated patio" next to the warming outdoor fireplace. Unless you and they are lucky, they mean heavenly stars if there's no fog. Great treats in this bistro, which has been popular here for fifty years, include Chef Mohamed Rabbaa's lunch starters such as grilled polenta with wild mushrooms ($5.75), fried Monterey calamari with cilantro basil aioli and Japanese horseradish ($6.50), and a chilled Castroville artichoke. Salads range from baby spinach with grilled prawns and Caesar to goat cheese or portobello mushroom salad. Eggs bennie and omelettes are served all day, with a wide range of special carnivore and vegetarian sandwiches, mostly under $9.00.

At dinner try the fresh crab ravioli with scallops ($18.25), paella for two ($35.25), an interesting tandoori rack of lamb ($27.00), double garlic chicken ($16.50), or blackened venison medallions ($23.25).
➥ *Village Corner, Sixth Avenue and Dolores, Carmel 93921; (831) 624–3588. Open 7:00 A.M.–11:00 P.M. daily. Visa, MasterCard. Wheelchair accessible.*

Now turn right (north) up Dolores for some more interesting shops and galleries. **PITZER'S OF CARMEL** is a newish large gallery featuring American contemporary art, from impressionism to realism: oils, watercolors, pastels, and bronze sculpture. Look for landscapes, florals, Western scenes, and aviation and marine subjects. We especially love the huge bronze dolphin (only $27,000). Rob Pitzer ran a gallery in Greenwich, Connecticut, before opening his own gallery here in Carmel.
➥ *Pitzer's of Carmel, Dolores es near Sixth Avenue, Carmel 93921; (831) 625–2288. Open 10:00 A.M.–6:00 P.M. Monday–Saturday, till 5:00 P.M. Sunday. Visa, MasterCard, Discover. Wheelchair accessible.*

Just up from Pitzer's is another huge gallery, GALLERIE AMSTERDAM, start-ed ten years ago by Holland native Tony Vanderploeg. Enjoy the expert lighting that sets off the intriguing work and the exceptionally friendly and knowledge-able staff.

Gallerie Amsterdam features the work of eighty artists and emphasizes eigh-teenth-, nineteenth-, and early twentieth-century works, including that of Alexander Volkov and Hungarian artist Vida Gabor as well as Cals, Musin, Munn, Toussaint, and Fournier. Don't miss the "architectural eggs" by Russian architect Mikhail Rybins.

Gallerie Amsterdam, Dolores es between Sixth and Fifth, Carmel 93921; (831) 624–4355. Open 9:00 A.M.–6:00 P.M. Sunday–Wednesday, till 10:00 P.M. Thursday–Saturday. Visa, MasterCard, American Express. Wheelchair accessible.

STEFANO DI CARMEL is a gorgeous store full of products by American and Italian leather workers, owned by Al Zarzana and staffed by charming friends.

Stefano di Carmel, Dolores es between Sixth and Fifth, Carmel 93921; (831) 625–2998. Open 9:00 A.M.–7:00 P.M. Monday– Thursday, 9:00 A.M.–9:00 P.M. Friday–Saturday, till 6:00 P.M. Sunday. Visa, MasterCard, American Express, Diners Club, Discover, JCB. Wheelchair accessible.

Just up from the leather shop, visit small and pleasant RICHARD THOMAS GALLERIES, which specializes in contemporary masters from Italy, Spain, France, and the United States, including, again, Alexander Volkov. You'll also find sculpture and limited edition prints. You can't miss *Demetra* by Angelo Vadala or the romantic Romantic Renaissance paintings of Csaba Markus.

Richard Thomas Galleries, Dolores es between Sixth and Fifth, Carmel 93921; (831) 625–5636. Open 9:00 A.M.–6:00 P.M. Sunday–Thursday, till 9:00 P.M. Friday–Saturday. Visa, MasterCard, American Express. Wheelchair accessible.

North of the galleries is PILGRIM'S WAY BOOKSTORE, a welcome break in the gallery run along the north side of Ocean Avenue. Pilgrim's Way majors in New Age books on natural health, psychology, Native American studies, alter-native medicine, astrology, and other inspirational topics, and New Age music. Enjoying a strong local following, this bookstore welcomes browsers who don't even think they're interested in New Age stuff.

Pilgrim's Way Bookstore, Dolores es near Fifth Avenue, Carmel 93921; (831) 624–4955. Open 10:00 A.M.–6:00 P.M. Monday–Saturday, 11:00 A.M.–5:00 P.M. Sunday. Visa, MasterCard, American Express. Wheelchair accessible.

EM LE'S is an old Carmel cozy breakfast and lunch landmark with a fireplace. It's often been voted "Best Breakfast in Monterey County," as have a few other restaurants. Em Le's French toast is famous, and rightfully so. Divine. We love the real soda fountain and the way the staff turns this little cottage into a fantasy world at both Halloween and Christmas.

❧ *Em Le's, Dolores near Fifth Avenue, Carmel 93921; (831) 625–6780. Open 6:30 A.M.–3:00 P.M. daily, with lunch beginning at 11:00 A.M. No credit cards. Wheelchair accessible.*

Next enjoy another cluster of galleries, including Lindé Fine Art Gallery, Keller & Scott Antiques, Yellow Dog Gallery (no relation to the famous Gallerie Blue Dog, page 123), Carmichael Designs (glass), and Le Bijou.

Now cross Dolores to its south side for another slew of galleries, including those of the esteemed Carmel Art Association.

The Del Dono Garden Court of galleries begins with ATELIER CARMEL, where you will find a large selection of oil paintings from the eighteenth century forward, early California artwork, Italian sculpture, and loads of prints of the masters, from Rembrandt to Chagall.

❧ *Atelier Carmel, Dolores ws at Fifth Avenue, Carmel 93921; (831) 625–3168. Open 10:00 A.M.–6:00 P.M. daily. Visa, MasterCard. Wheelchair accessible.*

WILLIAM A. KARGES FINE ART specializes in early California impressionistic art with many local and not-so-local artists, many of whose paintings depict California when it was the pristine rolling hills we now see only in paintings and Western movies. Artists represented include Cornelius Botke, Dennis Doheny, and Clyde Scott.

❧ *William A. Karges Fine Art, Dolores ws near Fifth Avenue, Carmel 93921; (831) 625–4266. Open 10:00 A.M.–5:00 P.M. Monday–Saturday. Visa, MasterCard. Wheelchair accessible.*

S.R. BRENNEN GALLERIES has two floors dedicated to contemporary realism, impressionism, and Postimpressionism, with a vast array of interesting sculpture.

❧ *S.R. Brennen Galleries, Dolores ws near Fifth Avenue, Carmel 93921; (831) 625–2233. Open 10:00 A.M.–6:00 P.M. daily. Visa, MasterCard. Partly wheelchair accessible.*

Explore Plein Aire in the back, with garden art and accessories.

Just south of these galleries and Del Dono Garden Court is HIGHLANDS SCULPTURE GALLERY, which majors in contemporary indoor and outdoor sculptures in stone, wood, ceramic, glass, bronze, and other metals and created primarily by California artists. Highlands encourages you to touch the sculpture, and who could resist the convoluted curves of Norma Lewis' *EOS III?* Please do touch! We love David Herschler's *Space Ribbons* and the mesmerizing tinkle sounds of Charles McBride White's water sculptures. This is a good place to experience for the first time or get your modern art fix in a most tasteful, happy way.

❧ *Highland Sculpture Gallery, Dolores ws between Fifth and Sixth, Carmel 93921; (831) 624–0535, fax (831) 624–6676. Open daily, hours vary. Call or fax for an appointment to be sure. Visa, MasterCard. Wheelchair accessible.*

As you leave Highland, turn right (south) and you immediately come to the beautiful sculpture garden introducing you to the highly respected **CARMEL ART ASSOCIATION GALLERIES**. The eighty-year-old institution serves as unifier and artistic home to Carmel's artists. The association is owned and run by more than 120 local artists who exhibit their fine work in all media here at Carmel's oldest gallery. Manager Janet Howell and friends are extremely hospitable and informative. This is where you find the work of true, actively practicing local artists.

❧ *Carmel Art Association Galleries, Dolores ws betweeen Fifth and Sixth, Carmel 93921; (831) 624–6176. Open 10:00 A.M.–5:00 P.M. daily. Visa, MasterCard. Wheelchair accessible.*

In Su Vecino Courtyard there are several galleries, including James J. Rieser Fine Art, Savage Contemporary Fine Art, and Josephus Daniels Gallery.

JAMES J. RIESER FINE ART features contemporary and not-so-contemporary artists who lived in Carmel, early California painters (including the famed Maynard Dixon), and Western women artists such as Alice Crittenden, Mary DeNeale Morgan, and Henrietta Stone. Current well-known locals such as Jane Goode and Edward Norton Ward also exhibit here.

❧ *James J. Rieser Fine Art, Dolores ws between Sixth and Fifth, Carmel 93921; (831) 620–0530. Open 11:00 A.M.–5:00 P.M. Visa, MasterCard. Wheelchair accessible.*

SAVAGE CONTEMPORARY FINE ART is named for owner/artist Sylvia Savage, who offers dynamic abstract painting and forceful, sensuous sculpture at extremely reasonable prices, a rarity in these parts. Enjoy David A. Stephens's mixed-media abstracts and Sharon Spencer's bronze and stone sculptures. We like the laid-back and welcome-to-touch ambience.

❧ *Savage Contemporary Fine Art, Dolores ws between Sixth and Fifth, Carmel 93921; (831) 626–0800. Open 10:00 A.M.–6:00 P.M. daily. Visa, MasterCard. Wheelchair accessible.*

Upstairs Josephus Daniels Gallery features collectible prints and photographs of high quality and good prices. (OK, history buffs. Who was the original Josephus Daniels? Answer: President Woodrow Wilson's Secretary of the Navy.) You can also find California coast and nature scenes photography at Gallery Sur, on the corner of Dolores and Sixth Avenue.

We suggest you turn right and head west on Sixth Avenue's north side to several galleries, including Weston Gallery, Phillips Gallery of Fine Art, D.E. Craghead Gallery, and Gallery Americana. Then cross to the south side of Sixth and begin to work your way back up the street, where you will find the Lynn Lupetti Gallery, Gallerie Blue Dog, Loran Speck Gallery, and the Lilliana Braico Gallery. This will bring you back to Dolores but a leisurely browse may take a good afternoon.

WESTON GALLERY, one of our favorites, exhibits the photographs of some of the west's great camera artists of the last one hundred years, including Ansel Adams, Edward Weston, Man Ray, Robert Mapplethorpe, Michael Kenna, Yousuf Karsh, and Brett Weston. Here you will enjoy the finest photography in originals, prints, books, posters, and portfolios. Margaret Weston and Amy Essick preside.

⁂ *Weston Gallery, Sixth Avenue ns near Dolores, Carmel 93921; (831) 624–4453. Open 10:30 A.M.–5:30 P.M. Wednesday–Monday. Visa, MasterCard. Wheelchair accessible.*

PHILLIPS GALLERY OF FINE ART, the newest gallery in town, started out with flair and lots of color, as in Isobel George's *Madame Joy*. Phillips now offers the haunting, otherworldly oils and serigraphs of Carmel wunderkind Andrew T. Jackson, who was voted "Best Local Artist" by *Coast Weekly* readers in 1997. Here you can also view the work of Harold Hitchcock, Howard Lamar, Ruth Basler Burr, Carole Fletcher, Isobel George, Lisette, Leonard Highcock, and Michael Swinnie. In concert with Muzimu Gallery, Phillips also shows exquisite Zimbabwean stone sculptures.

⁂ *Phillips Gallery of Fine Art, Sixth Avenue ns between Dolores and Lincoln, Carmel 93921; (831) 626–1126. Open 10:00 A.M.–6:00 P.M. daily, till 8:00 P.M. Friday. Visa, MasterCard, American Express. Wheelchair accessible.*

Next going west we come to **D.E. CRAGHEAD GALLERY**, which features figurative art, landscapes, florals and sculptures, oils and pastels, plein-air and photorealism, including the work of Don Craghead and William Selden.

⁂ *D.E. Craghead Gallery, Sixth Avenue ns between Dolores and Lincoln, Carmel 93921; (831) 624–5054. Open 10:00 A.M.–5:30 P.M. daily. Visa, MasterCard.*

Owners Bill and Jennifer Hill have rejuvenated **GALLERY AMERICANA**, at the corner of Sixth and Lincoln, by adding new painters and sculptors to the repertoire. You can see the work of more than sixty artists, including Gerald Balciar, Mark Weber, Ovanes Berberian, Mario Jason, and Dan McCaw. The 8,000-square-foot gallery is one of the largest in Carmel.

❧ *Gallery Americana, ne corner Sixth and Lincoln, Carmel 93921; (831) 624–5071. Open 10:00 A.M.–5:30 P.M., till 5:00 P.M. Sunday. Visa, MasterCard, American Express, Discover. Partly wheelchair accessible.*

Now cross Sixth Avenue, and go one-half block down the other side. Especially in drizzly weather you will enjoy the Little Swiss Café for cheese blintzes ($5.00), Swiss sausage and onions ($8.50), and other breakfast and lunch selections. Next door, duck into the Bohemian House Fine Arts.

LYNN LUPETTI GALLERY and her Magic People Productions exhibit Lynn's paintings of "harmony and relationships," from characters in literature to sensuous nudes. She also features the fantasia sculpture of J. A. Pippett (who once sculpted for the Jim Henson Studio), Kim Kori's bronze sculpture, and Howard Rubin's Tiffany-style lamps.

❧ *Lynn Lupetti Gallery, Sixth Avenue ss near Lincoln, Carmel 93921; (831) 624–0622. Open 10:00 A.M.–5:00 P.M. daily. Visa, MasterCard. Wheelchair accessible.*

Pop art gallery **GALLERIE BLUE DOG**, formerly known as Rodrigue Gallery after its owner, artist George Rodrigue, was renamed for Rodrigue's half-wolf creature with riveting yellow eyes. Yes, this is the blue dog you saw repeatedly in Xerox commercials during the 2000 Olympics. Rodrigue contracted polio in the third grade and spent a year and a half in bed with crayons and clay in New Iberia, Louisiana. Eventually, he studied at the Arts Center College of Design in Pasadena. Rodrigue became known primarily for his occasionally humorous and sometimes tragic paintings of his mesmerizing, ghostly blue dog. Both artist and dog are Cajun, from Louisiana's bayou country where Rodrigue still paints alone in his cabin on stilts in the Atchafalaya basin. Rodrigue also has galleries in New Orleans, Tokyo, and Munich, in case you want to drop by. Blue Dog paintings only cost $12,000–$250,000!

❧ *Gallerie Blue Dog, Sixth Avenue ss between Lincoln and Dolores, Carmel 93921; (831) 626–4444, fax (831) 626–4488; e-mail bluedog@mbay.net; www.bluedogart.com. Open 10:00 A.M.–6:00 P.M. daily. Visa, MasterCard. Wheelchair accessible downstairs only.*

One gallery up, and in total contrast to the Blue Dog next door, is **LORAN SPECK GALLERY**, where you feel as if you have stepped into the studio of an old Dutch or Italian master. This gallery is a one-man exhibition of the Renaissance paintings, oils, pastels, watercolors, charcoals, etchings, limited-edition prints, and posters of gallery owner Loran Speck. Are you surprised? All of his paintings are framed in hand-painted twenty-two-karat gold gilt (guilt?).
➳ *Loran Speck Gallery, Sixth Avenue ss between Lincoln and Dolores, Carmel 93921; (831) 624–3707. Open 10:00 A.M.–6:00 P.M. daily. Visa, MasterCard. Wheelchair accessible.*

Cross Dolores heading east (uphill) to the **THOM. GREGG, GOLDSMITH** gallery, which is also his working studio. Gregg's a fascinating fellow with degrees in engineering and architecture from University of California, Berkeley, who gave up his career in electronic research and development to turn his hobby of jewelry making into his newly chosen profession. Gregg designed and built his own display cases and works only in gold and platinum to create exquisitely simple rings, bracelets, and necklaces ($150–$15,000).
➳ *Thom. Gregg, Goldsmith, Sixth Avenue ss at Dolores, Carmel 93921; (831) 624–3588. Open 10:00 A.M.–5:00 P.M. Tuesday–Saturday. Visa, MasterCard. Wheelchair accessible.*

A few steps east is Chris Winfield's **WINFIELD GALLERY**, where he specializes in what he calls "midcareer" central California artists, a category that happens to include several present and retired professors of art at the University of California, Santa Cruz, such as Patrick Ahearn, Jack Zajac, and Don Wygandt. Winfield defines midcareer as having been sufficiently professional to have exhibited in museum shows. We enjoy the charming bronze animals by sculptor Gwynn Murrill, who created the mountain lions that guard the doors of the Ronald Reagan Building in Los Angeles, as well as the work of noted landscape artist Bill Martin.

Chris's father, Rodney Winfield, designed the Moon Rock Window in the National Cathedral in Washington, D.C.
➳ *Winfield Gallery, Sixth Avenue ss near corner of Dolores, Carmel 93921; (831) 624–3369. Open 11:00 A.M.–5:00 P.M. Monday–Saturday, opens at noon Sunday. Visa, MasterCard, American Express. Wheelchair accessible.*

After all this walking, you must be hungry. Among your gustatory choices is **FLAHERTY'S SEAFOOD GRILL AND OYSTER BAR**. The grill and the oyster bar, which serve from the same menu, are in two rooms divided by a passageway and with two pleasant but distinct ambiences. The oyster bar is larger, with wooden tables, stools, and a casual family atmosphere, while the seafood grill has white tablecloths and specials up to the surf and turf ($39). Flaherty's has been named "One of Northern California's Top Ten Fresh Catch Seafood Restaurants" by the *San Jose Mercury News.*

Locals and visitors have been enjoying Flaherty's for more than twenty-five years. Try chef Francisco Cocova's chowder pot selections, from New England or Manhattan clam chowders to Carmel Bay fish stew or Washington oyster stew, all under $10. All the seafood you can imagine is available and affordable here, from shrimp Louie salad ($9.75) and steamed mussels ($7.95) to Maryland crab cakes ($6.95), shrimp quesadilla ($10.95), Cajun catfish or a calamari Jack burger (both under $8.00), pasta with mussels or prawns, and hamburgers. And that's lunch!

Dinner offers chowders and shellfish appetizers galore, plus live Maine lobster ($27.95), whole cracked Dungeness crab hot or cold ($24.95), a mixed seafood grill ($21.95), and Flaherty's cioppino ($19.95). You can also indulge in chowder and salad for $8.95. Plus pastas like smoked salmon ravioli ($17.95), Santa Fe chicken ($13.95), or black Angus New York steak for all you carnivores ($21.95). Try that Key lime pie and check out the children's menu.

❧ *Flaherty's Seafood Grill and Oyster Bar, Sixth Avenue ss between Dolores and San Carlos, Carmel 93921; (831) 625–1500 or (831) 624–0311, fax (831) 625–2713. Open 11:00 A.M.–10:00 P.M. daily. Beer and wine. Visa, MasterCard, American Express. Wheelchair accessible.*

Down the lane from Flaherty's is **GARCIA GALLERY**, upstairs—up steep stairs. Mostly featuring the brass, jewelry, and acrylics of Danny Garcia, the gallery also shows work of other members of his family, and has since 1960.

❧ *Garcia Gallery, upstairs off Sixth Avenue ss between San Carlos and Dolores, Carmel 93921; (831) 624–8338. Open 10:00 A.M.–5:00 P.M. daily. Visa, MasterCard. Not wheelchair accessible.*

BIRKENSTOCK OF CARMEL is a unique shoe emporium that claims to "work with people's foot problems," and we believe it. This was the first Birkenstock shop in the United States. Founder Rennie Agee and her son Greg have made this a mecca for the footsore for two decades. Daily walker Kathleen particularly admires their computer-designed orthotics.

The Agees and Mike Maxwell carry more shoe lines than their beloved Birkenstocks, including Mephisto, Finn Comfort, and Theresia. They are also one of the few American shops that carry real Tilley Endurables hats, those wonderful brimmed Canadian cotton hats that protect from sun and rain and can be washed in any river.

❧ *Birkenstock of Carmel, Sixth Avenue ss between San Carlos and Dolores, Carmel 93921; (831) 624–5779. Open 10:00 A.M.–5:30 P.M. Monday–Saturday, 11:00 A.M.–4:00 P.M. Sunday. Visa, MasterCard, American Express. Wheelchair accessible.*

LINCOLN STEFFENS'S HOME, CARMEL

SIGNIFICANT OTHERS

Significant Others includes places and restaurants that may not be on your normal travel pathways but which we think are worth going out of your way to experience.

ROBINSON JEFFERS'S HAWK TOWER
NEXT TO HIS TOR HOUSE, CARMEL

In the city of Carmel, we hope you will drive by the house Lincoln Steffens lived in, Robinson Jeffers's Tor House and Hawk Tower, the Carmel Mission, and Point Lobos (4 miles south on Highway 1). On your way to or from Point Lobos, you may also enjoy both the Barnyard and Crossroads shopping centers, just east of Highway 1 south of Carmel.

To view the home of muckraker, journalist, and philosopher Lincoln Steffens and his wife, Ella Winter, go down Ocean Avenue almost to the bottom (beach) and turn left on San Antonio Avenue. The Steffens home is the second house on the left and is privately owned. You can read the plaque in front, but please don't disturb the residents.

To get to Robinson Jeffers's **TOR HOUSE** south of Carmel Point the pretty way (it's all relative here), go toward the beach on Ocean (west), turn left (south) on Scenic Road, which will wind along the ocean, giving you gorgeously distracting views of both the Pacific and some of California's most expensive real estate. Eventually turn left on Stewart, and left again on Ocean View Avenue. Both Tor House and Jeffers's Hawk Tower will be on your left.

Enjoy dreaming of Jeffers building these stone by stone and the fascinating stories volunteer docents tell about every piece of pottery and artifacts from around the world brought by interesting characters to decorate Jeffers's home. The shop on the property is a great place to view rare Jeffers photos and purchase Clint Eastwood's video on Carmel, *Don't Pave Main Street* ($29.95). We would have brought it home gladly, but we don't know how to run our 12:00-flashing VCR! Jeffers's daughter-in-law, Lee Jeffers, still lives on the property.

We suggest you plan a visit around the garden party the first Sunday in May, or around the annual Tor House Festival Columbus Day weekend in October for the fascinating poetry walk.

🌿 *Tor House, 26304 Ocean View Avenue, Carmel 93921; (831) 624–1813 Monday–Thursday, (831) 624–1840 Friday–Saturday during tours. Open for tours by reservation only, every hour 10:00 A.M.–3:00 P.M., Friday–Saturday. Tour fee $7.00 adults, $4.00 college students, $2.00 high- and middle-school students (must be twelve or older to tour). No credit cards. Not wheelchair accessible.*

One of our favorite restaurant discoveries is **GRASING'S**, the brilliant combo effort of master chef and radio broadcaster Narsai David and Chef Kurt Grasing, right across from the Carmel Fire Station on Sixth Avenue near Mission Street.

Grasing used to cook at Narsai's Restaurant (in Kensington, California), David's best-ever restaurant, then opened 231 Ellsworth in San Mateo, and cooked at the Clift Hotel in San Francisco, the Pierre Hotel in New York, Le Gavroche in London, and Ventana in Big Sur. David brings a wealth of experience to this friendship cum partnership as a well-known restaurateur, editor, and columnist for television, radio, and newspapers. Together they offer a simple and impressive menu featuring fine coastal cuisine based on central coast harvests and the best local wines.

Grasing the chef and Grasing's the restaurant well deserve their awards as "Best Chef" and "Best New Restaurant" in an *Adventures in Dining* magazine readers' poll. Everything here is perfect: elegant and casual, perfectly served with informal timing, incorporating adventuresome tastes with comfortable familiarity, not to mention finest quality at reasonable prices. Can we say more?

Kathleen loves it that there are actually anchovies on the Caesar salad, which there should be but seldom are ($6.25, $9.50 with chicken). For a taste delight try the bronzed salmon salad with warm roasted potatoes, spinach, and lemon-caper-dill vinaigrette ($10.50), the perfect grilled salmon sandwich at lunch with fries, potato, or delightful corn salad ($10.25), medallions of pork with shiitake mushrooms, bacon, peas, and polenta ($18.50), roast rack of lamb "Narsai," marinated with pomegranate and red wine over ratatouille ($25.75), seared duck breast with figs, pearl onions, and star anise ($19.50), or grilled swordfish with baby bok choy, ponzu, and sesame aioli ($21.50). Kurt also offers a three-course prix fixe dinner daily.

Grasing's superior wine list offers chances to taste the best of Monterey Peninsula wines and some rare older California vintages. All of this and you can dine inside or on the heated patio. The owners also have just opened The Carmel Chop House at San Carlos and Fifth.

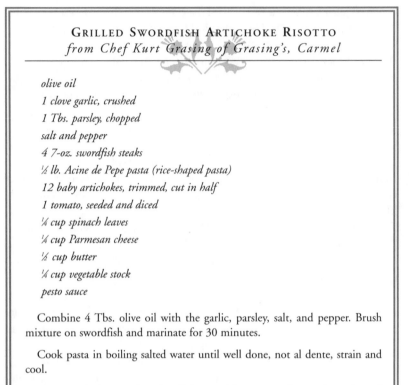

GRILLED SWORDFISH ARTICHOKE RISOTTO
from Chef Kurt Grasing of Grasing's, Carmel

olive oil

1 clove garlic, crushed

1 Tbs. parsley, chopped

salt and pepper

4 7-oz. swordfish steaks

½ lb. Acine de Pepe pasta (rice-shaped pasta)

12 baby artichokes, trimmed, cut in half

1 tomato, seeded and diced

¼ cup spinach leaves

¼ cup Parmesan cheese

½ cup butter

¼ cup vegetable stock

pesto sauce

Combine 4 Tbs. olive oil with the garlic, parsley, salt, and pepper. Brush mixture on swordfish and marinate for 30 minutes.

Cook pasta in boiling salted water until well done, not al dente, strain and cool.

Sauté artichokes in oil until well done. Add tomato and spinach; cook until spinach is wilted. Add cooked pasta, cheese, and butter risotto style (that is, stirring constantly). Add stock, if necessary.

Grill swordfish. Serve on top of risotto; drizzle with pesto sauce. Serves four.

❧ *Grasing's, Sixth Avenue ns near Mission, Carmel 93921; (831) 624–6562. Open 11:00 A.M.–10:00 P.M. daily. Beer and wine. Visa, MasterCard, American Express. Wheelchair accessible. Pets welcome outdoors, has heaters.*

A giant carved wood snail signals the driveway of **LOUTAS ON MISSION**, Kerry Loutas's hot new country French-American restaurant. Loutas is down a little driveway behind a small one-story professional building. Kerry spends the dinner hour in the dining room hosting you and serving his food, deftly crafted often by sous-chef Hans Starkweather.

Heavenly Prince Edward Island mussels, escargots ($7.00), smoked salmon with crème fraîche ($8.00), mouthwatering filet mignon ($24.00), chicken in black truffle Madeira sauce ($19.00), two-way duckling seared and roasted

($23.00), and bouillabaisse ($21.00) are among the delights you can expect without disappointment. You can also enjoy a prix fixe three-course dinner Sunday-Thursday for $24. Excellent local wine list. Run, don't walk.

❧ *Loutas on Mission, Mission ws between 4th and 5th, Carmel 93921; (831) 620-1942. Open 5:00–9:30 P.M. Sunday–Thursday, till 10:00 P.M. Friday–Saturday. Visa, MasterCard, American Express. Wine and beer. Wheelchair accessible.*

CREME CARMEL (not caramel) is down a little path in the Carmel Square courtyard between Ocean Avenue and Seventh. The teensy fourteen-table dining room truly makes you feel that you are in the special place that you are, with intimate music and a quiet, polite staff. The emphasis is definitely French but with the use of definitely California specialties, including rare Sonoma foie gras, Pacific salmon, and sliced breast of Sonoma duck. Entrees are mostly between $18 and $30. The wine list is worth the trip.

❧ *Creme Carmel, Carmel Square on San Carlos es between Ocean and Seventh, Carmel 93921; (831) 624–0444. Open for dinner from 5:30 P.M. Beer and wine. Visa, MasterCard, American Express, Diners Club, Discover, Carte Blanche. Wheelchair accessible.*

Heading south of Carmel on Highway 1, be sure to visit Carmel Mission, Point Lobos, and the Barnyard and Crossroads shopping centers.

We highly recommend that you visit CARMEL MISSION, whose formal name is Mission San Carlos Borromeo del Rio Carmelo. Majorca native Padre Junipero Serra, who founded nine missions while president general of the California Franciscans in the 1770s, is buried here. In 1961 Pope John XXIII designated the mission as a minor basilica, and in 1987 Pope John Paul II visited Carmel Mission to bless it and Father Serra.

To get to Carmel Mission either go down Ocean Avenue and turn left (south) on San Carlos Street, left (east) again on Thirteenth Avenue (which becomes Rio Road) to Lasuen, or take Highway 1 south and turn right (west) on Rio Road to Lasuen.

We guarantee that you will enjoy browsing around the gardens, courtyards, the church itself, historic rooms, and the shop of all religious shops.

❧ *Carmel Mission, Rio Road and Lasuen Drive, Carmel 93921; (831) 624–1271. Open 9:30 A.M.–4:30 P.M. Monday–Saturday, 10:00 A.M.–4:00 P.M. Sunday, September 1–May 31, 9:30 A.M.–7:30 P.M. June 1–August 31. Visa, MasterCard. Wheelchair accessible.*

Clint Eastwood's MISSION RANCH and THE RESTAURANT AT MISSION RANCH are somewhat quietly hidden down below Carmel Mission, on a cliff

MISSION SAN CARLOS BORROMEO DEL RIO CARMELO
(CARMEL MISSION)

over the Pacific Ocean. For now, enjoy the rocking-chair-on-the-porch atmosphere, the historic 1950s farmhouse, six tennis courts, a fitness facility, and the great restaurant with piano bar entertainment nightly. You can get here by taking Dolores south from downtown Carmel or wander around and around from the Mission. We recommend the former.

The original 160-acre ranch was owned by Jose Antonio Romero, former teacher and alcalde of Mission San Carlos Borromeo. In 1852 he deeded the property to William Curtis, a Monterey storekeeper, for a whopping $300, and the Marin family owned it for the next sixty years. When the Dienelt family owned the ranch, it was used as a private club and then as an officers' club for the Army and Navy during World War II, with the windows blackened to hide it from possible approaching Japanese ships. The ranch now has twenty-two acres, the rest having been sold to the Carmel School District and the State of California. Clint Eastwood bought the property in 1986 to save it from a condominium development, and since has had some development ideas himself.

Rooms range from $95 to $155 in the Farmhouse and Main Barn, and up to $275 in the Bunkhouse (some bunkhouse!).

The restaurant is open for dinner from 4:30 P.M. daily, and the Sunday Jazz Brunch from 9:30 A.M.-1:30 P.M. is a bargain at $21.95 for adults and $10.95 for children.

Dinner is casual and good, with appetizers such as baked goat cheese ($5.50), locally smoked salmon ($9.95), and quesadillas ($5.95). Try the unusual Dungeness crab soup ($6.95) or the "Wedge" of crisp iceberg lettuce with diced

THE FARMHOUSE AT CLINT EASTWOOD'S MISSION RANCH, CARMEL

tomatoes and blue cheese dressing ($5.50). Dinner itself may include king salmon ($15.95), swordfish ($19.95), an entree of Prince Edward Island mussels with tagliarini pasta and prawns ($15.85), house-smoked baby back ribs ($16.95), steaks, delicious blackened filet tips (when they are available, $16.50), and a couple of reasonable burgers and sandwiches.

✤ *Mission Ranch and* **The Restaurant at Mission Ranch**, *26270 Dolores Street, Carmel 93923; hotel (831) 624–6436 or (800) 538–8221, fax (831) 626–4163; restaurant (831) 625–9040, fax (531) 625-5502. Restaurant open from 4:00 P.M. Sunday–Friday, Saturday from 11:00 A.M., Sunday brunch 9:30 A.M.–1:30 P.M. Children's menu available. Full bar. Visa, MasterCard, Diners Club. Wheelchair accessible.*

Rio Road crosses Highway 1. On the east side of Highway 1 Rio Road takes you to both the Crossroads and Barnyard shopping centers. The **CROSSROADS** is a modern, jazzily polite shopping center with upscale restaurants, such as the Rio Grill and Chef Robert Kincaid's Bistro, as well as r.g. burgers and coffeehouses. There are also cooking, clothing, and home accessories shops, all of the finest quality. The only gas station in Carmel selling diesel gas is here also.

In contrast, the **BARNYARD** is a rustic, brown-shingled shopping center with an old-Carmel feeling—rather more like a little village than a mini-mall.

BIG SUR COASTLINE
Photo Courtesy Monterey Peninsula Visitor's
& Convention Bureau

Outdoor heated garden patios abound, with terraces and colorful flowerbeds creating a most pleasant and comforting atmosphere.

To get here, go east on Rio Road from Highway 1, turn left on Carmel Rancho Boulevard, and left again into the shopping center at the end of its own little road. Or turn left on Carmel Valley Road off Highway 1 and turn right on Carmel Rancho Boulevard.

Our personal favorite place here is **THUNDERBIRD INDEPENDENT BOOKSHOP AND THUNDERBIRD RESTAURANT**, a marvelously eclectic and useful bookshop with an excellent restaurant lined with the store's cookbook selections. We always stop at Carmel Valley Coffee Roasting Company for a mocha, but there are lots of other choices, including Allegro Gourmet Pizzeria (many Carmel residents' favorite pizza place), From Scratch Restaurant, Golden Buddha (for northern Chinese and Hunan cuisine), La Gondola Ristorante (Italian), Lugano Swiss Bistro, Pieces of Heaven handmade chocolates, Robata Grill and Sake Bar, Sherlock Holmes Pub, and the newish Polo Club, another in the Carmel group created by Csaba Ajan. This Polo Club, and its Polo Lounge are not related to Polo Clubs in other cities and countries.

Many other shops keep locals supplied with interesting cookware, jewelry, clothing, antiques, and artwork. This is where Carmelites shop.

Don't miss the Barnyard's annual wine festival, usually the second weekend in September.

BIG SUR

Big Sur, the dramatically beautiful, wild and lonely seacoast 28 miles south of Carmel on Highway 1, takes its name from the river that runs through it to the ocean, *El Rio Grande del Sur,* "Big River of the South." In the 1840s Governor Juan Bautista Alvarado owned the land grant and sold it to English trader (and Vallejo in-law) William Cooper. Cooper used Rancho Sur for cattle raising and smuggling to avoid American import taxes, but Mrs. Cooper refused to live there. Early American settlers included sailor William Post in 1859, followed by homesteaders Michael and Barbara Pfeiffer, who built a house here in 1869.

Gradually others followed, including David Castro and his wife, Amadia Vasquez, sister of notorious bandit Tiburcio Vasquez, who hid out at the Castro ranch between holdups. Until 1881 only a rugged trail meandered to the area from Monterey. Then local residents, led by Post, personally scraped out a road with a generous appropriation of $200 in county funds. Ranching had replaced smuggling as the principal business and the scattered population had grown sufficiently to support the practice of a young physician, Dr. John Roberts, who settled in Big Sur in 1881 after trying out Monterey for six months. By 1913, prodded by Dr. Roberts, the county built an improved road.

In 1934 Pfeiffer family descendants donated large tracts for state parks, which were later expanded. State Highway 1 down the coast came through Big Sur in 1937, giving it decent communication with the rest of the world. Poet Robinson Jeffers and members of the Carmel writers colony took an interest in the south coast in the early decades of this century, but none settled permanently, until iconoclastic writer Henry Miller arrived in the 1940s.

On the right side of the highway about 28 miles south of Carmel is NEPENTHE, a world-famous restaurant, with great views of the ocean from its deck, which began life as the hideaway of actor-director Orson Welles and his movie star wife, Rita Hayworth, in 1944. In 1949 it became a restaurant, worth a stop for a leisurely lunch. Call (831) 667-2245. Just behind the parking lot is CAFE KEVAH, (831) 667-2344, for a light meal, and THE PHOENIX SHOP, (831) 667-2347, for gifts and locally produced art.

For accommodations of a special nature—in a natural habitat—the choices are choice: **BIG SUR RIVER INN** has the Big Sur River running through its grounds and offers popular meals, (831) 667–2700; **POST RANCH INN**, opened in 1992, was built with stunning architecture and use of wood, stone, and glass, (831) 667–2200; **VENTANA RESORT** in the woods, (831) 667–2331; **DEETJEN'S BIG SUR INN** is a B&B in Norwegian style, (831) 667–2574.

Lovers of Henry Miller's work, or occasional literati, should visit the **HENRY MILLER LIBRARY**, 31 miles south of Carmel, at Graves Canyon on the east side of Highway 1. Lovingly established and maintained by Miller's longtime friend Emil White, the little library is loaded with Miller memorabilia. It is open every day except Monday at somewhat varying hours. Call (831) 667–2574. If that is not enough Miller, try the **HENRY MILLER GALLERY**, 33 miles south of Carmel, behind the **COAST GALLERY & CAFE** (interesting local art). Loaded with Miller pictures and books, both are housed in a giant water tank structure. For both, call (831) 667–2301.

Drive down to the village of Big Sur to appreciate the lifestyle of those whose love of the wild coast has drawn them here to stay. To breathe in the nature of the south coast, several parks are available: **ANDREW MOLERA STATE PARK**, 21 miles south of Carmel; **PFEIFFER BIG SUR STATE PARK**, 31 miles, and **JULIA PFEIFFER BURNS STATE PARK**, 37 miles (see Parks in "List of Lists"). All are well equipped for camping and hiking.

Finally, 41 miles south of Carmel is the world-famous **ESALEN INSTITUTE** aimed at the full development of "human potential." There are spas, baths, and saunas as well as workshops, discussions, and other valuable activities. Founded by Michael Murphy (who served with Jerry on the elected executive committee of Associated Students at Stanford umpteen years ago) in the 60s, Esalen attracts thousands of visitors each year, including business and public leaders who seek to recharge their personal batteries. Reservations are a must. Call (831) 667–3000.

You can continue south on twisting Highway 1 to Hearst Castle (San Simeon) or head back to Carmel and Monterey.

CHAPTER 5

SANTA CRUZ AND SOUTH

• Santa Cruz Area Wineries • Other Attractions in Santa Cruz • Soquel and Capitola • Aptos • Watsonville, Elkhorn Slough, and Moss Landing • Castroville • Marina, Seaside, and Sand City

*S*anta Cruz may be known as the ultimate Surf City U.S.A. but there really is more there there, to paraphrase Gertrude Stein's comment about Oakland.

Locals of Santa Cruz and its surrounding area include winemakers, software engineers who commute to the Silicon Valley, business and professional people, restaurateurs, university students and professors at University of California's freest campus (for its first several years no grades were given), artists, writers, and, of course, surfers and those who cater to every imaginable whim of surfers and surfer groupies.

Santa Cruz and Santa Cruz Mountain communities have suffered drastically and recovered admirably from two horrible earthquakes. The first, in 1791, destroyed Mission La Exaltacion de la Santa Cruz and much of the rest of the pueblo. The Loma Prieta earthquake of 1989 destroyed much of downtown Santa Cruz, as well as less-than-sturdy buildings from San Francisco to the north to Aptos to the south.

But somehow we visit Santa Cruz and never think of earthquakes. The distractions are too great: gorgeous Victorian homes; the sprawling white Cowell Beach; the just-up-from-the-county-fair Boardwalk with its Big Dipper, cotton candy, and T-shirt shops; the glitzy Coconut Grove ballroom; and loads of local artists' galleries. Santa Cruz Municipal Wharf has ten traditional restaurants and events, and eight gift and souvenir shops, as well as boat charters and kayak and boat rentals.

To get here, follow Highway 1 along the Pacific Coast, or take Highway 17 Southwest from Highway 101.

Santa Cruz is the northern gateway to the Monterey Bay Marine Sanctuary, which results in terrific whale watching between November and April when the huge mammals make their annual round-trip between Alaska and Mexico. For a fabulous marine learning experience, visit **SAVE OUR SHORES** at Santa Cruz Harbor. You might enjoy the interpretive center's *Hunting for Habitats* exhibit, view a marine-related video, or browse through the small resource library dedicated to marine education, research, and environmental policy. Save Our Shores is dedicated to preserving the coastal and marine environment of the Monterey Bay National Marine Sanctuary.

➴ *Save Our Shores, 135 Fifth Avenue (at Santa Cruz Harbor), Santa Cruz 95062; (831) 462-5660; e-mail sos@cruzio.com. Open when they are there. Wheelchair accessible.*

The **SANTA CRUZ HARBOR** itself, not to be confused with Santa Cruz wharf at the north end of the beach, offers free water taxis, self-guided walking tours, boat rentals and charters from among the 1,200 boats docked here, repairs and supplies, a boat launch ramp, several environmental learning experiences, RV spaces, and fun restaurants. On Wednesday evenings during daylight saving time, you might even get on as part of a pickup sailing crew during Santa Cruz's weekly sailing races.

➴ *Santa Cruz Harbor, 135 Fifth Avenue, Santa Cruz 95062; (831) 475–6161. Open daily 8:30 A.M.–5:00 P.M.*

At **LIGHTHOUSE POINT** north and west of Cowell Beach and the Boardwalk, you can visit the country's first surfing museum in the lighthouse. The beach here is surf central, the location of Santa Cruz County's most famous surf spot, "Steamer Lane."

➴ *Lighthouse Point, West Cliff Drive, Santa Cruz 95062; (831) 459–4308.*

SANTA CRUZ AREA WINERIES

The Santa Cruz Mountains first gained notice as a premium wine-producing region in the late 1800s, but few traces of those wineries exist because of Prohibition (1920–1933). The federal government recognized Santa Cruz Mountains Viticultural Appellation in 1981, making it one of the first American viticultural areas to be defined by geophysical and climatic factors.

The appellation encompasses the Santa Cruz Mountain range from Half Moon Bay in the north to Mount Madonna in the south. The east and west boundaries are defined by elevation, extending down to 800 feet in the east and 400 feet in the west. Microclimates created by the mountain terrain, marine influences such as mist and fog, distinctive soils, and low crop levels all con-

tribute to resulting intensely concentrated fruit, low yields, and specially selected handcrafted wines.

Most of the wineries are family-
owned and small compared to those
in the Sonoma and Napa Valleys,
with many attached or adjacent to
the family home.

The most convenient Santa
Cruz winery to visit is **STORRS
WINERY** in the Old Sash Mill right
downtown. From Highway 1 take
River Street south and turn right on
Portrero Street to the Old Sash Mill.
Co-winemaker and co-owner Steve
Storrs is also winemaker for Scheid
Vineyards in Greenfield, southeast
of Carmel Valley.

STORRS' GRILLED SALMON
from Pamela and Steve Storrs, Storrs Winery, Santa Cruz

---

1 salmon fillet
olive oil
honey mustard
2 Tbs. fresh or dried dill

Brush salmon fillet with olive oil on the skin side. Spread honey mustard evenly on flesh side of fillet. Sprinkle with fresh or dried dill. Grill skin side down over hot coals till done, about 5 minutes.

Both Pamela and Steve Storrs are graduates in enology from University of California, Davis, and Steve has an additional degree in viticulture. Together and separately they have apprenticed in Burgundian wineries and worked at several of California's best-known, including Domaine Chandon in Yountville.

The Storrses young sons ride the tractors and trucks during harvest time, which Pamela refers to as "a very Zen time of year when you live by the rhythm of the grapes. It also signals a time of rebirth for winemakers, even more so than spring."

They use only hand-harvested fruit and employ *méthodes anciennes* (barrel fermentation) for Chardonnays and open-topped vats with extended macera-tion for the red wines. As a result, *San Francisco Chronicle* Food Editor Michael Bauer calls Storrs Vanumanutagi Vineyard Chardonnay "the closest thing to a Grand Cru Chablis I've found in California." Their 1994 Santa Cruz Mountains Petite Sirah won the Best of Show Award at the 1996 California State Fair, other vintages having won "Best Varietal of the Region (Greater Bay Area)" and "Best of Wine Region."

The story of the vineyards that the Storrses lease goes like this. After Robert Louis Stevenson died in Samoa, his widow returned to the Monterey Bay area and named the overall ranch Vanumanutagi Ranch, Samoan for "Vale of the Singing Birds." She also named the vineyards planted on the ranch after her husband's books, Treasure Island (Chardonnay), Kidnapped (Petite Sirah), and Jekyll & Hyde, which Pam Storrs says "are as different as night and day."

Fine points: Featured wines: Chardonnay, Petite Sirah, Zinfandel. Owners: Pam and Steve Storrs. Winemakers: Pam and Steve Storrs. Cases: 9,000. Acres: 24 (leased from Scheid Vineyards).

❧ *Storrs Winery, Old Sash Mill, 303 Potrero Street, No. 35, Santa Cruz 95060; (831) 458–5030. Open noon–5:00 P.M. Friday–Monday. No tasting fee. Visa, MasterCard, American Express. Wheelchair accessible.*

A visit to Storrs Winery will also introduce you to the whole Sash Mill complex, once the Sinkinson Sash Mill. While it's on the other side of the tracks from mainline Santa Cruz, you can sit in a cafe and watch the Suntan Special roll in from Roaring Camp and browse through artists' studios and shops dedicated to water sports.

The pride and joy of three generations of the Italian immigrant Bargetto family, **BARGETTO WINERY** has two tasting rooms, one in Soquel at the winery and one on Cannery Row in Monterey. Since you are in the Santa Cruz area, let's visit the Soquel one.

Bargetto Winery is south of Santa Cruz proper near Soquel, offering a much different experience from the coziness of Storrs. To get here from Highway 1, take the Porter Street/Bay Avenue Exit, head east (toward the hills) for a half block, and turn right on Main Street. Continue on Main for 1 mile to the winery.

Lots of greenery on the outside, rich woods in the tasting room, and an art gallery showcasing regional artists set the tone for a fun experience. Bargetto, which opened in 1933, is the oldest California winery producing Santa Cruz Mountains wines.

Bargetto offers tours on weekdays at 11:00 A.M. and 2:00 P.M.; tours are available on weekends by reservation. The family also serves occasional summer brunches in the winery's courtyard, sponsors an artists' weekend (the third in August) at which thirty artists exhibit their work outdoors, merging fine art with food and wine, and hosts a holiday festival featuring handcrafted gifts and wine specials in the cellar.

Fine points: Featured wines: Bargetto Chardonnay, Pinot Noir, Cabernet Sauvignon, Merlot, Gewürztraminer; Chaucer's Mead, Ollallieberry, Raspberry, Apricot. Owners: The Bargetto family. Winemaker: Paul Wofford. Cases: 35,000. Acres: 29.

❧ *Bargetto Winery, 3535 North Main Street, Soquel 95073; (831) 475–2258, fax (831) 475–2664. Open 9:00 A.M.–5:00 P.M. Monday–Saturday, 11:00 A.M.–5:00 P.M. Sunday. Visa, MasterCard, American Express, Diners Club. Wheelchair accessible.*

For a delightfully eclectic and eccentric personal and wine experience, you must visit **BONNY DOON VINEYARD**. To get to the "enchanted kingdom of Bonny Doon," go 8 miles north of Santa Cruz on Highway 1 and take Bonny Doon Road for 3.7 miles—"a first-rate meandering country road that will take you through apple orchards, a redwood forest, and deposit you on our doorstep at 10 Pine Flat Road." Pine Flat Road turns left (northwest) from Bonny Doon at Bonny Doon Winery. Watch for the appropriately rustic tasting room building in the trees, and enjoy picnic tables in the redwood grove alongside Mill Creek, which runs beside the winery.

Randall Grahm, the "Mad Genius" and original "Rhone Ranger" of wine, follows his own quirky instincts, does exactly what he wants and not what others expect him to do, and creates wines that led others to call him crazy and nuts. Until they started to follow him.

Grahm attended what he calls "Uncle Charlie's Summer Camp," more widely known as the University of California, Santa Cruz, where he was "a permanent liberal arts major." Serving next as a confessed floor sweeper at the Wine Merchant in Beverly Hills, Grahm's incidental exposure to French wines turned him into a "complete and insufferable wine fanatic." After finishing the viticulture program at University of California, Davis, in 1979, he began to work out his obsession with Pinot Noir.

With his family's help Grahm bought and planted his vineyard in 1981, establishing the Lilliputian Bonny Doon wine facility in 1983. Deciding that coastal California was more suited to Mediterranean-type wines made in the Rhone style, especially varieties such as Marsanne, Roussanne, Syrah, Grenache, Mourvedre, and Cinsault, he soon switched to the less commonplace Rhone varietals.

GRILLED PEACHES WITH RASPBERRY PUREE
from Randall Grahm, Bonny Doon Vineyard, Bonny Doon

½ (10 oz.) pkg. frozen raspberries, slightly thawed

1½ tsp. lemon juice

¼ cup Fraise or Framboise

1½ tsp. brown sugar

¼ tsp. ground cinnamon

2 medium peaches, peeled, halved and pitted

1½ tsp. butter

Combine raspberries, lemon juice, and Fraise in food processor until smooth. Strain puree to remove seeds. Cover and chill. Combine brown sugar and cinnamon; spoon into center of each peach half. Dot with butter. Place peach halves on grill over medium coals and cook until heated thoroughly. To serve, spoon puree over each peach half. Serves two to four.

Be sure to try Bonny Doon's dessert wines, a type usually made in cooler climates. His Vin de Glacière, known as ice wine/eiswein and made from frozen-on-the-vine grapes elsewhere, is made by putting his grapes in a freezer before crushing. Oohh noooo!

Bonny Doon has developed a new 105-acre vineyard and winery in Pleasanton near Livermore southeast of Berkeley/Oakland.

Even if you don't like Rhones, you have to go to Bonny Doon just for the fun of it. Be sure to get on its newsletter mailing list to receive Grahm's hilariously stimulating wine-food-arts-literature epistles. Join the D.E.W.N. (Distinctive Esoteric Wine Network) by calling (831) 426–4518.

Fine points: Featured wines: Vin Gris de Cigare (thinking person's pink wine), Le Sophiste (Roussanne/Marsanne mélange), Clos de Gilroy (Grenache), Le Cigare Volant (Cryptoneuf-due-Pape or Chateauneuf du Pape), Cardinal Zin, Old Telegram (Mourvedre), Syrah (strong pink), Big House Red, Il Fiasco, and Ca' del Solo label Bloody Good Red, Malvasia Bianca, Il Pescatore, Barbera, Charbono, Grappa, Bonny Doon Cassis, Framboise, Muscat Vin Glaciere, Moscato del Solo, and Grappa del Fiasco. Owner: Randall Grahm. Winemaker: Randall Grahm. Cases: 145,000. Acres: 150.

❧ *Bonny Doon Vineyard, 10 Pine Flat Road, Bonny Doon 95060; (831) 425–3625, fax (831) 425–3856; e-mail bonnydoon@worldnet.att.net; www.bonnydoonvineyard.com. Open noon–5:00 P.M. daily April 1–September 15, Wednesday–Monday September 15–April 1. No tasting fee. Visa, MasterCard. Wheelchair accessible.*

Other Attractions in Santa Cruz

If you're not into surfing or hanging out on the Boardwalk, you might enjoy a few other attractions in Santa Cruz County, including the Antonelli Brothers Begonia Gardens, Casino Fun Center, Gizdich Ranch, Long Marine Laboratory and Aquarium, Mystery Spot, Neptune's Kingdom, and the Roaring Camp & Santa Cruz Big Trees Railroads, as well as the many art galleries downtown.

Santa Cruz's **Casino Fun Center** is a mecca for virtual realists who enjoy Sector 7 Laser Tag Arena, Virtual Link virtual reality, and arcade games. You can enjoy Daytona 500 racing, Gallazian Theatre, a "shooting gallery," food concessions, and loud noise.

❧ *Casino Fun Center, 400 Beach Street, Santa Cruz 95060; (831) 423–5590; www.beachboardwalk.com. Open 11:00 A.M.–7:00 P.M. daily beginning Memorial*

Day, 11:00 A.M.–11:00 P.M. daily July–Labor Day, 11:00 A.M.–7:00 P.M. weekends in winter. Visa, MasterCard, and Discover cards for purchases only. Wheelchair accessible.

For an exciting and tamed natural wonder experience, try the LONG MARINE LABORATORY AND AQUARIUM at University of California, Santa Cruz, where you can touch live sea anemones, sea stars, and hermit crabs. View an 85-foot whale skeleton, sea lions, and dolphins.

❧ *Long Marine Laboratory and Aquarium, University of California, Santa Cruz, 100 Shaffer Road, Santa Cruz 95064; (831) 459–3854. Open 1:00–4:00 P.M. Tuesday–Sunday. Admission: adults $2.00, seniors and students $1.00, children and anyone on first Tuesdays free. Visa and MasterCard. Wheelchair accessible.*

While you're visiting the UC/Santa Cruz campus, don't miss the world famous ARBORETUM to see its plant collections from Australia, South Africa, and New Zealand. You can even buy drought-tolerant plants.

❧ *University of California, Santa Cruz Arboretum, 1156 High Street, Santa Cruz 95064; (831) 427–2998. Open 9:00 A.M.–5:00 P.M. daily, plant sales 10:00 A.M.–4:00 P.M. Tuesday–Saturday, 1:00–4:00 P.M. Sunday. Free admission. Visa, MasterCard, American Express. Wheelchair accessible.*

MISSION SANTA CRUZ is a 1931 half-size replica of the original built in 1791 (where the nearby Holy Cross Church stands now), but it is still worth seeing. The original, which was destroyed in 1857, was the twelfth mission built in California. The mission's Galleria gift shop features interesting period antiques and gifts representing California's Spanish and Native American heritages.

❧ *Mission Santa Cruz, 196 High Street, Santa Cruz; (831) 426–5686. Chapel open 9:00 A.M.–5:00 P.M. daily, Galleria gift shop open 10:00 A.M.–4:00 P.M. Tuesday–Saturday, 10:00 A.M.–2:00 P.M. Sunday. No admission fee. Mostly wheelchair accessible.*

For leather lovers, the A. K. SALTZ TANNERY is a real treat. Walk in and inhale that mouthwatering leather smell! Wow! Saltz has been the largest tannery west of the Mississippi since 1865, and makes the finest leather goods right here. You can even take a tour if you call ahead, and don't miss the store.

❧ *A. K. Saltz Tannery, 1040 River Street, Santa Cruz 95060; (831) 460–3434. Open 10:00 A.M.–5:00 P.M. Monday–Saturday, tours Monday–Friday. Visa, MasterCard, Discover. Wheelchair accessible.*

The **MYSTERY SPOT** is a spookily freaky spot discovered in the Santa Cruz redwoods in 1940 where you can consciously experience gravity, balance, perception, height, and light all seeming to be reversed. Balls roll uphill! Thirty-five-minute guided tours leave every fifteen minutes.

To reach the Mystery Spot, take Ocean Avenue off Highway 1 and follow signs. (If you're on Highway 17 as you arrive in Santa Cruz, it becomes Ocean Avenue.)

Mystery Spot, 1953 North Branciforte Drive, Santa Cruz 95065; (831) 423–8897. Open 9:00 A.M.–8:00 P.M. summer, 9:00 A.M.–5:00 P.M. winter. Visa and MasterCard in gift shop only, not for tours. Partly wheelchair accessible.

One of the most interesting and thrilling non-Boardwalk things to do in the Santa Cruz area is to ride the Santa Cruz Big Trees & Pacific Railway and the Roaring Camp & Big Trees Narrow-Gauge Railroad.

The **SANTA CRUZ BIG TREES & PACIFIC RAILWAY COMPANY** travels from the original 1891 Southern Pacific Felton depot to the 1893 Santa Cruz Union depot. You experience 1900 and 1930s passenger diesel trains for the two-and-a-half-hour excursion through dense forests of native flora and fauna on the Suntan Special to Roaring Camp, Big Trees, the Garden of Eden, Rincon, and Sashmill—the ride includes hanging 150 feet directly over the river below. In Santa Cruz you cruise by Victorian homes right down to the carousel and arcade at the Boardwalk.

On the **ROARING CAMP & BIG TREES NARROW-GAUGE RAILROAD**'s historic steam passenger train you ride for an hour to Bear Mountain via one of the steepest railroad grades in North America. After leaving from the old-fashioned depot in the tiny crossroads town of Roaring Camp, you pass through dense redwood forests, Big Trees, Indian Creek, Grizzly Flats, Deer Valley, and one of the most drastic switchbacks in North America via Spring Canyon and Hallelujah Junction. Once you're atop Bear Mountain, you can get off and picnic, returning to Roaring Camp on a later train. You might want to indulge in the railroad's Chuckwagon Bar-B-Q under the trees, featuring three kinds of steak, chicken, ribs, and apple cider from a nearby cider mill for a charge of $5.00–$15.00, depending on your choice of entree.

Roaring Camp & Big Trees Narrow-Gauge Railroad, P. O. Box G-1, Felton 95018; (831) 335–4484; fax (831) 335–3509; e-mail Rcamp448@aol.com; www.roaringcamprr.com. Open 11:00 A.M.–4:00 P.M. daily in summer, weekends in winter. Visa, MasterCard, Discover only at Roaring Camp (no credit cards if boarding on the Boardwalk). Roaring Camp & Big Trees Narrow-Gauge Railroad is accessible for three wheelchairs; the Santa Cruz Big Trees & Pacific Railway is not accessible.

For your dining pleasure, we will highlight a few Santa Cruz restaurants. Most winemakers and romantics favor **CASABLANCA**, a historic and elegant 1920s estate that is now an inn and restaurant high above bustling downtown Santa Cruz. Sunset and dusk from the gleaming dining room can be exquisite in good weather. Four hundred wines, both California and imported, augment chef Scott Cater's creative local cuisine, which features seafoods, rack of lamb, classic grilled duck, and smoked salmon. Pastas with fresh seafood—some even without cream—are masterly. We especially like the excellent Dijon vinaigrette salad dressing. Desserts range from healthy to worth-the-splurge pastries.

Casablanca, 101 Main Street, Santa Cruz 95060; (831) 426–9063. Open from 5:30 P.M. daily, Sunday brunch. Full bar. Visa, MasterCard, American Express, Diners Club. Barely wheelchair accessible.

Right along the beach at Santa Cruz Harbor, the **CROW'S NEST** is a great spot to view the yacht harbor and Wednesday evening sailing races. Locals flock here, and many head straight upstairs to the bar for meeting and greeting, live music and dancing on weekends, and the oyster bar. Downstairs wall-to-wall windows give great views to accompany the excellent local fish right off the nearby dock or the aged midwestern corn-fed beef and fabulous salads. Children are welcomed, with their own menu to prove it.

Crow's Nest, 2218 East Cliff Drive, Santa Cruz 95062; (831) 476–4560. Open for lunch and dinner daily. Full bar. Visa, MasterCard, American Express, Diners Club, Discover. Wheelchair accessible.

The **BEACH STREET CAFE** right across the street from the Coconut Grove features a gallery of original Maxfield Parrish paintings and a dining room of good, clean food to warm the senses at breakfast and lunch.

Beach Street Cafe, 399 Beach Street, Santa Cruz 95060; (831) 426–7621. Open 8:00 A.M.–3:00 P.M. daily. Beer and wine. Visa, MasterCard, American Express, Discover. Wheelchair accessible.

BLACK'S BEACH CAFE is the baby of Santa Cruz native and California Culinary Institute–trained Robert Morris, who does an excellent job merging his local roots, foreign travels, and culinary training into extremely satisfying meals. Morris uses local ingredients almost exclusively in many dishes with Pacific Rim influences. Since we are ahi tuna fans, we love his many choices of preparations, from salads and sandwiches to entrees. The huge sandwiches are for even the most active surfers as well as gourmands, so be hungry. There's outdoor seating facing the beach.

❧ *Black's Beach Cafe, 1 Fifth Avenue and East Cliff Drive, Santa Cruz 95060; (831) 475–2233. Open for dinner 5:00–9:00 P.M. Tuesday–Sunday, for breakfast and lunch 9:00 A.M.–2:00 P.M. Saturday–Sunday. Beer and wine. Visa, MasterCard, American Express. Wheelchair accessible.*

Downtown Santa Cruz is cheek to jowl with pubs and clubs featuring music of all genres (swing to funk, folk to hip-hop, jazz to salsa). Try a tour of Pacific Avenue, Front, Beach, and River Streets.

Food fans will definitely enjoy the fresh local produce at the **DOWNTOWN FARMERS MARKET** of Santa Cruz at the corner of Cedar and Lincoln Streets from 2:30 to 6:30 P.M. Wednesdays rain or shine. Local flowers (!), vegetables, fruits, eggs, honey, seafoods, cheeses, and olive oils abound.

Santa Cruz's unique festivals humor and entertain visitors of many tastes, from its Fungus Fair in January featuring wild varieties of mushrooms (not wild mushrooms) to the Clam Chowder Cook-off on the Boardwalk in February. Then there's the Burrito Bash in June and India Joze's International Calamari Festival in August. The Aloha Outrigger Races and Polynesian Festival take place in August on the municipal wharf, and thousands of people run the Wharf Race between the Santa Cruz and Capitola wharves in July.

SOQUEL AND CAPITOLA

Once separate and very independent communities, Soquel, Capitola, and Santa Cruz have spread their borders and now run into each other, although none has lost its identity.

Both Soquel and Capitola are easily reached from well-marked exits off Highway 1. Soquel borders Santa Cruz on the east side of Highway 1, and Capitola touches it along the beach to the south of Santa Cruz proper. Parking can be a problem in all of these communities, which is why we prefer to visit them in the off-season, that is, well after Labor Day and well before Memorial Day.

What Soquel loses to Capitola in beaches, it makes up in antiques stores, housing loads of dealers along its Soquel Drive and side streets. Antiques fans should make a point to find their way over here.

Capitola, on the other hand, has an extremely well-scaled small artful village right down at the beach, as well as shopping centers and malls on the land side of the world. Dating from 1869 as Camp Capitola, the village is logically located where Soquel Creek flows (when it flows) into the Pacific Ocean at Capitola Beach. The beach itself is popular with locals and visitors, partly because it lacks Santa Cruz's extreme glitz, partly because the waves and people are a little quieter than they are in Santa Cruz, and partly because of its children's beach and the nearby shops, galleries, and trendy, interesting restaurants adjoining the beach's esplanade. ZELDA'S (831–475–4900) restaurant patio runs onto the beach and serves surprisingly good hamburgers and fish sandwiches, while MARGARITAVILLE (831–476–2263) swings with margaritas and Mexican food evoking Jimmy Buffett's memories.

Professional and home gardeners won't want to miss the ANTONELLI BROTHERS BEGONIA GARDENS, between Santa Cruz and Capitola, featuring the bright colors of tuberous begonias, fuchsias, ferns, and other shade plants. Antonelli's produces more begonia seed than any nursery in the world, with peak show months in August and September.

❧ *Antonelli Brothers Begonia Gardens, 2545 Capitola Road, Santa Cruz 95062; (831) 475–5222. Open 9:00 A.M.–5:00 P.M. daily April–October. Visa and MasterCard. Partly wheelchair accessible.*

For an unusual festival experience (something Santa Cruz County seems to specialize in), try the CAPITOLA BEGONIA FESTIVAL in September, during which little floats covered with thousands of colorful begonias glide down Soquel Creek. Usually works of art and hilarious ingenuity, the floats have to fit under the Stockton Bridge, which allows only about a 9-foot clearance. Some floats are rigged to duck under the bridge in a limbolike gesture, occasionally sabotaged by friendly rival teams, or weighted down by wet onlookers who jump onto the floats to sink them enough to fit under the bridge. Check out the sand castle building contest too.

You may also want to plan a visit around the CAPITOLA ART & WINE FESTIVAL, usually the second weekend in September, to enjoy great food from local restaurants, fine wines from Santa Cruz Mountain vintners, music, arts and crafts (831–475–6522).

Capitola's waterfront has restaurants for every taste, from Asian to take-away fish and chips, to sports bars with hamburgers and California seafood specialties.

Nearly everyone's favorite restaurant and hangout with great food in Capitola is GAYLE'S BAKERY AND ROSTICCERIA. Joe and Gayle Ortiz turn out some of the most delightful breads, cakes, tarts, and croissants anywhere. You actually have to take a number, but who cares? Wait with an excellent espresso or glass of wine and your dreams. We especially like the oak-roasted chicken and fabulous salads, while others prefer hearty vegetarian dishes and fabulous breakfasts. Dine here indoors or out on the heated patio, or take your favorites back to your hotel or to the beach.

❧ *Gayle's Bakery and Rosticceria, 504 Bay Avenue, Capitola 95010; (831) 462–1200. Open 6:30 A.M.–8:30 P.M. daily. Beer and wine. Visa, MasterCard. Wheelchair accessible.*

One of everyone's favorite newer discoveries in Capitola is the **OSTRICH GRILL**, selected "Best New Restaurant" in a local poll and given *Wine Spectator's* Award of Excellence. The wood-fired grill turns out terrific chicken, steaks, pizzas, pastas, and local seafood.

❧ *Ostrich Grill, 820 Bay Avenue, Capitola 95010; (831) 477–9181. Open for lunch 11:30 A.M.–2:00 P.M. Monday–Friday, and dinner nightly. Full bar. Visa, MasterCard, American Express, Diners Club, Discover. Partly wheelchair accessible.*

SHADOWBROOK RESTAURANT has been called "Northern California's Most Romantic Restaurant" by *San Francisco Focus* magazine and by the *San Jose Mercury News*, and for good reason. The setting and gardens are meticulously managed and manicured, as are the service and food. You might want to wander down from the road to the restaurant past dripping waterfalls and gardens that make you take a deep breath and enjoy the peaceful moment. Then on your way out of the restaurant, you can ride Shadowbrook's famous cable car back up to the road. Or you can ride both ways or walk both ways. Comforting ivy and other vines trim the building.

Heavy stone walls, a romantic fireplace, beamed ceilings with enormous glass windows, and a deck overlooking Soquel Creek set the tone in which to admire Chef Tom Grego's California cuisine with the freshest local seafood. Locals come regularly for their fixes of prime rib with horseradish sour cream sauce (reminiscent of our mothers' Sunday dinners), as well as fresh pastas and hearty salads. Visit the bar upstairs or enjoy a selection from the excellent wine list at your table.

❧ *Shadowbrook Restaurant, 1750 Wharf Road at Capitola Road, Capitola 95010; (831) 475–1511. Open for dinner daily, Sunday brunch. Full bar. Visa, MasterCard, American Express, Carte Blanche, Discover, Diners Club. Wheelchair accessible.*

APTOS

Kathleen used to spend weeks at a time on Aptos's private beach while staying with her parents in an architect's home, strolling alone along the water and watching an occasional Japanese fisherman. Today the beach is gated and fenced in. (How can individuals or homeowners' associations *own* parts of our country's coast?) But there is public beach available nearby, thank heavens.

In the fifties Aptos village was all there was; but now you have to look for it between the shopping centers. To find it, if you can, take the Rio Del Mar Boulevard exit off Highway 1 and turn left at Soquel Drive. While making this trip, you might see a wee cloud of steam rising as long-toed salamanders breed away in a swamp. Local enviromentalists stopped plans to widen the freeway here because the new addition would have disturbed the salamanders. Now the deeds of neighboring properties actually include salamander easements to guarantee their lifestyle and lives!

You may want to visit nearby **FOREST OF NISENE MARKS STATE PARK**, a 10,000-acre preserve of second-growth redwood trees. You can get there by taking Aptos Creek Road next to Aptos Station (near the Bayview Hotel). Bike racks make hiking and biking compatible adventures in the park, which was the epicenter of the 1989 Loma Prieta earthquake that devastated parts of Aptos as well as many buildings throughout Santa Cruz County and way beyond.

❧ *Forest of Nisene Marks State Park, 201 Sunset Beach Road, Watsonville 95076; (831) 763–7062. Open from dawn to dusk.*

In Aptos notice the huge, one-hundred-year-old magnolia tree and its protector, the restored Bayview Hotel. The nearby Village Fair with its multitude of antiques shops and soda fountain fill what was once the local apple-packing plant.

Right across from the hotel, try the **CAFE SPARROW**, whose sandwiches and salads at lunch attract locals over and over, and whose dinner menu reminds us of the hearty fifties when we first went to Aptos. Super filet mignon, venison from New Zealand, grilled chicken perfectly done, fried or sautéed breaded oysters, and all the cholesterol you could ever dream of made irresistible.

Recipient of the *Wine Spectator's* "Award of Excellence" and voted "Best Restaurant" by the local *Good Times* readers' poll, Cafe Sparrow is a must try.

❧ *Cafe Sparrow, 8042 Soquel Drive, Aptos 95003; (831) 688–6238. Open for breakfast and lunch 8:00 A.M.–2:00 P.M. Monday–Saturday, dinner 5:30–9:00 P.M. daily, Sunday brunch 9:00 A.M.–2:00 P.M. Beer and wine. Visa, MasterCard. Wheelchair accessible.*

Another don't-miss in the Aptos area is **CHEZ RENEE**, the baby of Jack and Renee Chyle, both graduates of California Culinary Academy in San Francisco. The elegant, soft pinkish peach dining room is reminiscent of Claude Rouas's late L'Etoile in San Francisco's Huntington Hotel or of Anton & Michel in Carmel. This elegance is tempered with casual comfort, combined as it is with a colorful patio just outside the dining room.

Renee entertains everyone with her charm, which keeps locals and visitors returning in droves. She and Jack have owned this fine restaurant since 1983, so they should be around for a while.

French influences show in the excellent wine list, which also features some of Monterey's and Santa Cruz's finest, as well as in the subtle sauces combining fruits and wines, especially remarkable when spooned over crisp duck that seems as if the fat has disappeared. The port sauce warming the filet mignon with Stilton cheese is worth forgetting vegetarianism or cholesterol. Seafood specials are light as the air, and be sure to try Jack's specials, whatever they are, to experience Italian and California influences as well.

We have friends who go here just for the single malt Scotch collection.
Chez Renee, 9051 Soquel Drive, Aptos 95003; (831) 688–5566. Open for lunch Tuesday–Friday, dinner Tuesday–Saturday. Full bar. Visa, MasterCard. Wheelchair accessible.

WATSONVILLE, ELKHORN SLOUGH, AND MOSS LANDING

Riverside Drive off Highway 1 will lead you into Watsonville, the self-proclaimed "Strawberry Capital of the World" and "Apple City of the West" (some Washington staters may question the latter). Watsonville is a classic flat farm town in the Pajaro Valley. Here immigrant families from several nations coexist in a fun community enhanced by the nearby Pajaro Dunes luxury condominium development (which has its own restaurant and clubhouse).

You might enjoy the downtown plaza, the many Victorian homes that survived both the 1906 and 1989 earthquakes, the ethnic stores and restaurants, a performance at the new Henry Mello Center for the Performing Arts (built after the 1989 Loma Prieta earthquake), or the West Coast Antique Fly-in at Santa Cruz County's only airport.

A food lovers' delight, pick-your-own farms surround the town. You will find strawberries, olallieberries, raspberries, apples, lettuce, Brussels sprouts (oh, come on), and splendiferous flowers. Be sure to buy produce on your way home so that it survives the car's heat.

Food lovers with kids might enjoy a visit to the **GIZDICH RANCH** 1.5 miles east of the County Fairgrounds, where you can experience a small family-run farm, picnic at tables in the orchards, pick apples and berries if they are in season, play in the farm's park, indulge in sumptuous pies, or just snoop around the bake shop. U-pick opportunities abound except in January.

*♨ *Gizdich Ranch,* 55 Peckham Road, Watsonville 95076; (831) 722–1056, fax (831) 722–2458. Open 9:00 A.M.–5:00 P.M. daily; pie shop open January–March only. Visa, MasterCard, American Express. Partly wheelchair accessible.

While you're in the Watsonville area, visit the SIERRA AZUL NURSERY AND GARDENS to view and discover drought-tolerant plants ideal for California's Mediterranean climate. Californians get great garden and growing advice for any location in the state. View two acres of plants, demonstration gardens, and Mount Madonna.

*♨ *Sierra Azul Nursery and Gardens,* 2660 East Lake Avenue (Highway 152), Watsonville 95076; (831) 763–0939. Open 9:00 A.M.–5:30 P.M. daily. Visa, MasterCard. Wheelchair accessible.

For water lovers, nearby Elkhorn Slough affords boat and raft trips to observe breathtaking shorebirds, including ducks, loons, and elegant egrets. Santa Cruz County also boasts more state parks than any other county in California, the two closest to Santa Cruz being Wilder Ranch State Park just up the coast from University of California, Santa Cruz, and Henry Cowell State Park along winding Highway 9 in the Santa Cruz Mountains.

As you drive back and forth across the Pajaro River, you are basically also crossing the Santa Cruz/Monterey county line. We highly recommend that you plan time (at least a couple of hours) to visit ELKHORN SLOUGH NATIONAL ESTUARINE RESEARCH RESERVE, a 1,400-acre reserve in the middle of 2,500 acres of wetland that include 500 acres coddled by the Nature Conservancy. The slough gets fresh water from the hills, which meets with salt water at Moss Landing, resulting in salt pads, marshes, and gooey mudflats—plush hotels for marine and flying species of wildlife.

To get to the visitors center, take Dolan Road off Highway 1 through high-tension-wire forests to cattle country and redwood forests. Turn left (north) on Elkhorn Road for about 2 miles and turn left into the visitors center. Inhale, folks. Take a deep breath, relax, and open your eyes and ears as wide as possible. Blue herons, egrets, harbor seals, and thousands of shorebirds sing back and forth.

The vast trail system through the slough begins just west of the visitors center. Be sure to ask questions, such as what special animals you might see or look for the day you visit. Trail loops range from .8 mile to 2.2 miles, with docents available as guides. Wheelchair users might try the accessible trail at Kirby Park along the eastern side of the slough nearly 4 miles beyond the visitors center. Please travel with respect for your surroundings.

✢ᵹ *Elkhorn Slough Reserve Visitors Center, 1700 Elkhorn Road, Watsonville 95076; (831) 728–2822. Open 9:00 A.M.–5:00 P.M. Wednesday–Sunday. Admission: $2.50 adults, unless you have a California Wildlife Campaign pass or a hunting or fishing license; kids free. Visa, MasterCard. Bookstore and one ¼-mile (paved) trail are wheelchair accessible.*

ELKHORN SLOUGH SAFARI cruises, run by Yohn Gideon, take you on a 27-foot pontoon boat through slough ecology and history with a naturalist guide. Refreshments too. The safari cruises depart from Moss Landing and provide a rare opportunity to observe and photograph nesting birds, feeding sharks, giant slugs, and endangered animals. West Coasters may recognize the safaris from "Bay Area Backroads" on KRON-TV or from *Sunset* magazine. Reservations are required.

✢ᵹ *Elkhorn Slough Safari, P.O. Box 570, Moss Landing 95039; (831) 633–5555; www.elkhornslough.com. Fee: $26 adults, $24 seniors, $19 for children fourteen and under; group discounts available.*

Downtown Moss Landing seems to be dominated by the enormous towers of the Moss Landing Pacific Gas & Electric plant, which, along with local fishing, used to be the prime source of employment in town. Now a plethora of strictly local Americana antiques and collectibles stores in interesting century-old buildings along Potrero and Moss Landing Roads complement the gray cement Monterey Bay Aquarium Research Institute buildings and a few holdout crusty and colorful fishers. Wander along the boatyards and fishing supplies stores to get the old-time smells and flavors.

Halfway between Monterey and Santa Cruz, Moss Landing was originally established as a whaling station in 1864 by one Captain Charles Moss. Now the boats are primarily yachts at the Tres Pines Yacht Club. Most of the antiques dealers fled the high rents and glitz of Cannery Row to lead a supposedly more sane life out here in Moss Landing, so you will find many treasures, from people to stuff.

To get a real feeling for the place, we suggest you try lunch or a snack at PHIL'S FISH MARKET AND EATERY, a chain-link fenced-in fish market and short-order fish joint at which you can sit inside or outside under colorful umbrellas and sample great fish and chips, oysters, fish sandwiches, salads, coffee, and ice cream, with everything under $10. Try the crab cake sandwich on sourdough or an English muffin or the calamari sandwich, both under $8.00, or the cracked crab salad, or the local albacore salad, all of which come with garlic bread. Don't miss Mama Nina's cioppino. Owner Phil DiGirolamo says, "We are always looking for new recipes to tantalize your tastebuds," and he gladly takes your suggestions for marinades.

Fresh-caught fish from boats across the street may end up as cracked crab, stuffed prawns, a hearty cioppino and chowders, stuffed sole, Sicilian-style marinated squid or octopus, smoked fish, and shellfish cocktails. The local French bread makes it all irresistible. You can even bring in your own catch—Phil's will prepare it, or crack your crab. The fish market sells local fish, from sand dabs to halibut, skate wings, butterfish, several varieties of shark, tuna, and mackerel, smelt, opah (not Oprah), luvare, Monterey Bay prawns, and more. Other (formerly) wild fish are flown in. Great kids' menu under $5.00. Obviously informal. *Phil's Fish Market and Eatery, 7640 Sandholt Road, Moss Landing 95039; (831) 633–2152, fax (831) 633–8611; www.philsfishmarket.com. Open 8:30 A.M.–8:00 P.M. Sunday–Thursday, until 9:00 P.M. Friday–Saturday. Beer and wine. No credit cards. Wheelchair accessible.*

Drop into Yesterday's Books down the street from Phil's for books on California and maritime history, as well as children's and art books.

On Moss Landing Road, antiques and collectibles fans will enjoy Moss Rose, and Beth Haughton's and Michel Tsouris's handmade jewlery, sculpture, and paintings, at Karthia.

CASTROVILLE

If you like extremely fresh produce and artichokes, you'll want to make Castroville a stop on your visit to the Monterey Peninsula.

Castroville is just 14 miles north of Monterey and easily reached by taking Highway 156 just off Highway 1. The town is surrounded by gray-green, long-leafed artichoke plants and lettuce fields. Farming and artichokes are the culture here, with the downtown serving local farmers and immigrant workers.

If you love or even like artichokes, don't miss **GIANT ARTICHOKE**, right off the highway at Merritt Street. Here you'll find fresh artichokes of every size grown, as well as frozen or deep-fried artichokes. You can also get breakfast, lunch, and dinner. Merritt Street runs perpendicular to Highway 1, and Castroville's metal name tag arches over Merritt Street, Castroville's main.

In Giant Artichoke's market, you can select from about six sizes and prices of artichokes to take home. Local growers say that for freshness, look for chokes with the leaves tight to the body. They say too that there are only fifty calories to a choke—it's what we put on them that adds up. Here you will also find an excellent selection of local wines, four varieties of artichoke pasta sauces, frozen fried artichoke hearts, and a wide variety of cheeses.

❧ *Giant Artichoke, Highway 1, Castroville; (831) 633–3204. Open 7:00 A.M.–7:00 P.M. Monday–Friday, 7:00 A.M.–8:00 P.M. Friday–Saturday. Visa, MasterCard, American Express. Wheelchair accessible.*

Local businesspeople, farmers, and Rotarians also gather at **LA SCUOLA RISTORANTE**, a very local and good Italian restaurant serving Tuscan specialties such as veal, yummy homemade gnocchi, tiramisu, and their own pastas and local fish. It's located downtown in Castroville's first school (1860)— hence its name.

❧ *La Scuola Ristorante, 10700 Merritt, Castroville; (831) 633–3200. Open for dinner only from 5:00 P.M. daily. Full bar. Visa and MasterCard. Wheelchair accessible.*

Try any other artichoke stand, especially southwest of Castroville. Don't miss the annual Artichoke Festival the last weekend in September for a smallish fun festival featuring artichokes cooked every delectable way imaginable and an artichoke eating contest that may ruin the participants' intestines once and for all. The festival has an annual Marilyn look-alike contest honoring its first Castroville Artichoke Queen, Marilyn Monroe.

MARINA, SEASIDE, AND SAND CITY

Back on Highway 1 heading south, you can visit Salinas River State Wildlife Area to the west. Six miles south of Castroville you come to Reservation Road,

> *There is a beautiful view from the Carmel grade, the curving bay with the waves creaming on the sand, the dune country around Seaside and right at the bottom of the hill, the warm intimacy of the town.*
>
> —John Steinbeck, *Cannery Row*

which leads to **MARINA STATE BEACH**, its wheelchair-accessible boardpath and its Osprey Coffee trailer at the north side of the parking lot, where parking is free. The beach's sand dunes often blow above head level, so be ready to protect your eyes and keep your teeth clenched while you order that latte. Marina State Beach is also the hang-gliding hangout of California. You might enjoy watching the show from the parking lot, but don't wash your car before you go.

Marina, the youngest of the Monterey Peninsula's cities, is primarily a shopping center town with huge commercial strips and rows and rows of housing developments, new and old, originally for military families stationed at Fort Ord. Now Marina and Seaside also have large populations of retired and working people who enjoy the sea air. With the closure of For Ord as an army base, Marina acquired from the Army a new municipal airport, a 26,000-square-foot sports arena, tennis courts, and a fifty-acre park. Several companies at the Marina Airport offer aviation recreation adventures such as sailplanes, skydiving, and helicopter rides.

The Marina dunes are home to more endangered species than any other sand dunes in California.

Enjoy the drive through the ice plant–veined sand dunes as you pass through what was Fort Ord and what is now California State University at Monterey. Then you come to Sand City, where sand is still mined industrially, and Seaside, where shoppers' dollars are mined hourly. Costco marks the spot on the east side of Highway 1, along with one of the largest Borders bookstores anywhere, along with representatives of most of America's modern chain stores.

Seaside is the fastest-growing and most populous city on the Monterey Peninsula, partly due to students and faculty at the Cal State campus, and partly because it offers affordable housing compared to pricey Carmel and Monterey. The people who work in the Monterey Peninsula's posh establishments have to live somewhere! Visitors in search of a little exercise might enjoy Laguna Grande Regional Park at Canyon del Rey Boulevard and Hilby Avenue. The park includes a sixty-acre restored wetlands area with a twelve-acre lake in the center that is encircled by a 1-mile bicycle path, nature trails, picnic tables, volleyball courts, and public rest rooms.

If you are in Seaside, you will enjoy the new Fishwife and Turtle Bay Tacqueria right next to each other. Beats fast food by a mile or two!

CHAPTER 6

THE GRAPE ESCAPE: TOURING AREA WINERIES

*C*alifornia wines of the Monterey Peninsula and central coast are usually underknown, underappreciated, and underlauded.

We hope to help you find some excellent wines, some interesting people, some new knowledge, and lots of fun. You might want to plan your tour around the MONTEREY WINE FESTIVAL, the first weekend in April. It includes stimulating and scintillating workshops for both amateur and professional wine tasters and servers, a new release party at the Monterey Bay Aquarium, special tasting events, winemaker luncheons and dinners, special dinners and focused tours, a "big bottle auction," a sparkling wine brunch, and cooking demonstrations.
Monterey Wine Festival, Box 1749, Monterey 93942; (800) 656–4282, fax (831) 649–4124; e-mail: 76543.1635@compuserve.com; www.montereywine.com.

MONTEREY WINERIES

The climate on the Monterey Peninsula is cooler than that of most other California wine-growing regions, benefiting from the blessed fog that rolls in from the Pacific Ocean and Monterey Bay. The fog and soft breezes contribute to the long, slow ripening season, leading to intense varietal flavors.

Nearly 40,000 acres of Monterey County are planted in premium varietal grapes, with many tons sold to premium Napa Valley vintners, and the countryside is dotted with wineries that actually make and bottle wine for Napa and Sonoma wineries.

Monterey County appellations include Carmel Valley, Santa Lucia Highlands (running along the western side of Salinas Valley), San Lucas, and Hames Valley.

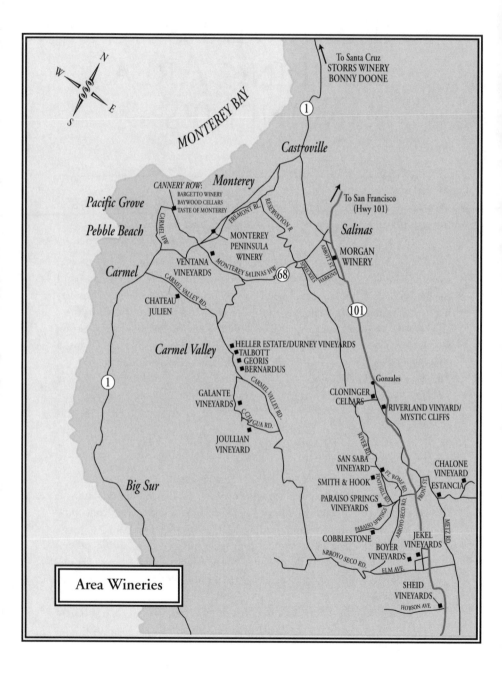

Area Wineries

We begin right in downtown Monterey, since tasting rooms are easiest to get to here if your time limits you from venturing out into Carmel Valley or the Salinas Valley.

If you won't be exploring beyond the immediate cities of Monterey and Carmel, be sure to visit **A TASTE OF MONTEREY**, where you can sample wines of thirty-three local wineries, many of which are not open to the public.

A Taste of Monterey, upstairs in the 700 Cannery Row Building, offers a fabulous panoramic view of Monterey Bay from Monterey to Santa Cruz, local produce plates and appetizers ($5.50), a gift shop well stocked with local gourmet foods (including Gilroy garlic products), wine accessories, and a good selection of wine-related cookbooks. Be sure to check out the cooperage and winemaking photo displays.

☙ *A Taste of Monterey, 700 Cannery Row, Monterey 93940; (831) 646-5446, fax (831) 375-0835. Open 11:00 A.M.–6:00 P.M. daily. Tasting fee: $5.00 for six tastes, applies to wine purchase. Visa, MasterCard, American Express. Wheelchair accessible.*

> *A Taste of Monterey serves and sells wines from most Monterey County wineries, but it is the only place where you can taste the wines of some wineries that don't have tasting rooms. Those include:*
>
> *Chateau Christina*
> *Estanzia*
> *Kendall-Jackson Monterey Winery*
> *Lockwood*
> *Maddalena Vineyard*
> *Monterey Peninsula Winery*
> *Monterey Vineyard (until supply runs out)*
> *Monterra/San Bernabe Vineyard*
> *Morgan*
> *Pavona*
> *Richard Boyer*
> *San Saba Vineyard*

On the first floor of the same building, you can VISIT **BARGETTO WINERY TASTING ROOM**. Bargetto's is a Santa Cruz Mountains winery, but offers tastings here in Monterey. Bargetto brothers Phillip and John emigrated from Piedmont, Italy, and began their winery in 1933. Today third generation Bargettos— Beverly, Tom, John, and Martin—direct the winery, which they say is "the oldest California winery producing Santa Cruz Mountains wines." The cool Santa Cruz climate creates low-yield but potent grapes, resulting in rich wines.

Besides making interesting varietals, Bargetto also produces mead, olallieberry, and other fruit wines under its Chaucer's brand.

This is a busy, lively tasting room with loads of gourmet foods and books, and it's certainly easy to get to. (For information on the winery, see "Santa Cruz Wineries" in chapter 5.)

❧ Bargetto Winery Tasting Room, 700 Cannery Row, Monterey 93940; (831) 373–4053. Open 10:30 A.M.–6:00 P.M. daily. Visa, MasterCard, American Express, Diners Club. Wheelchair accessible.

Also on Cannery Row and across from the Monterey Plaza Hotel you might enjoy sampling **BAYWOOD CELLARS'** wines in the interestingly elegant tasting room with Oriental rugs, a metal Porsche model, and a sports art gallery featuring signed photographs of former 49ers Coach Bill Walsh, and other football and golf memorabilia. Michael Simas entertains one and all.

Baywood sells fruit to many prominent wineries, including Sutter Home and Robert Mondavi (for its Woodbridge label wines). In addition to using its own Monterey and central coast vineyards, Baywood imports grapes from the Napa Valley. Cigar buffs will find a well-cared-for collection to go with their wines.

Winegrowers since 1966, the Cotta family says their wines have won "over 400 awards in national and international competitions," including recent gold and silver medals at the Orange County Fair for their Monterey County Chardonnay.

Fine points: Featured wines: Las Vinas Monterey, and Las Vinas Brut Champagne, Blanc de Noir, Symphony, Chardonnay, Cabernet Sauvignon, Syrah, Merlot; and Baywood Cellars Chardonnay, Gewürztraminer, Zinfandel, and Vintage Port. Owners: John and James Cotta. Winemaker: John Cotta. Cases: 40,000. Acres: 3,100.

❧ Baywood Cellars, 381 Cannery Row, Suite C, Monterey 93940; (831) 645–9035, fax (831) 645–9345. Open 11:00 A.M.–8:00 P.M. daily. Tasting fee: $3.00 for five wines, extra $1.00 for two tastings of champagnes. Visa, MasterCard, American Express, Discover. Wheelchair accessible.

CARMEL VALLEY WINERIES

Just 1.4 miles south of Carmel on Highway 1, turn left onto Carmel Valley Road to experience some of California's great beauty, great resorts, and fine wines. Kathleen spent many summers in Carmel Valley in a decade when hardly any of the luxurious resorts were here and one could ride a horse right up to the grocery store. She's not dating herself or anything—it was, thank heavens, just before investors from elsewhere decided that perhaps Carmel Valley really wasn't too far to lure visitors out to enjoy themselves.

The first attractions you come to going out Carmel Valley Road sit in juxtaposition to each other: the elegant Quail Lodge Golf Resort, the Fatherhood Park Farm Stand, and the Baja Cantina and Produce Stand. Quail Lodge offers

CHATEAU JULIEN, CARMEL VALLEY

the ultimate in elegant dining at the Covey and sumptuous lodging in all configurations from rooms to cabins and villas, swimming, tennis, golf, hot tubs, hiking trails, and general luxury.

At both the farm and produce stands you can get equally gorgeous local produce, but you have to cook it yourself. The Baja Cantina offers down-home, fun and neon-lights Mexican food, in an atmosphere where locals of all stripes hang out. A few Quail Lodge guests have actually been spotted trying it out!

About 5.6 miles east on Carmel Valley Road from Highway 1, you can't miss the new French design of **CHATEAU JULIEN**, one of the most pleasant wineries we have visited. There is a large parking lot to the right of the driveway. (Monterey-Salinas Transit buses stop right outside the winery.)

We accidentally explored the new building just beyond the parking lot, which is Chateau Julien's "chai," a space built one story into the ground with 15-inch-thick walls to provide the ideal climate to house its 2,000 French and American oak barrels. The last time we visited, the staff was setting up for a fabulous dinner and dance amid the barrels.

The winery's great hall features a dramatically soaring cathedral ceiling, stained-glass windows, cut stone floors, and a wonderfully warm fire. The adjoining conservatory has a real glass ceiling worth having a look at, but no one breaks through this one.

Well-informed staff members pour tastes at the central dining table as if you were a guest in their home, and a small sign reminds all that you can't pour wine for yourself according to California law. As few wineries do, Chateau Julien

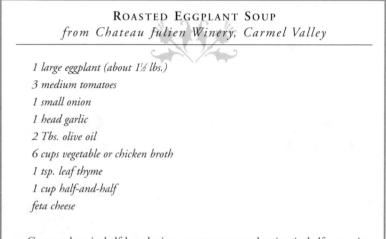

ROASTED EGGPLANT SOUP
from Chateau Julien Winery, Carmel Valley

1 large eggplant (about 1½ lbs.)
3 medium tomatoes
1 small onion
1 head garlic
2 Tbs. olive oil
6 cups vegetable or chicken broth
1 tsp. leaf thyme
1 cup half-and-half
feta cheese

Cut eggplant in half lengthwise; cut tomatoes and onion in half crosswise. Cut ¼ inch off top of garlic head. Place vegetables on foil-lined baking pan. Brush lightly with olive oil. Bake in a 400 degree oven for 45 minutes. (Don't worry if some browned or burned spots appear.) Let vegetables cool. Scoop eggplant, tomatoes, and onions out of their skins before placing them in a soup pot. Add broth and thyme. Bring mixture to a boil; reduce heat and simmer 45 minutes.

Puree ingredients in blender or food processor. At this point, soup can be refrigerated in a covered container until the next day. When ready to serve, return soup to pot and heat gently to a simmer. Stir in half-and-half. Serve in wide rimmed bowls and garnish with crumbled feta cheese. Serve with Chateau Julien Pinot Grigio or Sangiovese. Serves 8–10.

thankfully offers a menu of domestic and imported cheeses and fresh fruit trays ($8.00), as well as wines by the glass ($4.00 specialty wines, $ 6.00 private reserve wines), all making an elegant picnic at their outdoor tables.

We also found an excellent collection of food, wine, and cigar books, as well as the best of current fad fine cigars and a Cigar Collector's Guild through which aficionados over twenty-one can order.

You will find variety in both price and availability in their Chateau Julien (Monterey County grapes), Emerald Bay Coastal (coastal grapes and easily available), Garland Ranch (central coast grapes), and Mirage Vineyards (grapes from throughout California) labels.

Chateau Julien also puts on more interesting events than most wineries, including an art and wine festival in April, a spring winemaker dinner in May, a cigar and wine dinner in June, a summer jamboree, a winemaker dinner and seminar in the fall, and a December holiday cooking class.

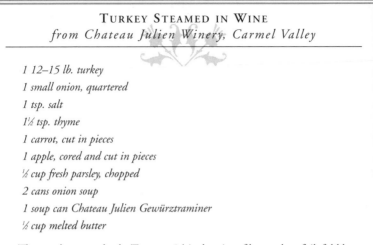

TURKEY STEAMED IN WINE
from Chateau Julien Winery, Carmel Valley

1 12–15 lb. turkey
1 small onion, quartered
1 tsp. salt
1½ tsp. thyme
1 carrot, cut in pieces
1 apple, cored and cut in pieces
½ cup fresh parsley, chopped
2 cans onion soup
1 soup can Chateau Julien Gewürztraminer
½ cup melted butter

Thaw turkey completely. Tear two 24-inch strips of heavy-duty foil, fold long edges together, and seal well. Oil foil. Place turkey on foil.

Place onion and salt in neck cavity. Fold skin flap over cavity opening. In large cavity, place next six ingredients. Baste turkey with butter. Place another sheet of foil over turkey, like a tent. Keeping foil from touching turkey, pinch edges of foil together, sealing well. Place on lowest shelf of oven. Bake at 400 degrees 5 minutes per pound plus 15 minutes covered, and then five minutes per pound plus 15 minutes uncovered. And now, get ready to serve the moistest turkey you have ever prepared. Note: It is the steam that cooks the turkey so quickly, so make sure the foil is sealed well.

Fine points: Featured wines: Chateau Julien Chardonnay Sur Lie, Pinot Grigio, Syrah, Zinfandel, Cabernet Sauvignon, Merlot, Sangiovese, Port, Cream Sherry. Owners: Bob and Patty Brower. Winemaker: Bill Anderson. Cases: 80,000. Acres: 165.

❧ *Chateau Julien, 8940 Carmel Valley Road, Carmel Valley 93923; (831) 624– 2600, fax (831) 624–6138; www.chateaujulienvalley.com. No tasting fee, charge for full glasses. Open 8:00 A.M.–5:00 P.M. Monday–Friday, 11:00 A.M.– 5:00 P.M. Saturday–Sunday, tours by reservation. Visa, MasterCard, American Express. Wheelchair accessible.*

As you leave Chateau Julien, turn right (east) on Carmel Valley Road. You might want to stop at the flower farm right next door, or at the shopping center to pick up some picnic supplies. In another mile Anna Makowska has an interesting open art studio next to the Farm Center. You can even detour for a hike 2.5 miles past Anna's studio in Garland Ranch

Regional Park, a 4,400-acre, trailed splendor of trees, natural growth, herons, deer, and wild turkeys. Spring wildflower fans will love the perfectly named Lupine Loop, an easy 1.4-mile multisense experience. Walk in groups, as mountain lions occasionally surprise explorers.

Back on Carmel Valley Road, you next pass on the left two of Carmel Valley's best old venerables, Carmel Valley Inn and Los Laureles Lodge. Both places welcome day-trippers, so you don't have to stay overnight to enjoy their dining, swimming, and tennis experiences. Both have poolside food service and more formal restaurants inside.

In another half mile you see the Boronda Adobe, which just may be where oft-copied Monterey Jack cheese began. Maria Juana Boronda, whose husband Don Jose Manuel built the adobe, started to make cheese to sell out of minor desperation after he was injured bullfighting. Her friends and neighbors liked the white cheese she made from the old family recipe, and along came good old eagle-eye Monterey leader David Jacks (See "History of Monterey"), who talked her out of the recipe and, of course, tried making it on his own. So, guess what? He called it Monterey Jack Cheese.

In another .7 mile you pass Villa Bella Donna, the ranch and private residence of Leon Panetta, former U.S. congressman and former chief of staff to President Bill Clinton.

BERNARDUS LODGE opened perfect, and hardly ever can anyone say that. As a luxurious country resort with a complete spa and salon, Bernardus Lodge is the second hospitality child of former race car driver Ben Pon, the first baby being Bernardus Winery.

As you enter the lobby, you feel as if you are in a large living room with an open bottle of wine and glasses to welcome you. Enjoy it in the salon to your left, while staff register you for your stay. The bungalows are pleasant, earthen adobe colors, with purple bougainvillea climbing everywhere. The fabulous patio with a huge fireplace overlooks the croquet lawn and competitive-size swimming pool. Room rates range from $245 to $1,690 in low season, and $375 to $1,900 in high season, with special guest packages from $450 to $2,888 for accommodations, meals, spa services, wine tasting, hikes, croquet lessons, tennis, golf, and horseback riding.

Both of Bernardus's restaurants are excellent. Wickets, the more casual, has a bar (with Greek olives with rosemary in terra-cotta saucers) and a view of the patio, and serves breakfast, lunch, and dinner. Specialties include house-smoked salmon carpaccio ($10), house pâtés, rillettes, and terrines, pizzas ($10–$12), salads, pastas, grilled Sonoma chicken ($15), steak tartare with pommes frites ($13), a Bernardus wine flight ($12), and lovely pastries.

Marinus is the more elegant of the two restaurants, with yellowfin tuna tartare ($12) if you dare, Maine lobster salad ($15), Big Sur chanterelle salad with prosciutto and toasted rosemary focaccia ($10), portobello mushroom soup ($9), sautéed foie gras ($17), spotted skate wing ($26), beef short rib ($26), Sonoma duck ($30), and superb cuts of prime beef grilled over mesquite and oak.

Splurge!

❧ Bernardus, 415 Carmel Valley Road, Carmel Valley 93924; (831) 658–3400, fax (831) 659–3529, reservations (888) 648–9463; www.bernardus.com. Full bar. Visa, MasterCard, American Express. Wheelchair accessible.

John Gardner's Tennis Ranch is open to overnight guests only, but you can drive in and take a look. Reservations are usually required, but you are almost

BERNARDUS LODGE, CARMEL VALLEY

guaranteed to run into celebrities of some sort. This is the ultimate pampering pleasure tennis ranch in the area.

In just another .3 mile, you come to the exquisitely renovated tasting room and art gallery of HELLER ESTATE/DURNEY VINEYARDS, which you will recognize by owner Toby Heller's fabulously sensual *Dancing Partners* sculpture on the front lawn. Heller Estate/Durney Vineyards is a must-stop for a multipleasing experience. In case the kids (parents?) need a break, the public library between and behind the tasting room and restaurant offers a story time from 10:30 to 11:00 A.M. Fridays.

In 1998 Heller Estate/Durney Vineyards received a top one hundred wines rating for its 1992 Carmel Valley Cabernet Sauvignon in the *Wine & Spirits*

CHILLED TOMATO SOUP WITH AVOCADO & CRAB
from Cal Stamenov, Executive Chef, Bernardus Lodge

5 lbs. tomatoes, divided	½ jalapeno pepper
1 onion, sliced	4 Tbs. salt
2 garlic cloves	½ cup sherry wine vinegar
3 red peppers	¾ cup extra virgin olive oil
1 green pepper	Tabasco to taste
4 cucumbers, peeled and seeded	1 lime
3 celery stalks	2 lemons
1 bunch fennel	1 lb. crabmeat
½ cup basil and ½ cup cilantro chopped	2 avocados, peeled and sliced
and wrapped together in cheesecloth	at last minute

Cook 1 lb. tomatoes, onion, and garlic until cooked through. Puree red and green peppers, cucumbers, celery, fennel, and jalepeno; combine with the cooked tomato, remaining 4 lbs. of fresh tomatoes, wrapped herbs, and 4 Tbs. salt. Refrigerate overnight.

Strain soup through medium strainer. Add vinegar, olive oil, Tabasco. and the lime and lemon juice; season to taste and keep chilled. Serve in a chilled bowl or large martini glass. Add sliced fresh crabmeat and avocado. Garnish soup with diced cucumber and diced tomato. Serve with Sauvignon Blanc. Serves eight.

Buying Guide. The *Wine Enthusiast* gave a gold medal to its 1994 Late Harvest Johannisberg Riesling. Other critics and publications rave about the Chenin Blanc and Chardonnay. Heller Estate/Durney Vineyards wines are produced entirely from their own organically grown (without pesticides or herbicides) estate vineyards, and all wines are aged in French oak barrels. Quality is the key here. Their wines dance on your palate, evoking interesting and substantiated fantasies.

Fine points: Featured wines: Chenin Blanc, Chardonnay, Late Harvest Johannisberg Riesling, Cabernet Sauvignon, Cachagua Cabernet Sauvignon, Pinot Noir (Burgundian style). Owners: The Heller family. Winemaker: Rex Smith. Cases and acres: owners prefer not to disclose.

❦ *Heller Estate/Durney Vineyards, 69 West Carmel Valley Road, Carmel Valley 93924; (831) 659–6220 or (800) 625–8466, fax (831) 659–6226; e-mail durney@redshift.com; www.usawines.com/durney. Tasting fee $3.00 applied to purchase. Open 10:00 A.M.–4:00 P.M. Monday–Friday, 11:00 A.M.–5:00 P.M. Saturday–Sunday. Visa and MasterCard. Wheelchair accessible.*

Carmel Valley's culinary level has risen enormously in the last few years. Walter Georis's **CORKSCREW CAFE** replaced a Thai restaurant and is perfectly located right between Heller Estate/Durney Vineyards and Robert Talbott Vineyards' tasting room. If you are curious about the Corkscrew's name, wander through the courtyard or around the corner to Georis Winery's tasting room.

Fans of Georis's Casanova Restaurant in Carmel (see p.112), as well as those who haven't made it there yet, won't want to miss the Corkscrew. Georis has again created cozy and fun dining rooms and niches with early Monterey and Mission influences in the decor.

Chef Wendy Little has created unusual small plates, including a salad Lyonnaise of frisee lettuce, bacon, roasted potatoes, and poached egg ($6.95), roasted chile filled with three cheeses and avocado salsa ($6.95), and duck and pistachio pâté ($7.95). Large plates include porcini mushroom ravioli with roasted vegetables, mushroom gravy, and white truffle oil ($16.50), steamed cockles and mussels in chorizo-saffron broth with grilled bread ($16.50), seared quail stuffed with Italian sausage accompanied by caramelized figs and soft polenta ($18.00), and grilled Hawaiian swordfish with braised Swiss chard, crispy potatoes, and lemon caper butter ($18.95). Desserts range from pumpkin crème brûlée ($6.00) to warm apple crepes, drunken chocolate cake with chocolate frosting and white chocolate ice cream, or aged goat cheese with honey and seasoned walnuts (each $6.50). Enjoy special after dinner wines by the glass or bottle, and purchase a whole artful Corkscrew plate to take home ($7.50). Excellent local wine list with some imports.

Corkscrew Cafe, 55 West Carmel Valley Road, Carmel Valley 93924; (831) 659–8888. Open for dinner from 5:00 P.M. Wednesday–Sunday, and for lunch Saturday–Sunday. Wine and beer. Visa, MasterCard, American Express. Wheelchair accessible.

In the same building as the Corkscrew Cafe, make sure to visit **ROBERT TALBOTT VINEYARDS,** the true love of Cynthia and Robb Talbott of Carmel's beautiful and elegant Talbott Tie Company, right at the corner of Carmel Valley Road and Pilot Road.

Talbott's tasting room showcases their excellent wines, neckwear, bathrobes, shirts, and other accessories in equal elegance. The warm, early California–style patio is a great place to sip Talbott wines, and from it you can step around the corner to try Georis Winery's best vintages.

Long, thin Italian breadsticks help cleanse your palate between selected wine tastes of Talbott's small production quality wines under the labels Talbott, Kali-Hart, Diamond T, and Logan, with bottlings to 5 liters.

Fine points: Featured wines: Chardonnay, Cuvée Cynthia, Pinot Noir. Owners: Cynthia and Robb Talbott. Winemaker: I. C. (Sam) Balderas. Cases: 25,000. Acres: 824.

❧*Robert Talbott Vineyards, 53 West Carmel Valley Road, Carmel Valley 93924; (831) 659–3500, fax (831) 659–3515, www.talbottvineyards.com. Open 11:00 A.M.–5:00 P.M. Thursday–Sunday. Tasting fee: $3.00 for daily selection, $6.00 to taste and keep glass. Visa, MasterCard, American Express. Wheelchair accessible.*

ROBERT TALBOTT VINEYARDS TASTING ROOM,
CARMEL VALLEY VILLAGE

Just around the corner from Robert Talbott Vineyards' tasting room is **GEORIS WINERY**, specialist in luscious Merlots from Walter Georis's own organic vinyards. Do not miss Georgis's eclectic gift shop full of corkscrews, Mexican imports, books about corkscrews, and other fun junque. This is one place where food and wine together are definitely appreciated. Georis's Casanova Restaurant in Carmel has one of the most praised wine lists on the central coast.

Fine points: Featured wines: Merlot, Cabernet Sauvignon, Cabernet Franc. Owner and Winemaker: Walter Georis. Cases: 1,200. Acres: 28.

❧ *Georis Winery, 4 Pilot Road, Carmel Valley 93924; (831) 659–1050, fax (831) 659–1054. Open 11:00 A.M.–5:00 P.M. daily. Visa and MasterCard. Wheelchair accessible.*

Many locals and visitors love the reliable restaurants right along Carmel Valley Road in the Village, such as WILL'S FARGO DINING HOUSE AND SALOON for a western Victorian dining experience with big chandeliers, heavy mahogany, tinkling crystal goblets, and huge or not-so Angus beefsteaks cut to order. Most people order big—big steaks and big potatoes—but you can also have pasta, seafood, and salads, and there is an excellent menu for kids. Great martinis.

&%& *Will's Fargo Dining House and Saloon, Carmel Valley Village, Carmel 93924; (831) 659-2774. Open for dinner Tuesday–Sunday. Full bar. Visa, MasterCard, American Express. Wheelchair accessible.*

We strongly encourage you to experience lunch or late grill at WHITE OAK GRILL, where you can taste **River Ranch Vineyards'** rare wines.

Self-taught chef Terry Terflinger and his partner, Marilyn Beach, opened White Oak Grill in 1997 to accolades from *Wine Spectator* and *Sunset* magazines as well as from the *San Francisco Chronicle.*

The small white frame building (1890) originally processed milk from Los Laureles Dairy Ranch, which was eventually transported to the old Del Monte Hotel in Monterey. Monterey Jack cheese was first made in this building, and it has also served as a post office, stagecoach stop, inn, art gallery, and decorator's studio.

Terry and Marilyn have created a casually elegant small-room restaurant where one can happily sit in a chair on the front porch to wait for a table if necessary. Through the front door you walk into the small lobby and River Ranch Vineyards wine shop.

Everything here seems perfect, from the pommes frites to grilled vegetables ($4.00) or avocado with tomato and Bilfiore mozzarella ($8.00) for starters. Entree salads are around $8.00, bistro and grilled sandwiches are under $10.00, and the salmon ($10.50) and steak frites ($12.00) are divine. We especially like the solid white tuna sandwich with organic field greens (the best outside our kitchen!), the grilled marinated lamb sirloin sandwich ($10.00), the grilled portobello mushroom sandwich ($9.00), and the juicy Gorgonzola cheeseburger with pommes frites ($10.00).

Late grill starters include spicy prawns ($9.00), small rack of lamb ($14.00), and sautéed mushrooms ($8.00). Entrees include soup of the day or organic field greens salad with a larger grilled rack of lamb ($24.00), fourteen-ounce rib eye steak ($23.00), farm-raised salmon ($19.00), and a portobello mushroom grilled and stacked with seasonal vegetables ($16.00). You can purchase the sharp Dijon mustard served at each table for just $10.00.

RIVER RANCH VINEYARDS is one of the smallest wineries in Monterey County and is a combined effort of Bill Stahl and Sam Balderas of Robert

Talbott Vineyards. You can taste River Ranch wines at your table in White Oak Grill for $7.00 and then purchase them to take home.

Fine points: Featured wines: Chardonnay, Pinot Noir. Owner: Bill Stahl. Winemaker: C. I. (Sam) Balderas. Cases: 500. Acres: 2

➳ *White Oak Grill and River Ranch Vineyards, 19 East Carmel Valley Road, Carmel Valley 93924; (831) 659–1525, fax (831) 659–5472. Open for lunch 11:30 A.M.–2:30 P.M. Thursday–Monday, for dinner 6:00–8:30 P.M. Thursday–Sunday. Wine and beer. Visa, MasterCard, American Express. Wheelchair accessible.*

WHITE OAK GRILL AND RIVER RANCH VINEYARDS,
CARMEL VALLEY VILLAGE

RUNNING IRON RESTAURANT AND SALOON offers another take on the Wild West with a long list of burgers (try the Lonesome Burger), steaks, more than two dozen sandwiches (even some vegetarian), various grades of man-eating chili, terrific baby back ribs, and a few salads for those health freaks. This is a loud, fun bar with animal heads and a stuffed mountain lion, as well as hundreds of cowboy boots, hanging from the ceiling.

➳ *Running Iron Restaurant and Saloon, East Carmel Valley Road (just east of most stores) at Via Contenta, Carmel Valley Village 93924. Open for lunch and dinner, Sunday brunch. Full bar. Visa, MasterCard, American Express. Wheelchair accessible.*

WINTER BRUSCHETTE
from Chef Terry Terflinger, White Oak Grill, Carmel Valley

2 medium golden beets
olive oil
salt and pepper
1 large red bell pepper
butter
2 Tbs. chopped shallots
3 Tbs. chopped garlic, divided
½ cup chicken stock
6 cups Swiss chard, shredded
2 Tbs. grated Romano or Parmesan cheese
8 slices rustic bread or large baguette

Heat oven to 375 degrees. Place beets on ovenproof pan, drizzle with olive oil, season with salt and pepper. Roast until just tender, about 1 hour. When beets are tender, remove from oven, let cool, remove skin, chop into small cubes, and set aside.

Roast bell pepper over open flame until charred. Place in bowl, cover with plastic wrap for 10 minutes to cool and to sweat skin. Remove skin, cut in half, remove all seeds and membrane, and dice fine; set aside.

Heat 2 Tbs. oil and 1 Tbs. butter in pan large enough to hold all Swiss chard. Add shallots, 1 Tbs. garlic, and the chicken stock, and sauté for 1 minute. Add Swiss chard and sauté until limp, 2–3 minutes. Remove from pan; drain and set aside.

To assemble, combine beets and Swiss chard in a mixing bowl. Season with salt and pepper. Mix in cheese. In a saucepan, over low heat, combine 2 Tbs. olive oil and 2 Tbs. garlic. Heat just enough to sweeten and soften the garlic, about 1–2 minutes.

Dip bread slices in mixture, place on cookie sheet, and broil until just colored, or place on grill, oil side down, until lightly grilled. Spoon about 1 Tbs. of mixture on each slice of toasted bread. Sprinkle with roasted pepper, arrange on plate to accompany an entree or serve as an appetizer. Serves eight.

We happen to like **PLAZA LINDA**, a strip mall-ish successful attempt at Mexican riviera charm and seafood run by Dean and Josie Diaz. Bright colors highlight the decor, and the big surprise is the interior heated patio that truly feels like one in Mexico. If it's too hot or cold, sit at a window table and at least soak in the Mexican ambience.

Everything is made to order, including the tortillas, so keep yourself alive with excellent warm chips and even warmer salsas. The Plaza Linda Mexican salad features Salinas Valley greens topped with broiled chicken, cheddar and Monterey Jack cheese, guacamole, tomatoes, green onions, olives, and your choice of dressings ($7.95). The nachos are huge and scrumptious and can even come as a Macho Nacho Dinner with shrimp, tri-tip steak, or chicken for an additional dollar or two. Check out the El Fisho Menu with blackened fish of the day ($15.95), grilled fish or lobster tacos ($13.95), Dungeness crab enchilada, or grilled jumbo prawns wrapped in bacon with pico de gallo (both $14.95). We love the pulled meats. No shortcuts here, so enjoy to the fullest, and arrive hungry! Margaritas are available in several colors and flavors, ranging from normal to adulterated and virgin.

Plaza Linda was originally recommended to us by a Carmel woman who comes here with loads of others for the jazz on Saturdays, when the Buddy Jones Jazz Trio plays from 6:00 to 9:00 P.M. Fourth-generation patrons are served by third-generation employees, who "have not used lard for over twenty years."

A few others who have discovered this place include Doris Day, Paul McCartney, Ringo Starr, John Madden, Joan Fontaine, Sting, Alexander Haig, Joan Baez (there's a contrast or two), Merle Haggard, and Cheryl Tiegs.

➳ *Plaza Linda, 9 Delfino Place (behind the market), Carmel Valley 93924; (831) 659–4229. Open for lunch Monday–Friday, dinner Monday–Saturday, "closed every Sunday for life." Full bar. Visa, MasterCard, American Express. Wheelchair accessible.*

At Carmel Valley Village shopping center you will find Bon Appetit Pizza, Sole Mio Caffe, Trattoria Cucina Italiana, gas stations, Summerhouse and Chatterbox restaurants, Talbott's Ties outlet, and a woodworking shop, among many others.

One of the most elegant restaurants in the area is the Ridge Restaurant at Robles del Rio Lodge up the hill from the village. It's worth a drive up to see the historic resort and the views from it. *Note:* The resort has been closed for renovation and is expected to re-open in spring 2002.

As you leave town continuing eastward, immediately on your left is BERNARDUS winery, a busily popular tasting room with charm that belies its cement exterior. (It once housed a bank.)

Bernardus owner Ben (Bernardus) Pon is a Dutch magnate, six-time Le Mans Porsche race car driver, entrepreneur, world traveler, and international businessman who, with his wife, Ingrid, succumbed to Carmel's charms in 1980, adding a home here to those in Amersfoort, Holland, and Somerset, England. His father, Ben Pon Sr., imported the first Volkswagen bug to the United States and created the design for the VW bus.

Pon caught the winemaking bug and purchased 220 acres of land and a small winery formerly owned by Robb Talbott of Talbott Vineyards and Winery.

Striving to make great Bordeaux-style red wines, Pon also finds the challenge of making wines in an underknown appellation region exciting. He aims to make wines comparable to those of Bordeaux, rather than to those of the Napa and Sonoma Valleys. Toward his immediate goal of making great wine, Pon hired winemaker Mark Chesebro.

Bernardus wines consistently gain ratings of ninety or better from *Wine Specatator* and many other experts and wine critics in a wide variety of publications.

In the tasting room we especially enjoyed looking at photos of Pon's racing Porsches, as well as a large photo on one wall that shows the altitudes of Bernardus and other Carmel Valley wineries' vineyards. (Just for fun, it shows Georis at 600 feet, Galante at 900 feet, Heller Estate/Durney at 1,200 feet, Bernardus at 1,250 feet, and Joullian at 1,400 feet.)

Framed letters and invitations on the walls show that Bernardus's 1995 Chardonnay was served for a Gladys Knight performance in the Clinton White House in 1998, as well as for a dinner honoring President Roman Herzog of the Federal Republic of Germany. Ample breadsticks help retain sobriety and cleanse the palate, and Scharffen Berger chocolates tempt.

Fine points: Featured wines: Pinot Gris, Sémillon, Marsanne, Marinus, Chardonnay, Sauvignon Blanc, Merlot, Cabernet Sauvignon, Pinot Noir. Owner: Ben Pon. Winemaker: Mark Chesebro. Cases: 42,000. Acres: 220.

❧ *Bernardus, 5 West Carmel Valley Road, Carmel Valley 93924; (831) 659–1676 or (800) 223–2533, fax (831) 223–2533. www.bernardus.com. Open 11:00 A.M.–5:00 P.M. daily. Tasting fee: $3.00, which counts toward purchase over $25.00. Visa, MasterCard, American Express. Wheelchair accessible.*

The other two Carmel Valley wineries are in what's called the Cachagua Valley, about 18 miles from Highway 1. The valley remains home to descendants of the Esselen Indians who inhabited this area. To reach the wineries, turn right (south) on Cachagua Road about 4.5 miles east of Carmel Valley Village. It will loop around and land you back on Carmel Valley Road, about 6 miles east of where you left it.

About 5 miles up Cachagua Road, you will come to GALANTE VINEYARDS AND ROSE GARDENS, a feast for at least three senses. Incredible Jack Galante is as passionate about his 12,000 rose plants (including ninety varieties that he grows commercially for designers and retailers around the country) as he is about his wines. Love it, love it, love it!

Follow the wine bottle signs to the tasting room, designed to look like a barn because Jack's father, Clemente Galante, has made "wine in the old barn by the farmhouse for years." Galante senior wisely bought the 700-acre ranch to raise cattle in 1968. A native of the island of Rhodes and of Italian heritage, Galante senior owned the wonderful and late Maison Mendesolle women's clothing shop in San Francisco's St. Francis Hotel. (Kathleen used to shop there occasionally with her mother, or rather her mother shopped there with Kathleen in tow.)

Galante and his wife, Jane, a concert pianist whose grandfather was Carmel founder Frank Devendorf, thought Carmel Valley would be good for the kids, and was it ever. Galante gave up on the cattle business and decided to try grapes, soon selling his tonnage to wineries before the grapes even formed on the vines. He also developed the rose business.

After years of making wine for themselves and selling most of their grapes to other wineries (which attained great success with them), the Galantes decided to try making wine for sale. Even though Jack and his wife, Martha, and their sons John and Evan live primarily in Marin County, no one could be more involved in the winery, roses, and Cachagua community than Jack Galante. He raises money for all community needs. His press kit even includes a brochure about fund-raisers for the Cachagua community center and volunteer fire department.

You might want to plan a visit around the concerts held on the Fourth of July weekend and on the first and last weekends in August, complete with great food. The mid-July Music Gumbo Festival is said to be one of the best in the region.

You can order rose plants or elegant cut roses by the stem or by the dozen, and if you are a rose lover, don't miss Galante's annual mid-September Days of Wine and Roses, which include walking tours of the rose gardens, wine tasting, and an outdoor western barbecue, along with music and wine- and rose-related games. You can even rest your weary feet in their rose-petal-filled tubs!

In the unique climate of the Cachagua Valley, it can get very hot during the day and very cold at night, with temperatures ranging from the mid-thirties to the low hundreds in the same day. The temperature in the winery building remains at fifty-five without air-conditioning—a fan in the cupola draws the cool night air through automated louvers low on the walls.

 Fine points: Featured wines: Black Jack Pasture Cabernet Sauvignon, Red Rose Hill Cabernet Sauvignon, Rancho Galante Cabernet Sauvignon. Owner: Jack Galante. Winemakers: Greg Vita and Jack Galante. Cases: 7,000. Acres: 60.

❧ *Galante Vineyards and Rose Gardens, 18181 Cachagua Road, Carmel Valley 93924; (800) GALANTE, fax (415) 331–2039; e-mail web@galantevinyards.com;*

HARVEST LAMB
from Jack Galante, Galante Vineyards, Carmel Valley

1 large butterflied leg of lamb

1 cup olive oil

2 cups Galante Vineyards Rancho Galante Cabernet Sauvignon

4 cloves fresh garlic, chopped fine

¼ cup green onions, chopped

1 cup crumbled feta goat cheese

¼ cup dried Greek oregano

¼ cup fresh mint leaves, chopped and packed

1 tsp. white peppercorns, crushed coarsely

1 tsp. green peppercorns, crushed coarsely

1 tsp. black peppercorns, crushed coarsely

BASIC PREPARATION:
Marinate the lamb in ½ cup olive oil, Cabernet Sauvignon, 2 cloves chopped garlic, and green onions for 2 hours. Prepare a mixture of the feta goat cheese, oregano, mint, and remaining garlic. Cut deep pockets in the leg of lamb to stuff the mixture into. Rub the outside of the lamb with the remaining olive oil mixed with the three kinds of peppercorns. Grill on a covered barbecue, turning occasionally, at 375 degrees until desired doneness. Serves six.

HARVEST (GRAPE) PREPARATION:
Marinate the lamb in freshly crushed Cabernet Sauvignon grapes, 2 cloves garlic, and green onions for 2 hours. Prepare a mixture of the feta goat cheese, oregano, mint, and remaining garlic. Cut deep pockets in the leg of lamb to stuff the mixture into. Rub the outside of the lamb with ½ cup of olive oil mixed with the three kinds of peppercorns. Grill on a covered barbecue, turning occasionally, at 375 degrees until desired doneness. Keep the lamb smothered in freshly crushed Cabernet Sauvignon grapes. The grape juices will penetrate deeply into the lamb. Serves six.

For a variation, barbecue and smoke a ham smothered at all times with Sauvignon Blanc grapes.

www.galantevineyards.com. Tasting fee: $5.00 per person for groups of six or more. Visa, MasterCard. Wheelchair accessible. Rose orders and inquiries: (831) 659–2649

The town of Cachagua is about 1 mile up Cachagua Road from the vineyard. Don't miss both the natural country General Store and Princess Camp, a great characters–great drinks local bar. From here go up the road to the Cachagua Community Park, where you can park the car to explore Los Padres Reservoir and the trails in Los Padres National Forest, all enhanced by the rippling Carmel River. Oh, those crawdads we used to catch!

Slightly further along Cachagua Road comes Comsat's (Communication Satellite Corporation) Earth Station, all very amusing to Kathleen, who received Comsat stock for graduation from UC/Berkeley and has seen it stay at the same price for a very long time.

In 2 miles along this narrow, winding road lined with sycamores, oaks, and wildflowers, you come to **JOULLIAN VINEYARDS**, created by the Joullian and Sias families of Oklahoma City, Oklahoma, with the goal of making world-class wines. Former Peace Corps volunteer and Joullian general manager and winemaker Ridge Watson loves to show off his site with its dramatic view. The winery is open only by appointment and makes primarily Bordeaux varieties.

Every year Watson and his wife, D'Tim, who is originally from Thailand, host a popular picnic at Joullian for good customers and friends—often one and the same. This tri-tip roast cooked by D'Tim is everyone's favorite. She recommends that you use a barbecue with a lid.

Fine points: Featured wines: Chardonnay, Sauvignon Blanc, Sémillon, Cabernet Sauvignon, Merlot, Cabernet Franc. Owners: The Joullian and Sias families. Winemaker: Ridge Watson. Cases: 15,000. Acres: 655.

Joullian Vineyards, 20300 Cachagua Road, Carmel Valley 93924; (831) 659–2800. Open 11:00 A.M.–3:00 P.M. Monday–Friday. Tasting fee: $3.00 applies to any purchase. Visa and MasterCard. Wheelchair accessible.

SALINAS AREA WINERIES

Next we will visit wineries of the Salinas Valley. Continue on Cachagua Road around 1.5 miles to Carmel Valley Road, from which point you have a choice of two routes. If you turn right, you take an extremely winding way to the Salinas Valley. If you turn left, you will go back to Laureles Grade over to Highway 68, also known as the Monterey-Salinas Road. This latter is our preferred route because it gives us a chance to stop at Ventana Winery and at Tarpy's Roadhouse, one of our favorite restaurants.

If you start in Monterey or Carmel, take Highway 68 east. Otherwise, take Highway 101 toward Salinas. As you head eastward from Monterey and Carmel, Ventana is the only winery you can visit along Highway 68 between Monterey and the turnoff near Salinas. Talbott's new tasting room is actually in

---

TRI-TIP ROAST
from D'Tim Watson, Joullian Winery, Carmel Valley

---

1 2-lb. tri-tip roast
½ cup soy sauce
¼ cup Joullian Cabernet wine
4 cloves garlic, minced
freshly ground black pepper to taste
¼ cup chopped cilantro

Place meat in a lidded, plastic container and cover with remaining ingredients. Cover and refrigerate overnight, even two nights. Shake container periodically.

To barbecue, heat coals to red-hot stage. Cook roast for 25 minutes covered, then remove lid and cook 40–50 minutes on open fire or until required doneness is achieved. The meat should attain a dark caramel color, while still remaining pink and juicy on the inside.

Serve with a green salad, crusty bread, and barbecued beans. Serves six to eight.

Carmel Valley, and we urge you to venture out there (see page 165).

But we love the people at **VENTANA VINEYARDS**, which is known as the "Most Award-Winning Vineyard in America." It is also one of the most innovative in the world. The tasting room and Tarpy's Roadhouse restaurant are in the same stone building just west of the intersection of Highway 68 and Canyon Del Rey Boulevard.

Washington native J. Douglas Meador grew up in an agricultural family that specialized in cattle, wheat, apples, and other fruit trees. After graduating in mathematics and econometrics from the University of Washington, he spent seven years as a naval officer and aviator that included two combat tours in Vietnam.

In 1972 Meador was on his way home to be "an apple baron" when he was lured into stopping off for a minute to install 2,500 acres of vineyards here in Monterey County, and basically never left. Soon he acquired the property known since as "Ventana" and began a life of research and exploration of new techniques, resulting in his midwifing the birth of the Monterey wine region. Since the 1977 harvest, wines made from grapes grown by Ventana have won gold medals every year.

Among Doug Meador's many innovations are close vine spacing and the vertical shoot system, splint-canopy trellising, malolactic fermentation in American white winemaking, and planting of America's first French oak trees

VENTANA VICE PRESIDENT LUANN MEADOR

for barrel making. What some of this means is that he plants vines in rows 6 feet apart and forces them to grow straight up, allowing fruit to hang in the open with less danger from mildew.

LuAnn Meador feels like a native Californian, having moved here at a tender age from Milwaukee, Wisconsin. A business graduate of Cabrillo College and San Jose State University, LuAnn worked her way through the banking industry, ultimately becoming vice president of Wells Fargo's Carmel branch.

Partly because of her marketing and sales experience, Doug talked LuAnn into switching to the wine business. She now serves as vice president of the winery.

LuAnn is often near or in the cozy tasting room, which is upstairs and in good supply of well-chosen wine trinkets, shirts, and books. Be sure to try the Orange Muscat for a fun and different taste experience. (The only other winery where we've seen it is at Villa Mt. Eden in the Napa Valley.) Ventana encourages you to bring and enjoy a picnic on the gorgeous, brilliantly colorful, flower-strewn patio.

Fine points: Featured wines: Sauvignon Blanc, Chardonnay, Dry Rosado, Dry Riesling, Chardonnay, White Table Wine (only $5.00), Gewürztraminer, Riesling, Chenin Blanc, Orange Muscat, Monterey Rosé, Red Table Wine, Merlot, Cabernet Sauvignon, Cabernet Franc, Syrah, Muscat d'Orange; Meador Estate Syrah "Maverick," Chardonnay Block 9, Sauvignon Blanc Block 3, Dry Chenin Blanc "Old Vine." Owners: Doug and LuAnn Meador. Winemaker: Doug Meador. Cases: 40,000. Acres: 400.

CHOCOLATE HAZELNUT CHEESECAKE
*from Chef Michael Kimmel of Tarpy's Roadhouse,
Monterey*

2 cups hazelnuts, toasted for 10 minutes, then rubbed together to remove skins

1 cup sugar

*1 pkg. chocolate wafer cookies, toasted for 10 minutes, processed in food
processor*

24 oz. French vanilla chocolate, chopped fine

6 lbs. cream cheese

1½ cups heavy cream

12 eggs

3 cups sugar

1 Tbs. vanilla extract

1½ cups hazelnut flavoring

Process the skinned nuts and 1 cup sugar until very fine. Wipe clean three 1-inch springform pans. Wrap in heavy-duty foil. Brush with softened butter. Distribute the chocolate wafer crumbs into each pan. Roll around to coat the sides, then shake for even coat at the bottom. Melt French vanilla chocolate over simmering water.

Place cream cheese, cream, eggs, 3 cups sugar, 2 cups hazelnuts, vanilla, and hazelnut flavoring into the mixer bowl. Run on low speed to blend ingredients, shut machine off, then switch to high and allow to run for about 1 minute. With machine off, add melted chocolate, run again for another 15 seconds to blend, shut machine off and scrape down sides of bowl. Run again for another 15 seconds.

Evenly divide the batter among the three pans and put them in a large roasting pan. Place the roasting pan in a 350 degree oven and pour very hot tap water about halfway up the sides of the springform pans. Bake for about 1 hour or until the cakes wobble when shaken. Remove from the oven to cool. Refrigerate at least four hours before serving.

Ventana Vineyards, 2999 Monterey-Salinas Road (Highway 68), Suite 2, Monterey 93940; (831) 372–7415 or (800) BEST–VIN, e-mail info@ventanawines.com; www.ventanawines.com. Open 11:00 A.M.–5:00 P.M. daily. No tasting fee. Visa, MasterCard, American Express. Not wheelchair accessible.

TARPY'S ROADHOUSE, MONTEREY

And now for **TARPY'S ROADHOUSE**, an architectural and dining experience we wouldn't want to miss. Tarpy's shows humor in its decor, staff, and colorful patio. It's also worth a special trip from Monterey, just five to ten minutes out the Monterey-Salinas Road (Highway 68). Here grown-ups get crayons to color on the tablecloths, and Tarpy's wine list has won *Wine Spectator's* Award of Excellence. Definitely a winning combination! (Tarpy's is part of the Downtown Dining group, which also owns Rio Grill in Carmel's Crossroads shopping center and Montrio on Calle Principal in Monterey.)

Tarpy's name comes from a guy named Matt Tarpy, who, among other things, emigrated from Ireland in 1826, got involved in local democratic politics, and founded the Pajaro Property Protective Society vigilante group. In a property dispute following the sale of part of his land to Murdock and Sarah Nicholson (1868), Tarpy moved a cabin onto what Nicholson thought was his property, and Sarah Nicholson and two men went to claim it. Tarpy packed his guns, and went out to settle the matter. Several versions of the story conflict as to who started what, but one fact is clear: Sarah Nicholson got in the way and was shot dead.

Tarpy turned himself in and went to the county jail in Monterey. Rumor spread like wildfire, and the next morning 400 men overpowered the sheriff, dragged Tarpy from jail, and hanged him from a tree at Tarpy Flats. So there—Western justice at its simplest.

TARPY'S CRAB CAKES
from Chef Michael Kimmel of Tarpy's Roadhouse, Monterey

5 lbs. crabmeat with cartilage removed, don't break up pieces

1 red bell pepper, diced small
1 yellow bell pepper, diced small
1 medium carrot, peeled, diced small
1 medium yellow onion, chopped fine
1 Tbs. shallots, chopped fine
4 stalks celery, chopped fine
1 Tbs. butter for sautéeing

1 bunch scallions, sliced thin
1 bunch cilantro, chopped fine
4 lemons, grated and juiced, no seeds
1 Tbs. kosher salt
1 Tbs. black pepper, ground
6 dashes Tabasco sauce
1 cup dry, toasted bread crumbs, toast in the oven, then grind
2 Tbs. Old Bay seasoning
3 cups mayonnaise

6 eggs
flour to coat

Carefully pick through crabmeat to remove pieces of shell and cartilage without breaking up pieces.

Sauté the second set of ingredients in butter till soft, allow to cool, then toss with the third set of ingredients and mix well.

Gently fold in crabmeat, trying not to break up large pieces of crab. Portion into 2-oz. cakes (use scoop) until they are thin and flat. Set up a breading station with beaten eggs in one pan, and another pan of flour lightly seasoned with salt and pepper. Dip crab cakes carefully into beaten eggs, then into seasoned flour. Shake off excess flour and deep-fry or sauté in olive oil in skillet just before serving. Makes about twenty crab cakes.

A Mobil three-star restaurant, Tarpy's truly combines history with "creative American country cuisine." Bill Cox and Tony Tollner now own and run the place, showcasing Chef Michael Kimmel's innate skills in creative foods without getting too nouvelle for many tastes. We love the cozy niches, large patio, and crayons on every table for us to release the scribbles in all of us.

Try the chili-crusted chicken breast with apricot barbecue sauce and Gruyère scalloped potatoes (lunch $9.50, dinner $14.55) or the famous baby back ribs ($11.95–$18.51). We also highly recommend Tarpy's grilled vegetable plate with sweet corn succotash (lunch $9.97, dinner $11.95), classic meat loaf with mushroom gravy and roasted garlic mashed potatoes ($11.95), as well as the herb crusted salmon (lunch $12.50, dinner $17.95). At lunch Kathleen loves the seared ahi tuna on field greens and sesame noodles ($9.70), while Jerry prefers the Black Angus rib eye steak sandwich with Hunan barbecue sauce ($9.95). We can hardly resist the haystack onion rings ($4.15). Don't miss the chocolate espresso bread pudding or the lemon and fresh ginger crème brûlée (both $5.95).

If you didn't bring your picnic to enjoy at Ventana, be sure to try Tarpy's, or make a special trip out here, regardless of the weather. Good weather means romantic seating outside, bad weather means romantic seating and warm fireplaces inside. Also, everything on the menu is available as takeout. Sunday brunch too. Enjoy!

➹✧ *Tarpy's Roadhouse, 2999 Monterey-Salinas Road (Highway 68) at Canyon Del Rey, Monterey 93940; (831) 647–1444, fax (831) 647–1103; www.tarpys.com. Open 11:30 A.M.–10:00 P.M. daily. Full bar. Visa, MasterCard, American Express, Discover. Mostly wheelchair accessible.*

Once you've visited Ventana and had lunch at Tarpy's, you should be well set to tour a few wineries between the Laureles Grade and Salinas. Simply travel east on Highway 68 (Monterey-Salinas Road) and turn south at River Road, which winds slightly along the slopes and base of the Santa Lucia Mountains along the west side of the Salinas Valley and through some of the most beautiful terrain we have seen. Emergency provisions are available at locally popular Mo's River Road Market.

As you continue along River Road, notice the repainted old school buses, deep in the fields, with portable toilets attached to the back, parked deep into the fields. These buses transport Mexican farm workers from a central pickup spot to where the work is, with their entire sanitation facilities in those portable outhouses.

The first winery you come to is **MORGAN WINERY**, which you can visit by appointment only, but try to plan ahead. Dan and Donna Lee opened Morgan in 1982. A Central Valley native, Dan was studying veterinary medicine at UC/Davis when he discovered enology and found that it satisfied his interests in both science and agriculture. You can either make a reservation to visit two weeks in advance or taste Morgan's wines at A Taste of Monterey (see page 157).

Soon after completing Davis's graduate program in enology, Dan went to work at Jekel, became winemaker, and, at a meeting of the Monterey County Winegrowers Association, shared with a banker his vision of moving Monterey County into world-class wine production. The banker encouraged him to open his own winery, became his business adviser, and then his wife.

While Dan was still making wine at Durney, the Lees opened Morgan "in their spare time" at home. In 1984 they moved to their state-of-the-art Morgan facility here in Salinas. They began conservatively making a Chardonnay and worked to perfect it, striving for quality instead of quantity, a goal they have achieved as its many honors attest. Their simple philosophy: Use the best grapes and let the fruit determine production techniques to enhance the natural flavor rather than overpower it.

 Fine points: Featured wines: Chardonnay, Sauvignon Blanc, Pinot Noir, Zinfandel. Owners: Dan and Donna Lee. Winemaker: Dean DeKorth. Cases: 35,000. Acres: 65.

Morgan Winery, 590 Brunken Avenue, Salinas 93901; (831) 751–7777, fax (831) 751–7780. Tours 8:00 A.M.–4:30 P.M. by appointment only, must be reserved two weeks ahead. Visa, MasterCard. Wheelchair accessible.

If you visit Morgan, go back to River Road and head south. Otherwise, continue on River Road. When River Road turns right, be sure to follow it, and soon you pass a large vineyard owned by Estancia Winery, but there's no visiting or tasting here. In just another .2 mile you come to CLONINGER CELLARS, which puts out one of the most amusing homemade winery newsletters, called *From the Bench.*

Cloninger's location affords a gorgeous view of Salinas Valley lettuce fields with a backdrop of oak-covered hills. The tasting room and winery are in a cream-colored building with antique wooden benches, two very protective sleepy cats, and a pretty pond, complete with windmill. Cloninger invites you to bring a picnic and enjoy the view.

Loren Cloninger grew up in the Salinas Valley, which was then dotted with dairies. He says that part of a dairyman's salary was a free supply of homemade wine, which he learned to enjoy traveling farm to farm with his grandmother. Many of the farmers were Swiss-Italian, and red wine from family wine cellars "was always at the table." Loren became a fan and learned to make wine, which many friends loved, and they in turn became fans.

In response to friends' repeated requests for his wines, he joined in a partnership with Boskovich Farms to create Cloninger Cellars in 1988. They started small—at first their wines were sold only at local grocery stores and restaurants.

CABERNET SORBET
from winemaker Dave Paige, Cloninger Cellars, Salinas

five quart ice cream freezer

half a bottle Cabernet Sauvignon

*3 qts. berries (blackberries, blueberies, and raspberries, all together sometimes),
can be frozen*

sugar to taste

"I blend most of the berries in a blender, using some of the wine to help liquefy the fruit. After combining about three blenders' worth of this puree in a large mixing bowl with a pint or two of whole berries, I start tasting. Unless you have been using canned berries, you undoubtedly need to mix in a fair amount of sugar. I always do this to taste, and you should too, because not all Cabernets or all berries will have the same strength. At least it's nonfat!

"At this point . . . the mixture will seem a little flat when tasted frozen, so to liven it up I always add a little lemon juice, to taste, to brighten the fruit flavors . . . and sometimes some black pepper.

"Now you just need to remember how to use your ice cream freezer.

"P.S. By popular demand, there will probably always be some type of sorbet at our open houses. In the fall, look for sorbet made from fresh Chardonnay or Pinot Noir juice!"

In 1996 they opened their tasting room and winery, and also added a new winemaker, Dave Paige, who had worked in the Sierra Foothills, Australia, at Sterling Vineyards in the Napa Valley, and most recently at nearby Jekel Vineyards. Enjoy the biscotti balls covered with thick chocolate, and take home some grape-seed oil along with wine and lots of local lore.

Cloninger won a gold medal at the California State Fair (1998) for its 1996 Chardonnay, as well as Best Chardonnay of the Central Coast Region.

 Fine points: Featured wines: Chardonnay, Pinot Noir, Cabernet Sauvignon. Owners: Loren Cloninger and the Boskovich family. Winemaker: Dave Paige. Cases: 4,000. Acres: 51.

❧ *Cloninger Cellars, 1645 River Road, Salinas 93908; (831) 675–WINE, fax (831) 675–1922; www.cloningerwine.com. Open 11:00 A.M.–4:00 P.M. Monday–Thursday, till 5:00 P.M. Friday–Sunday. No tasting fee. Visa, MasterCard, American Express, Diners Club, Discover. Wheelchair accessible.*

Although you will probably be continuing on from Cloninger Cellars, we wanted to alert you to **SAN SABA VINEYARD**. One of Monterey County's interesting wineries, it is not yet open to the public, but call in case you can visit on a good day. While its main office is in Dallas, Texas, the winery is strictly Salinas style, small and friendly if you get there when someone's around.

When River Road forks, bear right, onto Foothill Road, where our first stop is at San Saba.

Retired plastic surgeon Dr. Mark Lemmon planted his first vines in 1975 and released his first vintage in 1981. Created in the Bordeaux style, the Cabernet Sauvignon brings back memories of small wineries in France—it is aged at least two years in French oak barrels. All San Saba's wine grapes are estate-grown, handpicked, and hand-harvested from twenty-year-old vines.

The painting on San Saba's unusual label comes from an original oil, *The Lions,* created by nineteenth-century French artist Rosa Bonheur and purchased by Lemmon from a gallery in France. Lemmon believes that the image conveys strength, power, elegance, and finesse, all characteristics he hopes will be in evidence in San Saba wines.

Fine points: Featured wines: Chardonnay, Merlot, Cabernet Sauvignon, Pinot Noir. Owner: Dr. Mark Lemmon. Winemaker: Joel Burnstein. Cases: 5,000. Acres: 65.

❧ *San Saba Vineyard, Foothill and Fort Romie Road, Salinas 93902, or 3131 Turtle Creek Boulevard, Suite 1010, Dallas, TX 75219; (800) 998–7222, fax (214) 520–0545; www.sansaba.com. Open by appointment only. Visa and MasterCard. Wheelchair accessible.*

Eight miles south of Cloninger, take the soft right onto Foothill Road (not well marked) and follow the little white WINE TASTING signs to **SMITH & HOOK AND HAHN ESTATES.** The road quickly becomes washboard bumpy, so either extreme devotion or a four-wheel-drive vehicle is recommended.

If you want an approach that is easier on your car, from Highway 101 take Arroyo Seco Road exit, follow Arroyo Seco Road to Fort Romie Road, turn right on Fort Romie Road for .8 mile, turn left on Colony Road and right on Foothill Road, and the winery will be on your left.

Both Smith & Hook and Hahn wines are made here at the winery, and the interesting tasting room once served as a 420-gallon aging barrel for Almaden Winery. You are most welcome to picnic under the trees and inhale the vast Salinas Valley from this 1,000-foot elevation. You can almost smell the lettuce growing.

Fine points: Featured wines: Smith & Hook Viognier, Baroness Chardonnay, Merlot, Cabernet Sauvignon; Hahn Estates Chardonnay, Merlot, Cabernet Franc, Cabernet Sauvignon,

Meritage. Owners: The Hahn family. Winemaker: Art Nathan. Cases: 105,000. Acres: 1,000.

➣ *Smith & Hook and Hahn Estates, 37700 Foothill Road, Soledad 93960; (831) 678–2132, fax (831) 678–0057; www.hahnestates.com Open 11:00 A.M.–4:00 P.M. daily. No tasting fee. Visa, MasterCard, American Express, Discover. Wheelchair accessible.*

We suggest you go back to Fort Romie Road from Smith & Hook and Hahn Estates and turn a sharp right. In just .2 mile you come to the driveway of **MISSION NUESTRA SENORA DE LA SOLEDAD** (Soledad Mission), one of the lesser-known California missions.

Soledad Mission was founded October 9, 1791, and was the unlucky thirteenth in the chain—unlucky because it has been largely ignored in the restoration process. Something of an outpost originally and currently, the mission itself looks lonely and weepy. Considered a hardship post by the missionaries, the last padre stationed here practically passed out at the altar. He had to be carried the 30 miles over the Santa Lucia Mountains to be buried at Mission San Antonio de Padua at what is now King City.

You can enjoy a small museum of local farming and mission artifacts, as well as annual fiestas and wine tastings on the mission grounds. The restored chapel is pleasant and offers a real contrast to the more popular Carmel Mission. Plan time to take a peaceful break here. You can really imagine what it must have been like surviving here two centuries ago, as you picnic on the garden benches amid the ruins of the mission's neglected adobes.

➣ *Mission Nuestra Senora de la Soledad, 36641 Fort Romie Road, Soledad 93960; (831) 678–2586. Open 10:00 A.M.–4:00 P.M. Wednesday–Monday. Admission by donation. Partly wheelchair accessible.*

To get to **PARAISO SPRINGS VINEYARDS & COBBLESTONE** from the mission, continue south on Fort Romie Road, which ends at Arroyo Seco. Turn right onto Arroyo Seco, and then keep going. You are now on Paraiso Springs Road. Go almost 1 mile straight, cross Foothill, and then go up the steep little hill as the road turns to the right.

As you arrive at Paraiso Springs' parking lot at the top, the winery is on the left, and the brown-shingled house to the right with the great view of the Pinnacles in the Gabilan Mountain range is the tasting room. You can picnic on the lawn or at the cafe tables inside.

The minute you walk into this tasting room you feel at home. Friendly people and thoughtfully designed hats, shirts, and books create a friendly ambience.

PARAISO SPRINGS PORT BROWNIES
from Paraiso Springs Vineyards, Soledad

2 cups flour	2 tsp. vanilla
2 cups sugar	2 eggs, slightly beaten
2 sticks butter	1 tsp. baking soda
½ cup water	1 bottle Paraiso Springs Vineyards Port
¼ cup cocoa	½ cup buttermilk

Sift together the flour and sugar. Heat butter, water, and cocoa. Boil and pour over dry ingredients. Beat thoroughly. Add vanilla, eggs, baking soda, ½ cup Port and buttermilk and mix well. Bake in a greased and floured 15"x10"x1" jelly roll pan for 20 minutes at 350 degrees.

Meanwhile reduce the remaining Port until it has the consistency of honey (roughly 45 minutes). Let brownies cool, then drizzle the Port reduction sauce over the top. (Oh my!—KTH)

No wonder the owners won the honor of an Agriculture Leadership Award from the Salinas Valley Chamber of Commerce and Pacific Coast Farm Credit.

Rich and Claudia Smith; their son Jason; daughter Kacy; Jason's wife Kim; and Kacy's husband Dave—all graduates of UC/Davis—grow the grapes, make the wine, and work in distribution, as well as in an impressive variety of community endeavors. The family grows 2,800 acres of wine grapes throughout the Salinas Valley, and their company, Grape Harvest of California, harvests 3,000 acres of vineyards for other wineries, many of which are some of California and the Napa Valley's best known.

Rich and Claudia have been selfless givers to the Monterey wine, agriculture, and tourism communities for years. Both have served as president of Monterey Wine Country Associates. Rich has also served as president of the Monterey County Farm Bureau, Monterey County Grape Growers Association, and numerous other organizations. He has also been an adviser to many university wine programs. Claudia also served as president of the Salinas Valley California Women for Agriculture and is the founder of the Monterey County Agricultural Education.

Rich planted their vineyards here in 1973 and has grown premium varietal grapes for other wineries ever since. Winemaker Philip Zorn was born in New York and grew up in West Berlin. He trained in enology and viticulture in Bad Kreuznach, Germany, and interned in the Nahe region with Weingut Baeder & Son in Rudesheim/Nahe and at Pieroth Winery in Langen Ronsheim. Closer to home, he worked at Schug Cellars in Sonoma, Sunny St. Helena Winery, Gauer Estate Vineyards, and Mountain View Vintners. In addition to the Paraiso Springs and Cobblestone label wines he produces here, he produces Tria wines with his partner in that endeavor, winemaker Bill Knuttel of Chalk Hill Winery.

Paraiso Springs is known partly for its specialty wines, most of which are available only in the tasting room, including a Reserve Pinot Blanc in a special bottle commemorating the births of the Smiths' first granddaughters in December 1995, an unusual Souzao Port wine, as well as Late Harvest Riesling and Pinot Noir. Most of their wines have earned high ratings from *Wine Spectator, Wine Enthusiast,* and other respected rate setters.

 Fine points: Featured wines: Chardonnay, Pinot Blanc, Pinot Noir, Syrah, Riesling, Souzao Port, Baby Blush, Late Harvest Riesling, Pinot Blanc Reserve, Late Harvest Pinot Noir, Cobblestone Chardonnay. Owners: Rich and Claudia Smith. Winemakers: Philip Zorn and David Fleming. Cases: 20,000. Acres: 400 estate, manage 3,000 others.

🍇 *Paraiso Springs Vineyards & Cobblestone, 38060 Paraiso Springs Road, Soledad 93960; (831) 678–0300, fax (831) 678–2584; e-mail psvwine@aol.com. Open noon–4:00 P.M. Monday–Friday, 11:00 A.M.–5:00 P.M. Saturday–Sunday. No tasting fee; tours $5.00 per person for groups of more than ten. Visa, MasterCard. Wheelchair accessible.*

PARAISO SPRINGS VINEYARDS & COBBLESTONE, SOLEDAD

JEKEL VINEYARDS, GREENFIELD

From Paraiso Springs we recommend that you make your way south to **JEKEL VINEYARDS** in Greenfield. It really isn't as far as it sounds. You can go the pretty back road way, or take the highway.

The pretty back road way: From Paraiso Springs, head east on Paraiso Springs Road. Turn a sharp right on Arroyo Seco and go south to Elm Avenue. Winter rains often wash mud over the road, meaning you should drive carefully along eerily beautiful Elm because you are likely to find either the mud or dust. Despite what local maps say, Elm veers off to the left like an unannounced fork in the road at the base of a steep hill, exactly 8 miles south of the intersection of Paraiso Springs and Arroyo Seco. Cross the green iron bridge and pass Central Avenue. Still on Elm Street, believe it or not (this is no mid-America Elm Street, baby), you come first to Fourteenth Street and then Thirteenth. Turn left on Thirteenth to Walnut, turn east on Walnut.

The highway way: From Highway 101, take the Walnut Avenue exit in Greenfield, head west on Walnut Avenue for 1 mile, and the entrance to Jekel Vineyards will be on your right at the stone pillars.

The two-story dark brown building with white trim and wisteria-covered balcony railings gives a comforting feeling. Its lawns and flowers are shaded by large trees. The small, cozy tasting room faces the bottling room, and you can duck around and watch production and actually talk to folks. You can't miss the fact that Jekel is an active sponsor of the Pebble Beach Golf Links tournaments and sells wines, of course, as well as attractive T-shirts and caps. Consider a picnic under the shady gazebo.

Right next door is Gravelstone Vineyards, where all of Jekel's Chardonnay is grown. Bill Jekel began planting vineyards in 1972 and built the winery in 1978, releasing his first vintage, Johannisberg Riesling, the same year. Winemaker and general manager Rick Boyer joined Jekel in 1994 after graduating from UC/Davis in plant science viticulture (and making All Conference

Defensive Back in football as a senior). He later worked in grower relations for E & J Gallo Winery and as production manager at Ventana Vineyards.

Fine points: Featured wines: Chardonnay, Johannisberg Riesling, Merlot, Pinot Noir, Cabernet Sauvignon, Cabernet Franc, Petit Verdot, Malbec, Meritage. Owner: Bill Jekel. Winemaker: Rick Boyer. Cases: 85,000. Acres: 322.

Jekel Vineyards, 40155 Walnut Avenue, Greenfield 93927; (831) 674–5525, fax (831) 674–3769. Open 11:00 A.M.–4:00 P.M. daily. No tasting fee. Visa, MasterCard. Wheelchair accessible.

Replacing Monterey Vineyard is lovely **RIVERLAND VINEYARDS/MYSTIC CLIFFS**, an unusual wine and big-star entertainment venue alongside Highway 101 with traffic and wind blowing by. Despite the noise, the grounds are expansive and beautifully cultivated, with burbling fountains, lots of natural woods in the tasting room, the best prices for shirts and hats anywhere, and an enormous output of wine for its New York owners.

To get here, take the Alta Street exit off Highway 101 to its west side, turn right immediately and go north to the winery "just before the tracks."

Riverland/Mystic Cliffs bottles wine for its own labels, as well as for Mondavi's coastal wines, Monterey Vineyard, Deer Valley, and Dunnewood.

RIVERLAND VINEYARDS/MYSTIC CLIFFS, GONZALES

SCHEID VINEYARDS, GREENFIELD

You can now taste and purchase Monterey Vineyard wines at A Taste of Monterey on Cannery Row (see page157).

Fine Points: Featured wines: Mystic Cliffs Dry Riesling, Sauvignon Blanc, Chardonnay, Pinot Noir, Merlot, Cabernet Sauvignon. Owner: Canadagua/Constellation Wine Company of New York. Winemaker: Ed Filce. Cases: 2.6 million. Acres: 1,500 and contract out.

Riverland Winery/Mystic Cliffs, 800 South Alta, Gonzales 93926; (831) 675–2481. Open 11:00 A.M.–4:00 P.M. Wednesday–Sunday. Visa, MasterCard, American Express. Wheelchair accessible.

We suggest you retrace your steps to Highway 101 and point yourselves south toward **SCHEID VINEYARDS**, the most southern of the Monterey County wineries that is open regularly for tasting. On Highway 101 go 5.3 miles south to Hobson Avenue, and turn west (right). Scheid is one-half block on the right in a little blue one-hundred-year-old restored barn. We were there in the fall, and a very friendly scarecrow guarding the Halloween pumpkins nearly blew into our arms.

Scheid has the most spectacular labels we've seen, designed by Dominic Man Kit Lam, whose autographed book of paintings is available in the tasting room for $55. The exquisite small tasting room has yellow walls with blond maple floors and a brass bar rail to rest one tired foot at a time. Don't miss

---

CORNFLAKE CHICKEN
from John Allore for Scheid Vineyards, Greenfield

½ cup honey

2 Tbs. Dijon mustard

1 tsp. paprika

pinch of cayenne

1 tsp. garlic powder

1 cup corn flakes, crushed

¼ cup pecans, crushed

4 chicken breasts, skinless

Mix honey, Dijon mustard, paprika, cayenne, and garlic powder. In a separate bowl, combine corn flakes and pecans. Dip chicken in honey mixture. Roll chicken in corn flakes and pecans. Bake at 350 degrees for 40 minutes. Serve with 1996 Scheid Chardonnay. Serves four.

---

the charming Talavera Mexican pottery on the shelves of the tasting room. We firmly endorse Scheid's claim to have the prettiest women's rest room of Monterey County wineries, including its white tile with ivy-grape leaf tiles, rolled hand towels, and flowers!

Scheid offers a simple and elegant brochure that explains the grape-growing and winemaking process season by season. Scheid, one of the few publicly traded wineries (NASDAQ) in Monterey County, makes most of its money by managing other people's vineyards, such as for International Distiller and Vintners of North America, Canandaigua Brands, the Hess Collection, the Chalone Wine Group Ltd., Gundlach-Bundschu Winery, Joseph Phelps, Morgan Winery, and Independence Wine Company.

Fine points: Featured wines: Chardonnay, White Riesling, Gewürztraminer, Merlot, Cabernet Sauvignon, Pinot Noir. Owner: Canadagua/Constellation Wine Co. of New York. Winemaker: Steve Storrs (Storrs Winery in Santa Cruz). Cases: 3,500. Acres: 5,000 owned or managed.

❧ *Scheid Vineyards, 1972 Hobson Avenue, Greenfield 93927; (831) 386–0316, fax (831) 386–0127;www.scheidvinyards.com. Open 11:00 A.M.–6:00 P.M. daily summer, till 5:00 P.M. daily winter. No tasting fee. Visa, MasterCard, American Express. Wheelchair accessible. Executive office: 13470 Washington Boulevard, Suite 300, Marina del Rey 90292; (310) 301–1555, fax (310) 301–1569.*

BLUE CHEESE FLAN
from Lynn at Chalone Vineyard, Soledad

¾ cup crushed buttery crackers

2 Tbs. melted margarine

2 8-oz. packages cream cheese (room temperature)

2 4-oz. packages blue cheese crumbles

1 Tbs. sugar

1⅔ cups sour cream, divided

3 eggs

⅛ tsp. pepper

orange or lemon yogurt (optional)

Combine cracker crumbs and margarine. Spread on bottom of springform pan and bake in 350 degree oven for 10 minutes. Combine cream cheese and chopped blue cheese until well blended, add sugar, ⅔ cup sour cream, eggs, and pepper. Mix well. Pour into springform pan and bake in 300 degree oven for 45 minutes.

Combine yogurt (if desired) with remaining sour cream. Spread over cake and bake for an additional 10 minutes. Cool and unmold. Serve with fruit and crackers or French bread. Can be prepared a few days in advance, and keeps very well. Serves an army.

To complete our Salinas Valley wine loop, get back onto Highway 101 and point yourselves northward, back toward Soledad, Gonzales, and Salinas to get to **CHALONE VINEYARD**. From Highway 101, take the Highway 146 exit heading east, which is the canyonesque road to the Pinnacles National Monument. Go 6.1 miles and turn left (north) onto Stonewall Canyon Road for about 1 mile to Chalone's tasting room.

Home of the oldest vineyard in Monterey County, Chalone is widely famous for its outstanding Chardonnays and Pinot Noirs, all estate grown. Founded by innovative Richard Graff, who was killed tragically in a private plane crash in 1997, Chalone now includes Acacia in the Carneros District (Sonoma–Napa Valleys), Carmenet in Sonoma, and Edna Valley Vineyard in San Luis Obispo.

Chalone's remoteness is one of its prime assets. Don't miss the cave's wine cellar or the annual wildflower walk, warehouse sale, or winemaker's dinners.

Fine points: Featured wines: Chardonnay, Chenin Blanc, Pinot Blanc, Pinot Noir. Owner: Chalone Wine Group. Winemaker: Dan Karlsen. Cases: 35,000. Acres: 309.

🌱 *Chalone Vineyard, P. O. Box 518, Stonewall Canyon Road via Highway 146, Soledad 93960; (831) 678–1717 or (707) 254–4200; www. chalonewinegroup.com. Open 11:30 A.M.–5:00 P.M. Saturday and Sunday; call for appointment Monday–Friday. Tours by appointment. No tasting fee. Visa, MasterCard, American Express. Wheelchair accessible.*

To return to Monterey or Carmel, get back to Highway 101, head north to Salinas, and turn west to Highway 68 and Monterey/Carmel.

CHAPTER 7

TRAVELS WITH STEINBECK

*J*ohn Steinbeck was a Stanford dropout who won the gold medal given by the California Commonwealth Club for best novel by a California author, a Pulitzer prize, and the Nobel prize for literature. Movies based on his work received twenty-nine Academy Award nominations. Maybe if he'd gone to Cal (UC/Berkeley) he would have made something of himself.

JOHN STEINBECK
Photo courtesy of Pat Hathaway Collection and National Steinbeck Center

STEINBECK IN SALINAS

Any complete tour dealing with the author of *Travels with Charlie, Tortilla Flat, East of Eden,* and *Cannery Row* should begin in the city of Steinbeck's birth, Salinas. Yes, Salinas, Monterey County, California, whose welcome sign says WELCOME TO SALINAS—UPTOWN STYLE, DOWNTOWN CHARM. It's all relative.

Salinas is about 20 miles (one-half hour) east of Monterey and 105 miles south of San Francisco. It is an excellent place from which to visit many Monterey County wineries and to sample a couple of good restaurants.

To get here from Monterey, take Highway 68 east 17 miles to downtown Salinas, resisting all turnoffs and following the signs to Main Street. The National Steinbeck Center is at the end of Main Street in old-town Salinas, as are many of Steinbeck's favorite spots.

From San Francisco and San Jose, take Highway 101 south to Salinas and take the Main Street exit. Go east on Main Street, which here turns into Salinas Street, turn left (south) on West Gavilan Street, and then turn east on Main Street, which is one-way and ends at the Steinbeck Center. There's a good parking lot just to your left.

From Los Angeles take Highway 101 north, take the John Street exit, turn left on John Street to South Main, turn right on South Main and go 5 blocks to the Steinbeck Center.

NATIONAL STEINBECK CENTER, SALINAS

John Steinbeck Jr. was born February 27, 1902, of German and Irish ances-
try. His father, John Steinbeck Sr., served the public as county treasurer, and his
mother worked as a teacher, sometimes in the public schools and sometimes at
home, nurturing her son's interest in reading and literature.

As a youth, Steinbeck worked during school vacations as a hired hand in the
fields of nearby ranches. After graduating from Salinas High School in 1919, he
went off to Stanford University intending to major in English. Eventually, however, he developed an "independent major," which allowed him to attend classes
only sporadically.

In 1925 Steinbeck left Stanford for New York in an attempt to break into
the big time, but he didn't succeed and returned to California, where he wrote
his first three novels, *Cup of Gold*, *The Pastures of Heaven*, and *To a God
Unknown*. They all bombed.

In 1930 Steinbeck married Carol Henning, and they lived in Pacific Grove,
where he gathered much of his material for *Tortilla Flat* and *Cannery Row*.
Tortilla Flat, which was published in 1935, won the highly respected Gold
Medal for best novel by a California author and thus changed the Steinbecks'
lives. In 1938 he won the New York Drama Critics' Circle Award for his play
adaptation of *Of Mice and Men*, based on his 1937 novel. Then in 1939 *The
Grapes of Wrath* won the Pulitzer prize for fiction, and Steinbeck received the
American Booksellers' Award and became a Member of the National Institute
of Arts and Letters. After a second brief marriage, Steinbeck married the love of
his life, Elaine Anderson Scott, on December 28, 1950.

During World War II, Steinbeck served as a war correspondent for the
New York *Herald Tribune* (some of his pieces were collected into *Once There
Was a War)*. In the fifties he wrote campaign speeches for Adlai Stevenson's
presidential campaign. In 1962 he was awarded the Nobel prize for literature,
specifically for *Travels with Charley*, but really as a lifetime achievement award.
He was awarded the United States Medal of Freedom in 1964 and also became
a Trustee of the John F. Kennedy Memorial Library. In 1966 he served as a
member of the National Arts Council. Steinbeck died in New York City
December 20, 1968. His ashes reside in the Garden of Memories Cemetery in
Salinas, should you wish to visit them. In 1979 the U.S. Post Office issued a
Steinbeck commemorative stamp. In 1984 the American Arts Gold Medallion
was given in his memory.

In the meantime, several of Steinbeck's books were banned by Salinas
Valley schools because of their accurate depictions of real life in the fields;
he received numerous death threats; and his books were burned twice on
Salinas's Main Street. It now seems poetically just that the public library in
Salinas bears his name.

So we start at the **NATIONAL STEINBECK CENTER**, a truly rare literary center, ironically and wonderfully funded largely by descendants of the leading farmers who once wanted Steinbeck's books banned. One of the first photos you see in the main exhibit hall is that of Pat Covichi, Steinbeck's agent.

Here you and the kids can browse through seven themed interactive, multisensory galleries and exhibits of scenes from Steinbeck's novels. You can feel the cool air of the lettuce boxcar in *East of Eden*, smell the fish and hear the seagulls in *Cannery Row*, climb on or pet the Red Pony in the barn, and listen to classical music in Ed "Doc" Ricketts's "lab." Seven theaters show clips from Steinbeck films, and you can use the computers to try your hand in the Art of Writing Room, access Steinbeck's works on CD, or look at videos. We especially love walking around Rocinante, Steinbeck's actual green camper from *Travels with Charley.*

On the right side of the entryway, be sure to walk to the back and visit the gallery of rotating exhibits of early California artists, the art of the Americas, and local history and culture.

Even if you have never read any of Steinbeck's work, the museum store is an excellent place to begin, with small and inexpensive volumes of his writing, as well as collectors' goodies ranging from clothing and books to cards, glassware, jewelry, journals, posters, and other Steinbeck stuff.

JOHN STEINBECK'S 1960 CAMPER NAMED ROCINANTE
Photo courtesy National Steinbeck Center

If you need a resuscitating break, try the Steinbeck Center's One Main Street cafe, where chef Dwight Collins uses his considerable culinary experience (Stanford Research Institute, Apple Computer, Intel, Fairchild Semiconductor, Bon Appetit Management Company, and more) to create fresh California foods at affordable prices using the produce grown on nearby farms. Try Sea of Cortez Fisherman's Stew, Tortilla Flat Black Bean Soup, a Cannery Row club sandwich with either grilled calamari or salmon fillet, Chicken Castroville, or steamed artichokes with lemon aioli. All are under $10.

As you leave the National Steinbeck Center, stand on the front stairs, take a deep breath, and look down Old Main Street where this Nobel prize winner's books were burned. Notice the mural on the building wall to your left, depicting Steinbeck and the people about whom he wrote. Farmworkers and farm owners still dress up in their best boots and cowboy hats to come to town. A few even wear suits, or at least a tie once in a while.

✢↺ *National Steinbeck Center, One Main Street, Salinas 93901; (831) 775–4720 or 796–3833, fax (831) 796–3828; www.steinbeck.org. Open 10:00 A.M.–5:00 P.M. daily, except Easter, Thanksgiving, Christmas, and New Year's Day. Admission: adults, $7.95; seniors. $6.95; ages thirteen to seventeen, $5.95; ages six to twelve, $ 3.95.*

STEINBECK MURAL,
OUTSIDE NATIONAL STEINBECK CENTER, SALINAS

In just a couple of blocks of walking you can pass by several of Steinbeck's favorite buildings, some of which he frequented and wrote about in various books.

As you look down Main Street from the Steinbeck Center, you can see many buildings Steinbeck mentioned in *East of Eden*. Interesting addresses in the 100 block of Main include No. 150, whose incarnations over the years as Abbott House and the Cominos brothers' hotel appear in *Travels with Charley*. *East of Eden* sites include the San Francisco Chop House, which once stood at 116 Main, and Krough's Drug Store at No. 156. Griffin's Saloon was near the Old White Theater at No. 157 across the street.

> ## FISH HOUSE PASTA
> *from Salinas Valley Fish House, Salinas*
>
> ---
>
> ½ cube butter
> ⅛ cup green onions, chopped
> ¼ cup black olives
> 1 Tbs. shallots, chopped
> ¼ cup diced Roma tomatoes
> ½ lb. baby bay shrimp
> ½ cup clam broth
>
> Melt butter and sauté green onions, olives, and shallots. Add tomatoes and clam broth and simmer for a minute; add shrimp last. Simmer 5–10 minutes and serve over cooked linguini.

In the 200 block, *East of Eden* scenes include the Monterey County Bank building at the corner of East Gabilan (after 1906 earthquake), Porter and Irvine's at Nos. 210–214, Bell's Candy at No. 242, and the old Elks building at No. 247, which was mentioned as Farmers Mercantile.

While you are in this area, we highly recommend you try local restaurants, two of which are extremely convenient to the Steinbeck Center. **SALINAS VALLEY FISH HOUSE** is deceptively plain in decor and simple in menu. But locals and Steinbeck center staff recommend its calamari ($6.95), pastas, steaks, and salads highly. The most expensive items on the menu are Sicilian Holiday Pasta or rib eye steak at $12.95 for either entree. Salads range from $2.95 for spinach to $3.95 for Caesar or local greens (with shrimp, add $3.00). The wine list offers a good representation of local wines, reasonably priced, and you can't miss with the crème brûlée, tiramisu, Death by Chocolate, or cannoli at only $3.50. All pastas are made here.

✣ *Salinas Valley Fish House, 172 Main Street, Salinas 93901; (831) 775–0175, fax (831) 753–9623. Open for lunch 11:00 A.M.–2:30 P.M., dinner 5:00–9:00 P.M. daily. Full bar. Visa, MasterCard, American Express, Discover. First floor is wheelchair accessible.*

We highly recommend **SPADO'S**, the baby of John Spadoro, who also is involved with Tutto Buono in Monterey. Spado's is the best and only with-it feeling restaurant in Salinas, and the food matches the exciting but not threatening decor.

As you walk down its entryway from West Alisal Street, there are outdoor tables on a dais protected in hot weather by awnings and in bad weather by awnings, heaters, and curtains.

The walls are warm yellow, the crowd is bustling and local, and the food is hugely spectacular. Before you order from the menu, check out the antipasto bar at the back of the room. Here you will find fabulous polenta, marinated tomatoes, thin delicate pizza slices, salads of several kinds, marinated beets, grilled peppers, pastas, risottos, and marinated mushrooms. You can indulge or overindulge in some of the best Italian delicacies here at lunchtime ($7.50).

The Salinas chopped salad is an excellent salad of the best local greens, but they aren't what we would call chopped ($5.99). The steak over chilled iceberg hearts with blue cheese and spicy nuts is also terrific ($5.95). There are several combos of pizza and Caesar salad, stuffed grilled portobello mushrooms, stuffed grilled eggplant, and pasta of the day with salad ($6.99).

We enjoyed the five-clove garlic chicken sandwich with melted provolone and homemade potato chips (like no others anywhere) at $6.99 and the tri-tip steak on garlic bread. Spado's stew and special pastas change daily and are unbelievably good. Be sure to check the large wall blackboard for daily specials, as well as the mural honoring local produce workers. All pizza topping combina-

---

BRAISED LAMB SHANKS
from John Spadoro of Spado's, Salinas

2 10-oz. lamb shanks	*32 oz. tomato sauce*
2 cups flour	*2 cups red wine*
1 yellow onion, chopped	*1 lemon peel, grated*
3 cloves garlic	*1 cup water*
3 carrots, chopped	*½ cup Dijon mustard*
½ stalk celery, chopped	*1 cup Asiago cheese, grated*
2 cups oil	

Dredge lamb shanks in flour. Sauté onion, garlic, carrots, and celery in oil in deep oven-suitable pan, then add lamb shanks and pan-sear until brown. Add tomato sauce, wine, lemon peel, and water. Bake at 400 degrees for 3 hours. Remove lamb shanks and brush with Dijon mustard, then roll them in cheese, and return to pan. Bake 15 minutes longer. Serves 2-4.

STEINBECK HOUSE, SALINAS

tions are also offered as calzones (under $10.00). The sand dabs are mouthwatering ($11.99), as are the steaks and lamb shanks. Lots of veggie alternatives and mother's macaroni and cheese, only better ($9.99).

🌻 *Spado's, 66 West Alisal, Salinas 93901; (831) 424–4139, fax (831) 424–6574. Open from 11:00 A.M. Beer and wine. Visa, MasterCard, American Express. Not wheelchair accessible.*

While we love Spado's, your tastes may take you to **STEINBECK HOUSE**, John Steinbeck's birthplace, where you can tour the house and enjoy a rather tearoomlike luncheon served by enthusiastic and well-versed volunteers of the Valley Guild.

The house was built in 1897. Steinbeck lived here for nineteen years, and it was here that he wrote his first stories and also worked on parts of *The Red Pony, Tortilla Flat,* and the short stories *The White Quail* and *The Chrysanthemums.*

To get to the Steinbeck House from the National Steinbeck Center, go west on Central Street to Stone—the house is on the corner. Park anywhere on the street or in the small lot off Stone just beyond the Best Cellar gift shop. Be sure to make a reservation for lunch during high tourist season (meaning warm weather).

CALIFORNIA CASSEROLE
from the Valley Guild, Steinbeck House, Salinas

INGREDIENTS FOR THE CASSEROLE:

2 lbs. ground chuck	1 Tbs. salt
¼ cup oil	½ tsp. garlic powder
1 cup onion, chopped	1 Tbs. chili powder
½ cup green pepper, chopped	1 tsp. cumin
1 16-oz. can tomatoes	¼ tsp. black pepper
1 8-oz. can tomato sauce	½ cup cornmeal
1 12-oz. can whole kernel corn	1 cup pitted ripe olives, sliced

INGREDIENTS FOR THE SPOON BREAD:

1½ cups milk	½ cup cornmeal
1 tsp. salt	1 cup grated cheddar cheese
2 Tbs. butter	2 eggs, slightly beaten

PREPARATION FOR THE CASSEROLE:

Brown meat in oil. Add onion and green pepper and stir until onion is golden. Add tomatoes, tomato sauce, corn, salt, garlic powder, chili powder, cumin, and black pepper. Simmer 15 minutes. Mix together some water and cornmeal and add to the meat mixture. Cover and simmer 15 minutes more. Add ripe olives. Pour mixture into 3-quart casserole dish.

PREPARATION FOR THE SPOON BREAD:

In saucepan, heat milk, salt, and butter over low heat. Slowly stir in cornmeal and cook, stirring constantly until thick. Remove from heat and stir in cheese and slightly beaten eggs. Mix well and pour over meat mixture. Refrigerate until 1 hour before serving time. Bake at 350 degrees for 1 hour. Serves twelve to fourteen.

The restaurant's prix fixe lunch menu changes daily and is printed monthly. It includes soup or salad and a vegetarian and carnivore entree ($7.50). Desserts are $3.00 and beverages are $1.00. All tips go to charities.

Explore and read all you want, although the upstairs bedrooms where all the action happened (including writing) are off limits. Be sure to check out the Best

JOHN STEINBECK'S GRAVESTONE
AND HAMILTON FAMILY PLOT,
GARDEN OF MEMORIES CEMETERY,
SALINAS

Cellar gift shop for unusual Steinbeck books (including some first editions), memorabilia, the Steinbeck House Cookbook, and individual recipes for sale in a rack in the back.

➳ *Steinbeck House, 132 Central Avenue, Salinas 93901; (831) 424–2635. Open 11:30 A.M.–3:00 P.M. Monday–Friday, till 2:30 P.M. Saturday. Lunch open seating 11:30 A.M.–2:00 P.M. Monday–Saturday. Beer and wine. Visa, MasterCard. Not wheelchair accessible.*

You may want to visit the **JOHN STEINBECK LIBRARY**, which is actually the Salinas public library, renamed in March 1969. Here you will find a fascinating archival collection that includes original manuscripts, rare editions, correspondence, photographs, taped interviews, and other Steinbeck memorabilia. These archives, which are slated to be moved to the National Steinbeck Center, are open only by appointment, but you can visit the Steinbeck Room to see part of the collection.

➳ *John Steinbeck Library, 350 Lincoln Avenue at San Luis, Salinas 93901; (831) 758–7311. Open 10:00 A.M.–9:00 P.M. Monday–Wednesday, till 6:00 P.M. Thursday–Saturday. Wheelchair accessible.*

While there are many other sites around Salinas to drive by, the only other really significant one to visit is the **GARDEN OF MEMORIES CEMETERY**, Steinbeck's burial site. His ashes are buried in his mother's Hamilton family plot No. 1, where he is surrounded by his parents, his sister Mary, William "Uncle Will" Hamilton, friends, and neighbors, many of whom appear in *East of Eden*. Universal Studios used Hamilton Plot No. 2 for a funeral scene in the television movie *The Harness*.

To get to the cemetery, drive south on Main Street and turn left on East Romie Lane, continue longer than you think you should, and turn a rather difficult right onto Abbott Street. Then turn right onto Memory Lane in the cemetery, and then right again after the mausoleum. Pass a little road (called the "old road" in *East of Eden*) and turn right onto the one real-looking road. Park quietly before you get to the flagpole near the marker that points thataway to Steinbeck's grave. Walk back (it's nearly impossible to miss graves here) to the Hamilton plot and voilà!

STEINBECK IN MONTEREY

John Steinbeck hung out a lot in Monterey, primarily at the foot of Alvarado Street, much of which has been replaced by the Monterey County Convention Center. It's still worth exploring, though, particularly during the farmers' market on Alvarado on Tuesday evenings, when you might see a few characters remotely resembling Steinbeck's friends and fictional creations.

Jimmy Trucia's Tavern at 242 Alvarado was one of his favorite hangouts, while he and his wife frequented Hermann's Inn at 380 Alvarado. In *Cannery Row* Doc Ricketts buys a hamburger at Hermann's, originally the Jacinto Rodriguez Adobe and now the Monterey County Convention and Visitors Bureau. Some biographers say Steinbeck wrote most of *The Pearl* in an upstairs

COLTON HALL, MONTEREY

Courtesy of Monterey County Convention and Visitors Bureau

BRONZE MEMORIAL TO JOHN
STEINBECK, STEINBECK PLAZA

room of the Monterey County Trust and Savings Bank, once at 399 Alvarado. In *Travels with Charley* Steinbeck suggested that the last time he was in Monterey he strolled down Alvarado.

The Poppy, which was at 444 Alvarado, appears as the Golden Poppy in *Cannery Row* and as the restaurant where Suzy works in *Sweet Thursday*. The Pirate in *Tortilla Flat* appears on Alvarado, and Joe eats steak at Pop Ernest's (then at No. 441) in *East of Eden.*

The MONTEREY POST OFFICE, 565 Harnell Street, was the first post office in California and west of the Rocky Mountains. The current building, which was built in 1932 by the Works Progress Administration, has two interesting ceramic murals featuring Sebastian Vizcaino and John D. Sloat in the act of landing at Monterey. This and the Fremont Headquarters Adobe north of this property are described in the Josh Billings incident in *Cannery Row.*

COLTON HALL, which we've mentioned several times in this book, on Pacific Street between Jefferson and Madison, is where the California Constitution was signed. Next to Colton Hall is the old Monterey County jail, completed in 1854, and mentioned in *Tortilla Flat.*

Currently the MONTEREY INSTITUTE OF INTERNATIONAL STUDIES (private) at 460 Pierce Street occupies the old Lara/Soto Adobe where John Steinbeck and his family lived in 1944 and where he wrote part of *The Pearl.*

Steinbeck and pal Ricketts's Western Flyer trip left from OLD FISHERMAN'S WHARF on March 11, 1940, for the Gulf of California, also known as the Sea of Cortez. On paper Doc and Suzy have dinner on the Wharf in *Sweet Thursday.*

And then there's Cannery Row, oh yes, oh my!

CANNERY ROW, the "Sardine Capital of the World," once had eighteen sardine canneries cranking and packing. Whew! Besides the sardines, Cannery Row yielded material for John Steinbeck's *Tortilla Flat, Cannery Row,* and *Sweet Thursday,* as well as *The Log from the Sea of Cortez.* Until 1953 Cannery Row was called Ocean View Avenue.

Steinbeck's favorite friend and character in his books, Edward F. "Doc" Ricketts, is memorialized with a bronze bust at Drake and Wave Streets near where the Del Monte Express train hit Ricketts's car and killed him in the dark on May 8, 1948. Ricketts was Steinbeck's pal, mentor, and model for at least six characters, as well as a nationally recognized leader in modernizing marine biology.

You can see a fairly accurate bronze bust of John Steinbeck in the little Steinbeck Plaza, which now serves as the entrance to McAbee's beautiful beach at the foot of Prescott and Cannery Row.

The "vacant lot" that was a favorite gathering place for "The Boys" in *Cannery Row* is now covered with attractive flowers. ("Why it is called vacant when it is piled high with old boilers, with rusting pipes, with great square timbers, and stacks of five gallon cans, no one can say," Steinbeck wrote.) The Cannery Workers Shacks adjoin the lot, which is next to the Sea Pride warehouse at Bruce Ariss Way and Cannery Row.

What is now **MACKEREL JACK'S TRADING COMPANY** at 799 Cannery Row was the Lone Star Cafe, a house of ill repute run by popular madam Flora Woods, who was well known locally for her well-placed political and often anonymous charitable donations. Steinbeck renamed the Lone Star the Bear Flag Restaurant and also changed Woods's name to Dora Flood. Flora-Dora closed her house in 1941 and died penniless in 1948.

CANNERY WORKERS' SHACKS, CANNERY ROW

ACROSS FROM DOC'S LAB 1986"
Mural by Bruce Ariss   Sponsored by DICK BRUHN A Man's Stoi

BRUCE ARISS MURAL PORTRAYS
"ACROSS FROM DOC'S LAB 1986," CANNERY ROW

Biologist Ed Ricketts's Pacific Biological Laboratories marine lab actually existed across the street at 800 Cannery Row. In *Cannery Row* Steinbeck called it both the Western Biological Laboratory and Doc's Lab. Renovated from a residence to a lab in 1929, it burned in 1936 and was rebuilt. In 1993 the city of Monterey purchased the property to preserve it as an important historic site and opens it for occasional tours by the Cannery Row Foundation. Call (831) 372–8512.

Across from the lab and down a little, at **835 CANNERY ROW**, the two-story brown wooden building with white trim was once the Wing Chong Market opened in 1918 by Won Yee and eleven other Chinese-American investors as a dry goods and grocery store to serve the rapidly expanding canning industry. In *Cannery Row* Won Yee becomes Lee Chong. The market now houses a souvenir shop and **ALICIA'S ANTIQUES** in the back. It's hard to find Alicia's open, unfortunately, but when it is, you can visit the Steinbeck Remembrance room, which contains Steinbeck and Ricketts manuscripts, first editions, and an eclectic assortment of memorabilia.

For forty years **KALISA'S LA IDA CAFE** at 851 Cannery Row has been a very legitimate and somewhat eccentric cafe run by Kalisa Moore, who serves good, cheap food and good characters too. We have heard some pretty wild stories from men who "grew up" in this place. Originally a boardinghouse built in 1929, it became a real bordello, called La Ida Cafe in *Cannery Row*. This is where Steinbeck's Eddie used to pour leftover drinks into a jug for Mack and "The Boys" at the Palace Flophouse.

STEINBECK IN PACIFIC GROVE

Remember, Monterey and Pacific Grove run together, so at times you may not know if you are in one or the other.

For instance, to get to **POINT CABRILLO**, formerly known as China Point, you just follow Ocean View from Monterey. Get on it just west of the Monterey Bay Aquarium and wind along the coast. Ocean View will actually take you all the way around Pacific Grove to Lighthouse Avenue, Pacific Grove's main street, where Ocean View turns into Sunset Drive and leads you to the Asilomar Conference Center.

Point Cabrillo houses the Hopkins Marine Station of Stanford University, which Steinbeck mentioned simply as the Hopkins Marine Station in *The Log from the Sea of Cortez* and *Sweet Thursday.*

KALISA'S LA IDA CAFE AND
WING CHONG/LEE CHONG MARKET, CANNERY ROW

Once you are in hard-core Pacific Grove, turn left (up) Fountain to Lighthouse Avenue to see what was **HOLMAN'S DEPART-MENT STORE**. If you come into Pacific Grove on Lighthouse, it is the biggest store on your right at Fountain. It's now an antiques collective. John Steinbeck, who loved to putter in the hardware department, mentioned Holman's often in *Cannery Row*.

You can drive by the house at 147 Eleventh Street, which Steinbeck's father built as a summer home in 1903. It is now a private residence, so please show respect for the people lucky enough to live there.

Steinbeck often came to Pacific Grove with his family when he was young, and he came back here to live with his first wife, Carol, in 1930. This is where he wrote *The Pastures of Heaven*, *To a God Unknown*, *Tortilla Flat*, *In Dubious Battle*, and *Of Mice and Men*, and where he completed *The Red Pony*.

> ### MALT SHOP PIE
> *from the Valley Guild,*
> *Steinbeck House, Salinas*
>
> 1 pint vanilla ice cream
> 1 Tbs. milk
> ½ cup crushed malted milk balls
> 1 9-inch graham cracker or
>   chocolate cookie piecrust
> 1 cup whipping cream
> 3 Tbs. instant chocolate-flavored
>   malted milk powder
> 3 Tbs. marshmallow topping
> malted milk balls for garnish
>
> Stir the ice cream to soften. Add milk and malted milk balls; stir to mix. Spread in pie crust. Freeze.
>
> Whip cream until soft peaks form. Add milk powder and marshmallow topping to whipped cream. Spread whipped cream mixture over ice cream layer. Sprinkle pie with additional crushed malted milk balls and freeze.

Steinbeck built the fence and planted all the trees you see around the house. After he died in New York in 1968, his ashes were placed in the yard beside the house for two days before they were taken to the Garden of Memories Cemetery in Salinas for burial.

Two other Steinbeck homes nearby include one at 222 Central, where his maternal grandmother, Elizabeth Hamilton, lived and died (in 1918). Steinbeck and his brother built a workroom onto the main house for the writer. The house, just across the street from the elegant Gatehouse Inn, is now a bed-and-breakfast.

Grandmother Elizabeth appears as a major character in *East of Eden*. Notice that Steinbeck's grandparents lived on Central Avenue in Pacific Grove, and his parents lived on Central Avenue in Salinas.

222 CENTRAL AVENUE, PACIFIC GROVE, HOME OF STEINBECK'S
MATERNAL GRANDMOTHER, ELIZABETH HAMILTON

In 1941 Steinbeck lived at 425 Eardley Avenue, where he worked on *The Log from the Sea of Cortez*.

A visit to the **BUTTERFLY TREES** and **MONARCH BUTTERFLY SANCTUARY**, known locally as the Butterfly Grove, is worth the experience on its own, but has even greater significance if you remember it from Steinbeck's *Sweet Thursday*. To get here, go west on Lighthouse Avenue past downtown, then turn left (south) on Ridge. The Butterfly Grove's eucalyptus trees are right behind the Butterfly Grove Inn. Walk or roll down a little path just south of the inn.

EL CARMELO CEMETERY, at the corner of Lighthouse Avenue and Asilomar Boulevard, is also adjacent to the Lighthouse Lodge and across Lighthouse from the Lighthouse Suites. This is the "pretty little cemetery" of *Cannery Row* where Steinbeck's pal Edward F. Ricketts's funeral was held and where Ricketts's parents are buried. Steinbeck also mentions Ricketts's funeral here in *The Log from the Sea of Cortez*.

Just west of the cemetery (across Asilomar) is the **POINT PINOS LIGHTHOUSE**, completed in 1855 and one of the oldest on the Pacific Coast. The lighthouse has had two women keepers in its life, one of whom Steinbeck describes in *To a God Unknown*. The lighthouse itself shows up in both *Cannery Row* and *Sweet Thursday*.

CREAMY LETTUCE SOUP
from the Valley Guild, Steinbeck House, Salinas

2 Tbs. butter	3 cups water
1 small onion, chopped	dash Tabasco
2 Tbs. flour	2 cups half-and-half
2 Tbs. dry chicken soup base	¼ head iceberg lettuce

In 2-quart pan heat butter. Add the onion and sauté until soft. Stir in flour and add chicken soup base, water, and Tabasco. Cook 15–20 minutes.

Add half-and-half; heat but do not boil. Shred iceberg lettuce and add to soup just before serving. Lettuce must retain fresh, crisp texture and flavor, so do not cook.

The only single dwelling at the Asilomar Conference Grounds is at 825 Asilomar Boulevard and was owned by Steinbeck's sister, Esther Rodgers, for twenty years. Steinbeck stayed in the cabin many times and worked on *The Log from the Sea of Cortez* while in residence.

STEINBECK IN CARMEL

Probably the most memorable place in Carmel for Steinbeck was the **PINE INN** on Ocean Avenue, where he met his third and last wife, Elaine Scott, in 1949. The hangout element of the Pine Inn has changed substantially since Steinbeck's time, because the restaurant is now run by the Il Fornaio chain.

From 1933 to 1936 Steinbeck used to visit muckraker Lincoln Steffens in his home on San Antonio, south of Ocean. To get here, go toward the beach on Ocean almost to the bottom and turn left (south) on San Antonio. The home, now called Meremar, is a private residence. Here Steinbeck met many liberals and humanitarians, particularly farm labor activists who inspired *The Grapes of Wrath* and *In Dubious Battle*.

Steinbeck spent some time with poet Robinson Jeffers at his TOR HOUSE, 26304 Ocean View Avenue. It is also said that Jeffers was one of the few contemporary poets whom he admired and respected.

And of course, even Steinbeck checked in occasionally (as we do) at **MISSION SAN CARLOS BORROMEO DEL RIO CARMELO** (Carmel Mission), founded in 1771 by Father Junipero Serra, now buried at the foot of the basilica's altar. Steinbeck described the mission in *The Pastures of Heaven*.

To get here either take Junipero south from Ocean Avenue to Rio Road and Lasuen, or take Highway 1 south of Carmel and turn right on Rio Road to Lasuen and the mission.

Now that you are out here near Highway 1, we suggest you follow it 2.2 miles south from the Carmel Valley turnoff to **POINT LOBOS STATE RESERVE**, the country's first undersea preserve. Twelve trails take you throughout its land portion.

Here Edward F. "Doc" Ricketts collected specimens, as described in *Cannery Row* and *Sweet Thursday.* Steinbeck and his sister Mary spent loads of time here, and the first leg of his trip with Ricketts to the Gulf of California skirted Point Lobos, as he wrote in *The Log from the Sea of Cortez.* In fact, Steinbeck's widow Elaine and his son Thom brought his ashes here on Christmas Eve 1968, just four days after he died, for a memorial service at his favorite Whalers Bay.

Here you can enjoy much of what they saw, thanks to preservation efforts of individuals and the state of California. You might see California sea lions, harbor seals, Brandt's cormorants, brown pelicans, deer, squirrels, elephant seals, sea otters, gray whales, and many more. The reserve has very strict rules, so pay attention to the brochure (with excellent trail maps) handed out at the entrance gate.

WHALERS BAY, POINT LOBOS STATE RESERVE

❧ **Point Lobos State Reserve**, *Route 1, Box 62, Carmel 93923; (831) 624–4909; www.pt-lobos.parks.state.ca.us. Open 9:00 A.M.–7:00 P.M., with hours varying by season. Admission: free if you walk in, $7.00 per car, or $6.00 per car driven by senior. Some areas are wheelchair accessible.*

STEINBECK AT THE MOVIES

John Steinbeck's stories were a favorite of motion picture producers and directors and were popular with the moviegoing public. Beginning with Of Mice and Men *in 1939, eight Steinbeck novels have been adapted for the screen. In addition, Steinbeck wrote screenplays, including* Viva Zapata!

Of Mice and Men *(1939) starred Burgess Meredith as George, who tried to protect the slow-witted Lennie, played by Lon Chaney Jr. It also featured Betty Field and Charles Bickford. All performed brilliantly. Sensitively directed by Lewis Milestone, it is still stirring, enhanced by composer Aaron Copland's first movie score. For some reason someone in Hollywood thought it necessary to make new versions in 1981 (with Robert Blake and Lew Ayres) and in 1992 (with John Malkovich and Gary Sinese), both good but unnecessary.*

The Grapes of Wrath *(1940), one of the stellar movies of all time, won Academy Awards for director John Ford and for Jane Darwell as supporting actress, for her portrayal of Ma Joad (scarcely a glamour role). Henry Fonda was unforgettable as Tom Joad, especially in his closing speech on courage. As director, Ford was courageous in taking on the topic of the plight of the dust bowl migrant farmers, so often still scorned as Okies in 1940. John Carradine also appeared in this classic, given immediacy by the gritty black-and-white cinematography.*

Steinbeck wrote the narration for **The Forgotten Village** *(1941), a documentary about an impoverished Mexican village, whose filming he had supported from the moment he heard of the concept. The film was well done but was banned by the New York State Board of Censors as "indecent" because it showed a woman nursing a baby and depicted a woman giving birth (though not the actual birth). This kept it from being reviewed by New York critics. The ban was eventually lifted in 1942.*

Tortilla Flat *(1942) brought together a remarkable cast, including Spencer Tracy, Hedy Lamarr (then considered one of the most beautiful women on film), John Garfield, and Frank Morgan (fresh from playing the Wizard of Oz), all directed by Victor Fleming. One catalog calls it an "absolute gem," but refers to Monterey as "a poor little California fishing village." For some reason the Chinese grocer was made into a Mexican in the screenplay.*

The Moon Is Down *(1943), Steinbeck's wartime novel about the German occupation of a Norwegian village (the only Steinbeck book that was not about the West Coast of North America or the United States), should not be dismissed as a piece of propaganda about the hateful Nazis. It is dramatic and human, with a topflight ensemble cast, including Sir Cedric Hardwicke, Henry Travers, Lee J. Cobb (who gives one shivers as the German commander who picks out hostages by chance), and Dorris Bowden.*

Steinbeck wrote the original screenplay for **Lifeboat** *(1944), a popular movie directed by Alfred Hitchcock, based on the concept that the characters would be stuck in a lifeboat for the entire film. Hitchcock had the screenplay substantially rewritten, however, giving Steinbeck screen credit for "the story."*

The Pearl *(1948) is the exquisitely photographed tale of the poor fisherman, played by Mexican star Pedro Armendariz, with Maria Marques, and directed by Emilio Fernandez. Just an hour and seventeen minutes long, it is a compelling rendering of the short novel.*

In **The Red Pony** *(1949) a star-studded cast (Myrna Loy, Robert Mitchum, Peter Miles, Louis Calhern), the direction of Lewis Milestone, and a musical score by the legendary Aaron Copland combine to make this charming movie about a man and his horse. In 1973 a television version was made with Henry Fonda.*

Steinbeck wrote the screenplay of **Viva Zapata!** *(1952) for director Elia Kazan. The movie has some great lines and an impressive cast headed by Marlon Brando, Jean Peters, and Anthony Quinn, who was awarded an Oscar for best supporting actor. The script caught the cadence of the language and the feelings of Mexican peasants revolting against a dictatorship.*

East of Eden *(1955), an epic movie of Steinbeck's epic novel, was directed by Elia Kazan. The cast included James Dean (in his second and next-to-last major role), Julie Harris, Raymond Massey, Jo Van Fleet (who won an*

Academy Award for best supporting actress as a bawdy house madam), Burl Ives, and Richard Davalos. The Cain and Abel rivalry comes alive, with Kazan at the top of his game, and Dean adding to his brief legend—he would die in a car crash within a year. In 1981, **East of Eden** *was presented as a television miniseries, starring Jane Seymour.*

The Wayward Bus *(1957) is a pleasant but rather routine rendering of this allegorical story of a varied group of strangers on a wandering odyssey. It starred Joan Collins, Jayne Mansfield, Dan Dailey, and Rick Jason and was directed by Victor Vicas.*

Cannery Row *(1982) features fine performances by Nick Nolte as "Doc" (Ed Ricketts) and Debra Winger as his spacey girlfriend, but the plot as scripted is a bit disjointed. It could have used Steinbeck as a screenwriter.*

STEINBECK AT BIG SUR

John Steinbeck's mother, Olive Hamilton Steinbeck, used to teach school in one-room schoolhouses in Big Sur, one of the most beautiful places on earth. Characterized by its cliffs and Highway 1, which seems to hang over the ocean, Big Sur has been known as El Sur Grande and the Big South. The Santa Lucia Mountains climb almost straight up to the sky in some places, with the pounding Pacific Ocean down below.

To get here from Carmel, just head south on Highway 1 for 28 miles of occasional hairpin curves and beauty. If heights bother you, make the trip heading north from somewhere so that you are on the inside of the cliff.

Locals enjoy winters, when the highway washes into the sea, cutting them off from civilization—only to be rebuilt and reconnect them to the world. In the 1920s Steinbeck worked in a labor gang building a road south of here, and he referred to the area in "Flight," originally printed in *The Long Valley* and later made into a movie.

If you go, there are excellent restaurants to try, from Nepenthe and Ventana Inn Restaurant to small local cafes.

CHAPTER 8

HISTORY OF THE MONTEREY PENINSULA

n June 1542 Juan Cabrillo, a Portuguese military comman-der who had helped Cortez conquer Mexico and Guatemala, was sent north by sea by the viceroy of New Spain to explore the mythical California coast, which was totally unknown to the Europeans at the time. Sailing two small ships—San Salvador and Victoria—Cabrillo discovered the natural ports now known as San Diego (which he named San Miguel), San Pedro, and the Santa Barbara Channel Islands.

MONTEREY SEEN BUT NOT OCCUPIED

Unfortunately, just as Cabrillo spotted the southern point of Monterey Bay, his two little vessels were blown out to sea. From the deck of his ship he claimed the land for Spain and named the cape Punta de Los Pinos, for its forest of trees. Even more unfortunate for the intrepid commander, he broke his arm during a storm, the injury festered, and he died of gangrene. Constantly battered by storms and high winds, the little expedition eventually limped back to Central America, never having set foot in California.

It would be fifty years before the Spanish made another serious attempt to explore the west coast north of Baja California. Instead, they concentrated on developing trade with the Philippine Islands and other Far East ports.

The Spanish became alarmed when Sir Francis Drake, the English privateer, sailed around Cape Horn into the Pacific in 1577. He pirated Spanish treasure ships and claimed the land at Drake's Bay, north of the undiscovered Golden Gate. In 1595 *San Augustin,* a Spanish galleon under Captain Sebastian Rodriquez Cermeño, still loaded with goods from Manila, sailed north in search of a suitable port in California. Cermeño located Drake's Bay, only to have the *San Augustin* smashed on the rocks there, sending the treasure to the bottom. He and his crew got a good look at Monterey Bay from the small boat they slowly rowed and sailed back to Mexico.

VIZCAINO LANDS AT THE "NOBLE HARBOR"

Finally, in 1602, a serious expedition was organized to explore the California coast with three ships under the command of fifty-year-old Sebastian Vizcaino, a Spanish Basque who was willing to help finance the effort. Vizcaino set out from Acapulco on May 5, 1602, with the ships *San Diego, Santo Tomas,* and *Tres Reyes.* Among the 200 in his command were three Carmelite friars and a cartographer.

The little fleet struggled up the Mexican coast for a half year until it reached Cabrillo's San Miguel Bay, which Vizcaino renamed San Diego. The expedition was in trouble from head winds, leaking water barrels, and signs of scurvy.

On December 14, 1602, Vizcaino spotted mountains, which he called Santa Lucia (for the saint's feast day), and the next afternoon his three ships came around Cabrillo's Punta de Pinos and found themselves in a great crescent-shaped bay. The little frigate *Tres Reyes* scouted ahead toward the shore and reported to Vizcaino that this was a suitable harbor. Vizcaino dubbed it Monterey in honor of Gaspar De Zuniga y Acevedo, the Count of Monterey, who was the viceroy of New Spain.

The following morning some of the men went ashore and constructed an arbor beneath a great oak tree. Then all the crews gathered under its spreading

branches while one of the friars celebrated a mass from the bower. The Spaniards found forests with wood suitable for ship repair, plenty of water, and what Vizcaino called a "noble harbor," which, he reported to the viceroy, was sheltered—ignoring the winds from the northwest. He added that the temperature was "mild," the land fertile, and the game plentiful. The local Indians, who had given the Spaniards food, were "soft, gentle, docile, and very fit to be reduced to the Holy Church," according to Vizcaino.

SEBASTIAN VIZCAINO

Scurvy, the mariner's disease caused by lack of vitamins and other nutrients, racked his men, so Vizcaino put the worst thirty-four cases onto the *Santo Tomas* headed back to Acapulco, after the priests gave them all communion and many of them last rites. Only nine men survived the return trip.

On January 3, 1603, Vizcaino led a squad of men 9 miles over the hills to the southeast of Monterey Bay, where he discovered a small river coursing down a wide ravine to the ocean, which he named the river Rio del Carmelo in honor of the religious order of his three friars. His ships attempted to explore farther north, but were battered by storms, soon separated, and finally each headed home.

MONTEREY IGNORED FOR 160 YEARS

Viceroy Monterey was enthusiastic about Vizcaino's discoveries, but was replaced in 1603 by the marques de Montesclaros. The new viceroy fired Vizcaino and shelved a 1606 order from the King of Spain that he send Vizcaino back to Monterey with colonists. The marques even brought charges of embezzlement against Vizcaino's able cartographer, Captain Geronimo Martin de Palacios, and had him tried and hanged. The reports of the expedition were ignored. It would be more than 160 years before Monterey Bay was visited again by Europeans.

In 1765 King Charles III appointed bright, energetic, and mentally unstable Jose de Galvez as visitor general of New Spain. Exploration and settlement of Alta California (now San Diego and north) was high on Galvez's list of priorities. He established a port at San Blas, north of Acapulco on the west coast of Mexico, as a shipping point to California. At the same time King Charles (Carlos) expelled the Jesuits from all Spanish possessions in reaction to the Jesuit habit of assuming governmental and diplomatic functions. This left the Franciscans as the principal religious order in the Spanish territories.

PORTOLA FINDS THE BAY—TWICE

Visitor General Galvez appointed veteran army officer Captain Gaspar de Portola military governor of Baja California, and Portola eased the Jesuits out of control of the missions. Galvez met with Portola to plan an expedition to find Vizcaino's fabled Monterey Bay. In addition to his position as governor of Baja, Portola was given authority as governor of Alta California, with no constituents, except the natives.

It would be a two-pronged expedition: A march by land up the coast, with two ships to support and supply the marchers at San Diego and Monterey Bay. The plan called for Portola to lead the effort on land after it had made it to a base at San Diego, and naval Captain Juan Perez Hernandez would command the two ships coming up the coast. At San Diego they would establish a military presidio and a mission, with other missions to follow at Monterey and near Point Conception (to be Buenaventura).

Appointed to head the anticipated chain of missions was Father Junipero Serra, a 5-foot-2 Franciscan friar, who combined administrative talent with unrelenting religious fervor. He sometimes scourged himself to a point of painful ecstasy, and he limped through life with an ulcer on his leg from an old infected insect bite. Father Serra believed God had sent him to save the pagan Indians from hell in the hereafter.

Serra was ill with his sporadic leg infection, so he was lifted onto a mule in Baja. He managed to make it to San Diego Bay but could go no farther. He agreed to stay there to direct construction of a mission.

Departing San Diego on July 14, 1769, Portola's party included Friar Juan Crespi and another Carmelite priest, twenty-seven soldiers, fifteen Christian Indians, mule drivers, an engineer, and a dozen others, plus cattle for food. They passed through modern-day Los Angeles, San Fernando Valley, Ventura, and San Luis Obispo, hacking out a trail as they went. October found them struggling over the Santa Lucia Mountains, with dwindling supplies.

Portola and his men reached Punta de los Pinos eighty-three days after leaving San Diego. Based on Vizcaino's description of Monterey Bay as a sheltered port, and not a sweeping crescent of beach, Portola's party did not recognize it— particularly with the northern point shrouded in fog. They also were misled by the fact that Vizcaino's estimate of the latitude of Monterey Bay was inaccurate. They tramped onward and when they came to the Salinas River they reckoned it was the Rio Carmelo. Understandably, from that point on they were totally confused as to their position.

Portola held a meeting of his leading men, who voted to move on north despite increasing cold and near starvation.

Sergeant Jose Francisco de Ortega, the chief scout, was sent ahead with a squad of those able to make it to the top of the ridge of hills that lay ahead just north of Half Moon Bay. From there Ortega looked down on San Francisco Bay, never before beheld by a white man.

Portola led his men back the way they had come. They erected a cross near Punta de los Pinos on December 9, 1769, and at its base buried a letter that said they were "disappointed and despairing of finding the Bay of

Monterey" and were starting back to San Diego. Eating the mules one by one, the starving expedition managed to crawl back to San Diego by late January 1770.

Buoyed by the arrival at San Diego of the *San Antonio* with fresh supplies and men from Mexico in late March, the indefatigable Portola organized another expedition to locate Monterey. Naval captain Juan Perez Hernandez would sail up the coast with Father Serra, supplies, and some of the men, while Portola would retrace his land route northward.

In only thirty-seven days Portola's troop marched from San Diego to the Punta de los Pinos, arriving on May 24, 1770. This time Portola became convinced that this was Vizcaino's Monterey. He set up camp on Carmel Bay. Eight days later, the *San Antonio* sailed into Monterey Bay.

A MISSION FOUNDED AND A STOCKADE BUILT

On June 3 Serra celebrated mass beneath the same huge oak where Vizcaino's crew had said their prayers. Serra declared the founding of Alta California's second mission, which he named San Carlos Borromeo de Carmelo, for a sainted Italian cardinal (1538–1584) of the Medici family.

The party's engineer and cartographer, Miguel Costanso, laid out a square (now bordered by Fremont, Abrego, Webster and Estero Streets in downtown Monterey), where the men turned to building a stockade from pine logs cut in the nearby forest. Within a month they had erected a barracks, quarters for both officers and friars, storerooms, and a lean-to room for a chapel.

A week after the first mass, Portola turned over direction of the embryonic presidio to Lieutenant Pedro Fages and boarded the *San Antonio* for a sea trip back to Mexico. He never returned to Monterey, but governed from Loreto in Baja. Engineer Costanso, who had written a detailed diary, went with Portola, as did a letter from Serra to the viceroy asking that the mission be relocated near the Rio Carmelo. Left at Monterey Bay were Father Serra, Father Crespi, and eighteen soldiers under Fages. Among the soldiers were men who eventually established families whose names would echo through the years of California's future: Carrillo, Alvarado, Soberanes, Dominguez, Amador, and Yorba.

It did not take long for Serra and Fages to clash over the issue of whether the priesthood or the civilian/military government was in command. Fages had the upper hand due to his designation by Governor Portola and his having troopers (called "Leather Jackets" for their uniforms). Fages could order his men to complete adobe walls around the plaza, chink log buildings with mud, plant wheat (much of the provisions were rotten), and complete the outbuildings.

Father Serra Moves the Mission

In May 1771 the *San Antonio* returned with trained workmen and Franciscan friars to staff five more missions to be organized by Father Serra, who also received written permission to move Mission San Carlos Borromeo to Rio Carmelo. Father Serra wanted to shift the mission for several reasons. There was good water and soil by Rio Carmelo, and he would no longer be under the direct control of Governor Fages. The new site was closer to the Native American villages, where there was a ready supply of souls to be saved. Since he intended to establish housing for young native maidens, he wanted them removed from contact with the sex-starved soldiers. In fact, he made it a rule that California missions had to be established at least a mile from any presidio.

Within 30 miles of Monterey Bay there were at least five different language groups of natives, the largest being what the Spaniards called the Costanoans ("the coast people"), but the natives called themselves the Ohlone. Numbering at least 3,000, they lived in villages along the Salinas River and on the shore from Monterey to Big Sur. Inland were the Salinan, a trifle wealthier than the Ohlone. The Essalen dwelled in Carmel Valley, Tassajara Hot Springs, and Big Sur, and never numbered more than 1,000.

The cultures and mode of life of all these tribes and tribelets were similar. They were all splendid hunters with well-carved bows and straight arrows with which the men killed deer, elk, and other game. They gathered berries, roots, and the abundant acorns that the women ground into a flour baked into a crude bread. Fishing and scraping abalone from the rocks filled out their diet. Since hunting, gathering, and fishing were all seasonal, they left their simple huts—never more than 10 feet by 10 feet—on precise schedules each year to meet fish runs, pick ripened fruit, or track game. There was no agriculture. Their chiefs governed by consensus, based on customs evolved over thousands of years.

Although tolerant of premarital sex, once there was a marriage (usually arranged by families with the couple's consent) monogamy was expected among the natives. A chief might take several wives, but that was his special privilege. Men went naked except in the colder seasons when they wore cloaks made of animal fur, while women wore woven grass fiber skirts and fur capes. Tribes took care of the sick or those with other problems, and the concept of individual land ownership was unknown. Vizcaino had described them as "gentle and peaceable, friendly, of good stature, fair complexion, and the women possessed of pleasing countenance."

Serra made Carmel his headquarters as presidente of the missions and soon had five in operation. However, in two years he was able to baptize only one native, a young boy. He became frustrated at the lack of assistance from Mexico City and the failure of a supply ship to come to Monterey in the spring of 1772. When one did arrive in the fall, Father Serra boarded it for a long trip to Mexico City to demand more help, to lobby for the removal of Governor Fages, and to get authorization to found more missions. Viceroy Antonio de Bucarelli agreed to recall Fages, but named another tough soldier, Captain Fernando Rivera, as commandante.

Meanwhile, no supplies were delivered to Monterey in 1773; the ships were beaten back into San Diego by bad weather. Father Crespi's crops failed. When Father Fermin Lasuen came walking in from San Diego in November, the situation was desperate. Unlike the natives, the white friars had not stored dried fish and meat taken in season. Fages organized a grizzly bear hunt, which provided meat for the starving men.

CONVERSION AND THE END OF NATIVE CULTURE

Captain Juan Bautista de Anza appeared in Monterey on May 1, 1774, after an amazing trek across the southwest desert to the Mission San Gabriel (east of present-day Los Angeles), and then up the Portola route to Monterey. Then on May 9, the *Santiago* sailed in, carrying ham, wheat, wine, chocolate, a physician (Jose Joaquin Davila), and three families, who had among them three marriageable young women.

Two days later Father Serra arrived, having walked from San Diego on the last leg of his trip back from Mexico City. Within a week he performed weddings for three soldiers and their native brides. Some natives felt these intermarriages showed Spanish respect for the indigenous people and encouraged natives to become baptized, including Chief Tatlun of a village in Carmel Valley.

The natives were impressed by the Spaniards' equipment, guns, clothes, glass beads, ships, and other objects, as well as the apparent ability of the priests to commune with their god. Therefore, many came forward to be baptized in this new religion. Soon many of them were working in serflike peonage, their daughters were separated from their families, and the rhythm of their lives so necessary to hunting, fishing, and gathering was interrupted forever.

Fages's replacement, Captain Fernando Rivera, showed up in October 1774, after having trekked from Baja California with fifty-one women, children, and soldiers, including twenty-six-year-old Vicente Ferrer Vallejo.

Viceroy Bucarelli was very much pro-California and felt Alta California was more attractive than the blistering hot, rock hard peninsula of Baja California. On August 16, 1775, Bucarelli ordered the provincial capital of the Californias transferred from Loreto in Baja to Monterey, which was accomplished in February 1777. He also approved the governor giving deserving soldiers small plots of land to encourage permanent colonization. The first to receive a designated parcel was Manuel Butron, who settled near the Carmel Mission with his teenaged native bride, Margarita Maria.

DE ANZA BRINGS THE COLONISTS

De Anza was then instructed to raise a caravan of soldiers and their families from frontier garrisons in Arizona and lead them to Monterey via his trail before establishing a mission and presidio by San Francisco Bay. Only forty soldiers signed up, but with their wives and children, muleteers, horsemen, and two officers, the total in the caravan was 240. One woman died on the way, but eight babies were born and survived. They had no wagons, but drove herds of horses, mules, and cattle, totaling 1,000 head. Among the caravan were Lieutenant Jose Moraga and families Bernal, Berryessa, and Castro.

After a journey of nearly five months, these trekkers reached Monterey on March 10, 1776. A third of de Anza's colonists decided to settle in Monterey while the rest divided among the other northern missions. Adobe houses were built for the newcomers, and the presidio and Carmel Mission were enlarged. Crops were planted and cattle raising became a major occupation.

In February 1777 Felipe de Neve was named governor of the Californias. Father Serra did not get along with de Neve any more than he had with Fages or Rivera. The new governor gave priority to establishing pueblos, farms, and ranches, instead of missions. In the next five years Father Serra was able to open only one new mission, at Buenaventura. And to Serra's horror, Governor de Neve appointed natives as alcaldes (a Spanish mayor/judge) to administer tribal affairs and refused to let soldiers be used to hunt for Native American runaways. To add to Serra's woes, his loyal aide, Juan Crespi, died in January 1782.

THE DEATH OF FATHER SERRA

Serra died of cancer on August 28, 1784, and was buried next to Father Crespi at the Carmel Mission. Nine missions in Alta California had been established by the indefatigable Franciscan. He was followed briefly by his number two man, Francisco Palou, and then Fermin Francisco de Lasuen, who served as father presidente of the missions for the next eighteen years.

Meanwhile in the 1770s, Spanish domination of the Pacific was threatened by the appearance of British Captain James Cook, whose ships rounded Cape Horn in 1772, armed with two advantages. He was able to determine longitude (and thus know exactly where he was) by using the chronometer invented by Britain's brilliant clock innovator, John Harrison. Secondly, he had sauerkraut. Barrels of this preserved cabbage kept his men supplied with vitamins, and they no longer died of scurvy on long voyages. By 1777 Cook was back in the Pacific, and after he found the Hawaiian Islands, he began to explore the west coast of Northwest America.

In March 1778 Cook discovered the west coast of what became Vancouver Island, landed, and claimed for Great Britain a sheltered harbor he called Nootka Inlet. In 1789 British ships at Nootka were seized by Spanish captains. Spain and England were on the brink of war.

VISITS BY FRENCH AND BRITISH SHIPS

In 1786 Jean François de La Perouse, leader of a French geographical and scientific expedition around the Pacific, became the first non-Spaniard to visit Monterey. La Perouse was shocked by the use of the whip, stocks, and chains on "Indians of both sexes" for minor offenses like "neglect of piety" and called their huts "the most wretched anywhere." He reported that the mission fathers treated baptism as a pledge by the native to become an indentured serf of the mission who could be chased down and punished if he or she left. The mission Indians worked seven hours a day, six days a week, and had to pray for one or two hours every day.

In 1789 when the cannon signaled the arrival of a long-awaited supply ship, the wadding caught fire and fell on the thatched roof of the presidio. Half the buildings burned down.

In 1791 Alejandro Malaspina, a meticulous Italian explorer sailing for Spain, visited Monterey on his way to the northwest, looking for the mythical Northwest Passage across the top of the continent. Fortunately he had on board a fine artist, Jose Cardero, who drew pictures of Monterey, the Carmel Mission, and the people, which provide us with the best visual impressions of the period.

When the French revolution neutralized Spain's chief European ally in 1789, the Spanish had to negotiate settlement with the British. So in October 1790 the two nations entered into the Nootka Convention, in which Spain agreed to give up any claims to lands not in their actual possession or granted by treaties. To negotiate the details and recover British property at Nootka, England sent Captain George Vancouver. Peruvian-born Admiral Juan Francisco de la Bodega y Quadra sailed north from Monterey to represent Spain. The two captains met at Nootka during August and September 1792 and became instant friends. Bodega y Quadra arrived back in Monterey on his ship, *Avisa,* in early October and on November 25, 1792, Vancouver and his two ships, *Discovery* and *Chatham,* followed him into Monterey Bay.

Bodega y Quadra and the people of Monterey entertained Vancouver and the British sailors in an almost continuous fiesta for fifty days, with banquets, dances, drinking, horsemanship, native demonstrations of deer hunting, and general good fellowship. The Spanish even provided equipment for the *Chatham,* which was heading promptly for London.

The Vancouver observed that the indigenous people acted "with a mechanical, lifeless, careless indifference," in contrast to the friendly, vigorous natives described earlier by Vizcaino and Portola. Frontier life was hard on the missionaries as well. Of the four padres first assigned to assist Father Lasuen at Carmel Mission, one was recalled to Mexico City after he was charged with overuse of the whip on the natives; another retired in his thirties, "worn out"; a third went back to Mexico City with a case of "depression and melancholia"; and the fourth went outright insane.

SETTLEMENTS GROW AND NATIVES DECLINE

San Carlos Borromeo de Carmelo was built in its current dimensions in 1797. Father Presidente Lasuen founded nine missions between 1786 and 1798, starting with Santa Barbara. Santa Cruz Mission on the northern tip of Monterey Bay was dedicated on September 25, 1791, and completed in 1794. Nearby the army built a presidio, followed in 1797 by an experimental planned community within present-day Santa Cruz, called Branciforte, the name of the incumbent viceroy. To encourage settlement, the pioneers at Branciforte were given land to farm or raise cattle, tools, clothes, and low-rent housing around a plaza. The concept was to mix Spanish and mestizo settlers with local natives to encourage intermarriage and cultural interchange. To get enough settlers, minor criminals and prostitutes were shipped to Branciforte from jails in old Mexico. The rougher element assumed control and built a racetrack as Branciforte's first public improvement.

The native population continued to dwindle, primarily due to epidemics of European diseases.

GOLDEN AGE OF THE CALIFORNIOS

Cattle raising increased rapidly after the territorial government began to approve land grants to Californios (as the Spanish colonists of California were called) for ranchos in 1784. Large "concessions"—ranches with the right to use the property but without official title—were granted in the Monterey area first to the Soberanes and Castro families. Families like that of Corporal Manuel Boronda (whose adobe still stands in Carmel Valley) began moving out from the protection of the crowded Monterey presidio.

Within a few years cattle ranches around Santa Barbara and Monterey and other coastal valleys were producing thousands of hides, which became the underpinning of the wealth of Alta California. In the early 1800s American ships out of Boston began making regular stops on the California coast to buy hides at docks piled high with the leather. Otter skins were being taken and shipped to China at the rate of 2,000 a year.

Fandangos, bullfights, horse races, bearbaiting, music, extravagant weddings, Chinese fireworks, romance, and ease made this the golden age for the Californio ranchers and their extended families clustered around each central ranch house. Father Lasuen died in 1803, leaving the mission system without a strong leader. The Catalan Volunteers, the seventy-man infantry company at the Monterey presidio, were shipped back to Mexico in 1803 and 1804, no longer necessary for the protection of the pueblo and mission. Alta California was officially separated from Baja in 1804, approximately along the line where the American-Mexican border lies today. Monterey remained the capital for Alta.

The situation in the home country of Spain during this period was chaotic due to the rampages of Napoleon Bonaparte. Napoleon eventually installed his brother Joseph as King of Spain. Taking advantage of the turmoil at home and the failure to maintain supply lines, liberators arose in South America beginning around 1808.

On November 20, 1818, two frigates, *Argentina* and *Santa Rosa*, appeared on the Monterey Bay horizon. Under the command of Hippolyte de Bouchard, they flew the flag of Buenos Aires, the principal province of rebellious Argentina. Governor Pablo Vicente de Sola evacuated most Monterey civilians (especially the women) to inland missions. The ships raked the shore with cannon fire, and the three Monterey emplacements (directed by Corporal Jose Vallejo) fired back. Bouchard sent a landing party under a flag of truce to announce he had come to liberate Alta California from Spain. However, he and his crew were really pirates intent on liberating the locals' possessions. Bouchard demanded supplies and surrender. Sola refused—"not while there was a man alive in the province." The cannon duel resumed, but Bouchard stormed ashore with more than 300 crewmen, took the small Custom House (built in 1814), and forced the outnumbered Californios to retreat inland. For ten days Bouchard's pirates looted, vandalized, and burned, before sailing away.

MEXICO GAINS INDEPENDENCE

In 1815 leadership of the Mexican independence movement passed to guerrilla general Vicente Guerrero. When Agustin Iturbe, the commander of the troops fighting the rebels, switched sides, the Spanish viceroy had to agree to Mexican independence, which was granted on August 24, 1821. On April 11, 1822, Governor Sola announced Mexico's independence to the crowd that had assembled in the Monterey presidio plaza. The new Mexican flag replaced the Spanish, and with few exceptions the citizens swore loyalty to Mexico.

One of the first changes under an independent Mexico was legalization of trade with foreign citizens at Monterey and San Diego. By the summer of 1822, two partners, Englishman William Hartnell and Scotsman Hugh McCulloch, were importing, selling, and buying for export, with a virtual monopoly in trade with the missions. They were soon followed by former Boston fur trader William Gale and then sea captain Roger Cooper, who had been born in the English Channel Islands but raised in the United States. Cooper sold his ship *Rover* to the Mexican government and stayed on.

Hartnell, with a flair for languages, set up a store in which he hired a couple of youngsters, Mariano Vallejo and his cousin Juan Bautista Alvarado, and became friendly with leading citizens. Three years later he converted to Catholicism and married sixteen-year-old Teresa de la Guerra, whose father was the richest man in Santa Barbara. Cooper also was baptized Catholic as "Juan Bautista" Cooper, and married a younger Vallejo daughter, Encarnacion. In 1824 a Spanish Basque trader, Jose Amesti, landed and soon wed Prudenciana Vallejo. Thus, almost all trade was in the hands of a small group of immigrants with familial connections.

With independence, grants of land title in the hinterlands were confirmed to Ignacio Vallejo, Feliciano and Mariano Soberanes, and Jose Tiburcio Castro and his brother, Simeon. However, the largest landowners remained the missions. At the end of the 1820s only seven families owned ranches near Monterey.

During the remainder of the 1820s, the governments of Mexico and the two Californias were comic opera. In Mexico City, General Iturbide created the

Empire of Mexico and had himself named Agustin the First (and also the last). He was ousted by a revolt led by young General Antonio Santa Anna two years later. A republic followed in 1824 with a revolving door of presidents, either by election or rebellion. For Monterey, with a population of 300, presidential musical chairs meant neglect, nonpayment of soldiers, and repeated changes of governors and policies. In 1829, unpaid, hungry, and ragged soldiers revolted at Monterey but were put down by troops loyal to the governor. The ringleader, an ex-convict named Joaquin Solis, was packed off to prison in Mexico City.

LAND GRANTS, SECULARIZATION, AND TRADE

Between 1833 and 1835 Governor Jose Figueroa gave land grants to several leading families, including Rancho Punta de Los Pinos (Pacific Grove), Rancho Saucito (around Monterey Peninsula Airport), and Rancho los Tularcitos (Carmel Valley). Catalina Manzanelli Munras received Rancho Laguna Seca and hills in Carmel Valley, while her husband, Esteban Munras, was given title to almost 20,000 acres near the Soledad Mission. The widow Cristina Delgado was granted more than 2,000 acres near the mouth of the Salinas River, remarkable since she and her late husband were mission Indians.

More land was needed to reward friends and pioneers and to encourage ranches and businesses. The obvious source was the extensive mission land. Thus, the Mexican government decreed "secularization" in 1834, under which the mission properties were taken by the government, and the mission buildings became parish churches. Mariano Vallejo, just twenty-eight years old, was sent to take civilian control of the Sonoma Mission (the last to be established in 1823), 45 miles northeast of the Golden Gate.

Cooper's half brother, Thomas O. Larkin, settled in Monterey in 1832. Soon he was in business as a trader, moneylender, and respected leader of the handful of Americans. Larkin became expert in avoiding the prohibitively high duties on imports by unloading his ships at night and then reporting only a small portion of his cargo. He built the town's foremost

THOMAS LARKIN

residence in 1835, a Mexican colonial adobe with many New England touches. He also erected smaller buildings, warehouses, and offices. Downtown Mont erey was taking shape as new adobes were built and streets more clearly defined (although they were either dusty or muddy tracks, depending on the season).

In 1833 the British Hudson's Bay Company's *Beaver*, the first steamship on the west coast, puffed into Monterey Bay on its way to Fort Vancouver in present-day Washington. Local traders welcomed the opportunity to sell otter pelts and hides. In the next few years, Hudson's Bay officials often visited Monterey and Yerba Buena, where the company built a trading post.

Richard Henry Dana, the young writer from the East Coast, visited Monterey in 1836 on his shipboard tour. Although his *Two Years Before the Mast* (1840) was critical of the indolence of the people as a result of the easy life, he wrote that "Monterey . . . is decidedly the pleasantest and most civilized looking place in California." His writing stimulated greater American interest in California.

CHAOS FOLLOWED BY GOVERNOR ALVARADO

Popular Governor Figueroa died of a stroke in September 1835. The central government selected two unfortunate successors. The first, Mariano Chico, did not favor secularization, picked a fight with foreign merchants like Hartnell and Cooper, hinted at moving the capital to Los Angeles, tried to fire Monterey Alcalde Ramon Estrada, and flaunted a mistress he called his "niece." After three months, protesting citizens surrounded his house and literally ran him out of town, and he sneaked aboard an outgoing ship. Acting Governor Nicolas Gutierrez, a womanizer who liked to impose himself on young native girls, ordered the arrest of Juan Bautista Alvarado, primarily because the provincial House of Deputies (*Disputacion*), of which Alvarado was president, had recommended that the governors be elected by popular vote.

Alvarado and his cousin Jose Castro organized a rebellion against Gutierrez with the help of American roughneck distiller Isaac Graham and forty of his fur-trapping friends, plus seventy-five local men—but not Mariano Vallejo, who refused to be involved. On November 3, 1836, Castro deployed his handful of men on the ridge above the town, where they lit several campfires, beat drums, and sounded trumpets as if they had the Monterey presidio surrounded. The governor's troops began to desert, and Castro demanded that Gutierrez surrender. The governor refused. One cannon shot (the rebels had only one cannonball) through the roof of Gutierrez's house, and he decided to resign.

The *Disputacion* promptly chose Alvarado as governor—the first native Californio to hold that position. Mariano Vallejo was named commandante general of California, although he remained headquartered in Sonoma. While General Castro announced that California was a free state, the rebels settled for a form of autonomy within the Mexican nation. During his six years in office, Alvarado distributed twenty-eight land grants, including many around Monterey, Carmel Valley, and Salinas, but also in Sonoma Valley and Napa Valley (plus a large grant at the confluence of the Sacramento and American Rivers to a Swiss immigrant named John Sutter). Although the secularization law provided that half of the mission lands were to be distributed to former mission Indians, only a few natives received grants.

GOVERNOR JUAN BAUTISTA ALVARADO

Alvarado had problems with his brief allies, American Isaac Graham's shaggy gang, who had not received the land grants they felt they had been promised for helping to get Alvarado the governorship. They swaggered through town intimidating the Californios, invaded the governor's office and sneered at him, and announced freely that now that Texas was free of Mexico (as of 1836), "California is next." Vallejo urged Alvarado to shape up his military and make a show of force, but the governor was more worried about possible cabals in southern California. So Vallejo dressed his native ally, the 6-foot-7-inch Suisun Chief Solano in a Spanish uniform, and he and the chief led one hundred fierce-looking Suisuns riding through Monterey, scaring everyone to death. For a time thereafter no one challenged Alvarado's authority. In April 1840, when he found out that Graham's men were planning to invade Monterey and declare it free of Mexico, General Castro and his soldiers surprised Graham and his chief cohorts, who were deported to Mexico for trial.

General Castro was sufficiently upset by the threatened rebellion that he shipped several Americans to Mexico City with Graham. He also declared that foreign immigrants were not welcome, which stimulated thoughts of Texas-like independence in the minds of many American settlers, who now constituted 10 percent of the California population.

American Thomas O. Larkin contracted with the California government to reconstruct the Monterey Custom House in 1841. Although he was never paid,

Larkin turned the building to good use, and it was soon the center of business, civic activity, and major celebrations. For his part, Governor Alvarado had built *El Cuartel*, the block-long barracks for his troops.

THE GREAT GAFFE OF COMMODORE JONES

When American Commodore Thomas Catesby Jones anchored at Callao, Peru, he picked up a rumor that the United States had declared war on Mexico. He promptly steered his two warships toward Monterey, arriving on October 19, 1842, and sent a small boat to shore with a demand to surrender. Commandante Mariano Silva, with only a handful of ragged unpaid troops, agreed to turn over the town the following morning. Commodore Jones and 150 sailors marched up to El Cuartel with a band playing, took down the Mexican flag, and raised the Stars and Stripes. He announced that the United States was at war with Mexico, and he was taking possession of California.

Larkin and Hartnell questioned Jones that afternoon, and Larkin showed him recent communications from both the United States and Mexico that proved there was no war. The following morning the embarrassed commodore admitted his mistake to Commandante Silva, wrote a letter of apology to incoming Governor Manuel Micheltorena in Los Angeles, and pulled down the Stars and Stripes. Micheltorena invited Jones and his crews to a fiesta in their honor in Los Angeles.

The Mexican government had appointed Micheltorena as governor in 1842. He tried to maintain control with a company of 300 "cholos," made up

EL CUARTEL

of the dregs released from Mexican prisons. Following a confusing mock war between competing factions and a revolt by the combined forces of ex-governor Alvarado and southern Californian Pio Pico, Micheltorena resigned in 1844. Pico became governor and moved the capital to Los Angeles, but no one cared, since General Castro governed as military commander in Monterey. It was all sandbox politics that left California with no coherent government. Only Mariano Vallejo, in complete control of Sonoma and the surrounding valleys, stayed aloof from these machinations.

LARKIN'S DREAM OF AN AMERICAN CALIFORNIA

In April 1844 Larkin was appointed American consul in Monterey, with responsibility for helping American citizens and commercial interests. His hope was that California could be annexed to the United States without hostilities. In 1844 James K. Polk was elected president of the United States as an advocate of annexation of the Republic of Texas, which had fought its way free of Mexico in 1836. In his closing days as lame-duck president, John Tyler pushed through the annexation of Texas. In 1845 Polk offered Mexico $40 million for California and New Mexico. The proposal was rejected.

Putting sand into the gears of Larkin's hopes was U.S. Army Captain John C. Fremont, officially the chief of a party of sixty-two "topographical engineers" searching out routes to the West. Fremont visited Monterey without incident in

LARKIN HOUSE

December before heading back to Sutter's Fort. On March 1 he returned with his buckskin-clad, scraggily bearded, rifle-toting crew, camping out on William Hartnell's ranch. After a few days, three of his men rode over to the ranch of General Castro's uncle, and "insulted" his daughters. General Castro immediately sent Fremont a written order to leave California or be arrested. The mercurial Fremont responded by flying an American flag atop Mount Gavilan. Castro raised 200 volunteers. Larkin hustled out to convince Fremont to leave, despite the captain's offer to fight to the death. Finally Fremont headed north, and a relieved Castro took credit for the retreat.

An unusual meeting took place at Larkin's home later in March 1846. Among those present were William Hartnell, English merchant David Spence, Mariano Soberanes, and the three cousins—General Jose Castro, ex-Governor Jose Bautista Alvarado, and the tall imperious-looking Mariano Vallejo. While Larkin listened, each in turn expressed his opinion as to the future of California. English-born Hartnell declared in favor of making California a British protectorate, and Spence leaned the same way. Castro favored annexation to France, primarily because it was a Catholic country. Soberanes and Alvarado argued emotionally for a free and independent California. Speaking last, Vallejo delivered a carefully devised speech in which he detailed the reasons for California asking to be annexed to the United States. No consensus was achieved, except that none of the leaders favored remaining a part of Mexico.

Unknown to anyone in California, on May 13, 1846, the United States Congress had declared war against Mexico, on the pretext that there was a dispute over the Mexican-Texas border. On June 15 the United States agreed with Great Britain to divide "Oregon Country" at the forty-ninth parallel, but relented on the British desire to keep Fort Victoria on the southern tip of Vancouver Island. This relieved the United States from the threat of British naval interference in its Mexican War.

Fremont returned to Sutter's Fort and encountered a group of Americans from the Sacramento Valley who wanted to throw off Mexican rule. Using the news of a Castro declaration that only Mexicans could own property, Fremont urged them to intercept a herd of horses Vallejo was sending to Castro at Santa Clara, which they did. With fresh mounts the Americans rode toward Sonoma. In Napa Valley they added more men and at dawn on June 14, 1846, they galloped into the Sonoma plaza, arrested Mariano Vallejo (who served them wine and brandy) and three others. The captives were taken to Sutter's Fort where Fremont insisted they be kept in a makeshift prison.

COMMODORE SLOAT TAKES MONTEREY

On July 2 three American warships under the command of Commodore John D. Sloat appeared and anchored in the Monterey harbor. Sloat had orders to seize the ports of California if war had been declared, but he had no official report of war. Fearful of making an embarrassing gaffe like Commodore Jones, he consulted with Larkin. Learning that Fremont was leading a company of 200, including some Bear Flaggers, to seize control of California, war or no war, Sloat landed 250 marines and sailors midmorning on July 7. They marched in formation up to the Custom House and could find only Captain Mariano Silva, who had ceded the town to Commodore Jones in 1842. The American flag was raised, the navy band played, and each of the three ships fired a twenty-one-gun salute. Sloat made a diplomatic speech in which he promised full American citizenship rights to the Californios, announced his men would pay for supplies, and said that church properties would be protected. The locals cheered, for this gentleman seemed much preferable to the rude Bear Flaggers who held Vallejo in prison or to the impetuous Fremont and his "California Battalion," which had shot and killed two de Haro sons and their aged uncle, a Berryessa, when they had attempted to surrender near San Rafael.

As it turned out, there was almost no fighting in northern California. Sloat sent a small squad led by naval Lieutenant Joseph Warren Revere, grandson of Paul Revere, to Yerba Buena and Sonoma to raise the Stars and Stripes. On July 9 Revere pulled down the Bear Flag in Sonoma, thus ending the twenty-five-day regime of the California Republic and Sonoma's time as a national capital. Fremont came down to Monterey to consult with Sloat, and his men camped outside of town (to the great discomfort of the local population).

THE AMERICAN WAR WITH MEXICO

Sloat, still not certain he had acted legally, transferred his command to Commodore Robert F. Stockton the first week in August. As his last act, at the urging of Larkin and his half brother Cooper (Vallejo's brother-in-law), Sloat ordered Mariano Vallejo and his compatriots freed from prison and allowed to go home. A few days later an official dispatch reported that a state of war indeed did exist.

Probably the most unusual member of the American naval crew was its chaplain, Walter Colton. With a degree from Yale, he had been editor of the

North American Review. He unearthed a battered forty-five-year-old printing press and some scrambled type used by Governor Figueroa to print proclamations. With the help of 6-foot-8-inch Bear Flagger Robert Semple, who was both a dentist and a printer, Colton published California's first newspaper, the four-page *Californian.* Printed on tobacco paper, it appeared on August 15, 1846, just in time to report the text of the declaration of war. William Hartnell translated the news from English to Spanish in a parallel column on each page. Semple eventually moved the newspaper to San Francisco.

WALTER COLTON

Commodore Stockton advanced Fremont in rank and then sent him off to southern California, where the military action against Mexican resistance loomed. He also appointed Colton as alcalde of the Monterey area. Colton insisted that he be confirmed by a local election, set up a local court conducted in both English and Spanish, and substituted work for whippings as punishment.

Although the Mexican volunteers won the early skirmishes in southern California, eventually Stockton captured Los Angeles, and Fremont won the battle of Cahuenga Pass, ending Californio resistance to American occupation. An intramural dispute followed the end of the war. American General Stephen Kearny, commander of American armed forces in California, claimed the secretary of war had also given him civil authority over California. At one stage Stockton had named Fremont military governor, and Fremont would not relinquish his position to Kearny—giving California two competing governors. Kearny made his headquarters at El Cuartel for three months, finally ordering Fremont arrested and taken back to Washington, D.C., to face a court martial for insubordination.

CALIFORNIA CEDED TO U.S. AND GOLD DISCOVERED

While Kearny's successor as military governor, Colonel Richard Mason, ruled from El Cuartel, most of the American volunteer company was moved to Sonoma in late 1847. The Mexican War was concluded with the Treaty of Guadalupe Hidalgo, which was signed on February 2, 1848, and soon ratified by both the U.S. Senate and the Mexican government. California, Arizona, New Mexico, and Nevada became American territory, and U.S. citizenship was granted to all Californios. News of ratification by the Mexican government reached Monterey in August 1848.

In January 1848 gold was discovered at a mill being built for John Sutter at Coloma in the Sierra Nevadas. Soon Monterey was deserted by most of its male population, the remaining American soldiers joining the crowd in the mountains. The port village of Yerba Buena, now called San Francisco, soon dwarfed Monterey in population, as did Sacramento and San Jose.

THE CONSTITUTIONAL CONVENTION AT COLTON HALL

California, with an uncertain eastern boundary, was neither a territory nor a state, and lacked any official government. In June 1849 the new military governor, Brigadier General Bennett Riley, ordered an election to be held August 1 for delegates to a constitutional convention scheduled for September. Alcalde Colton had already directed the construction of a sturdy stone and wood town hall (now Colton Hall), which would be ready to serve as the convention site.

The forty-eight delegates chosen by each settlement trickled into Monterey during the first two weeks of September. Eight of the delegates were Spanish-speaking Californios, led by General Vallejo, with William Hartnell translating. Elected chairman was Bear Flagger/dentist/printer Robert Semple, the tallest man present, who was escorted to the podium by Vallejo and John Sutter. The delegates voted to apply for statehood and to structure the constitution as a state in which slavery would not be allowed. They chose to limit the eastern border to a line just beyond the Sierra Nevadas, on the practical basis that Congress would never approve a gigantic state extending eastward as far as Utah, as some suggested. The constitution gave the vote to white males only, which created a crisis since many of the Californios were of mixed Indian blood. The result was a compromise: The new legislature when formed could give the vote to all males of Indian blood by a two-thirds vote.

In the early morning hours of October 13, 1849, after a ball at Colton Hall, the delegates signed the California constitution. Soon an interim legislature was elected, but the first state capital would be San Jose, followed by Benicia (for a year) and then finally Sacramento. Monterey was once again a sleepy village, more Mexican than American. Congress admitted California as a state on September 9, 1850. Monterey County was one of the first twenty-seven counties established in the new state and was the first county seat, with Colton Hall as the courthouse. A city council of aldermen replaced the alcalde. In the first five years the council adopted a few ordinances, including requiring dog licenses, banning horse races on main streets, ordering fences around wells, and forbidding cattle slaughter in downtown. From 1853 to 1859 the council did not meet.

Although the peace treaty had provided for honoring existing rights of Mexican citizens, the great influx of settlers during the gold rush put the old land grants in jeopardy. A federal land claims court heard the title disputes, but evidence was hard to produce because title descriptions were vague and almost never based on surveys. Squatters—many formerly renters—took over sections of ranches, refused to pay rent, and then challenged the title in court. Often the cases dragged on for years—as many as thirty—and legal costs became prohibitive. Even when they won in court—which the majority did—the rancheros were ordered to pay for surveys, which they usually could not afford. Some squatters enforced their claims at the point of a gun, and several rancheros were shot from ambush. Many of the Californios lost their property by foreclosure after borrowing money at usurious rates (as much as 2 percent a month) and giving mortgages as security to immigrants with ready cash.

David Jacks Forecloses on Monterey

One of these lenders was a young Scot named David Jacks, who had come to San Francisco in 1849 and built up a small nest egg working for the Custom House. Jacks moved to Monterey in 1850 and soon became a lender to the old Rancheros. He was able to acquire land through foreclosure and bidding at sales for tax delinquency.

The City of Monterey owed attorney Delos Ashley just under $1,000 for legal work to confirm its land title, but the city had no funds. Somehow Ashley got a bill

DAVID JACKS

through the legislature authorizing the city to sell "any or all" of its lands to pay its debts. In 1859 Jacks and the lawyer published a notice of an auction for "all the lands belonging to the city of Monterey" (including 30,000 acres on the outskirts) in a Santa Cruz County newspaper. Ashley and Jacks were the only bidders. Jacks eventually bought out Ashley, who left town. Efforts to set aside the sale on the basis of lack of city powers to sell was thwarted by a law introduced by a legislator friend of Jacks. Legal appeals by the city failed all the way to the U.S. Supreme Court. Eventually Jacks would own more than 60,000 acres. Strangely, he could never understand why he was disliked.

MURDERS, LYNCHINGS, AND THE CROOKED SHERIFF

During one three-year period in the 1850s, there were at least twenty murders annually with no convictions. Ten of these were caused by a feud in which Monterey County Sheriff William Roach was the principal participant. Roach had been named administrator of the estate of the drowned husband of Concha Sanchez. Louis Belcher, who had put up Roach's bond, charged that Sheriff Roach was looting the estate. Concha's new husband, a lawyer, was gunned down by Sheriff Roach's brother-in-law in an argument over the sheriff's alleged dishonesty. Two men carrying the estate documents out of the county on behalf of Belcher were stabbed to death in November 1855, apparently by local roughneck Anastacio Garcia, who was in the pay of the sheriff. On June 15, 1856, Belcher, the bondsman, was shot in the back while drinking in the bar at the Washington Hotel, reportedly by Garcia. When a posse cornered Garcia, he shot and killed three of them, including leading citizen Jose de la Torre. Garcia was soon caught and put in the Monterey jail. Without resistance from Sheriff Roach, several men invaded the jail, threw a rope over a rafter, and lynched Garcia, thereby silencing him. Several years later, ex-Sheriff Roach, his tongue loosened by liquor, bragged of his role in this feud. Shortly thereafter his bullet-riddled body was found at the bottom of a well.

RAILROADS, GROWTH, AND MONTEREY PORT

Juan Bautista Castro, the young heir to the Simeon Castro grant, subdivided lots in a community he named Castroville in hopes of his town becoming the next stop for the Southern Pacific, which had reached San Jose. Castro even gave away some lots to attract businesses, but he demanded that the railroad pay for a right-of-way and acreage for a roundhouse, which the Southern Pacific refused to do. An English sheep rancher named Eugene Sherwood had purchased the old Soberanes land grant and Rancho Sauzal (once owned by the Castros) from Jacob Leese. In 1867, Sherwood joined with two other landowners to draw a 1-mile-square grid for Salinas and gave the Southern Pacific a free right-of-way as well as land for a depot. Salinas thus became the railroad hub in the county and the railroad gateway to the rails to southern California, while Castroville was only a quick stop station.

Faced with the Jacks debacle, Monterey became "unincorporated," leaving it with no machinery for civic improvements. (It was not reincorporated until 1889.) In November 1872, by a vote of three to one (1,436 to 448), the county seat was moved to Salinas, which had grown rapidly after the railroad arrived. Colton Hall, which had been the county courthouse, became an elementary school.

One of the few of the old Californios who survived economically was Catalina Munras, widow of Estaban Munras. She retained their near 20,000 acres around the small town of Soledad, which became a key station on the Southern Pacific. Brothers Alfred and Mariano Gonzales inherited a rancho, which became the community of Gonzales when they gave the Southern Pacific a free right-of-way.

ALVARADO STREET IN 1888
(From a glass plate in Pat Hathaway's collection)

Not many cried when David Jacks lost a bundle in the short-lived Monterey and Salinas Valley Railroad. It was a narrow-gauge line built to carry farm goods from Salinas to the Monterey wharf (which Jacks owned) at lower rates than the Southern Pacific. The Southern Pacific retaliated by chopping rates to farmers and in 1879 bought the new little railroad under foreclosure.

It was on the narrow gauge that itinerant Scottish travel writer Robert Louis Stevenson arrived in 1879 in pursuit of his beloved, Fanny Osborne, who was separated from her husband and twelve years Stevenson's senior. During his four months in Monterey, Stevenson caught pneumonia and nearly died, while Fanny pondered divorce, which she finally received in 1880. When Stevenson made his mark on the literary world with *Treasure Island,* the coastline of the book's island was patterned after Carmel Bay and Point Lobos.

Between 1855 and 1875 the principal moneymaker for the town of Monterey was the whaling business founded by sea captain J. P. Davenport, with headquarters in what is now the First Theater building and a reduction plant under Point Pinos. Soon there were three other companies, including a group of Portuguese whalers, harpooning the humpback and California gray whales on their migrations to and from Baja California. By the late 1870s, however, whaling dwindled due to overkill (including young calves) and the replacement of whale oil for lighting by kerosene and natural gas. By then a colony of about eighty Chinese fishermen with thirty boats was catching and drying salmon and squid that were shipped to San Francisco and inland. As a port for the county's growing grain industry, Monterey shipped at least a shipload of agricultural products each week in season.

Between 1860 and 1890 the population of Monterey increased by only nine souls, from 1,653 to 1,662. The real action by the end of the 1870s was in the areas bordering on the old town.

PACIFIC GROVE FOUNDED AS A CHRISTIAN HAVEN

David Jacks heard that the Methodist Retreat Association was looking for a site for a seaside resort, so he showed them Rancho Punto de Pinos, which he owned. They loved it, particularly since a couple of asthmatic ministers were miraculously cured while camping there. In 1875 Jacks donated one hundred acres to the newly formed Pacific Grove Retreat Association and loaned it $30,000 for streets. An amphitheater for camp meetings was built, lots were surveyed and sold for $50 on up, and the first cottages and tent platforms were erected. Of course, when the association could not make payments on the loan, the unsold lots reverted to Jacks. He willingly sold them to newcomers, subject

PAT HATHAWAY AND HIS PHOTO COLLECTION

Monterey photographer Pat Hathaway got hooked on historic photographs more than thirty years ago. His California Views now has a collection of 75,000 photos, some dating back to 1875, of Monterey, Carmel, Cannery Row, and John Steinbeck, as well as other subjects such as Yosemite and the 1906 San Francisco earthquake.

Hathaway has fortunately cataloged this collection so that the history buff or serious researcher can be directed to the subject matter of interest. His collection seems to overflow his combined shop/museum/laboratory. Pictures from his collection have been used for television documentaries, exhibits, and historical volumes. While historical societies and libraries may have some of these photographs, no one has such a complete collection. For a reasonable fee Hathaway will produce a print for you, of any size—some from original glass plates.

Hathaway also has a keen interest in historic preservation. With historic photos he richly illustrated preservationist Michael Kenneth Hemp's Cannery Row, *first published in 1986. He will readily turn away from his desk to discuss the need to save the heritage of Monterey. The conversation is worth a visit.*

California Views, the Pat Hathaway Collection, 469 Pacific Street, Monterey 93940; (831) 373–3811; e-mail hathaway@caviews.com; www.caviews.com. Open 11:00 A.M.–5:00 P.M. Tuesday– Saturday.

to the association's restrictions: There was an absolute ban on alcoholic beverages, gambling, and dancing, and no swimming or business was allowed on Sundays. The elders of the association took a particular interest in women's swimsuits, which had to be shapeless from "above the nipples" to "below the crotch." In fact they had to have "double crotches or a skirt" to cover the buttocks. Curfews were imposed and a gated fence (locked at night) was built around the community, which was open only to the ocean. The gate did not last long—it was axed to splinters by an irate judge who was locked out after curfew.

Pacific Grove's road to the Point Pinos Lighthouse (installed in 1855) was soon lined with businesses, including a dry-goods store owned by Renssalaer Luther Holman and a drugstore owned by Charles Tuttle. In 1888 at Lighthouse and Sixteenth there arose a new Methodist church, which also served as Chautauqua meeting hall and a school. Numerous Victorian homes were erected. In 1889 the town was incorporated and a board of trustees elected. It pledged to maintain the dry and pure nature of the community. The population approached 1,500, almost equal to Monterey. During summer when recreation and religious activities were at their height, another 5,000 flooded the town. Four small hotels, spare rooms, and campsites served vacationers in nearby Monterey through the 1870s.

THE SOUTHERN PACIFIC AND THE DEL MONTE HOTEL

David Jacks still owned much of the land around Monterey, including the 7,000 acres of present-day Pebble Beach and Del Monte Forest, which he had purchased from land grant heiress Maria Baretto for twelve cents an acre. The

PACIFIC GROVE METHODIST CHURCH AND MEETING HALL

"Big Four" owners of the Southern Pacific—Charles Crocker, Leland Stanford, Mark Hopkins, and Collis P. Huntington—bought this property from Jacks in 1879 for $5.00 an acre in the name of their new Pacific Improvement Company. The Southern Pacific rail line from Castroville to Monterey was completed in January 1880, linking Monterey to San Francisco (fare: $1.00) and the transcontinental railroad.

At the same time, the Big Four rushed the luxurious three-story Del Monte Hotel to completion in an amazing one hundred days, with hot and cold running water, gas light, an internal system of the newfangled telephones, swimming pools, gardens, a racetrack, and horse carriages to carry visitors around the roadway along the water's edge to the pleasant woods. This road eventually became 17-Mile Drive. The Del Monte Hotel had its own railroad station on the east side of Monterey, where the elite of the Bay Area and the world famous arrived in droves, year-round. The Pacific Improvement Company also bought a substantial ranch (the old Boronda ra7ncho) to provide the hotel with water from the upper Carmel River and with milk products (including a new cheese called Monterey Jack) from a dairy on the property.

When the Del Monte burned down in 1887, it was quickly replaced with an even grander version, this one including a dining room seating 750. The 1890s saw the addition of a golf course, which became the site of the state amateur championships. That same year the Pacific Improvement Company built another luxurious hotel, the 114-room El Carmelo, on Lighthouse Avenue in the heart of Pacific Grove. The hotel lasted until 1918 when it was torn down to make way for the Holman department store. Pacific Grove became the terminus of the railroad. Timothy Hopkins donated the funds for the Hopkins Marine Station, which was built on the shore of Pacific Grove in 1892.

The popularity of the Del Monte and El Carmelo Hotels had the side effect of encouraging the restoration of the Carmel Mission, which was visited by many of the guests, who paid fifteen cents each to a fund to improve that decaying relic. Mrs. Leland Stanford and Helen Hunt Jackson, author of *Ramona*, began raising money to rebuild the mission.

DEVENDORF DEVELOPS CARMEL-BY-THE-SEA

In 1888 Santiago J. Duckworth, a hopeful real estate developer of Monterey, purchased 324 acres in what is now downtown Carmel (between First and Eleventh and Monte Verde and Monterey Streets). This land was part of the Manzanitas Ranch owned by Frenchman Honore Escolle, proprietor of a store in the Stokes Adobe in Monterey. Duckworth's initial idea was to create a Catholic enclave similar to Methodist-based Pacific Grove. He filed a map with the county recorder for Carmel City, with square blocks drawn without reference to hills and gullies. He published a brochure, quickly sold 200 lots, and built the eighteen-room Hotel Carmelo, along with a few cottages.

The only other real estate agent interested in Carmel was a woman, Abbie Jane Hunter of San Francisco, whose family had built the Carmel Hotel and a fancy bathhouse at the beach at the end of Ocean Avenue—then just a dirt road. Joining forces with Duckworth to promote Carmel, Mrs. Hunter first used the name "Carmel-by-the-Sea" in a mailer.

JAMES FRANKLIN
DEVENDORF

But during the 1890s sales were stagnant and the project was losing money.

Duckworth went to see successful San Jose real estate broker James Franklin Devendorf in 1900 and offered to sell his remaining Carmel property. Devendorf proposed to pay by trading real estate he owned in Stockton, and Duckworth agreed. Devendorf, just forty-four years old, needed more money to develop Carmel. So he formed a partnership called the Carmel Development Company with thirty-eight-year-old Frank Powers, a wealthy San Francisco attorney. Powers would provide the money and legal work while Devendorf would spend weekdays in Carmel managing the project. They filed a new map, using the name Carmel-by-the-Sea. Then they put Hotel Carmelo on rollers, pulled it 5 blocks closer to the beach, and renamed it the Pine Inn. They also sold lots on generous terms ($5.00 down) and helped scrounge up building materials for small houses.

STERLING AND HIS BOHEMIANS SETTLE IN CARMEL

The rustic, unstructured town soon attracted a group of bohemian writers and artists, first organized by poet George Sterling, who was fed up with working in a San Francisco insurance office, and noted writer Mary Austin. They were joined by writer James Hopper (a former University of California football star) and were visited by Jack London, a good friend of Sterling's, who eventually stayed away because he could not keep up his writing pace in the midst of the drinking (and he was no slouch) and high jinks. Within the first decade of the century, well-known muckraker Upton Sinclair came to live in Carmel for a while, as did a young hopeful writer named Sinclair Lewis.

Carmel's Sterling/Austin gang often put on theatricals and farces, wrote funny poetry late into the night, and added to the gaiety of the community. The press pictured them as happy bohemians. There was a dark side, however. Austin became a hypochondriac certain she was dying, several marriages fell apart, and poetess Nora May French and later Sterling's wife both took poison and died. In 1914 Sterling and Austin left (separately). Eventually Sterling would poison himself in 1926.

At Lovers Point (originally "Lovers of Jesus Point") in Pacific Grove, William "Bathhouse" Smith dynamited the bluff to create space for hot-water swimming pools, a restaurant, and an auditorium. Nearby a Japanese garden with ocean views was built.

THE BURNING OF CHINATOWN

Clinging to the cliffs on the border between Pacific Grove and Monterey was a ramshackle village of Chinese fishermen and their families. It included shops catering to the Chinese and the Joss House, the hub of the community. The property had been leased by the Chinese from the Pacific Improvement Company, which wanted to develop the land. Many of the residents of Pacific Grove were bothered by the smell of drying squid. It was proposed that the entire Chinatown be moved to the community of Seaside, north of Monterey, but that fell through. The sheriff served eviction notices in February 1906, but no one moved.

On the evening of May 16, 1906, a fire—obviously arson—swept from a barn at one end of Chinatown. The water to the fire engines was mysteriously cut off, and looting of the houses and shops in the path of the flames became rampant despite the efforts of a couple of courageous Monterey and Pacific Grove police officers who tried to halt the mob of thieves. Within a few hours most of the village was smoldering ashes, with only the Joss House undamaged. Several residents were killed, while most escaped with only the possessions in their arms. Many of the Chinese population scattered, but some moved the Joss House northward to McAbee Beach, re-creating the Chinese fishing village. In 1917 Hopkins Marine Station took over the old village site and became affiliated with Stanford University.

One go-getter drawn to Carmel's artistic colony was young actor Bert Heron, who bought eighty acres and built a house for himself and his family. In 1910 he founded the Forest Theater in a natural wooded amphitheater that

Devendorf leased rent free to the Forest Theater Society, which Heron had organized. The theater became the venue for many popular productions, often based on plays written by locals. The Carmel Arts and Crafts Club also founded a theater, the Theater of the Golden Bough, which for eleven years was another popular scene of experimental drama. The building burned in 1935, but as a group the theater survived.

Carmel-by-the-Sea was officially incorporated in 1916. A board of trustees took over governmental functions from Devendorf, but he was still a major force in the direction of the town. He was not your usual developer. He planted cypress trees along Ocean Avenue, handed trees to lot buyers, donated buildings for a school and a library, gave a parcel for the Methodists' Church of the Wayfarer, and was lenient to slow payers. In an era of restrictive covenants, he sold several lots to a black woman from Michigan. In 1921 Devendorf conveyed the beach to the town for less than a third of its appraised value, thus scotching a plan for a resort on the oceanfront. The land that would become Devendorf Park was his gift to Carmel.

A southern section of Pacific Grove was dedicated as a sixty-acre campground for the YWCA in 1913, known as Asilomar. Its buildings were designed by architect Julia Morgan, most famous for Hearst's Castle at San Simeon. Eventually Asilomar was purchased by the state of California in 1936 and remains a popular conference center, suitable for contemplation in a sylvan setting.

OCEAN AVENUE, CARMEL, IN 1909
(Photo by Louis S. Selvin)

MONTEREY ATTRACTS ARTISTS AND VACATIONERS

In the 1890s, when the railroad made the trip more feasible, artists began coming to Monterey. The colony took more formal shape when University of California art professor Eugen Neuhaus, in conjunction with artists William Keith and Charles Rollo Peters (famed for his moonlit scenes), founded the Del Monte Gallery. They were followed by German-trained William Ritschel, who painted seascapes from his home on the cliffs; former North Sea sailor Armin Hansen; Paul Dougherty, who painted in the style of Winslow Homer; and dozens of other men and women of recognized talent.

By the 1920s the Chinese community at McAbee Beach had melted away as they left the fishing business. Sunseeking tourists began flocking to the 500-foot-long strand. When the elegant three-story Ocean View Hotel directly on the beach was opened by Mr. and Mrs. M. C. Wu in 1927, it became *the* place to stay. One could get the best of fish dishes in the dining room (and teacups filled with whiskey during Prohibition). Eventually the smell from nearby Cannery Row caused its decline and it was demolished in 1944.

MONTEREY BECOMES THE SARDINE CAPITAL

Three men combined to develop Monterey's canned sardine industry: Frank E. Booth, Knute Hovden, and Pietro Ferrante. In the 1890s Booth came often to Monterey to buy salmon (then Monterey's chief fish product) for his father's packing plant on the Sacramento River. He noticed the sardines in the bay were plentiful and larger than the European variety. So he moved to Monterey and opened a small plant in 1902 to process and can sardines by hand. His first cannery burned down, but he built a larger one with Chinese laborers, making the cans with tin snips and hand soldering irons.

Booth hired Hovden, a young Norwegian who had studied at Norway's National Fisheries College, as plant manager. Hovden had worked for several European fishing companies before emigrating to the United States. Here he developed nets that let fewer sardines escape, devised holding pens in the water to keep sardines alive until ready to be packed, and invented a can-soldering machine.

Ferrante, a native of Italy, had been fishing in the San Francisco Bay Area for about fifteen years when his boat burned. He came down to Monterey to work for Booth and soon introduced him to "lampara" nets, the type used in the Mediterranean, which scooped up and held entire schools of fish. Later Ferrante became the prime organizer of the fishermen's union and the boat owners' association. Ferrante Plaza at the entrance to Fishermen's Wharf is named for him.

Booth and Pacific Fish (owned by Booth-trained James Madison) combined produced a total of 70,000 cases of sardines by 1912, mostly shipped overseas. Third into the cannery field was Hovden, who started his Hovden Food Products Corporation in 1916. His inventive brain was still at work, for he developed a suction pipe to pull the sardines from boat to shore without having to brave the surf, and a steam cooking system to replace boiling the fish in olive oil. More than twenty-five fish-canning companies soon lined the waterfront.

The eight blocks of Cannery Row (officially Ocean View Avenue until 1953) became replete with processing plants of various sizes, interspersed with stores, cafes, a marine laboratory, a can company, a boat works, and a bawdy house. A meat shortage during World War I increased American consumption of sardines. The number and size of boats grew, as did the variety of backgrounds of the fishers—Italian, Norwegian, Mexican, Japanese, Greek, Portuguese, Chinese, Irish, Filipino—Americans of all colors. In 1926 the Southern Pacific built Municipal Wharf No. 2 to berth the growing fishing fleet. The Army Corps of Engineers constructed a breakwater to protect the boats, since many had been damaged or sunk in a 1919 storm.

The sardine catch reached an average of 250,000 tons a year, even through the Great Depression. Thousands of women—often in crisp white outfits—worked on the lines, processing and packing. The business became the keystone of the Monterey economy. Official fears of overfishing led to the outlawing of the lampara nets in 1926, but the large Norwegian purse seine nets soon took their place.

Meanwhile the Pacific Improvement Company sold all its Monterey peninsula holdings to the Del Monte Properties Company, which had been organized by young Samuel F. B. Morse in 1919. He set about renovating the then seedy Del Monte Hotel, spiffed up the Pebble Beach golf course and lodge, and opened Del Monte Forest to carefully regulated home sites. When the hotel burned down in 1924, Morse constructed a larger and more modern facility. Del Monte Properties also sold off more than 3,000 acres in Carmel Valley, particularly to two developers who subdivided a portion, built the Robles del Rio Lodge, and laid out the Carmel Valley Village. Only the Boronda adobe remained from Mexican days; it was lovingly restored by George Sims in the 1940s. However, much of Carmel Valley was still in working ranches like the old William Martin ranch and the new Holman ranch.

CARMEL'S ARTISTS, WRITERS, AND PERRY NEWBERRY

A new wave of artists flocked to Carmel, including Maynard Dixon, Jo Mora, and Elizabeth Strong, as well as authors Lincoln Steffens, Leon Wilson, Steven Vincent Benét, and Robinson Jeffers. Poet and playwright Jeffers, whose somber but lyrical poetry gained international fame, built a rock house and tower (called Tor House and Hawk Tower, respectively) overlooking Carmel Bay, where he (and his wife) could concentrate. The town was also home to photographers like famed Edward Weston (whose sons Cole and Brett followed in his photo steps) and Louis S. Selvin, who chronicled Carmel on film from 1903 to the end of the 1930s and who doubled as postmaster for many years. In the thirties Ansel Adams moved to Carmel Highlands; aging Jane Austin wrote the text for his first published photo collection.

Perry Newberry, a young bohemian playwright and writer for the *Carmel Pine Cone,* became the leader of what he called the "art element" in its confrontations with the "business element" during the 1920s. When the city trustees voted to pave Ocean Avenue, Newberry feared it would stimulate growth and change the character of the town of six hundred souls. He led a successful campaign to defeat bonds for a city hall, and then ran for trustee himself on a platform that wound up: "If you truly want Carmel to become a boosting, bustling, wide-awake, lively metropolis, DON'T VOTE FOR PERRY NEWBERRY." He won, and blocked side street paving, a noon whistle, and other symbols of urbanization. To this day there are no street numbers in downtown Carmel. After becoming editor of the *Pine Cone,* he argued against any highway through town as part of the planned Highway 1 to Big Sur and beyond. In 1928 he was again elected to the trustees and helped defeat traffic lights, parking limits, and amusement park proposals.

Newberry even wanted to build a fence around the town, but instead used the talent of city attorney Argyll Campbell to draft a general plan and zoning ordinance establishing that the town was "primarily, essentially, and predominately a residential city wherein business and commerce have in the past, are now, and are proposed to be in the future subordinated to its residential character." The tug-of-war between residential and commercial elements was not over, but keeping out tourists—with or without a fence around the town—was impossible. Carmel's population jumped from 638 in 1920 to 2,260 in 1930.

COMSTOCK, BACH, PLATT, AND DOWNIE

About this time builder/designer Hugh Comstock, inspired by his doll-making wife, designed a pair of fairy-tale-looking cottages (called *Hansel* and *Gretel*) with adobe-like walls and swooping faux thatched roofs. Others asked for similar designs and eventually more than fifty Comstock cottages and the Tuck Box Restaurant were built in that style. They became symbolic of the old-fashioned woodsy atmosphere of Carmel-by-the-Sea. Many of the town's significant buildings were constructed by M. J. "Rock" Murphy, including the Harrison Memorial Library and the community center. Transplanted Los Angeles architect Charles Greene (followed by his brother, Gordon) designed many of the town's popular bungalows and lodges.

In 1927 nineteen Carmel artists formed the Carmel Art Association (the old Arts and Crafts Club formed in 1905 had evaporated), and in 1933 the group bought a large studio on Dolores Street, which remains the association's showplace. In 1937 artist Armin Hansen (who had moved from Monterey) founded the Carmel Art Institute. Contemporaneously, the Carmel Music Society was born through the efforts of pianist Dene Denny, interior designer Hazel Watrous, and ubiquitous Bert Heron. They produced a three-day Bach Festival in the Sunset School auditorium in 1935 that proved to be a whopping success. The Bach Festival remains Carmel's number one annual cultural event.

Next door in Pacific Grove, Julia Platt, with a Ph.D. in zoology, returned in the 1920s to the town where she had worked at the Hopkins Marine Station twenty years earlier. In 1927 the energetic Julia led a successful campaign to adopt a city manager form of government. Four years later, at the age of seventy-four, she was elected mayor and pushed the creation of a bird sanctuary at Point Pinos. The census had reported a sharp rise from 2,974 in 1920 to 5,558 in 1930 when it leveled off.

In that decade a young Stanford University dropout from Salinas moved into a small house in Pacific Grove owned by his parents and began to write stories and novels about the area and its characters. His name was John Steinbeck.

The reconstruction of the Carmel Mission had poked along until the 1930s when restoration expert Harry Downie took charge. He meticulously re-created the mission as it was at its zenith about 1800. Downie even unearthed Father Serra's cross. Carmel artist and sculptor Jo Mora was commissioned to design and sculpt a sarcophagus for Serra, with a bas relief base illustrating early California history.

The year 1937 saw the opening of Highway 1 passing through the hills above Carmel southward, eventually to San Simeon, Santa Barbara, and Los Angeles. The Monterey Peninsula Airport was completed the following year.

STEINBECK, THE WAR, AND THE END OF THE SARDINE ERA

Since Monterey had changed little—some said "slumbered" (its population had actually declined in the thirties to 8,531)—more than a quarter of the adobes existing in 1850 were still standing in 1937. That year the Monterey History and Art Association called for a master plan to preserve and blend Old Monterey with new development. The city planning commission responded by retaining Carnegie Foundation engineer Emerson Knight, who developed a comprehensive plan to be phased in over twenty-five years. In 1939 Knight unveiled a sweeping proposal to preserve and display historic buildings, install parks and playgrounds, change the traffic pattern, build a municipal bathhouse, prohibit billboards, adopt strict height limitations, and create a beach promenade from the Custom House north to El Estero. Key to opening up the city to the oceanfront was removal of Fisherman's Wharf and abatement or lowering the profile of various waterfront buildings, including Booth's. The historic, civic, and artistic organizations loved the plan. But it gave the fishing community—from the most humble fishermen and plant workers to the owners of the canneries—a collective heart attack.

A bigger battle overseas put the discussion of revamping downtown Monterey on hold. A few miles north, 35,000-acre Fort Ord (named for Edward Ord, an American army officer stationed at Monterey during the Mexican War) became the assembly and training camp for tens of thousands of Army draftees and volunteers for World War II and decades afterward. The Del Monte Hotel was leased to the U.S. Navy in 1940 as a center for training future Navy pilots. After the war it became a hotel for six years before being sold to the government for the naval postgraduate school in 1951.

The servicemen's dollars were a shot in the arm for the local economy, except for Flora Woods's house of prostitution on Cannery Row. The Army wanted such places near bases closed, so in May 1941 California's attorney general, Earl Warren, ordered a crackdown on their operation, and by June, Flora closed up at the request of the chief of police. Fort Ord introduced thousands to the natural beauty of the Monterey area, as would the Defense Foreign Language Institute and the Navy postgraduate school.

Author John Steinbeck's popular *Tortilla Flat* (1935) and *Cannery Row* (1945) gave the reading public a taste, if somewhat tongue in cheek, of Monterey and Pacific Grove. The Monterey Chamber of Commerce protested that these novels improperly pictured Monterey as a town of lazy derelicts, spending much of their time drinking Old Tennessee ("Old Tennis Shoes") whiskey, and there was a serious effort to ban Steinbeck's books from the city library.

Then suddenly in 1945 the sardine catch dropped dramatically and within two years the sardines had virtually disappeared. Thirty years of taking the most the fishermen could net had taken its toll and killed the industry. Also dying was Edward F. Ricketts, dedicated director of Pacific Biological Laboratories, a world expert on fish, and friend of John Steinbeck, immortalized as "Doc" in *Cannery Row*. Ricketts's car was broadsided on May 8, 1948, by the evening Del Monte Express train at the Drake Avenue crossing (a block from Cannery Row), which had no signal. He lingered for three days and died on May 11, 1948, aged fifty-two. He left a beautiful and bright widow, Nancy, whom he had married in January.

TOURISM AND ALL THAT JAZZ

Monterey's salvation lay in stimulating tourism. While the town needed to take up the issue of city renovation left hanging when the United States entered World War II, the locals' first priority was a need to create events and attractions to compete for visitors' attention and dollars.

The Monterey Jazz Festival was founded in 1958 by Jimmy Lyons, California's leading jazz radio disc jockey and expert, who became its longtime general manager. Held at the Monterey Fairgrounds each September, within a decade the festival became one of the nation's premier musical phenomena, with greats like Dizzie Gillespie, Louis Armstrong, and Dave Brubeck performing. Those who saw and heard Janis Joplin belting out "Me and Bobby McGee" while drinking on stage or Jimi Hendrix winding up his set by burning his guitar will never forget it. In the late sixties a documentary film on the jazz festival was a hit.

Over the years other events filled the calendar, including the Monterey Bay Blues Festival, the Concours Classic Car Weekend, a Grand Prix Indy Car race, the Monterey Squid Festival, art and adobe walks, wine and art shows, and many other attractions. Pacific Grove celebrated flowers, the return of the monarch butterflies (adopting the nickname "Butterfly City"), and Victorian tours. Carmel concentrated on art, music, and lots of drama, from Shakespeare to avant-garde, at several venues. Dog and horse shows were popular in Carmel Valley, and its resorts installed championship-level golf courses.

In Big Sur a young Stanford grad, Michael Murphy, founded the Esalen Institute for meditation, study, relaxation, and inspiration. It draws thousands each year. Also drawn to the Big Sur coast was Henry Miller, whose critically acclaimed works had been banned from the United States for being too sexually explicit—although they are almost tame by today's standards. Big Sur sponsors a full marathon that currently attracts more than 3,000 runners.

Singer-actor-golf enthusiast Bing Crosby created and underwrote the Bing Crosby Pro-Amateur tournament. Besides top professionals, celebrities like Phil Harris and Jack Nicholson clowned between shots on the course and at the nineteenth hole at Pebble Beach. After Crosby's death the tournament was briefly run by his son, Nathaniel, before becoming the AT&T Pebble Beach National Golf Tournament.

Early in the decade of the fifties, almost half of the Cannery Row real estate was bought up by a local partnership called Cannery Row Properties, which waited for the city to propose a master plan for the area. When no plan was forthcoming, new businesses sprang up in some of the old properties, including three restaurants and a pizza parlor. Ed Ricketts's old lab, which was protected from destruction by a historic designation, was taken over by a group of locals who turned it into a private club that agreed to maintain the building.

MONTEREY STRUGGLES WITH PLANNING AND REDEVELOPMENT

City Beautification Month, spearheaded by Monterey City Councilwoman Marje Eliassen in 1956, saw Boy Scouts cleaning out weed-clogged sidewalk strips and downtown vacant lots. But Eliassen and many citizens had a larger goal: planning to blend old Monterey buildings with renovations and new structures along the concepts—if not the exact details—of the discarded 1939 plan. In 1957 Councilwoman Eliassen ran for mayor, calling for such planning, but lost by 300 votes to pragmatic incumbent Dan H. Searle.

Margaret Jacks, daughter of David Jacks, partially atoned for her father's greed by giving several historic adobes to the city of Monterey in the late 1950s. Meanwhile the city had established a redevelopment agency for urban renewal of the downtown. The agency was empowered to develop a plan, acquire properties by eminent domain if blighted or essential to the plan, and then to resell the property for new construction by private enterprise consistent with the redevelopment scheme. Two-thirds of the net cost would be paid for by the federal government.

The agency staff submitted its redevelopment plan to the city council for private review in the summer of 1960, and it was unveiled in December. While the city council was happy to see it completed, others did not consider the plan a Christmas present. One newspaper called it a "bombshell" and the *San Francisco News-Call-Bulletin* reported that "Salty little Monterey, three-century-old heartland of California, is about to be dismembered and put back together again." The plan attacked the blighted conditions of many small buildings, irregular property lines, undersized lots, and traffic problems by proposing the bulldozing of almost 140 structures, while saving all but one historic adobe. Gone would be a 115-year-old hotel, a popular liquor store, an old-timer's tailor shop, and an auto dealership. In their place would be a block-long eight-story garage on Calle Principal, a new street cut through by the old Custom House, and the hope that some buyer would build a huge hotel-motel complex overlooking the bay.

The city's planning director and some members of the planning commission objected that they had not been included in the process and that some elements were in violation of the general plan. Ex-councilwoman Eliassen called it a "hideous mistake" and feisty Margaret Jacks, by then ninety-three years old, criticized the agency for not sparing more buildings. The History and Art Association and Eliassen particularly disapproved of the giant garage. Wesley Dodge, a partner in Cannery Row Properties, found to his chagrin that the building where he had his office, the Old Whaling Station, was going to be acquired by the agency. Nevertheless, with minor adjustments, the redevelopment plan was adopted in June 1961.

During the following two years the bulldozers leveled acres of buildings in the downtown. The out-of-scale eight-story garage was never funded, the glossy illustration of a renewed Alvarado Street was not realized, and purchases of open lots were slow. Thus, for the better part of the next two decades, much of the redevelopment area was an irregular complex of dusty empty lots, only slowly filling up.

CANNERY ROW: RENEWAL, PRESERVATION, AND THE AQUARIUM

One of the buildings torn down under the redevelopment plan was the Booth Cannery. In 1973 a Cannery Row Plan identified buildings that should be protected because they were historic, unique architecturally, or featured in Steinbeck's novels. At the same time the Cannery Row Development Company organized by Ben Swig, owner of San Francisco's Fairmont Hotel, bought a substantial amount of property along the waterfront. Swig proposed a massive hotel and restaurant complex. The California Coastal Commission viewed it as harmful to the scenic beauty of the shoreline and refused a permit. Swig's company sold out in 1976 to local restaurateurs Bert Cutino and Ted Balesteri.

A bust of John Steinbeck (who had died in 1968), sculpted by Carol Brown, was donated to the city by Mr. and Mrs. Merle W. Strauch of Carmel in 1973. It was mounted on a pedestal in Steinbeck Plaza, facing the street with his back to the sea. Thus Cannery Row embraced Steinbeck, the man who had made it world famous but had been vilified by the good people of Monterey for depicting the street and its people, warts and all. Honoring the life and legend of Steinbeck was not only justified but good business.

In 1980 the Local Coastal Plan/Land Use Plan confirmed the identification of threatened buildings in the 1973 Cannery Row Plan. This new report, within the context of the state's 1976 Coastal Act, declared that the architectural character of Cannery Row buildings should be "respected" or the historic heritage of Cannery Row would be lost. With the approval of the Coastal Commission, several buildings were torn down in the eighties and nineties to make way for the Monterey Plaza Hotel, the Chart House, and other hotels and restaurants. However, these new buildings and renovations maintained a look generally consistent with the old Cannery Row.

At the same time Michael Hemp, who had been collecting oral histories of old denizens of the Row, organized the Cannery Row Foundation. The foundation, which Hemp insisted was not antidevelopment, persistently attempted to keep the city alert to maintaining the historic character of Cannery Row. As late as the summer of 1998, Hemp was publicly complaining that the city council was dragging its feet on historical designation of buildings for preservation and had failed to put a measure on the ballot that would have directed some hotel tax toward historic preservation.

The major change in Cannery Row (and Monterey itself), however, was the construction of the Monterey Bay Aquarium at the southern end of the street. The aquarium, one of the most remarkable in the world, brings marine life and the sea tide into the building. The concept was the 1977 brainchild of Hopkins Marine Station biologists Steve Webster, Chuck Baxter, Robin Burnett, and Nancy Packard (Burnett's wife), who is now its executive director. It became reality thanks to an initial contribution of $55 million by David and Lucile Packard (Nancy's parents). Opened in October 1984, the Monterey Bay Aquarium immediately became Monterey's pride—as well as a prime tourist attraction—averaging 1.5 million visitors annually. Incorporating the three-story Hovden Cannery building, the design maintained the integrity of the original structure and became the anchor to the revitalization of the 9-block strip. In the nineties an additional wing was added at a cost of $33 million.

Ironically, the first proposal for an aquarium had come from Frank Booth back in 1914. It would have been on a piece of waterfront land he wanted to lease from the city. Booth had envisioned it as both a scientific and tourist attraction. The city council, which suspected self-promotion by Booth, attached so many stipulations to the lease he abandoned the application. Knute Hovden, as chairman of the Pacific Grove Museum Board, had pushed a bond issue to fund the building of an aquarium in that town, but the voters turned it down.

OF PERMITS, PRESERVATION, ICE CREAM, AND CLINT'S DAYS

Carmel was the site of thirty hotels, motels, and inns before its city council refused to grant permits for any new hostelries. Over the years a political seesaw teetered between ardent preservationists like Mayor Gunnar Norberg in the seventies, who wanted to preserve Carmel as a "heritage city" in the Newberry mold, and those who opposed too many impediments to the operation of businesses, like three-term mayor Barney Laiolo. In 1985, with a council headed by Mayor Charlotte Townsend, a business that lost its lease could not move to a location that had been used for another type of enterprise. In August 1985, relocation of commercial water permits was barred. These limitations were employed to keep new tourist-oriented businesses from opening on Ocean Avenue.

The issue came to a head when the town's only ice-cream shop lost its lease and was turned down for a permit to take over other premises. Carmel became known throughout the world as a "scrooge city" that would not permit eating ice-cream cones. The spotlight on the ice-cream flap opened up the entire issue of business difficulties in getting permits and variances. One of those who had a problem was Carmel resident Clint Eastwood, famed actor and director. He had sued the city over its denial of a variance for an elevator in a building he owned next to his Hog's Breath Inn restaurant in the heart of downtown. Eventually the matter was negotiated, but Eastwood was still annoyed.

Eastwood ran for mayor in a campaign in which he hired a manager and spent $30,000, twenty times the incumbent. The expenditure was scarcely necessary, since his charisma, charm, and celebrity made him an easy winner. Eastwood served only a single two-year term, but his fame and no-nonsense manner focused attention on Carmel. His tenure marked a period of some relaxation of the permit process, but it was a shortage of water more than government action that slowed growth. Carmel voters remain politically schizophrenic. In 1993, a measure to expand the town's commercial zone passed by only ten votes.

The Mission Sanctified and the Natives Forgotten

Pope John Paul II paid a visit to Mission San Carlos Borromeo de Carmelo on September 17, 1987, to sanctify the mission and pray at the sepulcher of Father Serra, who would be beatified (one step from sainthood) the following year. Given invitations to the ceremony in the basilica of the mission were local public officials of all levels, the Knights of Columbus, the cloistered nuns of the Carmelite monastery who prayed with the pontiff, and prominent locals. Not invited were any of the descendants of the natives who built the mission or lived under its direction. Costanoan Tribal Chief Anthony Miranda called for a two-day prayer vigil in front of the mission to protest this exclusion. The vigil was dispersed by the sheriff's department on the grounds that Miranda did not have a permit, a ruling the board of supervisors and the diocesan bishop supported. No one asked the pope, who celebrated a mass at Laguna Seca for 100,000 people.

If the ghosts of the Ohlones, Salinans, and Essalens could look down on the land from Santa Cruz in the north to Big Sur in the south, they would be amazed at how mankind has altered the country in which they lived for several thousand years. But modern development could not destroy the "noble harbor" that Vizcaino sailed into four centuries ago, the lovely river tumbling to the sea next to Carmel-by-the-Sea, or the bluff where Father Serra insisted his mission must be. The stunning natural beauty of Point Lobos, the Big Sur Coast, and the Del Monte Forest remain. In some cases humans have actually enhanced the charm and made the area more accessible to the public.

This stretch of coast, its woods and waters, has inspired several generations of artists, writers, actors, and musicians. The Californios and their golden age are a hazy memory, and the silvery bonanza of sardines expired more than a half century ago, but there are those who know that their history is worth preserving. The spirit of Monterey and its satellite towns has survived fire, disease, invasions, financial disaster, and policy disputes. All who are drawn to this special place love it. May they all live in harmony with its nature, as did the first people.

CHAPTER 9

PLACES TO STAY ON THE MONTEREY PENINSULA

Note: The room rates are usually summer rates; off-season prices are lower. A two-day minimum stay is sometimes required, particularly on weekends. There are often discounts available for senior citizens, AAA members, and others.

Big Sur

Post Ranch Inn, Highway 1, P.O. Box 219, Big Sur 93920; phone (831) 667–2200, fax (831) 667–2512; www.postranchinn.com; $450–$755; historic inn with ocean views, pool, lounge.

Ventana Inn, Highway 1 South, Big Sur 93920; phone (800) 628–6500, fax (831) 667–2419; www.ventanainn.com; $340–$975; ocean view, pool, restaurant, lounge.

Carmel

Adobe Inn Carmel, Dolores Street and 8th Avenue, P.O. Box 4115, Carmel 93921; phone (831) 624–3933, fax (831) 624–8636; $130–$315; pool, continental breakfast, AAA 4 diamonds.

Best Western Carmel Bay View Inn, Junipero Street between 5th and 6th Avenues, P.O. Box 3715, Carmel 93921; phone (831) 624–1831, fax (831) 625–2336; www.bestwestern.com/carmelbayviewinn; $79–$189; pool, continental breakfast.

Best Western Carmel Mission Inn, 3665 Rio Road, Carmel 93921; phone (831) 624–1841, fax (831) 624–8684; www.bestwestern.com; $99–$369, $35 pet charge; pool, restaurant/lounge, just off Highway 1 near Carmel Mission.

Candle Light Inn, San Carlos Street between 4th and 5th Avenues, Carmel 93921; phone (831) 624–6451, fax (831) 624–6732; www.innsbythesea. com; $129–$240; some kitchens, sometimes special rates matching dollars to maximum temperatures.

Carmel River Inn, Highway 1 and Oliver Road at Carmel River Bridge, P.O. Box 221609, Carmel 93921; phone (831) 624–1575, fax (831) 624–0290; www.carmelriverinn.com; $110–$190, $25 pet charge; rustic decor, pool, near Carmel Mission.

Carmel Sands Lodge, San Carlos Street and 5th Avenue, P.O. Box 951, Carmel 93921; phone (831) 624–1255, fax (831) 624–2576; www.carmelsandslodge. com; $79–$169; pool, restaurant/lounge, smoke free.

Carmel Village Inn, Ocean Avenue and Junipero Street, P.O. Box 5275, · Carmel 93921; phone (831) 624–3864, fax 626–6763; www.carmelvillageinn.com; $79–$170 (one suite at $360); prize-winning gardens, continental breakfast.

Colonial Terrace Inn, San Antonio Street between 12th and 13th Avenues, P.O. Box 1375, Carmel 93921; phone (831) 624–2741, fax (831) 626–2715; $76–$236; ask for ocean view in this old traditional inn.

Cypress Inn, Lincoln and 7th, Carmel 93921; phone (831) 624–3871 or (800) 443–7443, www.cypressinn.com; $125–$275; elegant, cozy courtyard, lounge, afternoon tea, famed for owner singer-actress Doris Day, and as a pet-friendly inn ($20 for first pet, $12 for a second); pet meals and list of pet-sitters.

Dolphin Inn, San Carlos Street and 4th Avenue, P.O. Box 1900, Carmel 93921; phone (831) 624–5356, fax (831) 624–2967; www.innsbythesea.com; $99–$239; pool.

Horizon Inn, Junipero Street and 3rd Avenue, P.O. Box 1900, Carmel 93921; phone (831) 624–5327, fax (831) 626–8253; www.horizoninncarmel.com; $139–$259; pool, breakfast basket, fireplaces, completely renovated in 2000.

La Playa Hotel, Camino Real at 8th Avenue, P.O. Box 900, Carmel 93921; phone (831) 624–6476, fax (831) 624–7966; www.laplayacarmel.com; $135–$595; historic, no elevator, some cottages, dining room, outside dining on terrace, pool.

Lobos Lodge, Ocean Avenue and Monte Verde Street, P.O. Box L-1, Carmel 93921; phone (831) 624–3874, fax (831) 624–0135; www.loboslodge.com; $115–$200; Carmel's newest, fireplaces, continental breakfast in room.

Mission Ranch, 26270 Dolores Street, Carmel 93923 (just around the corner from the Carmel Mission); phone: (831) 624-6436 or (800) 538–8221, fax (831) 626–4163, www.missionranch.com; $95–$275; actor-director and onetime Carmel Mayor Clint Eastwood bought this forty-acre ranch to save from overdevelopment, and made it an attractive country inn with ocean views nearby, restaurant for dinner, Saturday lunch, and Sunday brunch.

Normandy Inn, Ocean Avenue between Monte Verde and Casanova Streets, P.O. Box 1706, Carmel 93921; phone (831) 624–3825, fax (831) 624–4614; normandyinncarmel.com; $79–$500 (3-bedroom house); French Country decor, continental breakfast, pool.

Pine Inn, Ocean Avenue between Lincoln and Monte Verde Streets, P.O. Box 250, Carmel 93921; phone (831) 624–3851, fax (831) 624–3030; www.pineinn.com; $105–$250; Carmel's famed historic hotel, no elevator, restaurant, patio dining.

Svendsgaard's, San Carlos Street and 4th Avenue, P.O. Box 1900, Carmel
  93921; phone (831) 624–1511, fax (831) 624–5661; www.innbythesea,com;
  $150–$275, discounts for Entertainment travel club; country decor, pool,
  continental breakfast.
Wayside Inn, Mission Street and 7th Avenue, P.O. Box 1900, Carmel 93921;
  phone (831) 624–5336, fax (831) 626–6974; www.innsbythesea.com;
  $99–$300; Colonial decor, some kitchens, continental breakfast, pets definitely OK at no fee.
Carmel Bed-and-Breakfasts: There are numerous charming bed-and-breakfasts
  in Carmel including: *Briarwood Inn* (831) 626–9056; *Carmel Fireplace Inn*
  (831) 624–4862; *Carriage House Inn* (831) 625–2585 with AAA 4 diamonds; *Cobblestone Inn* (831) 625–5222; *Sandpiper Inn at the Beach* (831)
  624–6433; *Stonehouse Inn* (831) 624–4569; *Sunset House* (831) 624–4890;
  Vagabond's House Inn (831) 624–7738.

Carmel Highlands

Highlands Inn, 4 miles south of Carmel on Highway 1, PO. Box 1700, Carmel
  93921; phone (831) 624–3801, fax (831) 626–1574; www.hyatt.com;
  $175–$895; great ocean views, 2 restaurants, historic, AAA 4 diamonds.
Tickle Pink Inn, 4 miles south of Carmel off Highway 1 at 155 Highland Drive,
  Carmel 93923; phone (831) 624–1244, fax (831) 626–9516; www.tick-
  lepink.com; $189–$459; great ocean views, terrace lounge and hot tub, continental breakfast, AAA 4 diamonds.

Carmel Valley

Acacia Lodge/Hidden Valley Inn (Country Garden Inns), 102 West Carmel
  Valley Road, P.O. Box 504, Carmel Valley 93924; phone (831) 659–5361,
  fax (831) 659–2392; www.countrygardeninns.com; $106–$249; free breakfast, smoke free.
Bernardus Lodge, 415 Carmel Valley Road, Carmel Valley 93924; phone
  (831) 658–3400, reservations (888) 648–9463, fax (831) 659–3529, www.
  bernardus.com; $425–$1,900; elegant country resort, spa, salon, developed
  by racing driver Ben Pon; pool, tennis, croquet, hiking, Wickets and Marinus
  restaurants.
Carmel Valley Ranch, One Old Ranch Road, Carmel Valley 93923; phone
  (831) 625–9500, fax (831) 624–2858; $130–$500; 18-hole golf course, 13
  tennis courts, pool, fitness center, restaurants, AAA 4 diamonds.
Los Laureles, 313 West Carmel Valley Road, P.O. Box 2310, Carmel Valley
  93923; phone (831) 659–2233, fax (831) 659–0481; www.loslaureles.com;
  $130–$500; restored ranch, restaurant, lounge; pets OK with deposit.

Quail Lodge Resort and Golf Club, 8205 Valley Greens Drive, Carmel Valley 93923, via Carmel Valley Road; phone (831) 624–1581, fax (831) 624–3726; www.quail-lodge-resort.com; $350–$685; 18-hole golf course, 4 tennis courts, restaurant, bar, whirlpools, AAA 4 diamonds; pets OK with $100 charge

Robles Del Rio Lodge, 200 Punta del Monte, Carmel Valley 93924; phone (831) 659–3705, fax (831) 659–5157; closed for major renovations until spring 2002.

Stonepine Estate, 150 East Carmel Valley Road, Carmel Valley 93924; phone (831) 659–2245, fax (831) 659–5160; www.stonepinecalifornia.com; $295–$750, $2,500 for a 4-bedroom cottage; complimentary breakfast.

Valley Lodge, Carmel Valley Road and Ford Road, P.O. Box 93, Carmel Valley 93923; phone (831) 659–2261, fax (831) 659–4558; www.valleylodge.com; $149–$319; dogs OK with $10 fee (once had lion cubs, but are not encuraged), whirlpool.

Monterey

Best Western De Anza Inn, 2141 Fremont Street, Monterey 93940; phone (831) 646–8300, fax (831) 646–8130; $59–$149; pool, continental breakfast.

Best Western Monterey Inn, 825 Abrego Street, Monterey 93940, phone (831) 373–5345, fax (831) 373–3246; www.montereyinn.com; $69–$229; continental breakfast.

Best Western Park Crest Motel, 1100 Munras Avenue, Monterey 93940; phone (831) 372–4576, fax (831) 372–2317; www.bestwesternparkcrest.com; $129–$249; pool.

Casa Munras Garden Hotel, 700 Munras Avenue, Monterey 93940; phone (831) 375–2411, fax (831) 375–1365; www.casamunras-hotel.com; $99–$199, restaurant, bar.

Colton Inn, 707 Pacific Street, Monterey 93940; phone (831) 649–6500, fax (831) 373–6987; $79–$250.

Doubletree Hotel, 2 Portola Plaza, Monterey 93940; phone (831) 649–4511, fax (831) 372–0620; $149–$299; near Fisherman's Wharf, 7 stories, restaurant, pool.

El Adobe Inn, 936 Munras Avenue, Monterey 93940; phone (831) 372–5409, fax (831) 375–7236; $49–$169; pets OK.

Holiday Inn Express—Cannery, 443 Wave Street, Monterey 93940; phone (831) 372–1800, fax (831) 372–1969; www.hiexpress.com/montereycalifornia; $89–$299; 3 blocks from Aquarium.

Hotel Pacific, 300 Pacific Street, Monterey 93940; phone (831) 373–5700, fax (831) 373–6921; www.coastalhotel.com; $229–$429; adobe style, near Conference Center, fireplaces, decks, AAA 4 diamonds.

Hyatt Regency Monterey, One Old Golf Course Road, Monterey 93940; phone (831) 372–1234, fax (831) 375–3960; www.hyatt.com; $150–$275; resort, restaurant/ lounge, golf, tennis, pool.

Mariposa Inn, 1366 Munras Avenue, Monterey 93940; phone (831) 649–1414, fax (831) 649–5308; $89–$129; pool.

Monterey Bay Inn, 242 Cannery Row, Monterey 93940; phone (831) 373–6242, fax (831) 373–7603; www.montereybayinn.com; $199–$339; free breakfast, ask for bay view.

Monterey Beach Hotel—Best Western, 2600 Sand Dunes Drive, Monterey 93940; phone (831) 394–3321, fax (831) 393–1912; www.montereybeach-hotel.com; $119–$319; restaurant/lounge, beach, pets OK for a "nominal" fee.

Monterey Hilton Hotel, 1000 Aguajito Road, Monterey 93940; phone (831) 373–6141, fax (831) 655–8608; www.monterey.hilton.com; $150–$249; tennis, pool, restaurant/lounge, pets for fee.

Monterey Marriott, 350 Calle Principal, Monterey 93940; phone (831) 649–4234, fax (831) 372–2968; www.marriott.com; $129–$269; 10 stories, opposite Conference Center, restaurants, pool.

Monterey Plaza Hotel, 400 Cannery Row, Monterey 93940; phone (831) 646–1700, fax (831) 646–5937; www.montereyplazahotel.com; $185–$960, with Presidential Suite up to $2,800; on bay, restaurant/bistro, AAA 4 diamonds.

Spindrift Inn, 652 Cannery Row, Monterey 93940; phone (831) 646–8900, fax (831) 646–5342; www.innsofmonterey.com; $199–$379; on water, complimentary breakfast.

Pacific Grove

Asilomar Conference Center, 800 Asilomar Boulevard, Pacific Grove 93950; phone (831) 372–8016, fax (831) 372–7227; www.visitasilomar.com; $87.40–$110, plus $12 for each additional adult; cabins and lodges, no phones, no TV.

Days Inn Suites, 660 Dennett Avenue, Pacific Grove 93950; phone (831) 373–8777, fax (831) 373–2698; $99–$169; continental breakfast, recently remodeled.

Deer Haven Inn, 740 Crocker Avenue, Pacific Grove 93950; phone (831) 373–1114, or (800) 535–3373, fax (831) 665–5048, www.montereyinns.com; $59–$309; fireplaces, continental breakfast. Deer Haven is one of several quaint inns in Pacific Grove, as part of the Monterey Inns group, including *Sunset Inn,* 133 Asilomar Boulevard; *Featherbed Inn,* 1095 Lighthouse Avenue; and *Seabreeze Inn and Lodge,* 1100 Lighthouse Avenue; all have similar rates and continental breakfasts, and all can be reached through same 800 phone number and can be viewed on same Web site.

Lighthouse Lodge and Suites, lodge at 1150 Lighthouse Drive, suites at 1249 Lighthouse Drive, Pacific Grove 93950; phone (831) 655–2111, fax (831) 655–4922, www.lhls.com; lodge $89–$139, luxury suites $185–$265; pool, complimentary breakfast.

Pacific Gardens Inn, 701 Asilomar Boulevard, Pacific Grove 93950; phone (831) 646–9414, fax (831) 547–0555; www.pacificgardensinn.com; $95–$190; some suites.

Pacific Grove Inn, 851 Pine Avenue, Pacific Grove 93950; phone (831) 375–2825, fax (831) 625–1210; $117.50–$187; Victorian, fireplaces, breakfast buffet.

Quality Inn, 1111 Lighthouse Drive, Pacific Grove 93950; phone (831) 646–8885, fax (831) 646–5976; $80–$180; pool, continental breakfast.

Rosedale Inn, 775 Asilomar Boulevard, Pacific Grove 93950; phone (831) 655–1000, fax (831) 655–0691; www.rosedaleinn.com; $125–$235; all have gas firplaces, Jacuzzi tubs, refrigerators, microwaves, redwood buildings, complimentary breakfast.

The Wilkies Inn, 1038 Lighthouse Drive, Pacific Grove 93950; phone (831) 372–5960, fax (831) 655–1681; $75–$115.

Pebble Beach

There are three sister resort inns on 17 Mile Drive nestled in the famed golf course. Information for all three can be found at www.pebblebeach.com; reservations and golfing dates can be made by calling (800) 654-9300. They are:

The Inn At Spanish Bay, 2700 17 Mile Drive, Pebble Beach 93953; phone (831) 647–7500, $375–$575; pool, dining room, restaurant, AAA 4 diamonds.

The Lodge At Pebble Beach, 17 Mile Drive, Pebble Beach 93953; phone (831) 624–3811; $375–$2,350; pool, several restaurants, small pets OK with a fee; AAA 4 diamonds.

Casa Palmero, 17 Mile Drive, Pebble Beach 93953; phone (831) 622–6650; $550–$1,750; elegant newly opened 24-room Spanish-style inn and spa nestled near its sister resorts.

Seaside and Marina

There are nine modestly priced solid motels in Seaside and two in Marina, including chains and franchises.

CHAPTER 10

LIST OF LISTS

ANTIQUES

There are dozens of sources of antiques on the Monterey Peninsula if one is willing and able to take the time. Those listed here are among the best in our opinion.

Carmel

Arcadia Antiques, Mission Street between 5th and 6th Avenues, P.O. Box 7352, Carmel 93921; phone (831) 624–5938; open 10:00 A.M.–5:00 P.M. daily; teacups galore, furniture, Oriental items.

China Art Center, Dolores and 7th Avenue; phone (831) 624–5868; open 11:00 A.M.–5:00 P.M. Monday–Saturday.

Chinese Art Gallery, San Carlos and 7th Avenue; phone (831) 624–9116; open noon–5:00 P.M. Monday–Saturday and 2:30–5:00 P.M. Sunday.

Robert Cordy Antiques, Lincoln Street and 6th Avenue, P.O. Box 5262, Carmel 93921; phone (831) 625–5839; open 11:00 A.M.–4:30 P.M.; English furniture, paintings, corkscrews.

Conway of Asia, Dolores between Ocean and 7th Avenue, Carmel 93921; phone (831) 624–3643; open 9:30 A.M.–5:30 P.M. daily.

Country Life Antiques, 204 Crossroads Boulevard; phone (831) 624–1895.

Forget-Me-Nots, Dolores and 5th Streets; phone (831) 624–9080; open 10:00 A.M.–5:00 P.M. Monday–Saturday.

Great Things Antiques, Ocean Avenue between Dolores and Lincoln Streets, P.O. Box 5455, Carmel 93921; phone (831) 624–7178; open 10:00 A.M.–5:30 P.M. daily; European, interior design.

Hildegunn Hawley Antiques, Dolores Street between 5th and 6th Avenues (Su Vecino Court), P.O. Box 1132, Carmel 93921; phone (831) 626–3457; open 11:00 A.M.–5:00 P.M. daily except Sunday and Tuesday; 18th and 19th-century European and Oriental furniture, porcelain.

Keller and Scott Antiques, Dolores Street between 5th and 6th Avenues, P.O. Box 1132, Carmel 93921; phone (831) 624–0465; open 9:30 A.M.–3:00 P.M. Monday–Wednesday (except holidays) and every other Thursday, 9:30 A.M.–4:00 P.M. Friday and Saturday; jewelry and Orientals.

Maxine Klaput Antiques, Mission Street and 7th Avenue (Court of the Fountains), P.O. Box 5628, Carmel 93921; phone (831) 624–8823; open

10:00 A.M.–5:00 P.M. Tuesday–Saturday, Monday by appointment; 18th- and 19th-century furniture, porcelains, sterling silver flatware.

LePetit Trianon, 7th and Dolores Streets; phone (831) 626– 6296; open 10:00 A.M.–5:00 P.M. Monday–Saturday, noon–5:00 P.M. Sunday; antiques and pine furnishings.

Life in the Fast Lane, San Carlos and 5th Avenue; phone (831) 625–2121; open 11:00 A.M.–5:00 P.M. daily; old advertising, art deco, old toys.

Luciano Antiques, San Carlos Street and 5th Avenue, P.O. Box 5686, Carmel 93921; phone (831) 624–0306; open 10:00 A.M.–5:00 P.M. Monday to Saturday, 11:00 A.M.–5:00 P.M. Sunday; European, Mid-East, Oriental items, bronze and stone garden pieces.

Magpie Antiques, Ocean Avenue and Lincoln Street (at the Pine Inn), P.O. Box 4545, Carmel 93921; phone (831) 622–9341; pine furniture, china, English linens and laces.

Off The Wall, Lincoln Street between 5th and 6th Avenues, P.O. Box 4561, Carmel 93921; phone (831) 624–6165; open 10:00 A.M.–5:00 P.M. Monday– Saturday, 11:00 A.M.–3:00 P.M. Sunday; architectural antiques.

Robertson's Antiques, Dolores Street and 7th Avenue, P.O. Box 2421, Carmel 93921; phone (831) 624–7517; open 10:00 A.M.–5:00 P.M. Monday– Saturday, 11:00 A.M.–5:00 P.M. Sunday; Victorian furniture, lighting fix- tures, porcelain, Oriental items.

Stonehouse Antiques and Art, San Carlos and 7th Avenue; phone (831) 620–1556; open 11:00 A.M.–5:00 P.M. daily; antiques, collectibles, art.

Tresors, 7th Street between Dolores and San Carlos Streets, P.O. Box 665, Carmel 93912; phone (831) 624–1115; open 10:00 A.M.–5:00 P.M.; French furniture, art, jewelry, silver.

Vermillion, 240 Crossroads Boulevard.; phone (831) 620–1502; open 10:00 A.M.–6:00 P.M. Monday–Saturday, noon–6:00 P.M. Sunday; Japanese antiques.

Carmel Valley

Carmel Valley Antiques & Collectibles, Carmel Hills Shopping Center (3.5 miles east on Carmel Valley Road from Highway 1), Carmel 93294; phone (831) 624–3414; open 10:30 A.M.–4:30 P.M. Wednesday–Monday; furni- ture, pianos, lamps, toys, jewelry.

Jan de Luz, 4 East Carmel Valley Road; phone (831) 659–7966; open 10:00 A.M.–5:30 P.M. Monday–Saturday, noon–5:30 P.M. Sunday; Basque linens and furnishings.

Kim 3 at Teeleet Antiques, 25 Pilot Road; phone (831) 659–1360; open 10:00 A.M.–6:00 P.M. Monday–Saturday, noon–5:00 P.M. Sunday; international, Asian, Pacific Rim, and European country pine furnishings.

T. B. Scanlon Antiques, Carmel Valley Village Center, P.O. Box 709, Carmel Valley 93924; phone (831) 659–4788; open 10:00 A.M.–4:00 P.M. or "until I'm tired of being there," Monday–Saturday; 17th- and 18th-century furniture and other items.

Village Antiques, 19 East Carmel Valley Road; phone (831) 659–1019; open noon–6:00 P.M. daily; "great stuff" from around the world and several centuries.

Monterey

Alicia's, 835 Cannery Row, Monterey 93940; phone (831) 372–1423; open noon–6:00 P.M. daily; jewelry, collectibles.

Cannery Bay Antique Mall, 471 Wave Street (2 blocks east of Aquarium), Monterey 93940; phone (831) 655–0264; open 10:00 A.M.–6:00 P.M. Monday–Saturday, 10:00 A.M.–5:00 P.M. Sunday; 170 dealers are gathered together in the giant former Carmel Canning Co. Warehouse.

Coast Collectibles, 142 Carmelito Avenue; phone (831) 375–4240.

Marsh's Oriental Art & Antiques, 599 Fremont; phone (831) 372–3547.

Pieces of Olde, 868 Lighthouse Avenue, Monterey 93940; phone (831) 372–1521; open 10:00 A.M.–5:00 P.M. Monday–Saturday; furniture, dolls, collectibles displayed in a classic Victorian.

Moss Landing

As a side trip going north on Highway 1 or going south from Santa Cruz, on the west side of Highway 1, turn on to Moss Landing Road to find the antiques shops in this shoreline hamlet: *Moss Landing Mercantile*, (831) 633–8520; Antiques Etc., (831) 633–0817; *Little Red Barn Antiques*, (831) 633–5583; and *Moss Landing Antique and Trading Company*, (831) 633–3988. Open every day except Wednesday, but hours often depend on the weather. You may find some gem of an antique here, but the entire funky village is an antique. Go see for yourself.

Pacific Grove

Blackburn's Collectibles, 157 Grand Avenue (Grand Central Station), Pacific Grove 93950; phone (831) 373–6699; open one week each month, last Monday through following Sunday, hours vary; jewelry and antiques.

Front Row Center, 663 Lighthouse Avenue, Pacific Grove 93950; phone (831) 375–6525; open 10:30 A.M.–5:30 P.M. Monday–Saturday, noon–5:00 P.M. Sunday; jewelry, furniture, china, books.

Patrick's Consignment Store, 105 Central Avenue, Pacific Grove 93950; phone (831) 372–3995; open 10:00 A.M.–5:30 P.M. Monday–Saturday, noon–5:00 P.M. Sunday; furniture, estate jewelry, and nonantiques.

Trotter's Antiques, 301–303 Forest Avenue, Pacific Grove 93950; phone (831) 373–3505; open 10:00 A.M.–5:30 P.M. Monday–Saturday; 18th- and 19th-century porcelains, dolls, pottery, Tiffany lamps, Oriental art.

BICYCLE RENTALS

Carmel/Carmel Valley

Bay Bikes; call (831) 655–8687 in Monterey and they will deliver a bicycle.
Carmel Bicycle, 7150 Carmel Valley Road, Carmel Valley 93923, next to Quail Lodge; phone (831) 625–2211; open 10:00 A.M.–6:00 P.M. Tuesday– Saturday.

Monterey

AAA Bike, Monterey Moped, and Olivercycle; 1250 Del Monte Avenue; phone (831) 373–2696; open 10:00 A.M.–4:30 P.M. daily, sometimes closed Wednesday–Thursday; electric bikes, scooters, cars, foot-powered bikes.
Aquarian Bicycles, 486 Washington Street, Monterey 93940; phone (831) 375–2144; open noon–5:30 P.M. Monday, 10:00 A.M.–5:30 P.M. Tuesday–Saturday, noon–5:00 P.M. Sunday.
Bay Bikes, 640 Wave Street, near Cannery Row, Monterey 94940; phone (831) 646–9090; open 9:00 A.M.–6:00 P.M. daily, during summer until 7:30 P.M.
Bay Bikes, 99 Pacific Street at Fisherman's Wharf, Monterey 93940; phone (831) 655–8687; open 9:00 A.M.–6:00 P.M. daily, during summer stays open as late as 7:30 P.M.
Joselyn's Bicycles, 638 Lighthouse Avenue, Monterey 93940; phone (831) 649–8520; open 9:30 A.M.–6:00 P.M. Monday–Friday, 9:30 A.M.–5:30 P.M. Saturday, 11:00 A.M.–5:00 P.M. Sunday.

Pacific Grove

Winning Wheels Bicycle Shop, 223 15th Street, Pacific Grove 93950; phone (831) 375–4322; open 10:00 A.M.–6:00 P.M. Tuesday–Friday, 10:00 A.M.–5:00 P.M. Saturday and Monday, closed Sunday.
Adventures By The Sea, at Lovers Point, Pacific Grove 93950; phone (831) 372–1807; open 9:00 A.M.–6:00 P.M. winter, 9:00 A.M.–8:00 P.M. summer.

BOAT TOURS AND WHALE WATCHING

Glass Bottom Boat Tours, 90 Fisherman's Wharf, Monterey; (831) 372–7150; 25-minute tours every half hour (adults, $5.95; children under 12, $3.95), as well as special excursions; open when weather is calm; call for reservation.

Monterey Bay Whale Watch, 84 Fisherman's Wharf (from Sam's Fishing Shop), Monterey; (831) 375–4658; 6-hour trips May–November, depart 9:00 A.M. (adults, $39; children, $33), call for reservations, particularly since weather may not allow cruise; tours led by marine biologist.

Also see **Sport Fishing** for other boats that sometimes take parties whale watching.

BOATING

El Estero Boating, Lake El Estero, Del Monte Boulevard and Camino El Estero, Monterey; phone (831) 375–1484; rented paddleboats, canoes, or kayaks at $11.00 an hour, $7.00 a half hour; open summer 10:00 A.M.–6:00 P.M. daily, weather permitting; rest of year Saturday and Sunday, 10:00 A.M. to dark, weather permitting; a fun family outing.

For those with their own boats, two launching ramps are located in Monterey on the bay; one between the Coast Guard Pier and Breakwater Cove (by Cannery Row and the Monterey Yacht Harbor), (831) 373–7857, and the other between Municipal Wharf #2 and the Monterey Marina.

The Monterey Yacht Harbor has a few visitor's berths; (831) 373–7857. The Monterey Marina has 425 berths; (831) 646–3950 for berth.

BOOKSTORES

Carmel/Carmel Valley

Books Inc., Ocean Avenue and Mission Street (Carmel Plaza), Carmel; phone (831) 625–0440, fax (831) 625–9620, www.booksinc.net; open 10:00 A.M.–9:00 P.M. Monday–Saturday, 10:00 A.M.–6:00 P.M. Sunday; large inventory.

Pilgrim's Way Bookstore, Dolores Street between 5th and 6th Avenues, Carmel; phone (831) 624–4955; open 10:00 A.M.–6:00 P.M. Monday–Saturday, 11:00 A.M.–5:00 P.M. Sunday; philosophy, natural health, new age music.

Thunderbird Bookshop, 3600 The Barnyard, Highway 1 and Carmel Valley Road, Carmel; phone (831) 624–1803, (800) 94–BOOKS, fax (831) 624–9034; open 10:00 A.M.–9:00 P.M. daily; more than 35 years old, includes cafe in solarium and patio (624–9414).

Monterey

Bay Books, 316 Alvarado Street at Del Monte, Monterey; phone (831) 375–1855 www.montereybaybooks.com; open 7:30 A.M.–10:00 P.M. Sunday–Thursday, 7:30 A.M.–11:00 P.M. Friday & Saturday; coffeehouse, largest in Monterey.

Books & Things, 224 Lighthouse Avenue, Monterey; phone (831) 655–8784; open 10:00 A.M.–6:00 P.M. Monday–Saturday; bargains.

McWilliams & Chee Old & Rare Books, 471 Wave Street (in Cannery Row Antique Mall); phone (831) 656–9264; open 10:30 A.M.–5:30 P.M. Thursday–Tuesday.

Old Capitol Books, 639-A Lighthouse Avenue, Monterey; phone (831) 375–2665; open 10:00 A.M.–6:00 P.M. Monday–Saturday; large inventory of used and rare books.

Old Monterey Book Co., 136 Bonifacio Place, Monterey; phone (831) 372–3111; open 10:00 A.M.–5:00 P.M. Tuesday–Saturday; old and rare books.

Waldenbooks, 1301 Munras Avenue, Monterey; phone (831) 373–0987; open 10:00 A.M.–9:00 P.M. Monday–Friday, till 6:00 P.M. on Saturday and Sunday; popular mall-based bookseller.

Pacific Grove

Bookmark, 307 Forest Avenue, Pacific Grove; phone (831) 648–0508, (800) 648–0508, www.bookmarkmusic.com; open 11:00 A.M.–5:00 P.M. Tuesday–Saturday, except Wednesday open to 7:00 P.M.; specializes in books on performing arts—film, theater, dance, music.

Book Warehouse, 125 Ocean View Boulevard, Pacific Grove; phone (831) 375–1840; open 10:00 A.M.–6:00 P.M. Monday–Friday, 10:00 A.M.–8:00 P.M. Saturday and Sunday.

Bookworks, 667 Lighthouse Avenue, Pacific Grove; phone (831) 372–2242; open 9:00 A.M.–10:00 P.M. Sunday–Thursday, 9:00 A.M.–11:00 P.M. Friday and Saturday; coffeehouse, computer printouts on book and author information.

EpicWorlds, 213 Grand Avenue, Pacific Grove; phone (831) 655–1150; open noon–8:00 P.M. Monday–Friday, 10:00 A.M.–10:00 P.M. Saturday and Sunday.

Sand City/Seaside/Marina

Borders Books, 2080 California Avenue (Edgewater Center, just off Highway 1), Sand City 93955; phone (831) 899–6643; open 9:00 A.M.–11:00 P.M. Monday–Saturday, 9:00 A.M.–9:00 P.M., Sunday; includes cafe.

DIVE SHOPS

Aquarious Dive Shop, 32 Cannery Row, Monterey; (831) 375–6605; and 2040 Del Monte Avenue, Monterey; (831) 375–1933; boat bookings for instruction, underwater guided tours, rentals; call for reservations.

Bamboo Reef Enterprises, 614 Lighthouse Avenue, Monterey; (831) 372–1685; instruction, rentals and sales; extra large air compressor.

Manta Ray Dive Center, 245 Foam Street, Monterey; phone (831) 375–6268, (888) MANTA RAY, www.mantaraydive.com; open 9:00 A.M.–7:00 P.M. Monday–Friday, 7:00 A.M.–7:00 P.M. Saturday and Sunday; scuba diving equipment rentals and guided dive tours.

Monterey Bay Dive Center, 598 Foam Street, Monterey; (831) 655–1818, training center; 225 Cannery Row, Monterey; (831) 656–0454, retail sales; numerous classes, underwater tours ($50 and up), heated pool for training; call 24 hours early for tour.

Otter Bay Wetsuits, 207 Hoffman Avenue, Monterey; phone (831) 333–0234; custom wet suits.

EVENTS AND FESTIVALS

January

Rio Resolution Run, cross-country on roads, trails, and beaches around Carmel; (831) 642–4112 or 375–3750; January 1

El Dia De Los Tres Reyes, Hispanic candlelight procession down Calle Principal, Monterey; (831) 375–0095; January 6

AT&T Pebble Beach National Golf Tournament, on all the Pebble Beach courses off 17-Mile Drive; (800) 541–9091 or (831) 649–1533; starts last Wednesday

February

Masters of Food and Wine, cooking programs, demonstrations, tastings; Highlands Inn, Carmel; (831) 624–3801, ext. 147; last week

John Steinbeck Birthday Party, music, readings, nostalgia; Cannery Row, Monterey; (831) 372–8512; free; February 27

Monterey County Hot Air Affair, hot-air balloon races, rides, entertainment; Laguna Seca Raceway; (831) 649–6544; exact date varies, call ahead.

March

Dixieland Monterey, continuous Dixieland jazz in area of Fisherman's Wharf; check in at Doubletree Hotel; (831) 443–5260 or (888) DIX-MTRY, www.dixiejazz.com/monterey.html; first full weekend.

Pacific Repertory Theatre Spring Festival, Golden Bough and Circle Theaters; Carmel; Pacific Repertory Theatre, P.O. Box 222035, Carmel 93922; (831) 622–0100 (Tuesday–Friday, noon–4:00 P.M.), www.pacrep.org; eight weeks starting first full weekend

Colton Hall Birthday, Colton Hall, Monterey; historic plays, free birthday cake and punch; (831) 646–5640; March 8 or closest Saturday

Monterey Spring Faire, Custom House Plaza, Monterey; over one hundred West Coast artists; (831) 622–0700; Saturday and Sunday nearest middle of month

Beyond Boundaries, Steinbeck and the World, Monterey Plaza Hotel and Cannery Row, annual symposium focusing on multicultural life and history of Cannery Row; (831) 372–8512; third full weekend

Sea Otter Classic, Laguna Seca Park, Monterey; sports festival with mountain biking, bicycle road racing, roller hockey; (831) 755–4899; third full weekend

California Chocolate Abalone Dive, San Carlos Beach by Monterey Coast Guard Pier, divers plunge for 500 planted chocolate abalone; (831) 375–1933; third Saturday

April

Monterey Wine Festival, tastings, lectures, seminars at participating downtown Monterey hotels and restaurants; (800) 656–4282 or (831) 649–6544; first weekend

Good Old Days Celebration, parade with costumes, arts and crafts, quilt show; downtown Pacific Grove; (831) 373–3304; second full weekend

Toyota Challenge of Laguna Seca, Laguna Seca Raceway, AMA national championship motorcycle road races of AMA Superbike Series; (800) 327–SECA; third full weekend

Wildflower Show, Pacific Grove Museum of Natural History, Pacific Grove, annual event with more than 600 species; (831) 648–3116; third full weekend

Old Monterey Seafood & Music Festival, street festival in historic downtown Monterey, seafood, crafts, music; (831) 655–8070; third full weekend

Adobe Tour, annual tour of more than twenty-five adobes of Monterey, with costumed docents; (831) 372–2608; last Saturday

Springtime at La Mirada Art Museum, La Mirada Art Museum, Monterey, afternoon tea and tour; (831) 372–5477, 372–7591, or 372–2689; last Saturday and Sunday

A Garden Affair, Barnyard Gardens, seminars, lectures, garden tours, demonstrations; (831) 624–8886; last Sunday, 10:00 A.M. to 4:00 P.M.

Big Sur International Marathon, along Highway 1 from Pfeiffer Big Sur State Park to Carmel, more than 3,000 runners; (831) 625–6226; last Sunday

May

Orchid Faire, Crossroads Shopping Center (Highway 1 and Rio Road), display and sale of great variety of orchids; (831) 624–9003; first Saturday and Sunday

Robinson Jeffers Tor House Garden Party, Tor House and Hawk Tower, Carmel; poetry readings, refreshments, tours; (831) 624–1813; first Sunday

Carmel Garden and Design Show, Quail Lodge, exhibits of garden design; (831) 625–6026; second full weekend

Monterey National Horse Show, English Section, Monterey Fairgrounds, annual show featuring hunters and jumpers; (831) 372–5863; third full weekend

Carmel Art Festival, painting, sculpture, etching, photography, of local artists; (831) 625–2288; third full weekend

Del Monte Kennel Club Dog Show, lawn of Lodge at Pebble Beach, oldest show on Pacific Coast, varied breeds of blue-ribbon winners; (831) 624–5553; third Saturday

Great Monterey Squid Festival, Monterey Fairgrounds, cooking demonstrations, entertainment, arts and crafts; (831) 649–6544 or 649–6547; Memorial Day weekend

Pacific Repertory Theatre Summer Festival, Golden Bough Theatre, two plays in succession; (831) 622–0100

Carmel Art Walk, self-guided tour of Carmel art galleries, available at those displaying Art Walk sign; (831) 625–2288; mid-May through September, Fridays, 6:00 to 9:00 P.M.

June

Concerts in the Park, Devendorf Park, Carmel, (831) 626–1255; every Friday noon

Taste of Old Monterey, Alvarado Mall at Del Monte Street, Monterey, restaurants serving international foods, waiters' race, (831) 655–8070; first Thursday

California Cowboy Show, Carmel Valley Road, cowboy music, cowboy poetry, wine tasting, arts and crafts, sponsored by Carmel Valley Historical Society, (831) 624–9611; first Saturday, 6:00 P.M. (show starts at 8:00 P.M.)

Monterey Bonsai Exposition, Monterey Peninsula Buddhist Temple, 1155 Noche Buena, Seaside, Bonsai tree techniques and show sponsored by Bonsai Club, (831) 423–5522, 649–5934, or 624–4929; first Sunday, 11:00 A.M.–5:00 P.M.

Old Monterey Fine Arts Festival, on sidewalk along Alvarado Street, Monterey, painting, sculpture, photography, ceramics, jewelry, plus sidewalk show, (831) 649–1770; second full weekend, 11:00 A.M.–5:00 P.M.

Filipino Festival, Custom House Plaza, Monterey, entertainment, exhibits, arts and crafts, traditional food, all celebrating Filipino culture; also a free movie in the Maritime Museum Theater; (831) 449–1441, 883–2939, 372–9443 or 424–3134; second Saturday and Sunday, 10:00 A.M.–5:00 P.M.

California State Amateur Golf Championship, Pebble Beach and Spyglass Golf Courses, plus senior amateur championship on Thursday and Friday at Poppy Hills Golf Course; (831) 625–4653; third week with finals on Saturday

Downtown Celebration, Alvarado Street Mall from Cooper Molera Adobe to Del Monte Avenue, Monterey, live entertainment, arts and crafts, food; (831) 655–8070; third Sunday, 11:00 A.M.–5:00 P.M.

Monterey Bay Blues Festival, Monterey Fairgrounds, top blues performers, soul food; (831) 394–2652; last Saturday and Sunday

Monterey Bay Arts and Crafts Faire, Custom House Plaza, Fisherman's Wharf, Monterey, entertainment, arts and crafts, food, sponsored by Pacific Repertory Theatre to benefit summer Theatrefest; (831) 622–0700; last Saturday and Sunday, 9:00 A.M.–6:00 P.M.

Monterey Bay Theatrefest, at the wharf in Monterey, free theater festival; (831) 622–0700; starting last Saturday, through July

California Mountain Bike Championship, Laguna Seca Raceway, off-road bikers compete; (831) 758–3504; last Sunday and Monday

Films in the Forest, films made in Monterey County or with actors from the Monterey Peninsula; (831) 626–1681; Monday, Tuesday, Wednesday evenings, first showing to be announced

Outdoor Forest Theater Plays, locally produced and acted plays; (831) 626–1681; various dates June, July, and August

July

Fourth of July Flag-Raising and Parade, downtown Monterey, cars, clowns, music, food, games; fireworks over Monterey Bay at 9:15 P.M.; (831) 646–3866; July 4 at 10:00 A.M.

Sloat Landing Ceremony, commemoration of raising of American flag over the Custom House; (831) 372–2608; historical reenactments in Custom House Plaza, (831) 649–7118; Sunday closest to July 7

U.S. World Super Bike Championship, Laguna Seca Raceway; (800) 327–SECA; first full weekend

Monterey World Cultures Festival, sponsored by One Earth One People Peace Vision and American Indian Council & Global Peace Foundation, Monterey County Fairgrounds; (831) 623–2379; second Saturday and Sunday.

Monday Blues in the Park, Laguna Grande Park, Seaside, free concerts, arts and crafts; (831) 889–6270; second Sunday, continuing Sundays through third in August

Morgan Horse Show, Monterey Fairgrounds; (831) 649–1770; third full weekend

Carmel Bach Festival, Sunset Center Theater (San Carlos Street and Ninth Avenue), other venues; concerts, recitals, lectures, demonstrations, with professional musicians; (800) 513–BACH or (831) 624–2046; www.bachfestival.org; e-mail info@bachfestival.org; third Saturday, runs for 23 days

Monterey National Horse Show, Western Section, Monterey Fairgrounds; (831) 372–5863; fourth Friday and Saturday

Feast of Lanterns, Pacific Grove downtown; street dance, ice-cream social, pet parade, barbecue, boat parade, fireworks; (831) 372–7625; next to last Tuesday, weeklong

Pebble Beach Equestrian Classic, Pebble Beach; jumping, hunting, Grand Prix jumping for $25,000 prize; children's classes; (831) 624–2756; next to last Tuesday, runs two weeks

August

Carmel Shakespeare Festival, various venues; call Pacific Repertory Theater (831) 622–0100 (Tuesday–Friday, noon–4:00 P.M.), or write Pacific Repertory Company, P.O. Box 222035, Carmel 93922; www.pacrep.org.; first Saturday (or July 31 if a Saturday) through second weekend in October

Scottish Irish Festival & Highland Games, Monterey Fairgrounds; bagpipe bands, Celtic dancing, gathering of clans; (831) 375–8608; first Saturday and Sunday

Carmel Valley Fiesta Days, Carmel Valley Village; street dance, rides, games, barbecue, arts and crafts, 10K run and 5K walk; (831) 659–2038; first Saturday and Sunday

Concours Classic Car Weekend, historic car races, each day, Laguna Seca Raceway, (831) 648–5111; Concours Italian, Friday, Quail Lodge; (800) 538–9516; Concours D'Elegance, display of classic automobiles, Sunday, Pebble Beach; third full weekend

Monterey County Fair, Monterey Fairgrounds; rides, food, farm animals, local crafts; (831) 372–5863 or 372–1000; third Tuesday through Sunday

Ranchers Days, Carmel Valley, cattle herding, roping, riding; (831) 659–2472; third full weekend

Del Monte Kennel Club Dog Show, Carmel Middle School; (831) 624–5553; third Saturday and Sunday

Monterey Wine Country Winemakers Celebration, Custom House Plaza, Monterey, tastings, displays, wine-oriented recipes; Monterey County Vintners & Growers Association, P.O. Box 1793, Monterey 93942; (831) 375–9400, fax (831) 375–1116; tickets at A Taste of Monterey, 700 Cannery Row, Monterey, (831) 375–9400; third or fourth Saturday, noon–5:00 P.M.

Carmel Outdoor Art & Wine Festival, work of local artists, wine tasting; (831) 624–3996; last Saturday and Sunday

Mission Trails Peruvian Horse Show, Monterey Fairgrounds; (831) 484–2849; last weekend

Monterey Reggae Festival, Monterey Fairgrounds, live reggae performances, food, arts and crafts; (831) 372–5883; last Sunday

Greek Festival, Custom House Plaza, downtown Monterey; Greek food, dancing, music, crafts; (831) 424–4434; Labor Day weekend, Saturday–Monday, noon–7:00 P.M.

September

Taste of Carmel, (831) 624–2522; neither date nor place set

Toyota Grand Prix of Monterey Indy Car Races, Laguna Seca Raceway; touring Indy car World Series; (800) 327–SECA; first full weekend

Monterey Jazz Festival, Monterey Fairgrounds; clinics, seminars, jazz-oriented art, food; (831) 373–3366 or (800) 307–3378; montereyjazzfestival.org; third full weekend

Artists Open Studio Tour, self-guided tours of artists' studios in the Monterey area; (831) 372–4930, 375–6165, or 372–7591; last Friday and Saturday

Carmel Valley Gem & Mineral Show, Monterey Fairgrounds; demonstrations of jewelry making, fossil cleaning; (831) 659–4156 or 372–9215; last Saturday and Sunday

Barnyard's Annual Art & Wine Festival, Barnyard Community Room; local artists, wine tasting, refreshments, music; (831) 624–8886; date not set

Carmel Mission Fiesta, Carmel Mission; arts and crafts, games, BBQ; (831) 624–1271; last Sunday, 10:00 A.M.–5:00 P.M.

October

Carmel Performing Arts Festival, plays, music, dance at various Carmel locations; tickets by mail, phone, or at kiosk at Carmel Plaza; general information and tickets (831) 624–7675; get on mailing lists (831) 644–8383, fax (831) 622–7631; Carmel Performing Arts Festival, P.O. Box 221473, Carmel 93922; www.carmelfest.org; first two weeks, starting Friday

Annual Sand Castle Building Contest, anyone may enter; (831) 626–1255; place and date announced in September

Contemporary Carmel Performing Arts Festival, at various venues; dance, music, visual and oral storytelling, theater; (831) 647–0228; first Saturday through four weeks of the month

Butterfly Parade and Bazaar, Pacific Grove; children parade in butterfly costumes to celebrate return of monarch butterflies; (831) 646–6540; second Saturday

Old Monterey Historic Festival & Fair, adobe stops, food samples, outdoor
music, arts and crafts; (831) 655–8070; second weekend

Robinson Jeffers Annual Tor House Festival, Tor House, Carmel; (831)
624–1813; second full weekend

Victorian Home Tour, Pacific Grove; Victorian houses and churches; (831)
373–3304; second Sunday

Nikonos Shootout, Monterey waterfront; amateur photographers' underwater
competition; (831) 375–1933; third full weekend

Return to Anatevka—Jewish Food Festival, Congregation Beth Israel; food,
music, Israeli dancing in an eastern European village setting; (831) 624–2015;
third Sunday

Monterey Sports Car Championships, Laguna Seca Raceway, season finale;
(800) 327–SECA; fourth full weekend

Carmel's Annual Halloween/Birthday Parade & Barbecue, parade of costumed
children celebrate Halloween (and Carmel's birthday), barbecue at Devendorf
Park on Ocean Avenue; (831) 624–2781; October 31 or date close to it

Cherries Jubilee, Laguna Seca Raceway; a classic car festival of pre-1972, per-
fect-condition cars and trucks; (831) 759–1836; last full weekend

Big Sur River Run, 10K run along Big Sur River; (831) 624–4112; last Sunday

November

Great Wine Escape, wine tours, dinners, dance, wine tasting, jazz concert; various venues and prices in Monterey, Carmel, Pebble Beach, Pacific Grove,
Carmel Valley; Monterey County Vintners & Growers Association, P.O. Box
1793, Monterey 93942; (831) 375–9400, fax (831) 375–1116; second full
weekend

Pebble Beach Invitational Golf Tournament, Pebble Beach Resort & Golf
Links; (831) 484–2151 or 347–6216 for tickets; third Thursday through
Sunday

Carmel Home Crafters' Marketplace, (831) 659–5099; next to last Saturday

December

Carmel Lights Up the Season, lighting of Ocean Avenue and Christmas tree,
arrival of Santa Claus, open house at Carmel Plaza; (831) 624–2522; first
Friday

Vinyards Open Houses, first and second weekends; Chalone Vineyards (Saturday),
Riverland Vineyards (Saturday), Chateau Julien Wine Estate (Sunday),
Cloninger Cellars (Sunday), Smith & Hook Vineyards (Sunday), Jouillian
Vineyards (following Saturday), Scheid Vineyards (following Saturday).

Weihnachsfest, Barnyard Gardens; Carmel; Santa Claus, carolers, storytelling;
free admission; (831) 624–8886; first Sunday, all day

Christmas in the Adobes, Monterey; candlelight tours of adobes decorated as in Mexican times; (831) 847–6226; second full weekend

La Posada, Monterey streets; Christmas candlelight parade with Joseph and Mary searching for a place to stay, carols in Spanish and English, piñata party; (831) 646–3886; second Saturday

GOLF COURSES

Del Monte Golf Club, 1300 Sylvan Road, Monterey, (831) 373–2700; par 72, $65 plus cart; oldest golf course on West Coast

Laguna Seca Golf Club, 10520 York Road, Monterey, (831) 373–3701; par 71, $55

Pacific Grove Links, 300 Forest Avenue, Pacific Grove, (831) 648–3177; par 71, $25–$30

Naval Post Graduate School Golf Course, Garden Road, Monterey, (831) 656–2167; par 69, $6.00–$25.00

Links at Spanish Bay, Inn at Spanish Bay, 2700 17-Mile Drive, Pebble Beach, (831) 624–3811; par 72, $185 plus cart

Fort Ord Golf Club, Fort Ord, (831) 899–2351; 2 courses, both par 72, $8.00–$60.00

Pebble Beach Golf Links, 17-Mile Drive, Pebble Beach, (831) 624–3811; par 72, $275 plus cart

Peter Hay Par Three, 17-Mile Drive, next to Pebble Beach Golf Links; (831) 624–3811; 9 holes, par 27; fee is $10 for all day with entrance fee to 17-Mile Drive deducted from that, children under 12 are free (a bargain)

Poppy Hills Golf Course, 3200 Lopez Road, Pebble Beach, (831) 625–2035; par 72, $115–$130 plus cart

Spyglass Golf Course, 17-Mile Drive, Pebble Beach, (831) 624–3811; par 72, $225 plus cart.

Rancho Canada Golf Club, Carmel Valley Road, Carmel Valley, (831) 624–0111; 2 courses, east par 71 and west 72, $55 and $75 respectively

Carmel Valley Ranch Hotel (not public), One Old Ranch Road, Carmel Valley; par 70, $145 for hotel guest or referred by member, $175 for nonguest

Golf Club at Quail (not public), 8205 Valley Greens Drive, Carmel Valley; par 71, $80 accompanied by member or $185 with cart

HORSEBACK RIDING

Carmel Valley Ranch, One Old Ranch Road, Carmel Valley; (831) 625–9500, ext. 306; tour trail rides along Garland Regional Park with ocean views; reservations required

Molera Horseback Tours, Andrew Molera State Park, Highway 1, 22 miles south of Carmel, Big Sur; (831) 625–5486 or (800) 942–5486; trail tours all include beach ($25–$55), walk-ins OK, group rates, open daily April– December

Monterey Bay Equestrian Center, 19805 Pesante Road, Prunedale, near junction of Highways 101 and 158; (831) 663–5712; ride along bay sanctuary, group rates, petting zoo, lessons

Pebble Beach Equestrian Center, Portola Road and Alva Lane, Pebble Beach; (831) 624–2756; guided beach trail rides ($20 and up), ponies for children; open daily, tours at 10:00 A.M., noon, 2:00 P.M., 3:30 P.M.; reservations required

Stonepine Resort and Equestrian Center, 150 East Carmel Valley Road, Carmel Valley; (831) 659–2245; trail rides on 400 acres, lessons, dressage, call for riding information

The Holman Ranch, left on Holman Road 15.6 miles east of Highway 1 on Carmel Valley Road, (mail P.O. Box 149, Carmel Valley 93924; (831) 659–2640, stables (831) 659–6054, fax (831) 659–6055; historic private ranch with guided rides ($30–$100), ponies for children over 5; open daily; reservations required

Ventana Big Sur Trail Rides, Ventana Wilderness Area, Highway 1, Big Sur; (831) 625–8664; groups and children OK; open daily; reservations required

KAYAKING

A B Seas Kayaks, 32 Cannery Row, Monterey; (831) 647–0147; guided wildlife tour ($45); rental of kayaks ($25), seacycle ($13–$26), engine-driven inflatable boats ($49), and kayak-snorkel combination ($59), other boats, cruiser; call for reservations

Adventures by the Sea, 299 Cannery Row, Monterey and Lovers Point Beach, Pacific Grove; (831) 373–1807; bay tours ($45), kayak rentals ($25 and up)

Monterey Bay Kayaks, 693 Del Monte Avenue, Monterey; (831) 373–5357 (KELP); www.montereykayaks.com/tour; natural history tours, instruction, rentals and sales; tours of Monterey Bay ($45), Elkhorn Slough ($55), or Salinas River ($48); 2-day classes every weekend ($45–$140); rental of kayak, gear, and wetsuit $25; call for reservations

LAUNDROMATS

Monterey

Fremont Wash & Dry, 2319 North Fremont (across from Safeway); (831) 646–9195

Monterey Peninsula Launderette, Del Monte Shopping Center, Munras Avenue; (831) 373–1277

Monterey Peninsula Launderette, 617 Lighthouse Avenue; (831) 373–1277

Monte Vista Launderette, 23 Soledad Drive; (831) 372–9875

Surf N' Suds Laundromat, 1101 Del Monte Avenue; (831) 375–0874

Carmel/Carmel Valley

Carmel Laundry, Junipero Street and Third Avenue, Carmel; (831) 622–9274

Valley Maid Launderette, Midvalley Shopping Center, Carmel Valley Road, Carmel Valley; (831) 624–9905

Pacific Grove

Pacific Grove Coin Laundry, 709 Lighthouse Avenue; (831) 372–9582

Fairway Wash & Dry, 1128 Forest Avenue; (831) 372–9539

Isabella's Launderette, 1219 Forest Avenue; (831) 372–6589

Monterey Peninsula Launderette, 511 Lighthouse Avenue; (831) 373–1277

MUSEUMS

Maritime Museum of Monterey, Stanton Center, 5 Custom House Plaza, Monterey; (831) 575–2553 or 373–2469

Monterey Bay Sports Museum, 883 Lighthouse Avenue, Monterey; (831) 655–2363

Monterey Peninsula Museum of Art, 559 Pacific Street, Monterey; (831) 372–7591

Monterey Peninsula Museum of Art at La Mirada, 720 Via Mirada, Monterey; (831) 272–3689

National Steinbeck Center, One Main Street, Salinas; (831) 796–3833, fax (831) 796–3828

Pacific Grove Museum of Natural History, Forest and Central Avenues, Pacific
Grove; (831) 648–3116

Spirit of Monterey Wax Museum, 700 Cannery Row, Monterey; (831) 375–3770

PARKS

Big Sur

There are three major parks in the Big Sur area: *Andrew Molera State Park*
(2,154 acres), 21 miles south of Carmel on both sides of Highway 1; *Pfeiffer
Big Sur State Park* (2,944 acres), 31 miles south of Carmel on Highway 1;
and *Julia Pfeiffer Burns State Park* (1,725 acres), 37 miles south of Carmel
on Highway 1, turn east. All are geared to camping and hiking. Call (831)
667–2315.

Carmel

Carmel River State Beach, Scenic Road and Carmelo Streets, Carmel; (831)
624–4906; lovely beach; open dawn to dusk; free

Devendorf Park, bordered by Junipero Avenue, Ocean Avenue, Mission Street,
and Sixth Avenue, Carmel; open dawn to dusk daily and for events; free

Garrapata State Park, on Highway 1, on coast 10 miles south of Carmel; (831)
624–4909; primitive, great ocean views, trails; open dawn to dusk; free

Mission Trail Park, Rio Road near Ladera Drive, Carmel; (831) 624–3543;
three hiking trails and Rowntree Arboretum; open dawn to dusk; free

Point Lobos State Reserve, Highway 1 west side of highway, 2.5 miles south of
Carmel; (831) 624–4909; 1,200 acres, trails, old whaling harbor, otter and
seal viewing, scuba diving by appointment, some exhibits and guided tours,
open 9:00 A.M.–7:00 P.M. (closes 5:00 P.M. in winter); $7.00 per auto, $6.00
seniors; includes an ecological reserve of 750 acres under water that can be
explored by skindivers and undersea photographers with a permit obtained
at the entry gate

Carmel Valley

Garland Regional Park, 700 West Carmel Road, Carmel Valley; (831)
659–4488; 3,100 acres between Carmel River and Santa Lucia Range; open
8:30 A.M.–sundown; free

Monterey

El Estero Park, 45 acres facing Camino El Estero, between Del Monte Avenue
and Fremont Street; includes Dennis the Menace Children's Playground,

fields, barbecue areas, lake, fitness course, rest rooms; (831) 646–3866; open dawn to dusk

Fisherman's Shoreline Park, between Fisherman's Wharf and Coast Guard pier; (831) 646–3866; along the shore, lawns, benches, bay views; open dawn to dusk daily; free

Jack's Peak Memorial Park, on Holmstead Road from Highway 68 (25020 Jack's Peak Park Road); (831) 755–4899; hiking, barbecues, reaches highest altitude on peninsula (1,068 feet); open 10:30 A.M.–6:30 P.M. daily; $2.00 per car Monday–Thursday, $3.00 per car Friday–Sunday and holidays

Laguna Seca Recreational Area, 1025 Monterey-Salinas Highway, (831) 755–4899; hiking, bike trails, Laguna Raceway, 71 campsites, 98 RV hookups, concert amphitheater, shooting range; open daily, hours vary by use or event; shooting range open 11:30 A.M.–4:30 P.M. Saturday and Sunday; $5.00 fee per car, $6.00 to use shooting range; for range (831) 757–6317

Monterey State Historical Park, the Visitors Center in the Stanton Center at Custom House Square is a state park; (831) 649–7118; open 10:00 A.M.–5:00 P.M. daily; fees for guided tours, history movie is free

San Carlos Beach Park, along the shore behind Cannery Row; (831) 646–3866; open dawn to dusk; free

Veterans Memorial Park, Jefferson Street and Skyline Drive, Monterey; (831) 646–3865; 50 acres, including RV camping, hiking, playing fields; camping sites $15 each night; no reservations, no hookups

Pacific Grove

Asilomar State Beach, 800 Asilomar Avenue, Pacific Grove; (831) 372–4076; wooden boardwalk, trails, beach, tide pools, otter and whale watching; open dawn to dusk daily; free; fees for conferences

Berwick Park, Ocean View Boulevard and Tenth Street, Pacific Grove; (831) 648–3130; small park overlooking Monterey Bay, lawn; open dawn to dusk daily; free except use fee for large groups

Caledonia Park, Caledonia Street between Central and Jewell Avenues, Pacific Grove; (831) 648–3130; playgrounds, picnic tables; open dawn to dusk daily; free, except fee for larger groups

George Washington Park, six blocks on Alder Street between Sinex Avenue and Short Street, Pacific Grove; (831) 648–3130; forest, playing fields, barbecues, butterfly sanctuary (October–March); open dawn to dusk daily; free except fee for large groups

Jewell Park, Central and Forest Avenues, Pacific Grove; (831) 648–3130; small park with lawn across the street from Natural History Museum and next to library; open dawn to dusk daily; free, except fees for meeting room or gazebo upon application to city Recreation Department

Lovers Point Park, Ocean View Boulevard and Seventeenth Street, above the beach, Pacific Grove; (831) 648–3130; historic park with lawns, beaches, volleyball, picnic areas, ocean views, water fun; open dawn to dusk; free, but fees for larger events or groups

Monarch Butterfly Habitat, Grove Acre Avenue between Lighthouse Avenue and Short Street, Pacific Grove; (831) 373–7047; a tree-studded open space where Monarch butterflies spend the winter (October–March); phone to arrange docent tour; open dawn to dusk daily; free

Seaside

Laguna Grande Regional Park, Canyon Del Rey Road and Del Monte Avenue (turn east on Canyon Del Rey from Highway 1), Seaside; (831) 899–6270; lake, playground, picnic areas, summer jazz concerts; open dawn to dusk; free

REST ROOMS

Carmel

Junipero Avenue and Ocean Avenue, northwest corner
Lincoln Street and Seventh Avenue, northeast corner
Monte Verde Street and Sixth Avenue, northeast corner
Ocean Avenue, at western foot of Ocean, on north side
River Beach State Park, Carmelo Street and Scenic Drive

Monterey

Cannery Row Antiques Mall, 471 Wave Street
Casa Del Oro, south side of Scott between Pacific and Oliver
City Hall, Dutra and Madison
Stanton Center at Custom House Plaza, Scott, Calle Principal, and Alvarado
Visitor Center, Camino El Estero, between Anthony and Franklin

Pacific Grove

Best bet: a service station, a friendly restaurant, or a public park

SAILING CHARTERS

Carrera Sailing, 66 Fisherman's Wharf (at Randy's Fishing Trips), Monterey; (831) 375–0648; excursions of Monterey Bay Sanctuary on 30-foot sloop *Carrera*; two-hour trip at $25 per person, reservations required

Olympus Sailing Charters, 48 Fisherman's Wharf, Monterey; (831) 647–1957; excursions and tours on 67-foot yacht *Zeus;* private charter daily year-round, Monterey Bay Marine Sanctuary Tour, late December–March ($20 adults, $15 kids), afternoon tours (same price), Champagne Sunset Sail ($25 adults, $18 kids); call for reservations

SERVICE STATIONS

Carmel

Chevron Station, 2645 Rio Road; (831) 624–7764
Chevron Station, Rio Road and Highway 1; (831) 624–7413
George Giem Carmel Chevron, Junipero Avenue and Fourth Avenue; AAA towing; (831) 624–3827
Lugo's Shell-by-the-Sea, San Carlos Street and Fourth Avenue; (831) 624–0125

Carmel Highlands

Carmel Highlands Chevron, off Highway 1; (831) 624–5459

Carmel Valley

Carmel Valley Beacon, 14 West Carmel Valley Road Valley; (831) 659–4070
Carmel Valley Chevron, Carmel Valley Road and Village Drive; (831) 659–4149
Mid-Valley Chevron, Carmel Valley Road and Dorris Drive; (831) 624–7324
Lemos 76, Carmel Valley Road and Carmel Rancho Boulevard; (831) 624–2609

Monterey

BP Oil, 899 Hawthorne; (831) 372–0911
Bay Service Station, Tenth and Ocean Avenue; (831) 375–2580
Beacon Station, 700 Lighthouse Avenue; (831) 647–8910
Chevron Station, 351 Fremont; (831) 649–1060
Del Monte 76, 1401 Munras Avenue; (831) 375–6171
Flying J Gas, 2338 Del Monte Avenue; (831) 647–1981
Lighthouse BP, 191 Lighthouse Avenue; (831) 375–5128
Ryan's Monterey Car Wash, 312 Del Monte Avenue; (831) 375–7555
Abrego 76, Abrego and Fremont; (831) 372–0365
Monterey 76, 2045 North Fremont; (831) 375–8415

Pacific Grove

Forest Hill Mart, 1201 Forest Avenue; (831) 375–9189
Fraley's Coast Gasoline, 1152 Forest Avenue; (831) 375–2700
Lee's 76 Service, 1140 Forest Avenue; (831) 372–1478

SKYDIVING

Skydive Monterey Bay, 3261 Imjin Road, Building 518 (at Marina Airport via Reservation Road), Marina; (888) 229–5867 (BAY JUMP); training, call for prices, lessons, and reservation; first jump is in tandem

SPORT FISHING

Chris' Fishing Trips, 48 Fisherman's Wharf No. 1, Monterey; (831) 375–5951; 70-foot *Holiday* for salmon fishing

Monterey Sport Fishing & Cruises, 96 Fisherman's Wharf No. 1, Monterey; (831) 372–2203 for fishing, (831) 372–3501 for cruises; fishing, sightseeing, whale watching, several large boats

Randy's Fishing Trips, 66 Fisherman's Wharf No. 1, Monterey; (831) 372–7440; fishing, whale watching

Sam's Fishing Fleet, Fisherman's Wharf No. 1 at big red sign, Monterey; (831) 372–0577; 3 boats, deep-sea salmon

TENNIS COURTS

Monterey Tennis Center, 401 Pearl Street, Monterey; (831) 646–3881; 6 lighted courts, pro shop, lessons available for $40 and up; fees for extended use; open 9:00 A.M.–10:00 P.M. daily

Hyatt Regency Racquet Club, 1 Old Golf Course Road, Monterey; (831) 372–1234; nonvisitors can play for fee; reservations recommended; open daily

Via Paraiso Park, Via Paraiso and Herrmann Drive, Monterey; 2 courts; open 9:00 A.M. to dark daily

Cypress Park, Cypress and Hoffman, Monterey; 1 court; open 9:00 A.M. to dark daily

City of Pacific Grove Tennis Courts, 515 Junipero Avenue, Pacific Grove; (831) 648–3129; 5 courts, pro shop, fee of $4.00 per hour, lessons at $20 per half hour; open 9:00 A.M. to dark daily, reservations recommended

Spanish Bay Health and Tennis Club, 2700 17-Mile Drive, Pebble Beach; (831) 625–8507; guests and members only

Carmel Valley Racquet & Health Club, 27300 Rancho San Carlos Road, Carmel Valley, 2 miles east of Highway 1; (831) 624–2737; 18 courts (8

lighted) at a private club in which nonmembers can play for a fee, reservations recommended; open daily

Carmel Valley Ranch, One Old Ranch Road off Carmel Valley Road, Carmel Valley; (831) 626–2550; 12 courts (some clay), pool, fitness center; for members only, but memberships are available; call (831) 626–2510 for membership; open daily

John Gardiner's Tennis Ranch, 114 Carmel Valley Road, Carmel Valley; (831) 659–2207 or (800) 453–6225; famed total-immersion tennis resort with accommodations, patios, healthy meals, lessons one day to three weeks

WINERIES

Monterey

Ventana Vineyards, 2999 Monterey-Salinas Highway, Monterey 93940; (831) 372–7415, (800) 237–8846, fax (831) 655–1855; open 11:00 A.M.–5:00 P.M. daily

Baywood Cellars, 381 Cannery Row, Suite C, Monterey 93940; (831) 645–9035; open 11:00 A.M.–7:00 P.M. daily; tasting room only

Bargetto Winery Tasting Room, 700 Cannery Row, Suite L, Monterey 93940; (831) 373–4053; open 10:30 A.M.–6:00 P.M. daily; tasting room only

A Taste of Monterey Wine Visitors Center, 700 Cannery Row, Monterey 93940; (831) 646-5446; open 11:00 A.M.–6:00 P.M. daily; tasting and sales of local wines; www.tastemonterey.com

Lockwood Vineyard, 24600 Silver Cloud Court, Suite 104, Monterey 93040; (831) 642–9200; *see* A Taste of Monterey Wine

Pavona, P. O. Box 5664, Monterey 93944; (831) 646–1506; *see* A Taste of Monterey Wine

Carmel Valley
Going east from Highway One

Chateau Julien, 8940 Carmel Valley Road, P.O. Box 221775, Carmel 93922; (831) 624–2600; open 8:00 A.M.–5:00 P.M. Monday–Friday, 11:00 A.M.–5:00 P.M. Saturday and Sunday

Georis Winery, 4 Pilot Road, Carmel Valley Village, Carmel Valley 93924; (831) 659–1050; open noon–4:00 P.M. Thursday–Sunday

Bernardus Winery, 5 West Carmel Valley Road, P.O. Box 1800, Carmel Valley 93924; (800) 223–2533, fax (831) 659–1676; open 11:00 A.M.–5:00 P.M. daily, $2.00 fee for Marinus

Heller Estate/Durney Vineyards, 69 West Carmel Valley Road, P.O. Box 999, Carmel Valley 93924; (831) 659–6220; open 11:00 A.M.–5:00 P.M. Monday–Friday, 10:00 A.M.–5:00 P.M. Saturday and Sunday

River Ranch Vineyards, 19 East Carmel Valley Road, Carmel Valley 93924; (831) 659–1825

Galante Vineyards, 18181 Cachagua Road, Carmel Valley 93924, (800) GALANTE (425–2683), fax (415) 331–2039; call for appointment between 10:00 A.M. and 5:00 P.M., $5.00 fee per person for groups of 6 or more

Jouillian Vineyards, 20300 Cachagua Road, P.O. Box 1400, Carmel Valley 93924; (831) 659–2800; call for appointment

Nearby: Santa Cruz County to Greenfield
From north to south

Roudon-Smith Winery, 2364 Bean Creek Road, Scotts Valley 95066; (831) 438–1244; open 11:00 A.M.–4:30 P.M. Saturday or call for appointment

Hallcrest Vineyards, 379 Felton Empire Road, Felton 95018; (831) 335–4441; open 11:00 A.M.–5:30 P.M. daily

Bonny Doon Vineyard, 10 Pine Flat Road, Santa Cruz; 95060; (831) 425–4518, fax (831) 425–3856; open 11:00 A.M.–5:00 P.M. daily

Storrs Winery, 303 Portero Street #35, Santa Cruz 95060; (831) 458–5030; open noon–5:00 P.M. Friday–Monday

Bargetto Winery, 3535 North Main Street, Soquel; (831) 475–2258; open 10:00 A.M.–5:00 P.M. daily, tours 11:00 A.M.–2:00 P.M. Monday–Friday only

Devlin Wine Cellars, 3801 Park Avenue, Soquel 95073; (831) 476–7288; open noon–5:00 P.M. Saturday and Sunday

Soquel Vineyards, 7880 Glen Haven, Soquel; (831) 462–9045; open 10:30 A.M.–3:00 P.M. Saturday only

Monterey Peninsula Winery, 467 Shasta Avenue, Sand City 93955; (831) 394–2999; welcomes calls for appointment

San Saba Vineyard, 1075 South Main Street, P.O. Box 2154, Salinas 93902; (831) 449–8930; *see* A Taste of Monterey Wine

Morgan Winery, 590 Brunken Avenue, Suite C, Salinas 93901; (831) 751–7777, fax (831) 751–7780; open 8:00 A.M.–4:30 P.M. Monday–Friday, tours by appointment; *see* A Taste of Monterey Wine

Cloninger Cellars, 1645 River Road, Gonzales, mail P.O. Box 5, Salinas 93902; (831) 758–1686; open 11:00 A.M.–4:00 P.M. Monday–Thursday, 11:00 A.M.–5:00 P.M. Friday–Sunday

Riverland and Winery/Mystic Cliffs, 800 South Alta Street, P.O. Box 780, Gonzales 93926; (831) 675–4060; open 11:00 A.M.–4:00 P.M. Wednesday–Sunday.

Deer Valley Vineyards, 800 South Alta Street, P.O. Box 780, Gonzales 93926; (831) 675–2481

Robert Talbott Vineyard, 53 West Carmel Valley Road, Carmel Valley 93924; open 11:00 A.M.–5:00 P.M. Thursday–Sunday.

Smith & Hook and Hahn Estates, 37700 Foothill Boulevard, Soledad 93960; (831) 678–2132; 11:00 A.M.–4:00 P.M. daily

Paraiso Springs Vineyards, 38060 Paraiso Springs Road (at River Road), Soledad 93960; (831) 678-0300; open noon–4:00 P.M. Monday–Friday, 11:00 A.M.–5:00 P.M. Saturday and Sunday. Also taste Cobblestone

Chalone Vineyards, Stonewall Canyon Road (Highway 146), P.O. Box 518, Soledad 93960; (831) 678–1717, fax (831) 678–2742; 1:30 P.M.–5:00 P.M. Saturday and Sunday, Monday–Friday by appointment only

Boyer Winery, P.O. Box 7267, Spreckels 93962; (831) 674–2957; *see* A Taste of Monterey Wine

Jekel Vineyards, 40155 Walnut Avenue, Greenfield 93927; (831) 674–5522; open 10:00 A.M.–5:00 P.M. daily

Scheid Vineyards, 1972 Hobson Road, Greenfield; (831) 386–0316; open 10:00 A.M.–5:00 P.M. daily. Also taste San Lucas Vineyard

INDEX

$\mathcal{Q}$

$\mathcal{R}$

T

About the Authors

*K*athleen and Gerald Hill are fourth-generation Californians who divide their time between Sonoma in the northern California wine country and Victoria, British Columbia. As a team the Hills wrote *Sonoma Valley: The Secret Wine Country, Victoria and Vancouver Island: The Almost Perfect Eden, Northwest Wine Country: Wine's New Frontier, Napa Valley: Land of Golden Vines, The Real Life Dictionary of the Law, The Real Life Dictionary of American Politics,* and the international exposé, *The Aquino Assassination.* Kathleen is the author of *Festivals USA* and *Festivals USA—Western States,* and has written articles for the *Chicago Tribune, San Francisco* magazine, *Cook's* magazine, *San Francisco Examiner Magazine, James Beard Newsletter,* and other periodicals, while Gerald was editor and co-author of *Housing in California.* Gerald also practices law to support their writing habit.

Kathleen earned an A.B. at University of California at Berkeley, a degree in French from the Sorbonne in Paris, and an M.A. at Sonoma State University. Gerald holds an A.B. from Stanford University and a J.D. from Hastings College of the Law, University of California.